Worthy

DEYST.

An Imprint of WILLIAM MORROW

JADA PINKETT SMITH

thy

Author's Note

In recounting my journey, I have included scenes and conversations and descriptions of encounters with others that are not intended to be word-for-word reenactments, though I have attempted to the best of my abilities to recall those moments in the spirit in which they took place. In certain instances, I have changed the names of individuals to respect their privacy. To all who played meaningful roles in my life, I am forever grateful, and I hope to have remembered and researched names, spellings, and details faithfully.

I want to emphasize that I am not an expert trained in any form of therapy. Rather, my takeaways shared on these pages come from personal experiences in learning lessons along the way.

For anyone who may wish to know more about the properties of plant medicine, please do so by contacting and working with a trained facilitator. Do not try this work by yourself or in any recreational setting.

Finally, I want to say to anyone struggling with any mental health concerns, please know you are not alone and don't hesitate to reach out for help. For resources, please visit www.ourworthyjourney.com.

TO MY DAUGHTER,

and your daughters too.

TO MY SONS,

and your sons as well.

PROLOGUE

The Heroine's Journey 1

PART I

CHILDHOOD: THE ORPHAN

CHAPTER 1

My Grandmother's Garden 11

CHAPTER 2

The Blessed Child of Two Addicts 32

CHAPTER 3

Leaving the Garden 49

CHAPTER 4

University of the B-more Streets 64

CHAPTER 5

Advanced Degree 84

CHAPTER 6

A Gate to Many Roads 111

PART II

HOLLYWOOD

CHAPTER 7

Promise of a Perfect World 129

CHAPTER 8

Living the Dream 150

CHAPTER 9

Breakdown 171

CHAPTER 10

Trying to Find My Footing 181

CHAPTER 11

The Savior Prince 201

CHAPTER 12

Loss Unmourned 211

CHAPTER 13

The Reluctant Bride 226

CONTENTS

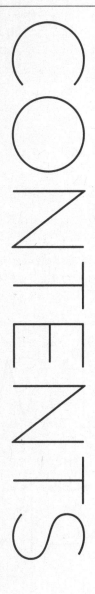

PART III

RIDE-OR-DIE

CHAPTER 14

Little Gurus 245

CHAPTER 15

Swallowing the Key 267

CHAPTER 16

Wild Banshee 281

CHAPTER 17

No Soccer Mom Here 304

PART IV

TO THE EXILED LANDS

CHAPTER 18

Feeling the Rain 331

CHAPTER 19

A Place at the Table 352

CHAPTER 20

Surrender 370

CHAPTER 21

The Holy Joke, the Holy Slap, and Holy Lessons 386

CHAPTER 22

Putting the Crown on the Queen of My Heart 401

Acknowledgments 407

I'M REALLY SCARED, AND MY HEART IS POUNDING HARD.

The Heroine's Journey

OJAI, CALIFORNIA
January 2012

I've pulled off the curving mountain road onto what turns out to be the top of a steep driveway leading down to the house of the Medicine Woman—whom I just met on the phone only a couple of weeks earlier. I'm sitting and staring down the driveway, between a thick overhang of foliage, on a beautiful clear night that should feel magical but instead feels full of dread.

I take a couple of deep breaths, trying to calm myself. I feel crazy. My mind, which was so focused on getting me here, is now suddenly betraying me, leaving me to feel vulnerable in ways that I hate. In this moment I'm pounded by the same terrifying feelings I felt in past experiences when I put myself in situations that it's a miracle I lived to tell.

The scariest aspect of those incidents was that whether I lived or died was in someone else's hands. And that lack of control may explain how I'm feeling here, in my car at the top of this driveway, as I try to get my bearings. I want to be grateful for this moment, for this opportunity, but a feeling of helplessness floods me.

All I can think to do is pray with all my heart, as sincerely as possible. My hands press together. I try desperately to steady my mind.

Don't be afraid, I tell myself. *You are in peaceful, beautiful Ojai. Why are you so scared? Because,* I answer right back, *what if THIS actually kills me?*

Three months earlier, in the wake of my fortieth birthday, my biggest worry was *Well, what if it DOESN'T?*

For two decades, I had been putting on a good face, going with the flow, telling everyone I was okay. Yet underneath, bouts of depression and overwhelming hopelessness had smoldered until they turned into raging hellfire in my broken heart. Unwelcome feelings—of not deserving love—made it harder to understand the disconnect between the so-called perfect life I had achieved and the well of loss I carried with me. Therapy helped up to a point. It got me to forty! But to what end?

I would later be diagnosed and informed that I suffer from complex trauma with PTSD and dissociation, but without this guidepost, I was a chronic mess with no fix, no possibility to heal. Every morning, waking up was like walking the plank of doom—could I make it to four p.m.? If I could, I had survived the day. I always wanted to sleep, but I never slept well. My children could put a smile on my face and were my only motivation to keep me going, but more and more, I could feel myself losing my grip of connection to them.

With all of this, I was slammed by the reality that I'd been checking off boxes meant to define being enough to deserve "having it all." What that meant to me was that I would be "enough" to be loved in a way that life didn't hurt anymore. Those boxes I'd been checking had not delivered the gifts that had been promised. I followed the rules . . . the rules we're told to follow. You work hard, make sacrifices for those you love. The rules tell you: Be a doting mother and a doting wife, do the work required, and life turns into paradise. NOPE. A loving relationship, harmony, peace . . . that happiness had yet to be delivered. "On paper," it all looked grand—I had the beautiful family, the superstar husband, the lavish lifestyle, fame and fortune. I had my own career, the freedom and support to pursue creative outlets. The sweetest part was my kids—Jaden, Willow, and my bonus son, Trey—my three favorite people in the world. They were, hands down, the best thing that ever happened to me. Yet none of that prevented me from hitting the wall I was speeding toward at a hundred miles per hour, knowing full well—this shit's gonna blow!

I had sought help everywhere you can imagine—from Goddess gatherings, silent yoga retreats, backpacking alone, studying every religion you can think of . . . you name it. I even went to Cuba and met with a Padrino (that was intense). None of it offered a lasting solution. Adding to my distress, Will and I weren't in a good place and hadn't been for a while. I couldn't make it right no matter how hard I tried. We couldn't hear or see each other—at all. Confiding in my close friends seemed unfair to them and to Will and me.

And so, by Thanksgiving, I'd fallen into despair and wanted to be on this earth less and less. This was not living.

Suicidal thoughts were not completely new to me. What was new: I'd begun to think about how to have a fatal accident that wouldn't look intentional—for the sake of my kids. If I remained the way I was, what good would I be to them anyway? Besides, I told myself, they would be okay. They would have their father, a devoted and great dad. Their being okay, in my mind, depended on me doing a good job of making my death appear to be conclusively accidental.

As grim as it may sound, the world had become less heavy now that I had a solution, a plan for my own exit, and I was resolved.

A somber steeliness took hold. Driving around a turn on Mulholland Drive a few times, I settled on a specific cliff that might work. I'd have to summon the courage to drive fast over the side—probably at night. Fatal car accidents happened all the time on Mulholland. My only hesitation was that I might not die.

Being practical, I pulled over to assess how steep the cliff was. Maybe in that moment I scared myself. Maybe I couldn't do it. I hated to imagine what would happen if it was a situation where I drove my car off the road and over the wrong cliff only to paralyze or disfigure myself. That would be a much worse nightmare for my children than losing me for good.

Clearly, I would have to find higher, steeper cliffs somewhere. Maybe outside of L.A. on my way to Big Sur. And that became the revised plan.

But before following through, the Universe intervened. In our living room, no less.

It was there that a conversation took place that got my attention. Moises, age seventeen, and his brother, Mateo, fifteen, are two of Jaden's very good friends and have been like surrogate sons to me. Out of the blue, Jaden summoned me from the kitchen into the living room because he wanted me to hear the story Moises and Mateo were sharing about their father. They started to tell me about a trip their father, Cesar, had taken to Peru. They were really excited to share news of Cesar's experience with me, knowing that I'm a spiritual seeker like their dad. Mateo and Moises proceeded to explain that the expedition Cesar had made to Peru for eleven days was to experience ayahuasca.

As I continued to listen, I became both hopeful and curious. Cesar happened to be in town, and I was eager to hear about his story firsthand, so we planned to meet at my house. He soon gave me a full graphic description of a *life-changing* experience. He explained that ayahuasca is a drink made from a plant that comes from the Amazon. His journey sounded daunting as he told me about it. Cesar, who is Colombian, speaks with a heavy musical accent. He described how ayahuasca was a deep psychological healer for him in ways he'd thought were impossible. He said it removed energy that masqueraded as physical ailments. I had known Cesar for a while, and I had never seen his eyes as clear—as bright—as they were at this meeting. He was evidence that "aya" isn't some newfangled recreational drug trip. Actually, it isn't a drug at all—it is medicine and has been for centuries.

The light in his eyes inspired me, his presence so glowing that I wanted whatever he had found. As soon as I started asking around, I was surprised by how quickly the Universe opened a door for me to meet Mother Aya. A therapist friend of mine said, "Oh yeah, I've done it several times." I couldn't believe it: "This is available right here in California? I don't have to go to Peru?" She explained that a medicine woman she had worked with lived fifteen minutes away, and she could arrange a journey for me as soon as I was ready.

I couldn't arrange my ceremony fast enough. At this point, my level of desperation was so all-consuming, all I could think was: *What do I have to lose?* If it killed me—great, mission accomplished. If not, thank God.

Yet here I am, one month later, just after New Year's Eve— coincidentally, the fourteenth anniversary of my marriage to Will— sitting in my car at the top of this hill, in Ojai, debating whether I should drive down this driveway or not.

A memory surfaces.

I *t was a hot, muggy Baltimore* summer day, on a weekend outing to Beaver Dam Park, where the rock quarry's cliffs supported a platform that could be used as a high dive into the freezing- cold water below. At age seven, I had daringly chosen to climb to the highest platform along with teens and adults. A sign was posted with the prominent warning "JUMP AT YOUR OWN RISK!" When I looked over the edge, I saw the risk I had chosen to take.

I stood there, frozen, for hours. I watched people jump off that wooden platform over and over. It started to become a thing that there was a little girl too afraid to jump. Everyone who climbed up tried to give me encouragement. "It's not bad at all," "It's easy," "You can do it," I heard as folks went flying off toward that cold water in playful summertime bliss. Many would yell back to me once they resurfaced: "See, it's fun!" "Go ahead and jump!" I stood there in limbo for so long that the point came when my mother yelled up at me: "Enough, you have to jump, Jada! Come on!" Finally, I walked to the edge and jumped.

Though I hit the water hard and it stung, I felt proud of myself that I'd done it, and the sting was worth the accomplishment. I'd con- quered fear. I swam to shore, and it was a great day.

W*ith that memory, I muster the* courage to get out of the car—after grabbing the apples, oranges, and flowers I have brought as an offering to Mother Earth and Mother Aya and to any other Divine energies out there willing to look over me tonight. I'm on my hands and knees at the top of the driveway, praying. *Please show me the truth I need to see, but please be gentle. Please, please show me if there is something wrong with me, and show me how to heal it, and give me the courage to do so.*

After getting back in the car, I take a deep breath and proceed slowly down the driveway, remembering Cesar's words: "Once you go in, you can't change your mind. No matter how hard it might get. The only way out is the way through."

Before I can tell you what transpired over the next four nights— and about the even more perilous but magnificent adventure that was to begin there—I must go back to the beginning. One of the biggest lessons I have learned, which is the main reason I wrote this book, is how important it is to share our journeys to self-worth.

Returning to the scene of the deepest betrayals of our heart, buried in our origin story, is a harrowing process. It is like crawling on our stomach through a jungle of thorns and roses. A lot of stories await us. In the words of Clarissa Pinkola Estés, whose *Women Who Run with the Wolves* has been a bible to me since I was nineteen years old, I am a "well-written-upon" woman. Most of us are. Many of us, as women, to one degree or another, don't recognize the insidious ways we are made to feel unworthy.

My belief is that every woman is worthy, a walking treasure, and deserves to live her life as the heroine of her own story. A woman has a right to her adventures, even if it means courting her shadows as guides to her brightest light. And she has a right to her pitfalls as well as her triumphs, and to the wisdom gained that leads to her self-actualization. When we as women have the courage to find keys to the treasure chest of ourselves, we find Divine freedom (a freedom that is not whimsical), and with this, our lives are deliberately and unapologetically crafted by our own hands.

My hope is that you will be encouraged and strengthened by the journey I'm about to share with you. The archetypal Heroine's Journey is less of a linear quest to go off and slay dragons and save damsels, as we know so well from the Hero's Journey paradigm, but more of a spiral out of chaos and into order, saving the damsel within ourselves, where each woman can learn how to be her own savior, and any man or woman (or any pronoun that fits) who loves her can learn how to support her in that.

This, then, is a book about a woman's quest to find the power of unstoppable, indestructible love for herself, the key to her true empowerment, and the acceptance of the journey that delivered her there.

PART I

CHILD
HOOD:
THE ORPHAN

CHAPTER 1

My Grandmother's Garden

*I*t's *close to midnight in the* warm summer darkness, and I feel wild and free. I'm doing something I have no business doing, and I'm loving it. Living on the edge is already a habit and, in the years to come, will be an addiction. I've just slipped out the kitchen's back door to an alley behind our modest row house on Price Avenue—a side street tucked in between two main thoroughfares in the working-class neighborhood of Northwest Baltimore's Pimlico Heights.

I press myself up and over the old metal gate and land on my feet like a cat. These are the moments when my dance and gymnastics classes come in handy. I charge down the alley, turning a sharp left to head south, then east, then north, in a kind of horseshoe direction.

I'm thirteen going on fourteen, and I'm on a mission to see my sixteen-year-old boyfriend, who works the overnight shift at the 7-Eleven. It's about a twenty-five-minute walk that by day is full of the noisy hustle and bustle of business and traffic but now is mostly quiet. Small sounds—a delivery truck here or a train rattling by over there—punctuate the silence. This is a working-class neighborhood that's butted up against a hood that is, let's say, *tricky*. All kinds of characters trickle into this area, especially at night. Gotta keep my eyes open and my guard up.

My route runs past the Reisterstown subway station, which is how I get around when moving to different parts of town, followed by a shopping mall with a Payless and a Kmart that my mother and I frequent, and then along sleepy residential blocks where many of the streetlights are out. At times it's so dark I can barely make out the homes of friends who live in the neighborhood. My stops and starts take me across two well-trafficked parkways, still in the darkness, and, finally, up a less dark stretch that will land me at the brightly lit glass doors of the 7-Eleven.

Dressed in jeans, a T-shirt, and sneakers—I'm tomboy cute right now—I have my hair pulled back into a sleek pony knot with the edges slicked down by Pro Styl gel. And because of the humidity, I probably hit 'em with a Tancho stick as well. I gotta be cute but not stupid.

Four years earlier, when I was nine, I was leaving my grandmother's house to walk to a nearby shopping mall. Her neighborhood is considered upper-middle-class, predominantly white, with a huge Hasidic Jewish community. At screaming distance from my grandmother's, I wasn't overly concerned when a young white guy driving a beat-up gray car pulled over next to me on the curb.

He leaned toward the open passenger window. "Hey!"

"Yes?" I answered.

"Have you seen a puppy around here?"

I leaned in a little closer. "No, I haven't seen a puppy."

"Do you know where Graveyard Street is?" As he spoke, I noticed him jerking off through the opening of his dingy trench coat.

"No," I muttered. And I kept walking.

The flasher didn't drive off immediately. By reflex, I glanced to my right without turning my head, making sure he didn't jump out and try to grab me. Right there, fortunately, was a synagogue parking lot. I moved toward it as if it were my destination—just in case. I kept strolling, and he pulled off. I turned to watch him leave and made sure he didn't turn the corner to come back around. He screeched off, but I kept my eyes on him until he disappeared.

In that moment, I learned you gotta have eyes in the back of your head, show no fear, and act like you're not fazed. You can tell the heart of a predator by what they hunt. Eventually, I learned that if you don't look like easy prey, cowardly predators will move on. Part of staying safe was hiding my feminine nature and taking on a more masculine bravado in how I carried myself. Even as a kid, I wasn't scared, I was disgusted. Disrupted, but not scared. It was moments like these that taught me I had to be rugged and super vigilant. Not only that, but yeah, I learned early that there ain't no such thing as a safe neighborhood.

What I appreciate about the hood I'm in tonight on my way to the 7-Eleven: There ain't no lies. It's not pretending to be something it's not—safe. I know what it is. My instincts are dialed in, and I've learned how to navigate this concrete jungle. I know how the various predators move, and I'm dressed to move quick, fight as hard as I have to, or retreat and hide.

But tonight, the air is full of excitement, and I can't wait to see my dude. It's the summer of 1985, and at thirteen, I'm coming of age on these streets. My mother, Adrienne, newly separated from my step-father, is an RN in a hospital maternity ward and has recently begun working the graveyard shift—from seven p.m. to seven a.m. She is like most single moms who work hard to keep the lights on and food on the table, who can only hope and pray that they put enough fear in their children to adhere to the laws they lay down about how to behave when they aren't present.

And, of course, I am not that child. In fact, I make it my business from seven p.m. to seven a.m. to ignore every law my mom ever thought of.

And that's how I feel on this balmy summer night. Free, un-guarded, unwatched, loving my wildness.

There is something comforting about the warmth of the air in these late hours. The muggy, oppressive heat of the day, when hu-midity levels tend to rise to miserable heights, is gone. Years later, I would often summon nostalgic memories of East Coast summer nights like this one. The thickness of that air can feel almost protec-tive, like a warm hug.

In hindsight, I thank all the powers of the Universe for hovering over me in these days. It's true that Pimlico Heights—so named for the neighborhood's proximity to the racetrack—had not yet fallen into the no-man's-land of the trickier hoods like Liberty Heights and Park Heights that bordered us. Like I said, there ain't no such thing as a safe neighborhood.

Yet when I catch my first glimpse of the warm and welcoming glow of the 7-Eleven, all I am ready for is the next chapter of young love.

Though Mark is not my first boyfriend, he's my most serious so far. He's also fun, and cute, with a little smidge of quirk. Black and Asian, "Blasian" before it was even a term, tall and skinny, he has a wide toothy grin and a deep voice that makes him sound much older than he looks.

Mark makes me laugh, and not because he's trying to be funny. For the last several weeks, I've been making this trek to visit him, and he says the same damn thing every time I arrive, swinging into the too bright 7-Eleven: "Jada, you know you shouldn't be down here."

I just look at him, grin back, and mutter something like, "Boy, yeah, you say the same thing every time I come in here."

"You know you crazy doing this." He presses this point, just like always. Sometimes, if his shift is over early, he'll walk me home or give me a ride. But not tonight. It doesn't matter—I'm gonna enjoy this time with him anyway, and I'm not afraid to walk home.

For the next nearly five hours or so, I hang right there next to the hot dog cooker and the Slurpee machine, making small talk with Mark. Snacking or not. Sometimes he tells me about his troubles at home, and sometimes I tell him about mine.

And then, before I know it, right before dawn, it's time to roll. The night has all but gone, and I'm barely on my way before the first streaks of morning light break across the sky.

The excitement I felt hours before is replaced by a sense of accomplishment mixed with melancholy that the night has ended. Now my focus is making it home before my mom does—because if she ever finds out where I have been, that's my ass. For real.

By six a.m., the grind of another hot, muggy summer day has begun. Traffic thickens on the parkways, and folks are heading out for early shifts. The sounds of news and music rev up from open windows and from car radios. All the more reason to hustle home. The irony is not lost on me that I watch out for unpredictable dangers by night, but by day I have only to fear the wrath of Adrienne.

As is my drill, I slip back inside our row house, locking the door behind me, and fly up the steps to my bedroom. When my mother arrives home around eight a.m., she doesn't come upstairs to check on me right away. Why would she? Her assumption, I'm sure, is that I'm safe and sound, fast asleep in bed—where I've no doubt been all night.

But "safe" is just one of many lies at this point in my life.

* * *

*W**henever I think of my origin* story, it's not really set on the streets of Baltimore. I think of Marion's garden. Marion was my mother's mother. Some of my earliest memories were formed at her side, out in her garden, learning powerful lessons I would use for the rest of my life.

Adrienne was the youngest of the four children born to Marion and her husband, Gilbert. My grandfather was an MD who served as the head of anesthesiology at Provident Hospital, which catered to a predominantly Black community. Grandfather maintained a private practice as a GP, smoked a pipe, said little, and adored his wife. I was the firstborn grandchild. Because my mother and my father, Robsol Pinkett, were only married for just over a year, and Mom was only seventeen when she became pregnant with me, we moved back into her parents' house when I was a toddler, and for all intents and purposes, that was home for much of my childhood. The house was nestled in a family-friendly upper-middle-class neighborhood.

We were one of two Black households in our immediate area, which was northwest of downtown Baltimore. In one direction, there were larger, more opulent single-family homes with big backyards. In the other direction, Lower Park Heights, was an area torn by the ravages of addiction, violence, and poverty. Directly across the street from us were large apartment complexes almost entirely inhabited by members of the Hasidic Jewish community. Our neighbors definitely had their own flow. Grandmother taught me very early about how the Hasidic community lived and the importance of respecting their customs. She explained that I should not be offended if they didn't socialize with us. Keeping to themselves was simply their way of life. Groups of Hasidic women—in wigs and long dresses—would walk up and down the neighborhood, nearly every day, pushing babies in strollers with other young ones in tow. The Hasidic men all had beards and wore big hats and prayer shawls tucked under their jackets with strings that hung below their pants pockets. I was always fascinated by their attire, not knowing the reasons behind these choices until many years later. I also liked watching the families out together on the street, coming and going, usually to and from the synagogue. In the process, I was taught to respect differences and that those differences didn't have to make us hate one another.

It was important to my grandmother that I could find common ground with anyone, no matter what. The value of being "well rounded" (as she would call it) was at the heart of how she crafted my education and experiences. She was the center of my world and the center of well-being for each of her four children, their spouses/ significant others, and my cousins. There was so much love in her house, as well as in her garden.

Throughout childhood, I was convinced that my grandmother had the biggest backyard in the universe. Her multi-tiered garden was, to me, as impressive as any park I had ever visited. There was so much space in the backyard, and Grandmother cultivated all kinds of smaller gardens within it—so much so that she always had flowers blooming or vegetables ready to be picked or leaves to be raked, no matter the season.

Going back to the age of five or six, I was given gardening jobs that allowed me to not just witness the cycles of growth but know that I had helped make them possible. During the fall, I would dutifully help rake leaves, which forever after made me love that time of year.

"Is this right?" I remember asking Grandmother—which, by the way, was the only acceptable way I could refer to her.

After inspecting the pile of leaves I had going, she gave me a small nod of approval and said, "Great job, Angel Pie," using the affectionate nickname she had for me.

The best part came next—leaping high into the air with my gymnastic skills and then falling backward into the multicolored piles. The smell of the crunchy leaves stayed with me long after I'd come up for air and scrambled out.

Sometimes the raking of leaves became a family affair. We'd all be out there with rakes—my grandparents, me, and some of my cousins. We would jump in the leaves and laugh together, making a full-on mess. Eventually, Grandfather—a handsome, slender man with a gentle might—would fling one hand as if shooing something away and say, "Okay, okay, that's enough now." And we would get back to work.

I was a very talkative and inquisitive child. When Grandmother and I were heading out to the garden, I would ask her all kinds of questions about all kinds of things. West Indian, and a Howard University graduate who went on to become a licensed social worker, Grandmother was a trailblazer, having been one of the pioneers in the teaching of sex education in Baltimore schools. Marion had a refined, melodic way of speaking—no patois, no hint of her Jamaican heritage. After all, she was born in Boston and had not lived with her immigrant family since she was thirteen years old.

One day on our way outside, I pointed to a photograph in the hallway. The pretty young woman in the picture was wearing an unusual style of dress. "Who is that?" I asked.

"Oh," she said, and beckoned me to continue outside with her to the toolshed, "that's me. In India."

India?

"Yes, I was an undergraduate at the time and received a fellowship arranged by the wife of Howard Thurman, Sue, to study in India for six months." Grandmother explained that the dress was called a "sari" and then described how exciting it was to travel all the way there in the mid-1930s as part of an invited delegation of African American leaders and students.

On that same trip, Howard Thurman—a theologian, professor, and civil rights activist who became a key influence in the work of Dr. Martin Luther King, Jr.—met with none other than Mahatma Gandhi to discuss the role that nonviolence could play in the overturning of oppression.

Howard and Sue, an activist and author in her own right, were so important to Marion that they became godparents to my aunt Sondra, my mom's oldest sibling. Grandmother and Sondra were present in 1963 for Dr. King's historic "I Have a Dream" speech at the March on Washington.

The little bit I knew about Marion's story after India was that Gilbert, her college boyfriend, asked her to marry him soon after her return. Gilbert didn't talk much, but he was a solid fellow, a provider and a consistent man of his word. Often I'd see him in his armchair reading or smoking his pipe. The fragrance of burning pipe tobacco is something I've loved ever since. I'd catch him with his eyes closed on occasion and finally asked one day, "Grandfather, are you sleeping?"

"No, I'm just resting my eyes," he replied, not bothering to open them at all. A brief smile passed across his face.

Resting his eyes? Hmmmm. Poor Gilbert. He must have been wondering, *Didn't we just get our grown kids out of this house? Now we have a little one up in here?* I was in everybody's business.

In my grandmother's house, our day-to-day life had an orderliness. Having set jobs to do made me feel I was contributing. They might have been hard, but they were never boring. That was because Marion Banfield understood how to turn the mundane into magic.

Looking back, I can see that she was, in fact, cultivating two gardens. One of them was the garden in her backyard. Her other garden was me. Grandmother poured *everything* she had into my cultivation, growth, and learning—just as I watched her pour *everything* into the soil of her garden. Literally.

Once, as we carried out the compost bucket, Marion egged on my curiosity: "What do you think is in there?"

I smelled. "Lemons?"

"Lemon peels, yes." In that bucket there were also fish heads, apple peels, coffee grounds, and whatever scraps had been collected in the kitchen. This was decades before composting became mainstream. "See, we're getting the earth ready. The worms will come and till the soil for us. In a few days, we can plant seeds."

My grandmother's garden was my school and my playground.

Outside in that backyard, I spent untold hours exploring, either by myself or with my cousins when they came to visit. The power of my imagination taught me how to entertain myself all on my own. One of my favorite solo games involved building a booming imaginary restaurant on the stone steps that separated the two tiers of the garden. There was plenty of dirt available for making mud pies that I'd cook up with weeds I picked and then decorate the tops with flower petals. Dandelion mud pies became the specialty of the house.

If I wanted to go on an adventure, I could hop on my Big Wheel and cruise across the small wooden bridge that separated two sections of the garden. Crossing from one part of the backyard to another was freedom.

Every day I found new treasures waiting for me outside. At that first tier was Grandmother's rose garden, and in the beauty of each bloom and in the thick thorns on each stem, I saw how nature created a boundary to protect its prize. Up above the roses was the vegetable garden. String beans, tomatoes, snap peas, and zucchini, all in abundance. To the right was the strawberry patch. There were other fruits, but I loved the strawberries the most because that was where the rabbits gathered and, in spring, where the baby bunnies would appear.

One spring day when I was five years old, I was in the strawberry patch, about to pick up one of the baby bunnies, and Grandmother stopped me, warning, "Angel Pie, don't touch the baby rabbits. If the mother smells your scent on her baby, she won't take care of that bunny."

"Okay," I said, disappointed. She had to remind me a few more times because I was so in love with the tiny rabbits. Instead, I resolved to take on the job of monitoring how many there were and making sure their little hollow was safe. Over the months that followed, I saw them grow up and eventually leave our garden, hopping off to other gardens to have bunnies of their own.

Everything grew if given enough sun, fertilizer, and the right amount of water. Evidence was in every patch of dirt. There were purple pansies and orange marigolds that I'd help Grandmother plant. There were tulips of many colors all around and another small herb garden where Grandmother grew mint.

Marion loved to drink fresh mint tea. She brewed it almost daily. Mint was one of the first things I planted when I became an adult and started my own garden. By that time, I had been away from Baltimore long enough to realize that what I'd thought was the biggest backyard in the universe was not nearly as big as it once seemed.

Marion always modeled a work ethic. Her point was that even the most basic chores—like weeding—required thought and effort. Grandmother ran a tight ship. She loved a spick-and-span house, and to this day, so do I. When I tell you that I was taught how to clean a house from floor to ceiling, I am not exaggerating. Cleaning the bathroom was not just scrubbing sinks and tubs and toilet bowls. It was a PROCEDURE, scrubbing and cleaning every inch of porcelain, including all the cracks around the base of the toilet.

Cleaning the floors and windows was not easy, but nothing came close to tackling the floorboards. She wanted those floorboards to look brand-new. Grandmother was not stern, but she was a serious taskmaster. "Angel Pie, I need you to make sure you SCRUB."

So I'd SCRUB. Instead of getting frustrated, I accepted these lessons as a challenge. I had a capacity to be meticulous anyway—I guess it has to do with being a Virgo. The real test, though, came when I finished one section of the floorboards and Grandmother put on a white glove and wiped her finger across the top. I'd hold my breath every time. If she raised a clean gloved finger, I could keep going. If not, as in most chores not done to her liking, Grandmother had no problem making me do the same section ALL OVER AGAIN.

The larger lesson was a lasting one—that how you apply yourself in the small daily tasks is how you will apply yourself in the big tasks of life. I learned all that she had to throw at me, dusting, washing windowpanes, setting and clearing tables, doing dishes, pots, and pans. Cleaning right was all about paying attention to details, but those floorboards, though—they had to be pristine. I fear a white glove to this day.

There was no spanking allowed in my grandmother's house. No tickling, either. And we were not allowed to play hide-and-seek. These rules were not random, and when challenged, Grandmother pointed out that spanking or beating children was reliving the horrors of slavery. Tickling had been used as a method of torturing prisoners of war in many cultures. As for hide-and-seek, she simply didn't like it because, as she explained, "I was once scared out of my mind when someone who had been hiding behind a door jumped out at me."

Her house, her rules, and no one dared to defy her.

Marion was remarkable at more things than I can count, but she was a terrible cook. She liked to create her own dishes, which sounded awful as she excitedly described them and were even worse when served: Braised cow tongue with sour cream, made in the Crock-Pot, comes to mind. If only Pero—the big black standard poodle I loved and rode around like a pony—had been allowed near the kitchen table when we ate, I could have sneaked him the food I didn't want. No such luck. If I didn't finish my plate, well, that's what I would be eating the next day, and the day after that if necessary. My grandmother did not play wasting food. Once I made the mistake of taking a bite of something she had prepared and saying, "Oooh, this is nasty."

"Don't say that word," she corrected me. "If you don't like it, you can say that it's 'unpleasant' or 'distasteful.'"

From then on, I primarily used "unpleasant" to describe much of Grandmother's cooking.

Grandmother's consistent response would be: "Food is not meant to be enjoyed. It should be eaten for nourishment."

Being a foodie (which has never been my thing) was not my grandmother's focus. Thankfully, Marion could pull off a classic breakfast, and because of her absolute joy in all family celebrations—birthdays, Thanksgiving, and especially Christmas—she could bake, in my view, like nobody's business (though her children would disagree). She taught me to bake a lot of the basics—cookies, cakes, and pies from scratch, not to mention different kinds of breads.

Marion was an endless source of fascination to me. She was a socialite, widely respected in the community. Forest Park Senior High School at one point named a library after her, and my middle school, Fallstaff, named a garden after her as well. She was outspoken and, throughout her life, remained active in the civil rights movement; she had been a key player in Baltimore's politics. So much so that she became the chair of Kurt Schmoke's campaign when he successfully ran as the first Black state's attorney of Maryland, which set him up to later become Baltimore's first Black mayor.

Grandmother had seen the world, traveling to places like Kenya and Ecuador and Russia. They seemed so exotic and so far away, I couldn't even imagine them. But then she would vividly describe her travels and give me a little souvenir—dolls from South America and necklaces from Africa—and those places would come alive. Many of those keepsakes live with me still.

As early as I could recall, Grandmother had me in tap dance, piano lessons, and pretty soon after that, tennis, gymnastics, and whatever else seemed enriching. She wanted me to read what she considered classic children's literature—*Alice in Wonderland; Roll of Thunder, Hear My Cry; The Learning Tree; Gulliver's Travels*. My reading was part of the summer school program she created just for me because she believed I could have summertime fun and still make room for learning. There was no such thing as taking a break from education.

Not everything she devised made sense to me, but here is what I was sure of—that my grandmother loved me to pieces. And it was no use resisting her will, because I wouldn't win. So, later on, when she decided to coordinate an after-school program to teach kids flower arranging at my middle school, I went with the flow—sort of. My inner monologue sounded something like: *Who does this?*

"We are going to learn pottery," Grandmother announced one day when I was eight. "It's wonderful to learn how to throw clay on the wheel." So wonderful, in fact, that she enrolled herself in an adult pottery class at the same time.

My mother rarely interfered with Grandmother's curriculum—except when I was in the first grade and was shamed by a ballet teacher for being disruptive in class. To make her point, the teacher took me out of my pink tutu, put me in a black tutu, and stuck me in a corner facing the wall.

When I told my mom about the incident, she saw red and confronted the teacher. My mother could not believe that the woman had the audacity to put the only Black child in her class in a black tutu as a punishment. My mother had no qualms about making that point in the fierce Adrienne tone that, to this day, is a sign to get out of the way. To add more fuel to her fire, it turned out that back in junior high school, my mother was also put in a corner for being talkative. Upon hearing about it, Marion had immediately gone to the school. So not only was Adrienne irate at the level of humiliation I had suffered, but putting her foot down was in her DNA.

Needless to say, that was the end of that ballet class.

During family gatherings, I was regularly enlisted by Marion to give a performance of some sort. For years, she would have me play "O Christmas Tree" for the holidays. I didn't always love playing the piano, but it was a tradition. One year I had the daring idea to write, direct, and star in a short play I'd conceived to celebrate the Nativity story.

Grandmother was pleased, and I took charge, making sure that every cousin (Brett, Jason, Garth, Tiffany, and even baby Trés, who appeared as Baby Jesus in the manger scene) had parts. I quickly wrote a script with lines for Joseph and Mary and a speech for myself. When it was time to perform, I called everyone to the living room, came out in front of my cousins, took a bow, and introduced the characters, concluding with "Thank you all for coming. Please enjoy the show!"

The adults tried to hide their laughter as I directed from the sidelines, whispering to Brett, "Go, go . . ." As per the script, he stepped forward and recited, "Now the Banfield children will present a program. The first number is 'Silent Night,' sung by Jada." We continued with five more songs until our finale, "The Twelve Days of Christmas," sung all together.

It was all sweetly ridiculous. But it was clear even then that I enjoyed performing.

Grandmother believed I was going to do something in this world. She would say, "Angel Pie, you are special."

In remembering this period, I often ask myself: *What was the thing she saw in me that made her say this?* I'm not sure, but she said it enough that I believed her. Marion planted every possible seed at her disposal in order for me to become whatever I so chose.

She didn't say, *Learn to challenge the status quo!* She didn't have to, because I watched her do it. She didn't say, *Don't take everything at face value.* She wanted me to value my own opinion. A light flicked on for me at a young age when we were walking through the supermarket and I asked if we could buy Nesquik, which I liked to put in my milk.

"We can't buy any Nestlé products anymore." She paused and explained, "We are boycotting Nestlé." The reason was that they were promoting their brand of baby formula in Africa and discouraging African women from breastfeeding. Babies in Africa were dying because the water used to make the formula wasn't clean.

I was horrified. And suddenly resolved: "We can never buy Nestlé products again!" I knew immediately that was the right thing to do.

This was one of my first lessons of activism.

Grandmother never talked to me about the horrors of racism she had witnessed and lived through. She was very optimistic about social change for Black people and always explained how we could support and uplift one another. Her belief was that a child's mind should be fed with hope so they would work for change as an adult. Yet she felt just as strongly that it was essential to know your history.

For that reason, in January 1977, she took exception to the iron-clad rule of my eight p.m. bedtime. This was for the miniseries *Roots*, adapted from the groundbreaking book by Alex Haley.

For those eight episodes, I sat at Marion's side and was spellbound. My reactions were complicated—fascinated and confused all at once. That big black chain around Kunta Kinte's neck and what it looked like for people to be whipped until they bled were images that stayed with me. My grandmother found it important for me to participate in this historical event—the unprecedented major TV broadcast of a critical part of African American history—even if it was painful to watch.

Whereas Marion was prominent in Dr. King's "combat hate with love" movement, my mother and my aunt Karen came of age throwing Black Power fists in the air. Either way, taking a stand against injustice was instilled in me early.

Marion called herself an atheist, but her mission was to expose me to all religions and philosophies so I could find meaning for myself. She did not believe in organized religion, but she believed deeply in one guiding principle: love. The ideal setting to learn love and acceptance, she decided, was the Ethical Society, where we attended meetings every Sunday. It was unheard-of for a Black West Indian family at this time to choose to not go to church. We were supposed to be up in some Baptist church somewhere. Not Marion. Status quo was out the door when it came to her truth.

Grandfather, Grandmother, and I would drive together in our yellow Volvo, which both my grandparents considered the safest and most reliable car on the road. The Ethical Society meetings were held in a modest home not far from us.

We'd enter the home and see that, as usual, chairs had been set up for a morning lecture with a podium in the middle. We would sing songs about the winds of change and peace and listen as different speakers talked about bringing humanity together through understanding and love. The children would later move to a smaller room upstairs and learn about different religions practiced in different settings and cultures.

Meetings of the Ethical Society exposed me not just to the teachings of Christianity, Judaism, Islam, Hinduism, Buddhism, and other faiths, but to the histories and cultural practices of their followers. It was enchanting to hear about far-off lands and the customs and rituals that expressed the mysterious communion followers found with their understanding of God.

Those Sunday meetings prepared me to become a lifelong seeker of spiritual knowledge. The more I learned, the more I believed that all forms of faith have valuable information to offer, but they all reflect one core belief—God is love.

Jesus could be a path, as could Allah and Buddha. But the fact was the Higher Power was going to make Itself available according to an individual soul's needs. It became my lasting view that the Higher Power, no matter what you call your Source, lives within the temple of your heart.

Of course, at such a young age, I didn't have the language to articulate these beliefs to my grandmother. I just knew that my heart and my mind were allowed to be open in that place, because Grandmother made the choice to take me there.

----

arion was always youthful in my eyes and very beautiful, with the most glowing cocoa complexion and a smile that could electrify any atmosphere. Yes, she was short, but a Powerhouse with a capital P. We were not a huggy, touchy family, but I do recall from when Grandmother held my hands or scrubbed my fingernails that she had beautiful soft, soft skin on her hands. Her hair was black and silky straight. She was Jamaican, with East Indian blood, as well as having a grandfather who was a Jewish man from Portugal.

Gilbert, whose family was from Barbados, had a true immigrant experience and could recall traveling to the United States as an only child with his parents through Ellis Island. He had striking good looks even in his later years.

Beauty ran in the family. My mother was always a true head-turner, and so, too, were her big sisters, my aunts Karen and Sondra. My uncle Leslie, like my grandfather, was very attractive. Marion would never boast about this, only acknowledging, "I have a handsome family." Anything more would have been vain. And she made it clear to me that looks were not something to rely on—yet one more reason to focus on cultivating our minds for success.

The idea that girls and women should not play on their looks was ingrained in me from an early age. The most revealing conversation I ever had with Marion took place one day when we were sitting together in the library/family room, and I asked about an old sepia-tone photograph on the first shelf above her desk. It was of a woman with a baby on her lap and a little girl standing next to her. The girl's expression was a bit somber, and the eyes of the adult woman were vacant.

"Grandmother, who's that?" was all I asked.

She took the photograph down, stared at it for a second, and then pointed to the woman in the photo, saying, "That is my mother." And then she pointed to the girl who was standing and said, "That's me." She was so cute in her little dress. Grandmother pointed to the child on her mother's lap. "That was my baby sister, but she died very young."

I was immediately sad but wanted to know more. Her mother, my great-grandmother, apparently suffered from paranoid schizophrenia and was institutionalized in Boston by her husband—my great-grandfather. I understood that Marion's mother was not available to really care for her children.

When Grandmother told me of her childhood trauma, I couldn't believe it. In my eyes, she had a perfect life. Grandmother worked very hard to give that perception, but it could not have been further from the truth. As an adult, I found out that Marion traveled back and forth to Jamaica during her childhood. During a visit when she was thirteen, she got pregnant. The details—under what circumstances she was impregnated—are not clear, but Aunt Karen, the family historian, and I came to the consensus that probably Marion wasn't aware of what sex was. She never gave the impression that she had been raped. It seemed as if she simply didn't know what was happening, and it was an innocent mistake. The fact that she was so adamant about teaching me, at an early age, how reproduction worked leads me to believe that ignorance was the biggest culprit in her teen pregnancy. It would also explain why she felt compelled to become a sex educator in the school system when it was still taboo.

It is painful to imagine the shame and rejection she faced being Black, the daughter of immigrants, thirteen, pregnant, and unwed. In the mid-1920s, no less. She was motherless, and her father wanted nothing to do with her, so she bore that child with little to no familial support. She gave her baby boy up for adoption and went into the foster care system, where she was placed with a white family. While she lived with them, she served as a maid to earn her keep. (This is likely where she learned how to clean a house so meticulously.)

The horror of her going through all of this as a child, alone, haunts me. Inside this proud, accomplished matriarch was a hidden history of a little girl made to feel unworthy, before I was even dreamed of. The miraculous part is that Marion did not let the poisons ruin her desire for a good life, picture-perfect, as the wife of a prominent doctor and one of Baltimore's more distinguished socialites.

Marion was far from perfect, but she was a woman of worth, and a hell of a heroine. She had built her life and extraordinary garden in spite of the past. By the time I came around, she was learning how to live not in her pain or her loss but in her own self-love and the love of the family she cultivated. Her house was a place of warmth and refuge not just for me but for the whole family. She had created a sanctuary for her children and her children's children—a lasting legacy of love.

In Grandmother's house, within her handmade haven, I saw how familial love could pull you through seemingly impossible times. I witnessed the miracles of healing in my grandmother's house for her grown children—each of whom, at different stages, needed to return home for a reprieve from the harsh world. She didn't always agree with her children, but she loved them fiercely. Her grace, tenacity, and devotion were constant reminders that no one is beyond the possibility of redemption.

This lesson of faith was the greatest gift of my young life. It was here in my grandmother's house, in my grandmother's garden, that life was right. Life had purpose, and life was full of love.

I heard it in the nightly sound of my grandmother at the piano playing Beethoven's "Moonlight Sonata" after she put me in bed. As much as I hated to have to go to bed, listening to her play that piece, in particular, was so soothing. She played it beautifully. I don't think she could go to sleep without playing it. I know I couldn't go to sleep without hearing it.

I am my grandmother's garden
—FROM A RECENT JOURNAL, JPS

We all have traumas in our childhood that can make us overlook the beauty that surrounds us. Oftentimes we believe we have to focus more on the negative events because they created so much pain. Some of us believe holding on to the negative is what protects us from not experiencing that pain again. That couldn't be further from the truth. Unfortunately, we tend to relive aspects of the negative experiences because we stay stuck, by consciously or unconsciously holding on to the negative thoughts our painful experiences birthed.

———————

Don't forget the beauty that surrounded you, that fed you and nourished your energy in a way that helped you get here, to where you are TODAY. Take time to remember the joy that existed so that we can reconnect our inner child to those pleasant moments that fed us the hope we needed, that gave us the strength to make it to this moment. You are so much more than your trauma.

———————

What I find helpful is exploring my memories and feelings with pen and paper. If you find some quiet time today, take an opportunity to write three beautiful memories from your childhood, or simply from your past, that helped you to nourish the beautiful YOU that you are.

———————

By the way . . . you are a golden soul.

CHAPTER 2

The Blessed Child of Two Addicts

W hen you gain the courage to go prowling within the murky memories of the past, you may choose to follow muddy footprints back to your origins. Those footprints can turn into either lotus leaves or pools of quicksand.

I am standing in the spacious converted attic living area that I share with my mother at her parents' house. In this early memory I am patiently—not my usual—waiting at Adrienne's side. She's in her early twenties at the time, so I'm likely about five or six years old. I watch intently as she stands looking into the mirror, putting on her makeup to go out for the night.

This converted attic is where I grew up, off and on, for most of my childhood. To get up here, we took the stairs that led off the kitchen. The attic housed my mother's bedroom, a long hallway, my bedroom, a common area where I could play, and another bedroom that had a large triangle window that looked onto the backyard. I always loved spending time in that room because it got so much sunlight. And my bedroom, though tiny, was ALL mine. The ceiling sloped over my bed, giving the room a cozy and warm feeling without becoming too claustrophobic.

In the attic, when it's just me and my mother, it is our safe little world, attached to the bigger safe world of my grandparents' home. And watching my mother study her reflection in the mirror while putting on lipstick always intrigues me.

Adrienne is pretty, with the same slender features and light brown complexion as my grandfather. After applying very little makeup, she lights up. Her eyes shine a bit brighter. All she needs now are high heels and a "night on the town" dress, and BAM, she is ready to make the scene.

Of course, I have all kinds of questions. "Where are you going, Mommie?" (This is how my mother taught me to spell that word, and I always will when I refer to her.)

"I'm going to Gatsby's. It's a club," she mumbles through puckered lips as she fixes her lipstick.

Ooooooo, I think. "Are you going with Aunt Jackie?" She is Adrienne's best friend and my godmother.

Adrienne brushes her eyelashes with mascara and answers with a smile, "Yup."

"What are y'all gonna be doing?"

"Now, that's grown folks' business." This answer, spoken with a tinge of impatience, is classic. But since I'm always hanging with her and her girlfriends, I am used to being in grown folks' business. And I love kick'n it with the big kids. Like an older sister, though, Adrienne is quick to remind me to stay in a child's place. You know how big sisters let little sisters be part of the mix with their friends for a while—and then quickly change their mind and need the younger siblings to stay in their lane? That's me and Mommie.

This memory repeats in other settings. There were stretches when Adrienne was able to save up enough to get us our own place to live. Those stints didn't last long. Once we were even evicted after she came up short on the rent. Whatever the situations were, we were blessed to be able to move back in with Marion and Gilbert. If there was any criticism from them, I didn't hear it. Instead, they encouraged Mommie to think about her career. My mother's fondest dream was to one day become a doctor, like her father. He approved of her interest but encouraged Mom to embrace the nursing field instead. Grandfather felt that because she was a young mother, the rigors of medical school would prohibit her from spending quality time with me.

Whenever I watched her getting ready for the night, the prospect of Adrienne going out to have a good time with her friends didn't register as my mother leaving to have a "fun" time without me. On the contrary, her smile made me feel that the future held those possibilities for me as well. As in—*Oh, I can't wait until the day comes when I'm old enough to put on makeup and go OUT, like Mommie!*

In years to come, these nights out took a turn. As I got older, I began to suspect that things which were made to appear to be normal and okay, in fact, were not. Those promising moments spent watching my mother in the mirror, all dressed up, would fade, replaced by more complicated scenes.

We both became masters at keeping up appearances. That's where the lotus leaves end and the quicksand begins.

----

ere's what I knew as a child: I was not planned. My parents, Adrienne Banfield and Robsol Pinkett, met in high school. After my mother became pregnant at age seventeen, the two were married a short time later. Their marriage lasted about a year, ending in divorce some four months after my birth on September 18, 1971. Adrienne gave me the name Jada, which was the name of her favorite actress, Jada Rowland, who starred for two decades on the soap *The Secret Storm*. Jada's character began on the show as a teenager and aged in real time. So, in a sense, my mother had grown up with her—even though Jada Rowland herself is white and doesn't have much in common with Adrienne or me. Still, you might say my mother's decision to name me after an actress could have been either prophetic or wishful thinking.

In any case, I couldn't have asked for a better name that was almost exclusively mine. My middle name came about a little differently. For that, Adrienne decided to pay tribute to her sister Karen—but changed the "a" to an "o" so I could have my own special version, Koren. When I was a kid, if I was pushing the envelope or in trouble—fighting in school? acting out?—I'd blame my alter ego, Koren. Later, it became a running joke with me and my friends that if Koren surfaced, everybody better take cover.

The chronicle of how I came to be the blessed daughter of two addicts was not a tale told for my or anyone else's consumption. Not for decades, at least. As a child, I was not aware of the tumultuous relationship and traumatic events that had taken place between my parents—incidents that were full of physical and emotional abuse. Where I once assumed that they were simply too young to make a marriage work, I would eventually learn that their issues ran far deeper.

Upon hearing that Adrienne was pregnant, my grandmother pulled from her own trauma and addressed the situation by doing for her daughter what no one had done for her—Marion confronted Robsol Pinkett and gave him three choices: (a) marry Adrienne or (b) we will arrange for an abortion or (c) the baby will be adopted.

When I eventually heard how Robsol gave a resounding "Yes, I will marry her," despite his parents' stance that he didn't have to do anything he didn't want to do, it made me realize, *Wow, that was a lifesaving decision for me, and the stand-up thing for him to do.*

His one action gave my life an anchor in this world yet also sent a message to Adrienne that she would have been of less value as an *unwed* young single mother. This was a message Grandmother had already suffered. The need to be perceived a certain way in the world was a trauma response for my grandmother and unintentionally passed on to her daughters. My mother revered her mother. And yet I wonder if it became too much over the years to have to live up to Marion's standards. I wonder if this burden damaged my mother's sense of self-worth over time.

Rob's erratic behavior could only have compounded her lack of self-esteem. In his early but escalating throes of alcohol and drug addiction, he could lurch into a level of violence that was terrifying and confusing. The abuse continued throughout their relationship, including when she was pregnant, and though she tried to cope by avoiding his outbursts, that soon became impossible. One day at her parents' house, shortly after I was born, an argument got out of hand. My grandparents weren't home at the time, and my mother put me on the floor to keep me safe as Rob, in a violent rage, backed her into another room and punched her in the stomach. In fear for her life, Adrienne distracted him by saying, "Rob, we left the baby in the other room." As he turned to come get me, she ran across the street to a neighbor's house.

I learned this many years after the fact, but it was no less heartbreaking to hear as an adult that she had no choice but to leave me on the floor in the house and escape his assault. She was certain I would be safe because "I knew your father was never gonna hurt you, Jada."

After that, my mother wasted no time moving us in with her parents and filing for divorce.

Despite the drama between them, my mother continued to believe, correctly, that Rob would never lay a hand on me and that he had the right to exercise his desire to be a father on the few occasions he chose to do so. My mother, to her lasting credit, never talked shit about my father in front of me, and whenever he made the effort to be in touch, she didn't make a fuss. She would take me to see him at the home of his parents, to whom she made sure I had a strong connection.

Robsol Pinkett was a stonemason by trade, highly skilled, extremely handsome, and brilliant. He was esoteric, and by this I mean multidimensional in unexpected ways. He was versed in nearly every subject you could name, a talented poet, and, with charisma for days, a natural performer—which I would later experience during his impromptu poetry readings. Rob was eclectic in his interests, colorful in his taste and style, and occasionally *really* out there. For example, when I was seven or eight, he sent me a birthday present that had everyone scratching their head. On first glance, it appeared that he had shipped me a family of brass elephants. They turned out to be brass bells made as different-sized elephants. For someone like me, who later became curious about Eastern mysticism and culture, the choice wasn't so off the mark. At the time, I don't know what had made Rob think that brass elephant bells would "ring" for a child. But that was the beauty of my father.

Although I saw Robsol only in short bursts, I recognized that we had traits in common. One thing I valued early on was how he was always in search of new thought, new answers—always right on the cutting edge of something, whether it was exploring alternate realities or sacred geometry. For someone who was often under the influence of drugs and alcohol, he rarely appeared to be inebriated when he was with me. In my presence, he had a Zen calm about him, just a smooth cat.

I do remember my father held a look of sadness in his eyes—a glimpse that he was carrying a certain weight. Or that was my take on it. He also had a beautiful laugh that sounded like music and a beautiful smile that felt magnetic. I don't know what haunted Rob, I just know it was there.

The one thing I never picked up on was his violent streak. But when I was about seven or almost eight, I got a hint of it when I noticed a scar on Mommie's lower back as she was getting dressed. This scar was not red or inflamed but more of a whitish, ghostly color. "Mommie, what happened to your back?"

My mother didn't even turn around to answer, just continued getting dressed. "Your father pushed me over a balcony when he was drunk." The statement was matter-of-fact, nonchalant, and she didn't go any further. I got the sense that while she wasn't going to lie, there was nothing more she was going to tell me in that moment.

Even still, my mom allowed me to see him whenever he requested, and she never, to my knowledge, asked that visits be supervised.

My paternal grandparents, on the other hand, made sure I was always supervised when Robsol planned to visit me at their house. And because Mommie knew that would be the case, she didn't have to ask. Besides, my grandfather, Grant Pinkett, a lawyer by profession who worked for the government, absolutely adored me, and nothing bad was ever going to happen to me on his watch.

Unlike the predominantly white and Hasidic neighborhood where I lived with my mother's parents, my father's parents' neighborhood, about twenty minutes away, was much more blue-collar and made up almost exclusively of Black folks. If I was at the Banfields' and went out on my own, on foot or on my bike, walking to Cross Country Elementary School, for example, I was often the only Black person on the street. The opposite was true in the neighborhood where I spent time visiting my father's parents.

I loved, loved, *loved* the neighborhood where Shirley and Grant lived. Everything about it made me feel at home. I loved how everybody knew everybody's name, knew everybody else's kids' names, and looked out for one another. The community was family. We were all a tribe.

Seven houses up from the Pinketts' was the home of Mommy Bobby. She was like a magical character from a storybook. Very pale—could have passed for white—she had big black hair done in a dramatic bouffant. She always wore polyester pants, had a variety of 1970s necklaces with medallions, and wore glasses with big black frames. Mommy Bobby LOVED children and owned a wonderful nursery school close by, which I attended at three years old after Grandmother Shirley recommended it to my mother.

I had my first starring role in Mommy Bobby's production of *The Wizard of Oz*. The best and most coveted role was, of course, the Wicked Witch of the West. And I threw myself into the part, complete with a witch costume and a face painted green. When it was time for my entrance, I ran down the aisle of a borrowed auditorium, delightedly speaking my lines at the top of my lungs: "I'm the Wicked Witch of the West! I'm the Wicked Witch of the West!"

Adults began to applaud for me as Mommy Bobby loudly, proudly joined in. That was IT—the bug bit me young. Mommy Bobby became like a third grandmother to me. She would always say to my mother, "That child is something. Watch out, world."

On the rare occasions when Shirley and I went to visit Mommy Bobby or the two of us were out on our front porch, my grandmother became very neighborly, greeting friends and acquaintances, catching up on the talk of the day. Someone might say, "Oh, did you hear what happened with . . . you-know-who?"

"No, nobody tole me!"

The person would then proceed to tell the story. The local grapevine worked like that in the Pinketts' neighborhood—especially in the summertime, my favorite time, with everyone outside on their stoop, visiting, washing cars, just kick'n it.

Shirley had her ways, and they were never to be questioned. After she taught me to play solitaire, I decided to test the format. Why pick up three cards at a time from the deck to see if you got a card you needed? It was more efficient to pick up cards one by one.

Grandmother Shirley stood over me and very clearly stated, "That's not how you play that game."

Hmmmmmmm. If I was playing on my own, who would it hurt if I changed a rule?

No, no, no, no. Shirley was real about rules. Especially with games. There was *one* way to do everything, and it was her way. A rule was a rule. When we played Boggle, as soon as the sand went through the hourglass, it was "Pencils down!"

My grandmother Shirley was charming but biting—a walking paradox. A teacher who at one point had been a school principal, Shirley had a love of books and words that went along with the importance she placed on education. Both she and my grandfather Grant were voracious readers.

My fondest memories of Grandmother Shirley take me back to her small, narrow kitchen around a small table that fit all of three people in total. She had a tiny TV in there, which was on 24/7. She was either watching the news, her favorite game show, or any one of her preferred soap operas.

I loved watching Shirley talk at the TV. If it was *Wheel of Fortune,* she'd shout out the phrases before the contestants could. She was quick on her feet and didn't even need vowels.

And she could throw down on some chicken. Whenever she baked her delicious salt-and-pepper chicken wings, I had the opportunity to witness my grandmother clean the meat off the bone like no other. She was not shy about cracking the bone open and sucking out the marrow. If she caught me staring, she would exaggerate the sucking sounds and attack those bones as if she hadn't eaten in a whole year. I would crack up laughing. She would smile back at me. We never acknowledged the humor of it all, which made it even more cool—it was our thing.

Shirley Holland Pinkett was a beautiful woman as well, with a lovely smile and a subtle magnetism. Some of my features come from Shirley, I believe, including her square jaw and the deep dimple in her chin.

After she retired, Shirley became a homebody. Other than going to church and an occasional walk outside, she presided over her kitchen in her ubiquitous housecoat with her hair either in curlers all over her head or tied up in a scarf. As she got older, Shirley became more and more resistant to going out. My grandfather Grant did all the shopping for her—her clothes, the food, and all the necessities of the household. But the crazy part was that when Shirley did decide to leave the house, she dressed to kill, in furs and fine jewelry and a snappy, stylish ensemble.

My mother used to drop me off at the curb in front of my grandparents' house when I was going there to spend a night or two. Before we stopped, I'd spot my grandfather waiting for me, sitting there on the porch—a sentinel on guard, saying little but all-knowing. Grant Pinkett was a man of even fewer words than Gilbert Banfield, but he held a love for me that was absolutely undeniable.

Grandfather Grant was probably as invested in my well-being as Marion Banfield. The funny thing is that at school functions where parents are supposed to come, it would often be my father's father and my mother's mother showing up for me. Maybe Grant could see that his son wasn't able to be the father figure that I needed, and so he stepped up in his son's place.

One December day when I was six years old and visiting, Grandfather Pinkett mentioned, "Christmas is coming—is there something you want?"

"Yesssssss" was my answer. "I want the Baby Alive doll, but I want her to be Black." My mother didn't allow me to have white dolls. The Baby Alive baby doll was the "IT" present that year. There was nothing I wanted more.

Grandfather Pinkett upped the ante. "Come on. Let's go find your doll."

All I had to do was smile. He scooped me up, we jumped in the car, and we scoured the city of Baltimore looking for this much-in-demand toy. Everywhere was sold out. We went home empty-handed that day, sadly, but he was resolute. Somehow he located that doll and surprised me with her on Christmas.

Grandfather Pinkett always went the extra mile. He took me with him to do the grocery shopping and on errands. Whenever I was with my grandfather, I could feel how much he liked my presence and that I was never a nuisance or a burden. And the way he conveyed that love for me was to capture every moment in photographs. He took photos of me everywhere, which became lasting proof of a part of my childhood that was innately joyful and full of love.

The Pinketts' home was a typical working-class multilevel row house—with the usual first floor and a second story, plus a bonus floor on the basement level that my grandparents eventually turned into a separate living area. Whenever Rob was allowed to be around, the basement was where he slept.

I have only vague memories of visiting with my father in my early years. One instance that stands out vividly was at a point when he was deep in his addiction and he came by but was not allowed in the house. Drunk, high—probably both—he banged on the front door, begging, "Ma! Lemme in! I'm hungry . . . I need a place to stay."

From the kitchen where I sat at the table, I could see Shirley in the entryway, calling through the front door, "Rob, you gotta get yourself together. You know you can't stay here."

He pleaded with her. I could feel his desperation even if I couldn't make out all his words. She pressed against the door, and the two continued to go back and forth in an exchange that seemed to soften her. She returned to the kitchen and took food from the fridge, placed some of it in sandwich bags, and then went back to the front door. I watched as she opened the door barely enough to drop a paper bag on the porch. Then she shut it and returned to her seat at the kitchen table, muttering, "Well, at least he'll have something to eat." Then she looked down at her game of solitaire and picked up where she had left off.

As an adult, especially after having children of my own, I meet this memory on the road as a stranger. The pain that Shirley tried to hide couldn't be ignored as she'd done the only thing she could by leaving food on the porch for her drug-addicted son, my father, whom she could not allow in the house. Shirley, knowing his violence and his condition, could be seen in the Buddhist parable of the armless mother who watches her son fall into the perilous, tumultuous, churning currents of life, with no way to save him.

Every mother's child in trouble lives through Rob, and every powerless woman who would die for her beloved son or daughter has to surrender to forces far beyond her control.

My father and his mother had an excruciatingly unbreakable bond. My father at his core was a momma's boy. He would tell me later that there was no one he loved more. But their dynamic was complicated.

Shirley coped with her son's addiction through faith and prayer. She was convinced that Jesus would take care of her son and, eventually, he would be saved. She believed what she believed and had a deep love for Jesus that held her through the dark passages. She had another son, my uncle Steven, her baby boy, who was brilliant, and who, for the majority of his younger years, avoided the traps that had ensnared my father. I never knew what traumas Shirley had survived. If I asked too many questions, she deflected. Sometimes Shirley could be mean and gave no grace for my curiosity. One or two beers, and she was on me for looking where I should not have been. "Don't go looking through drawers without permission! This is not your house!"

It was in these moments that I could sense Shirley had a story. My guess is that something in her childhood had made her feel unloved and uncared for. She and I had a complicated relationship, just as she had with her son, but I loved her. As time went on, it became evident that she had a complicated relationship with herself.

My grandmother believed that although my father's drinking and substance abuse was a problem, her heavy drinking wasn't. Shirley was a binge drinker, but she didn't see that as being an alcoholic. She made this clear at an AA meeting that the family attended to celebrate Rob's first anniversary of sobriety, which took place when I was in my teens. Rob went to both AA and NA in those days.

When it was time for Shirley to say some words at the podium about Rob's recovery, the first thing she said was "I don't know how Rob became an alcoholic." Mommie and I immediately looked at each other in disbelief.

I think Grandmother Shirley really believed she wasn't an alcoholic because, as far as I could see, she drank only on Friday evenings and on Saturday—never on Sunday, because that was the Lord's Day. Shirley was old-school in her definition of alcoholism: You drink every day, can't hold a job, and can't take care of your family. This definition kept her in denial. "Functioning alcoholic" wasn't a term familiar to her, but that's what she was.

Shirley could be extra huggy and kissy when she drank. Or, in episodes that were more frightening, she would go on long rants all by herself down in the kitchen, and I'd hear her shouting at an unknown antagonist for hours. *Who is she talking to? Why is she so upset?* I would quietly ask myself. Then there were times when she would be caught up in raucous laughter, fully entertaining herself alone.

In those times, I would hide. Behind a closed door, upstairs in an extra bedroom where Shirley kept shoes and costume jewelry, I distracted myself by playing dress-up. Downstairs, Shirley's volume kept rising as she ranted, becoming more and more slurry, and more and more frightening.

There were occasions when Grant felt compelled to step in and put his foot down if Shirley was really out of hand—he would resolutely tell her, "That's enough." Or "Shirley, just be quiet."

And then Grandfather Grant would return to his chair on the porch and continue reading his book. He spent many, many hours on that porch. If he wasn't there, he and I were out running errands. Somehow he always found a way to be gone. In most cases, I was with him.

A child can feel tension between adults, can become hyperaware of matters she doesn't understand when the matters involve a lack of control or safety. Without full understanding, the child can feel alone, stuck on their own emotional island. I know that feeling well.

As I grew up, I spent weekends at the Pinketts', trapped upstairs. Shirley's binges began to coincide with a growing sense of isolation I felt at home with Adrienne. At this time, my mother's drug use was not as apparent as Rob's, although it was there. All I knew was that there was a lot going on behind closed doors. My mother was young, and like any young person, she wanted to hang out and kick it with her friends or boyfriends. When we weren't at Marion's, there were plenty of mornings when she would sleep in really late, and I'd have to rummage in the kitchen to figure out what to eat and sometimes find myself experimenting like a mad scientist: *What if I eat my cereal with Pepsi instead of milk?*

I also had a lot of time on my hands. This is when my penchant for mischief turned up as I found things I was not meant to find. *Hmmm, weed seeds and weed paper, what do they do?* I wasn't old enough to recognize the world of an addict, but as I look back, I become a witness to how Adrienne's addiction was already in play and how it created an atmosphere of loneliness for me. It's interesting that both of my parents—although their addictions presented differently at this time—were never fully available to me.

When I go in search of the origins of my broken heart, it is this sense of not being a priority to the two people who gave me life that creates a fracture in my feeling of worth.

R*ob was an untapped treasure chest* of talent and knowledge, although he was mostly considered, well, weird. He was simply a man before his time. If he had lived long enough, he would have appreciated his grown grandchildren as his lost tribe. My fondest memories of Rob are of witnessing his passion for poetry. One of his poems he couldn't wait to share with me.

"It's called 'Nobody Gets Out of Life Alive,'" he announced during one of our visits. His delivery was dramatic as he dove in.

> Nobody gets out of life alive.
> You can hold on to those world possessions—
> Those things you earn each day—
> And know the reason you do your do—
> But know what folks will say—
> They'll say, "nowhere was a good one"

And mean it from their hearts—no jive.

But nobody, but nobody gets, out of life alive.

Now you can tell me what you think I mean—

I know the score of the game—

Make a million and go in bed, the end will be the same, but

    some of us will not listen and others will say I lie,

but nobody, nobody gets out of life alive . . .

The poem went on from there, all of it captivating. I loved the title of this poem from the moment I heard it because I knew it to be true, even as a child. When Rob performed, he always came alive and shook off whatever burdens he carried. As an adult, I received the gift of a handwritten book of poetry from him. It remains one of my favorite keepsakes today.

Rob also gave me one of the most important lessons of my young life. I was seven years old when he taught me about the power of honesty. It might have been fall. The day was excessively bright and sunny. The weather was pleasant with a slight chill, and we were taking a walk to Mondawmin Mall to go shopping or maybe to a movie.

As we walked along, I couldn't help but wonder why Rob was wearing such a big coat—it wasn't that cold outside. He had his hair in a brushed-back Afro that looked cool, but he also looked contemplative. That wasn't unusual. But today he seemed really deep in thought.

I felt real grown, walking at my father's side, because he didn't feel the need to hold my hand. That's another thing I liked about Rob—how he never related to me like an incompetent child, and he was never on some fake "I'm playing Daddy now that I'm with you" flow when he decided to see me. I respected that. He gave me life, but in his presence, I was my own person. That would be the one bit of parenting advice from him that I would carry with me.

As we were walking along, out of the quiet, I heard him say, "Listen, I'm a drug addict and a criminal." He paused for a moment. "So I can't be your father."

My reaction was a relieved acceptance. He wasn't telling me anything I didn't already know. I respected his honesty.

Finally. An adult in my life was not afraid to lift the wool from my eyes and just be—straight. My father gave me the lasting ability to withstand and eventually appreciate harsh truths.

Painful though it may seem, the finality of his statement never conjured the sadness you might expect. I didn't know what it was like to have a father in the first place, because he hadn't been around. So I had nothing to miss. Whatever devastating effects would come from his inability to be a father to me didn't present themselves for many years (especially in my intimate relationships with men).

Truth can be a blessing, but I can't overlook how it can be a burden to a seven-year-old. When I saw my cousins with their dads, I might have missed having a father who could do daddy stuff with me. But I resolved early that maybe that kind of daddy love just wasn't meant for me.

i found god in myself/and i loved her/i loved her fiercely
—NTOZAKE SHANGE

Many of us are born to parents and families who are already in the mix of trying to survive, withstand, move through traumas of their own. Some do so more easily than others, while most of us, as children, are left caught in the storms of our family's dysfunction. A lot of us had to feel the brunt of it, which left us feeling unsafe, unwanted, uncared for—unlovable. For many of the adults in our lives, this was not the intention, but this fact remains.

———

Consequently, this left us with the need to find solutions to remedy painful circumstances. Unfortunately, those same solutions can show up in our adult lives as repeated cycles of the dysfunction we tried to escape in our childhood. It's okay. We must comfort ourselves with the fact that, as children, we did the best we could, within circumstances out of our control—which left us to believe we weren't *enough*. In the process, we were inevitably robbed of some of the most precious aspects of ourselves—our joy, our trust, our innocence. We, in turn, learned to reject those qualities within ourselves.

———

As adults, we no longer have to do that. When we allow the little one within to heal and understand that we are enough to take care of ourselves, we no longer have to demand and be blameful when others can't care for us. We realize, through self-care, that we are enough to love ourselves thoroughly.

———

I eventually learned to reclaim and honor my vulnerability. One of the ways was to buy stuffed animals and allow the kid in me to enjoy them, cry with them, sleep with them. By reacquainting myself with the tender one within, I learned the power of my vulnerability.

———

Can you find the moment when you began to reject the precious child within yourself? You could take that further and write a list of the parts of yourself you might want to reclaim—that you didn't feel safe enough to embrace as a child. Give yourself the freedom to decide how you would like to express those parts of yourself on your journey to reclaim them.

CHAPTER 3

Leaving the Garden

Bullying *became a problem in the* second grade.

There was this big boy who had a mouthful of crooked teeth and who would not leave me alone. He got in my face one day and threatened, "You better bring me ten dollars tomorrow or I'm going to beat you up."

Ten dollars? Where am I going to get ten dollars?

In desperation, I took the money from a place where my grandfather kept cash.

It felt wrong, for sure, but as soon as I paid the bully, he backed off. His face lit up like I was his best friend. "You really got me the money." And he took off. He made the mistake of bragging on the playground and showing off his money. This came to the attention of the principal, who asked him where he got the ten dollars. He didn't hesitate to answer, "Jada Pinkett."

Grandmother received the call from the school and was initially APPALLED. There had to be a mistake. But when I tearfully told Grandmother the story, she knew I must have been very intimidated to have stolen money from my grandfather.

The bottom line for Marion Banfield was that the school could have done more to prevent the situation from escalating. In her view, every child ought to feel safe at school. Her conclusion was that I should go to private school.

I wasn't sure, because by this point, I'd reached the conclusion that there was a vast difference between how I was educated at home and how I was educated at school. Conventional structure did not work for me.

My mother's feeling was that I was just bad as hell at school. She felt strongly that I should at least be in a school setting with Black teachers, Black principals, and Black kids, and that was damn near nonexistent with private schools. But she was willing to explore options for my sake.

Marion arranged for me to have a trial with a Montessori school so they could assess me. My first assignment was to write a short story and illustrate it. Sounded fun! I decided to write a story reminiscent of authors I discovered on Mommie's bookshelf—like Stephen King. Such books were not necessarily appropriate for my age, but I loved horror and ghost stories all my life. So I wrote one that involved someone getting stabbed in a cave by an unknown monster, and I included a drawing. The teacher conducting my interview was disturbed, even though I could not have been prouder. First I was not protected from bullying, and now I was misunderstood by adults who didn't know me. My attitude was *No, there is nothing wrong with me, and you people are wrong.*

Was there something wrong with Stephen King? No, he was a genius.

Although I ultimately was accepted, I didn't last long at Montessori. Mommie and Marion believed I needed more structure because, ironically, I went from being bullied at one school to running the show at this one. All I wanted to do was play, talk, and tell the teachers what I would and would not do.

Our next attempt was another private school. The one-day trial experience there wasn't terrible, but I was not used to an all-white environment and felt like an outsider.

As soon as I saw Mommie, I told her, "I don't like it here." Thank goodness, I wasn't given enough time to prove how bad as hell I was.

Next, Mommie and Grandmother agreed upon a happy medium, a public school—Mount Washington Elementary, where the faculty and student body were diverse. This school was not too far from Grandmother's neighborhood, and even closer to the welcoming home of Uncle Leslie, Aunt Marsha, and Cousin Tiffany, where I walked every day after school.

The situation was better but not trouble-free. Being small, I got picked on all the time, by boys and girls alike. One day on the playground in the fourth grade, a much bigger girl approached me and, for no damn reason, grabbed a chunk of my hair and pulled so hard I thought she would pull it out by the roots.

When I returned home to Grandmother's house that evening, Aunt Karen was there, and I told her all about it and asked if she could come to school with me the next day.

Karen got that look in her eye that I sometimes saw with Adrienne. She said, "Don't come up in here tell'n me about some girl pull'n your hair. Somebody touches you, make sure they don't do it again."

I was quiet.

My aunt Karen was so beautiful, and she was just as tough. She had to be. In school, my aunt and my mother were both constantly having to prove: "Don't let these looks fool you." Karen had survived a few abusive relationships, at one point had her jaw broken by a boyfriend (whom Adrienne chased down with a baseball bat), and then had her son, my cousin Brett, taken from her by an ex. I will never forget hearing my aunt screaming for her child, my one-year-old cousin screaming for his mother, and my mother screaming at the police to do something. Aunt Karen didn't know where Brett was for two years.

The result of these traumas was that my aunt Karen and my mother carried the burden in their veins of "I'm not to be played with." The ghosts of their grief and the roots of their aggression left impressions on me, giving me permission to protect myself when necessary. And I learned by default whatever violence I could muster would keep me from—my hurt. Physical and emotional alike.

Karen's words stayed with me. I would of course avoid a fight if I could, and I never went looking for one. But as I got older, part of survival made fighting unavoidable, and if anyone wanted to test me, I had no problem meeting the call.

A lot of things happened in the summer of 1981. One of them was that my mother had started nursing school. Now that we had moved back in with my grandparents, she made the effort to spend time with me on weekends, spontaneously announcing outings like "Jada, we're going to the beach!" and off to Ocean City we would go.

One of the lasting gifts that Adrienne gave me was her love of music, all kinds of music. And that love came to live in my bones. Mommie loved everything—R&B, pop, a touch of rock, disco, and even country. She loved Kenny Rogers. On Saturday mornings, whenever we cleaned our living space in the attic, it was a party. Teena Marie's "Square Biz" or Cheryl Lynn's "Got to Be Real" joyfully filled the air. No matter where we lived, Mommie ALWAYS had a record player. Mommie bought vinyl records, and vinyl became my thing, too—to the point that as soon as I could get a job, it would be to buy albums of my own. My first purchase? Prince.

Going to go see *The Raiders of the Lost Ark* with my mom was a spur-of-the-moment adventure. I was nine, almost ten, but not prepared for those hideous, horrific face-melting images escaping from the ark. Mommie was going to go out afterward, and when she dropped me off at my grandparents', I admitted, "I don't want to sleep upstairs by myself tonight."

"I told you it was gonna be scary."

"But I'm *really* scared."

Mommie walked me into the house and promised, "I'll see you in the morning."

"Okay, can you see if I can sleep with Grandmother tonight?" I pleaded.

We tiptoed into my grandparents' dark bedroom, and Adrienne leaned around the doorway, whispering, "Ma, Ma . . ."

Marion sat up right out of sleep. "What's wrong?"

"Jada is scared to sleep upstairs. Can she stay in your room tonight?"

"Oh, for crying out loud."

My grandfather stirred, glanced at us, but chose to stay quiet and go back to sleep.

My grandmother might not have been happy about getting up and preparing her chaise lounge for me to sleep on, but she didn't leave me hang'n. Even if it didn't suit her rule that children should never sleep in bedrooms other than their own. The fact that she made an exception and allowed me to sleep on her beloved chaise was not at all lost on me.

It was in this era that Grandmother began to weave in reminders about the importance of not depending on a husband or any man as a sole source of support. "Always have your own money," she repeated on a few occasions. "Do not depend on a man for financial security." She was also very frank about the birds and the bees, saying to me as a preadolescent, "Know how to pleasure yourself. Your pleasure belongs to you and not to a man."

Perhaps my grandmother was preparing me for a time when she was no longer alive. No one ever said a word to that effect. In my mind, she was going to live forever.

T*he main event of the summer* of 1981 gave me a new leap of independence. Now nine years old, I already was a latchkey kid and walked myself from school daily, rode my bike everywhere, and had free rein in the neighborhood as long as I was home before dark. This summer I got a taste of the streets Cali-style. Mommie had arranged for me to fly out to visit Rob in his new home in California. He had a new wife and an infant son named Caleeb and a stepdaughter, Regina, who was a few years older than I was.

Rob was barely present during that trip because of his job. Plus, he had started drinking again. My stepmother was working all the time and had her hands full when she wasn't. This meant I mostly got to hang with Regina and all her teenage friends.

It was an adventure. Palm trees and sunny skies, and CUTE boys, from tall chocolate drops to lowriding cholos. In a short amount of time, I went from flying out in my tidy ponytail, dressed in a cute little outfit designed and made for me by my grandmother, to heading home to Baltimore in some Rick James–style cornrows with beads and all.

That hairdo changed my life! I felt like I was a real-deal teenager like Regina. I loved swinging my hair as the beads bounced against each other in a CLICK-CLICK-CLACK sound.

Spoiler alert: Grandmother took one look at me when I got back, had a fit, and made me take out the braids and beads on the spot. I had to resort back to my kiddie pigtails that in no way fit my new persona of "I ain't no lil kid no mo." But those cornrows left me with a different kind of confidence.

Not long after I returned from Cali, Mommie announced, out of the blue, that she was marrying Tony. They'd been dating awhile, and now the three of us were going down to the courthouse to make it official.

Mommie studied my face to gauge my reaction. I did not hide that I was unhappy. The thought of us sharing space with someone other than my grandparents was, let's say, not desirable. I was used to it being just her and me, and even though there had been a series of boyfriends in her life, they had never moved in. Plus, they were never around often enough to tell me what to do.

Now I was going to have somebody trying to be my daddy? And I'd have to vie for Mommie's attention and time? Nope.

My mother was so happy and sure that this was the right thing to do, I accepted that I had no say in the matter. I would just have to deal.

All I could do was smile, be as pleasant as I could, while I stood in that courthouse and posed for pictures. The last thing I wanted to do was rain on my mother's parade, but I just wasn't feeling it. Through all the smiles and romantic "I dos" and "forevers," I just kept thinking, *We'll see.*

T*ony wore my resistance down very* quickly, and I will forever be grateful that Mom brought him into our lives. He filled a void, without question, and much to my surprise, he was a kindred spirit. Tony was Mr. Go, Go, GO, as much on the move as I always wanted to be.

A lawyer who had worked in Tennessee and was studying for the Maryland bar while working as a legal aide, he had energy that was big and DYNAMIC. He was coming up in his field, soon to become prosecutor for the state's attorney, and he was completely in support of my mother's work to become a fully licensed RN. Tony was a big kid at heart with a twinkle in his eye, a fantastic sense of humor, and an infectious laugh. He had his own brand of charisma and could charm most people in an instant. Grandmother really dug him. He was a hungry, ambitious young lawyer with the potential to make it big, and he fit perfectly into Grandmother's picture of whom her daughter was meant to have as a husband.

Tony was undeniably fun. Plus, as a male figure, he brought a level of security to the dynamic with my mom that I hadn't felt before, outside of the influence of my grandfathers. I was new to this traditional kind of stability and consistency outside of Marion's house, and I had to admit, it felt very nice. Mommie and I would finally have a safe home of our own, full of family love.

The first place we shared with Tony was a roach-infested row house in Northeast Baltimore. No matter how often the exterminator came and sprayed that stinky, oily poison, the roaches just went to the row house connected to us that wasn't so clean, and they chilled until the coast was clear. They always returned. I love all living creatures, but I ain't no fan of roaches.

You can imagine how ecstatic I was to find out we would be moving into a brand-new house, also in Northeast Baltimore. Tony was climbing the ladder professionally, and his brother, a contractor, had renovated this home, and Tony was going to buy it! When he took us to see it the first time, Mommie couldn't hide her excitement. Tony glanced at me. "You like it?"

"Is this our new house?"

Tony nodded.

I was wide-eyed. It was an open plan, and everything was modern, airy, and bright. The house had a sparkling kitchen and a beautiful big backyard. My bedroom was like something from a magazine. I couldn't believe it. Tony was clearly on his way to being the ideal husband and father that I'd never had.

Tony was short, with a square little head and a sharp intellect. He was a criminal lawyer, so he could read a person or a situation in a flash. Oh, and he could TALK. TALK circles around people. But that was to be expected. That's what he did for a living.

I became fascinated with the law and loved how Tony strategized for every case differently. In his career, he worked as both a prosecutor and a public defender, but whichever side it was, these weren't small civil cases. These were hard-core crimes, including violent murders.

While Tony studied his latest case, I had a habit of snooping over his shoulder as he immersed himself in the paperwork. One time I found my eyes glued to a gruesome photograph in the evidence file he was reviewing, and he felt me looking. He glanced up from his work and asked, "Do you want to see?"

I excitedly nodded. He showed me the shots of a murder scene and gave me his theory of the case and his strategy for proving it.

From then on, I'd ask about his latest case, and he never shied away from giving me the full story and how he was going to prosecute the defendant. He even took me to court a few times because I was so interested. He loved how inquisitive I was and enjoyed how much I enjoyed what he did.

Not only did Tony spark in me a lasting interest in law, he also introduced me to my lifelong love of road trips. He was ready for an adventure whenever the mood struck. Mom couldn't just get up and go while working and attending school for her RN license at the same time. So Tony and I became full-time running buddies. I went wherever he went.

Road trip? *Hell,* yeah! We went all over the Northeast and the mid-Atlantic to visit his college buddies or relatives. It might be a day trip or a weekend ride, but we were on the road to somewhere exciting every chance we got.

Tony really did go every extra mile, no pun intended, to be a positive male presence in our household. With Mom's schedule, it sometimes seemed like Tony was my primary caregiver.

The highlight of the week came every Sunday, when we would go have dinner with Tony's mother, Mrs. White, who was gentle and kind, and whom I liked very much. Tony took a lot of pride in looking out for his mom, and I always admired that.

The least fun we had was doing homework, but he rose to the challenge—a treacherous task, because I was a struggling, easily frustrated student. English, social studies, and anything remotely connected to creativity were all easy. Math, though, made no sense. I could add, subtract, divide, and multiply, but math word problems offended me. A visual, tactile learner, I couldn't get a concept from being told how to get it; you had to show me. Tony was patient and consistent, but it didn't change the fact that I was neither.

We almost always got along, but inevitably, we had a classic father/daughter conflict that really upset me. In middle school, there was a boy, taller than I was and very thin, who taunted and bullied me every day. Whenever he railed on me, I tried to play it cool and reported it to my teachers. Nothing happened. Then one day, in the library, of all places, this fool got in my face while pushing past my physical comfort zone. His pointed finger almost touched my nose. Well, that's all I needed to jump on him. As if possessed, I went FULL RED. All I remember were the library aides pulling me off him.

We were immediately sent to the principal's office. The boy had visible scratches on his face and neck, which the principal took to mean that he had all the injuries, and therefore she needed to come down on me. I had lost several fights already in elementary school, with the scars to prove it, but not this one!

I pleaded, "I kept tell'n my teacher he was mess'n with me, and nobody did anything. He got in my face!"

My principal barked, "Watch your tone, or you'll be in more trouble than you are now."

I actually liked my principal. I found her fair. But in this case, she was wrong. I had a right to protect myself, and nobody was going to change my mind on that. It was what I had been taught.

When I got home, Warren Anthony Brown went in on me like he never had. Before I could finish my defense, he sternly countered, "Are you crazy? You were fighting a boy! He could have really hurt you if he wanted to!"

Tony went on and on. I sat in front of him unbothered because I knew I was RIGHT. All I could think about this tall skinny menace was: *Let him touch me again, I'mma do the same damn thing.*

Mommie didn't say much. She let Tony take the lead, and I was pissed about that, too. I wonder if she could see the bubble over my head: *Oh, now I shouldn't fight? You ain't raise me like that.*

Then the hammer came—I was *punished*. WHAT??????? Whatever! Punish me! Tony and I gave each other the silent treatment for damn near two weeks. My attitude was written on my face: *Who tells a person not to protect themselves when no one else will? This is stupid!*

This experience was an object lesson for my later journey as a mother. It taught me that one ought not combat a child's determination. Any child of mine would probably have strong willpower, and when the time came, I made a promise to work for understanding with patience instead of trying to break their resolve. And God gave me not one but three kids with fierce self-determination.

Time passed and all was forgiven. We moved on. Everybody got back to their hustle. And Tony's hustle was strong. Mommie's hustle was extra-strong at this time. She became an RN and, though Tony knew and I didn't really know it yet, a full-blown, high-functioning heroin addict who was holding it all together. The part I saw—their determination and drive—was a gift for me to witness because it revealed how discipline, self-confidence, and willpower can be a potent recipe for success. This example I would also take into my life. Have your kids on your hip on your hustle—you can better show them than tell them.

What was my hustle?

At twelve years old, I had a moment onstage that made me think performing could really be my thing. It was in a summer-program production. This time I had been cast as the lead, Dorothy, in *The Wizard of Oz*.

The house was packed, as I recall. My mother and Grandmother Marion were in the crowd, as was Tony, along with a lot of the family who had come to cheer me on. I was thrilled.

And just as I was launching into the final solo of "Somewhere Over the Rainbow," I forgot the words.

It was a moment when I could have crumbled and ruined the whole show. I could have decided to walk away from the stage forever. Instead, my confidence, willpower, and discipline kicked in as I announced, "I have forgotten the words to the song. Why don't you join in and sing them with me?"

And they did. It was as if the moment had been planned. It was as if I was shining a spotlight on the audience, which everybody loved. That became one of my proudest memories, because I made sure the show went on and barely missed a beat. It was a crash course in the power of "Don't let 'em see you sweat."

From then on, my performing aspirations became more serious. I had already begun attending an after-school program called TWIGS (To Work In Gaining Skills), at Baltimore School for the Arts, considered a stepping stone to getting into the performing arts high school.

Just before my thirteenth birthday, *Miami Vice* debuted on Friday nights. Tony and I watched every episode together, predicting storylines and delighting in the merger of the traditional cop-show format with the latest styles and scenes from MTV.

Those Friday nights, while they lasted, were magic. But they soon came to a grinding halt. Suddenly, the world was no longer safe.

T*he one-two punch came in early* 1985. Even though Marion had not been well for some time, it was never real to me that at some point she may not be with us—with me. She had survived cancer once, and when it reappeared as bone cancer, I expected that she would survive again. Grandmother was only seventy years old—relatively young.

The family was probably in as much denial as I was. As long as she could, Marion kept up with the celebrations for holidays and birthdays. I have a memory of one of the last Christmases that we celebrated. For the first and only time, Marion invited Shirley and Grant Pinkett for Christmas dinner with the Banfields. It was as if she felt the importance of closing the circles and fully making peace that year.

For all I knew, everything seemed right in the world.

Until the day my uncle Leslie came to pick me up from school. This was very unusual and gave me an immediate feeling that something was wrong. As I approached him, he calmly gave me the news that Grandmother had died. All I could say was "Okay." There was a part of me that believed he was mistaken, because my grandmother being gone was an impossibility.

When we got to her house, Aunt Karen was there and very distraught. Reality hit me hard, and I went upstairs to the attic to ground myself. Shortly after, Karen climbed the stairs and told me that she wanted me to come with her to say goodbye to Grandmother.

Nooooooooo was all I could think. I hadn't known that her body was still in the house. My heart shattered. "I don't want to," I told Aunt Karen. I was scared to see my grandmother dead. That would make it all too real.

Karen replied, "You have to. This will be your last chance to see her."

I know my aunt Karen meant well, but I wish that I had not gone to see her.

As I stood outside her bedroom door, I saw my lifeless grandmother lying on her bed. My grandfather was broken but doing his best to keep it together. My mother had just arrived, and she was inconsolable. I was frozen in the chaos of grief.

"Come in closer so you can see her, Jada," Karen urged softly.

I took three more steps in and vowed I would not step one foot closer. In that moment I had to admit it was good that all the pain caused by the bone cancer, all the moaning and discomfort she'd suffered through, was over. She looked peaceful. I accepted that my grandmother no longer existed in what now seemed to be a shell.

All I could do was question how death could be so cruel and not give me the chance to say goodbye.

Soon after I lost my grandmother, Tony and Mommie started the process of divorcing. All the solid ground under my little feet disappeared in less than six months. Tony did his best. He told me that although he and Mom were divorcing, "You are still my daughter."

Unfortunately, his reassurance dissolved before long, more or less after he met a woman who initially tried to be maternal toward me but soon forbade him any contact with his ex-wife's daughter. I'll never forget receiving a phone call from her when she told me, "Find your real father," and then hung up on me.

She harassed my mother and me endlessly until Grandmother Shirley gave her a call. Shirley told this woman that she knew people in high places and that if she bothered us ever again, she would make her life miserable. We never heard from that woman again, but with that, I didn't hear from Tony, either.

That rejection was brutal. He was the only active father I ever knew. Having him ripped out of my life was far more devastating than having a man who was my biological parent tell me that he couldn't be my father. Everybody always put so much emphasis on blood being the most important thing when it comes to familial bonds. In my case, the bond I had made with Tony was far more powerful than the blood I shared with Rob.

Something broke inside me. My grief was oceanic, so I put it on a library shelf labeled "unlovable" and tried to leave it there for good.

My thirteenth year was when my life changed drastically and when the Baltimore streets became my home—where I went in search of my power, sense of control, and love.

People are not meant to be perfect. We can mourn that fact,
but at some point, it's to our benefit to accept it. It's a mighty
invitation for healing.

—MY FRIEND'S MOM

Very rarely do we have the ability as children to see our parents as human, with their own hurts and battles acquired before we came into their lives. Nor do we have the ability to see that their wounds and unhappiness aren't our fault. Too often we have ideal pictures of how parents are supposed to be.

———

Even when we're adults, having to face our parents' humanness can be daunting and deeply painful. Yet the willingness to accept that delivers deep healing. It helps us let go of the childlike fantasy version of the Supreme Being parental figure. And when we dare to take our parents off their pedestals, we can recognize the influence of generational trauma. This is where knowing the history of our less than perfect parents can be liberating.

———

Many times, it is clear that our parents and their parents had unhealed stuff they passed on unwittingly. We then pass that on—unless we recognize the cycles. The conscious decision "This stops with me" is the first step. With that comes freedom, which brings internal chaos into order. Having awareness of these toxic cycles is a bold act of self-care.

———

Can you recognize patterns in your life and relationships that stem from inherited trauma cycles? If so, write down which cycles are most important for you to break. How does this awareness make you feel, knowing you don't have to carry that burden anymore?

CHAPTER 4

University of the B-more Streets

My midnight forays to go hang with my boyfriend at the 7-Eleven came to an abrupt halt in the fall of 1985, once the school year began. To this day, I cannot believe I kept that routine for much of the summer, considering the Baltimore city landscape at the time, which was far from the charmed description of "Charm City." This is Baltimore, *where you gots to B-more careful.* Don't get it twisted—*this ain't Mary-land. This is Murda-land.*

By the mid- to late 1980s, Baltimore was becoming known for having one of the most dangerous inner cities in the country per capita. This was especially true for kids my age, fourteen and fifteen years old, who were among the most likely in the country to be murdered by peers. It became the norm that a dude could get killed after simply stepp'n on someone's brand-new sneakers. Or not giving up their dookie chains or leather puff jackets. Don't think for a minute that girls were exempt from violence. One of my homegirls got stabbed to death with a kitchen knife in a family fight.

Hair salons seemed like a common place for dudes in a jealous rage to gun down their girlfriends. We also got jacked if we were too fly in the wrong place at the wrong time. And let's not even start on the drug game and the treacherous murders that inspired—we'll get to that. Now, not every block of every street was a war zone, but there was nowhere that you could go and not be on guard. This was true of where Mommie and I lived after her divorce—the row house on Price Avenue that she was able to buy with a small down payment. Though it was in need of a lot of work, it was surrounded by nice homes of working-class families.

This was life now. This was what we had been given, and the streets of B-more were an initiation. They surely prepared me for my future in ways I did not expect. To make your way, if you were young and Black, the streets were unavoidable. The curriculum this university had to offer set you up to fail if you let it. The need to survive was a given. But for me, that wasn't enough. In my mind, I had to learn what it took to thrive. The University of the B-more Streets seemed to offer opportunity, a way to make it big, and, for some, to be on top. I took to those streets to find my come-up.

After the double blows of my grandmother's death and Tony's departure, I was lost, in a state of mourning, and in need of a new sense of safety. It was now apparent that Adrienne was in the throes of her addiction and was mostly unavailable, leaving me, for all intents and purposes, on my own. In my community, there was an epidemic of orphaned children and teens, maybe not in the traditional sense of "orphan," but we had to figure it out without parental guidance. We had to grow up before our time.

When I lost my virginity at age fourteen, not long after Marion died, I was probably the last of my girlfriends to do so. I remember there were girls in middle school having sex with grown men. We all grew up fast, wild'n out in ways that adults in our lives never suspected.

We might have been orphaned, but we had one another while trying to figure out life skills we needed to survive the concrete jungle we'd been given. We had to clique up to help each other make it through. What I needed was a level of independence so I could create my own safety. Home no longer gave me that. The way forward, I decided right away, was to make my own money and my own rules. To do so, I had to learn the lay of the land. Ironically, in thinking this was how to keep myself safe, I walked closer and closer to the edges of danger, becoming addicted to the constant adrenaline rush.

How did I manage this, you ask, as an only child of a street-savvy young mother? For one thing, in the aftermath of her mother's death and her divorce from Tony, Adrienne was thrust into a state of deep grief that pushed her into becoming a full-fledged heroin addict. She had no one to answer to, no one to keep *her* accountable. And guess what? Because of her addiction there was no one keeping me accountable either. There was a lot of trouble for me to find during the hours of her graveyard shift. On top of that, trouble had a way of finding me while I was just minding my own business.

I*t is late summer or early* fall, at the beginning of the school year. Mom and I are sitting outside on the steps of our row house on Price Avenue when one of my homeboys comes driving up in a brand-spanking-new red BMW M3. This homeboy is a little corny, but he is fun.

With the music bump'n hard, he rolls down the driver's window and calls to me, "Yo! What's up?"

"Not much." I smile and throw his question back at him: "What's up?"

"I got a new ride. Where you try'n to go?" He smiles. The car is fly as hell, and I wouldn't mind being seen in it.

There's a beat. By this time, one thing my mother knows is that I'm always on the go, whether I'm at school, hanging out at the skating rink, or at any one of my jobs—the record store or Merry-Go-Round or the Gap. Or just doin' me.

I look to my mother. "You were just say'n you wanted some french fries from McDonald's. You want us to go get you some?"

"Who's he?"

"He's just my homeboy. Do you want some french fries or not?"

"Yeah, and stop at the store and bring me a Pepsi," she says.

"I'll be back." I hop up off the porch and call out, "All right, take me to McDonald's real quick." And make a dash for his dope-ass car.

In a flash, I'm in the car, sitting up front, window down, feeling fly as hell—mobb'n.

After a few minutes of hitting the main drag of Reisterstown Road, WHOOOOWHOOOOooooooo! Here come the COPS, from two directions, with lights flashing and sirens blaring.

Next thing I know, my homeboy—who, I will come to find out, has picked me up in a m-fing STOLEN car—GUNS the gas pedal and SPEEDS off, launching us into a full-blown CHASE.

This is the kind of shit you see in the movies, with a swarm of cops and helicopters chopping it up overhead. Now, this dude is not fazed in the least, 'cause he's a car thief PRO (I'd find out later).

"What the fuck is going on? You gonna get us killed!"

"No, I'm not!" he shoots back calmly.

He is calm. His being calm makes me believe he has a plan, and it is going to work, but . . . we are in a full-on chase. I've never seen a car chase in the movies where the people actually get away.

He manages to speed through traffic with such velocity and finesse that he somehow DITCHES the cops. Instead of finding some alley to hide in (too obvious), he pulls off into a residential cluster of streets that he races through like a stealth bomber.

My heart is about to pound out of my chest when he pulls over and says, calm and steely, "Get out the car." I start to do as he says, and he adds, "Anybody asks, act like you're walking home from a friend's house after watching some movies."

Well, by this point, I'd begun to question his advice and was worried that I'd draw attention to myself as a little lost Black girl in an all-white residential area. So, fast on my feet, I took off running at full speed until I quickly scouted for a hiding spot behind a family home, down a flight of steps to a basement. No one could see me from any angle at the bottom of those stairs. After a bit, not hearing anything, I figured the coast was clear.

Once I left the stairwell where I'd been hiding, I walked cautiously through a couple of backyards until it looked safe for me to weave back onto the street. Once my feet hit the sidewalk, I regained my fourteen-year-old strut. Everything seemed cool until I got to the corner.

Let me tell you, there is no jolt to the system like being a teenager who did nothing wrong, other than wanting to go get some fries, but finds a black-and-white police car waiting for you at the corner like a cobra about to strike. The next jolt was realizing that they must have had a police car at every corner of this residential area.

Be cool, I told myself, and tried to act curious, walking right toward a waiting police car.

Two cops approached me. One asked, "So, where you coming from?"

"I'm coming from a friend's house."

"What friend?"

I told them I'd been watching a movie at one of my girlfriends' houses. Real convincing.

The second cop shook his head and leveled with me: "We got your friend."

Of course, I played it out, asking, "What friend?"

Their attitude was "The jig is up, we have your friend, and he told us everything, so you better not lie."

My attitude was "I don't know what you're talking about, I went to a friend's house."

The officers sort of sighed, as if I had forced their hand, and put me in the back of a patrol car to go down to the station. The POLICE station!

The first person I saw when I walked in, looking glum, was . . . guess who? Homeboy didn't say a word. The cops took me over to a desk, sat me down, and asked, "Now do you want to tell us what happened?"

"Officer," I said, telling the absolute truth, "I don't know anything. All I know is that he picked me up. And we were going to McDonald's, and then the next thing I knew, we were being chased."

They conferred and decided, unsurprisingly, I guess, to call my mother.

A short time later, Mom showed up, annoyed as hell, but she believed me when I told her that I knew nothing and therefore had done nothing.

The big lesson here was: Don't ask questions . . . EVER! The less you know, the better. I found out only after the fact that this dude was a much-sought-after car thief. What would I have said if I had known the car was stolen? Thank God I didn't know nuth'n. That kept me safe and helped me keep my homeboy's business out of my mouth when talking to the police. I truly had nothing to tell them. Note taken for this part of the curriculum.

Truth be told, I was way more afraid of Adrienne, anyway.

Come to find out, the police had been on my homeboy's neck for months. He had been in foster care and was now sent to juvie. He was simply another orphaned heart trying to graduate the University of the B-more Streets.

The police sent me home with my mother and offered their stern advice to be more careful about getting into random cars. Funny enough, the incident may have caused my mom to question me less for a time because I had done nothing wrong. This would not always be the case.

Not by a long shot.

B *y the time I started ninth* grade at Baltimore School for the Arts, I had been attending the TWIGS program there for about a year. This free after-school program was for students between second and eighth grade who were hoping to gain experience in music, dance, theater, visual arts, and other creative disciplines. Every year more than one thousand arts students auditioned for Baltimore School for the Arts—a pre-professional arts training high school with an academic component—and only one hundred or so were admitted. As many as half of those who got in had gone to TWIGS.

Even though the school had only been in existence since 1979, the halls felt hallowed, being housed in two historic buildings, one of which was an old brownstone and the other the former Alcazar Hotel on the corner of Cathedral Street and Madison Avenue. The total enrollment was about four hundred students, a relatively small student body for a Baltimore public school, and because we took most of our classes in our particular areas of focus, those were the fellow students we got to know most.

Acting was always the thing that I most excelled at, and seemed to be a viable professional path, although my passion for self-expression lent itself to a range of other interests. Whenever possible, I'd take every dance class I could. Modern, ballet, African, jazz, you name it. I loved visual arts, too. Because voice, like movement, was so much a part of the actor's instruments, I managed to get vocal training as well.

I was very lucky to have a special person early on who encouraged me to see my own possibilities. He was Donald Hicken, the head of the theater department. Donald was kind but firm, willing to go to bat for me when and if the situation warranted. There came a point, however, when I most surely began to test his patience—after he looked the other way too many times as my attendance record increasingly left much to be desired. That point was when I basically went missing along with my schoolmate Cory Washburn.

We weren't actually missing at all. Cory and I had just decided that we should get ourselves to New York City because another BSA schoolmate, Josh Charles, was living there in his own apartment and everything as a full-on working professional actor. This was after he scored a small part in the John Waters movie *Hairspray,* shot in Baltimore, though his breakout movie role would be a bit later, in *Dead Poets Society*. It seemed like an excellent idea that we should head to New York to hang out with Josh and learn the ways of having a real-deal gig in show business.

Josh Charles, who may be best known for his stellar work as one of the leads of the TV series *The Good Wife,* was already cool as hell back then. He and I had been friends since elementary school. At age nine, Josh had swag and was the coolest white dude we knew. After attending different middle schools, he and I reunited at Baltimore School for the Arts. Early in high school, he started booking professional jobs as an actor and, soon after, left BSA to go live and work in New York, which to me was dope as hell.

When I called Josh and asked, "Can Cory and I come to New York and hang?" he, being who he was, was completely down to host us. We couldn't wait to see his New York City apartment and all the trappings of making it big. In our eyes, he was living the dream.

The sticking point was what to tell my mother, who was starting to wonder how much I could be trusted, especially after I stole her rental car, a Ford Escort, when she was out of town one weekend. There was no malice aforethought. As in not premeditated. It was just that I needed some wheels to go to the skating rink. I was still in the ninth grade and had no license. I had driven only in a parking lot a few times with Tony, but I managed to drive the Escort through the streets and pick up my friend Warren, a senior, who drove to pick up the rest of our friends. We went all the way to Crystal Skate Palace, a rink in Temple Hills—as far as you could go without leaving Maryland at the eastern border of D.C.—where we skated, and then dropped off everybody back at Warren's house.

From there, I got behind the wheel and returned to Price Avenue without incident. Except . . . I didn't know how to parallel park. In a panic, I drove back to Warren's house and made him come home with me and parallel park the rental car and take the subway home.

Phew.

Not exactly. The first thing Adrienne said when she returned was "Did someone move my rental car?"

"What?" I acted cool, like—*how is that possible?*

She seemed to accept that logic, but then—thinking it over—shook her head, saying, "I know that's not where I parked that car when I left."

She let it go, but I realized I had to get smarter. So, about a week before Cory and I planned to take the train to visit Josh, I brought the subject up: "Yeah, Ma, you know my class is taking a trip to New York, and we'll be gone for about three days."

"What's the trip for?"

Without overtalking the subject, I explained that we were all going to be participating in an Alexander Technique workshop. It was really a brilliant cover story, if I did say so myself, because my mother didn't question any of the logistics, just gave me permission to go and agreed to drop me at the train station at the appointed time.

Once inside Baltimore's Penn Station, I spotted Cory, packed and ready, and we went to buy our tickets. Before we knew it, our Amtrak train was chugging off to New York City's Penn Station.

What happened next is something of a blur. We definitely had fun for a day or so, hung with Josh, and walked the big-city streets like we'd brushed shoulders with fame. Then, for some reason, the school happened to call my mother that day about my absence. They had never done this before, even though I was always skipping out on school. I have no clue why they chose that day.

My mother explained my absence: "Oh, that's because she's with the rest of her class on the trip to New York to do the Alexander Technique workshop."

She was promptly informed that there was no such trip. Adrienne went BALLISTIC. First thing she did was to call her sister Karen, screaming in a panic, "Jada's in New York by herself, and I have no idea where she is!"

All hell broke loose. Mom was clear that I had lied to her and there was no trip. Her next mission was to locate me. Somebody got a message to somebody who rooted us out, and I eventually had to call my mother from a pay phone.

Her rant went something like this: "Jada! What the hell were you thinking? How dare you lie to me like that? And you had the nerve to have me drop your ass off at the train station. You need to come home NOW!"

Contrite, I said, "I'm sorry, Ma," and then went on to tell her how badly we wanted to experience what it was like to have a professional career like Josh.

"Jada! Get home!"

My mother was NOT having it, and she could have cared less about my reasoning. Her child was in New York with no supervision, and she had no way to get her arms around this situation other than to insist we IMMEDIATELY return to Baltimore. Cory's family had been contacted about our escapade, too, and we were both in major trouble.

Because it was already late, we were told to take the train home in the morning. For all my bravado, I'll never forget how scared I was to go back and face the righteous indignation that was to come. The wrath of Adrienne met me at the train station: "Get yo ass in the car!"

Adrienne is pissed to this day.

T here is nuth'n like walking into a popp'n club when you are fifteen/sixteen years old, no ID requested, and you feel like you own the spot. It's dark, it's moody, and all kinds of possibilities await.

But my focus was the dance floor, and at Club Fantasy, as with other clubs like Signals, Godfrey's, and Odell's, the music was what made it. In these days, Baltimore had a very specific kind of house music—local artists like Miss Tony, a drag queen ("How U Wanna Carry It" and "Pull Ya Gunz Out"), were big. Records like "The Dominatrix Sleeps Tonight" by Dominatrix ("Dot-dominic, dot-dominic, dot-dominic, dominic-tricks") or the classic "It's Time for the Percolator" became collector's items.

Hearing any of those joints always got me hyped for the dance battles.

Once I arrived at a club—say, Fantasy—I'd be waved in (at most places, I knew everyone from the bouncers to the owners to the bartenders). Along with my homegirl Fawn—whom I met at my job at Merry-Go-Round—I'd go directly to the dance floor, which had already been taken hostage by some of the boldest dancers in the house. The floor was packed, battles underway, and I'd jump right in. Winners were determined by crowd responses, with calls of "OOOOOH" and "DAMN YO," and a sound level that rose the better you did.

In the early days, they didn't see me coming. I was petite and considered tomboy-cute in my pink hair, Girbaud baggy jeans, and a pair of fresh, clean white Reebok Princess sneakers. My style set me apart.

On the floor, I had absolutely no fear or hesitation to go at all the boys who were dominating the battles. I'd whirl in with some of my hip-hop mixed with house moves, going from Running Man or the Cabbage Patch, until I'd arch my back into some African moves that I learned at BSA, stomping my feet as my torso turned rapidly, twisting from right to left. As the crowd started to cheer, I'd throw in a little modern dance, with a sprinkle of some pirouettes, and finish with a bit of house footwork, and jokas trying to get one up on me were thrown. Even if my moves weren't always the best, I was a performer, and my showmanship was always hard to beat.

Eventually, I earned a reputation as a formidable dance battle threat.

Any chance I got to perform, I took it. Dance battles came hand in hand with lip-synch competitions, where I could pull off a damn good Prince impersonation, leading to local and even national talent shows.

These were unforgettable good times.

My greatest joy was found at the skating rink, Painters Mill, where I practically lived for most of my high school years. They'd play everything from the S.O.S. Band—with songs like "Just Be Good to Me" or "Tell Me If You Still Care"—to the Gap Band's "Yearning for Your Love," which was a couples-skate favorite. Then there was Michel'le's "Something in My Heart." But nothing fills me with nostalgia more than a song by Keith Sweat called "Make It Last Forever." Everything about that song is just so East Coast. It's summertime, and it's young, wild, and free.

I'm so grateful that my generation grew up in the early days of hip-hop. Rap music had always been about merging influences that weren't being represented in the mainstream. MCs had to bring an individual style to the mic, as well as clever rhymes. What I loved about hip-hop at the time was that it was an outlet for rebellion with an Afrocentric focus, which gave us education about our Black history that we weren't getting elsewhere. Our history education in school was a joke. For the most part, we weren't learning about our roots, about social injustices in our communities, or about our heritage in African civilizations. We couldn't even get the full scope of slavery, so we were left to the brilliant minds in hip-hop like Rakim, KRS-One, and Public Enemy, Sister Souljah, the X Clan, MC Lyte, Queen Latifah, Salt-N-Pepa, Sugar Hill Gang, Grandmaster Flash, Poor Righteous Teachers, and so on. They infused the culture with pride.

Through their lyrics, rappers were also walking middle fingers to the systemic barriers that told us we were unworthy of equality and prosperity. And that resistance reverberated down our streets through our speakers. The messages were different depending on who was rapping, and the more individual you were in your presentation and delivery, the greater chance you had of cutting through a lot of competition. The women rappers who started coming to the fore in my teens were phenomenal. They could hold their own with any of the male rappers and then some. Their rhymes sent messages of female empowerment in contrast to the misogynistic messaging that would soon dominate hip-hop. They taught us to take ownership of our voices, our lives, and our bodies.

On top of dope rhymes, we had dope style. Like most of us, I had a sneaker collection, and every pair was as pristine as the next. From there I could rock a Russell sweatsuit with Reeboks that matched the color, or Fila sneaks with a Fila sweatsuit with my hair electric blue (before that was the thing to do), the side of my head shaved and a rat-tail down to my ass, along with the complement of gold herringbone necklaces, nugget rings, bamboo earrings, and even small gold ropes around my ankles. But I had no problem rolling into the rink with a skirt over vertically sliced-up jeans and a bleached denim jacket full of buttons with images of Prince, Madonna, and Duran Duran.

Prince's style, in dress and music, was audacious and unapologetic from the start, and made me a lifelong fan. And he was a masculine dude who wore makeup and high heels. His high-pitched whines and screams contrasted with baritone vocals—a riveting combination. Just lip-synching to songs like "I Would Die 4 U" or "Let's Go Crazy" was so much work. I could only imagine what it was like for him to actually perform them. Prince was one of my first artistic examples of the electrifying beauty of mixing different worlds and energies. He proved that they not only could mix but were a necessary recipe to create something unique and different.

These influences taught me that being fly wasn't just being pretty. BE a movement. A living, breathing testament. Not only was your art your life, but your life itself was the greatest masterpiece of all. How you walked through the world was as important as what you were creating. Trust and believe me when I tell you, I learned how to walk in the world and create an entrance.

The clubs, skating rinks, and parties weren't only for fun and good times. They were also where I would meet some of the more learned professors of the University of the B-more Streets.

B altimore *was infested with every kind* of drug, but heroin reigned. Starting in the 1970s, drugs had sent an avalanche of money into the predominantly Black neighborhoods of every major city. It was also a time when legit jobs that used to support families, connecting communities, were vanishing, major industries shutting down, leaving less opportunity for working-class folks, young people, and so on. Many would turn to the drug business to make ends meet or for a quick come-up or even to support their own habit. There was so much product flooding urban neighborhoods that nearly everyone in them was connected—selling, buying, or using. In the mid-1980s, a cheaper form of coke known as crack, which was easy and cheap to make and said to be far more addictive than cocaine itself, began to take hold in Baltimore.

The idea that I could gain some financial freedom by selling drugs just seemed practical to me—to make a way for myself in a landscape where so many awful things were happening. With the distorted reality that I had, selling drugs was the norm and didn't seem as extreme as the horrors taking place every day—like the time one of my homeboys was shot multiple times and left dead in the middle of the street from one a.m. to seven a.m. the next morning. I'll never forget the sound of his mother and sister wailing in the streets all night as they stood by his body.

There is a certain kind of quiet that hits a place in the aftermath of murder—when the morgue is not willing to come to that part of town to retrieve the body of a young man stolen by violent bullets. Even the hood has its own way of mourning and paying its respect when its own is left to rot on the concrete under the midnight sky.

This was real life, brutal and unfair. The best you could do was to win—by any means necessary. Is that selfish? Yes. But that was survival. When you live in an environment where you are seen as unworthy and you feel unworthy, you are going to treat others that way, too. These kinds of dog-eat-dog conditions can turn anyone selfish, which could make selling drugs simply part of the game of life. This was my way to financial stability and mobility. I wasn't going to become a hustler's girlfriend. I had seen with my own eyes the level of control and enslavement that came from being financially dependent on a man. Some of the girls in my circle looked to their drug-dealer boyfriends to give them places to stay, cars, jewelry, and clothes so they could have a better life, but at the cost of enduring cycles of betrayal and abuse that were unthinkable to me.

Fuck that. If anyone was going to give me the trappings of the good life, it was going to be me. I came to the conclusion that I could be as successful a drug dealer as any man. In my view, I could work my way to running a whole operation—be a queenpin.

The fact is, I didn't want my hands tied by no dude, and I surely didn't want my hands tied because of the system. A generation earlier, the strivers became doctors and lawyers, like my grandfathers and Tony. Now the most successful people in my hood were drug dealers. They had the life we all wanted. If you were strong enough, and if you could survive, it could be yours, too.

Those attitudes collided with my growing concerns about being left to fend for myself should something happen to my mother. My aunt Karen was worried enough about this that at one point, she asked my mother for guardianship should Adrienne overdose or worse.

In these years, Mom did try at times to get clean. She would go to rehab and get sober, but staying clean was another story. Before long, she was back to using. My need for vigilance at home kicked into high gear as my mother became more and more unreliable.

My aunt Karen had also been an addict but had kicked the habit and stayed clean. A key to her sobriety was attending NA meetings. In fact, it was in those same meeting rooms where Robsol found the support he needed to stay clean after he came back to Baltimore from California in the mid-1980s. When I worried that my mother would never reach her bottom and stop using for good, I found faith in the 12-step rooms and the testimonies of people who had come through hell on earth, by the grace of God. Their stories were seemingly un-redemptive. Some had lost their families, their jobs, and their homes, even sold their children for drugs. Yet in those rooms I saw the miraculous power of God to help the most powerless find redemption, love, and forgiveness, and begin their lives anew. These testimonies gave me hope that Adrienne and I would be okay. But after feeling hopeful and then being let down, again and again, you just get numb, and you stop allowing yourself to feel anything other than apathetic.

One day when I was at my part-time gig at Merry-Go-Round, my mom came in so high I couldn't believe she had managed to drive to the store without an accident. She wanted to put a leather trench coat on layaway so she could give it to me for my birthday.

I had never felt embarrassed in public by her, but when she started talking to the dude who ran the store—whom she knew and who had come over to say hi—and nodded off standing upright, I felt that shame.

"Ma?" I shook her arm; she opened her eyes and took a deep breath, reached into her purse for the cash to put down for the coat on layaway, and made an excuse that she was tired after a long night at the hospital.

Nobody said anything to me after she left. I made no effort to explain what we had just witnessed. We all knew what it was, and there wasn't one person in that store who hadn't been touched by the epidemic of addiction. Although I knew I wasn't alone, it didn't make the moment any less painful. Seeing her condition in the isolation of our home gave a false sense of normalcy, but in public, I could not ignore the severity of my mother's addiction. It was clear that something was really wrong with her, with me—with us.

My resentment didn't surface until an incident with one of Mom's boyfriends. Adrienne had always been careful about bringing the men in her life home, especially after her divorce. That changed when she started seeing Anthony, the definitive tall, dark, and handsome type who also happened to be a full-blown heroin addict. He was at our house often, and eventually, things started going missing.

Between Adrienne and me, in terms of jewelry, clothes, and cash, we were a decent lick for someone who knew where to look. Otherwise, the narrow three-story row house was no invitation to a thief. It had doors that closed only when wedged with newspapers, a kitchen with a dirty, stained yellow linoleum floor (which never improved no matter how much you scrubbed it), rusted metal cabinets we never wanted to store food in, wood floors in need of replacement, and barely any furniture. It wasn't so much a home as a place to lay your head. The door to my bedroom didn't even have a doorknob, let alone a way to lock it.

At one point, a shopping bag full of new clothes and some money of mine disappeared, and my mother mentioned that she couldn't find a necklace of my grandmother's that she shared with my aunt Karen. Our next-door neighbors informed my mother that they had seen Anthony climb through my bedroom window to enter the house and leave with some items. My mother confronted Anthony, and he confessed to stealing from us in order to cop some drugs.

My mother felt terrible. She made Anthony apologize to me, but what broke my heart was that my mother felt, because he had apologized, it was okay to let him back into the house. Feeling angry, unprotected, and disregarded, I was shocked. My space had been violated. If I couldn't be safe in my own home, then I wasn't safe anywhere.

And that was the second that I decided I needed even more control over my life. Whatever money he took and clothes he stole, I could get back. *No problem,* I thought, *I'm not going to trip.* It was this incident that not only justified why I sold drugs but ramped it up.

Why? Because I wanted out. I didn't want to be part of this, but I couldn't abandon my mother. That's a hell of a conflict.

I only vaguely recall how I started sling'n dope. I do remember that there were a lot of hustlers at the skating rink, and I started making connections there with the lower-level dudes whose egos were waiting to be stroked. I caught my first fish on some "I need a mentor" ish, someone to show me the ropes because I needed to make some money.

At first, M (we'll call him M) asked if I wanted to make a drop for him.

I told him, "Naw. You should give me something on the arm, and if I do right by it, we'll take it from there."

I knew I didn't want to be a mule. I didn't want to put myself in a position where a dude had his boot on my neck. Mules never called the shots. I wanted to call shots.

M smirked and stared at me for a minute. I don't think he took me seriously, but he wanted to humor me and himself. Finally, he laughed. "Aight, shorty."

He gave me a lil something to get started. Before long, I worked my way up to BP (we'll call him BP). He was a handsome midlevel hustler who taught me how to use a gun, how to look out for myself, and later helped set me up at a spot in Cherry Hill where I could sell dope out of a first-floor apartment window. I was soon introduced to Chet, who was making his way to kingpin status and would eventually serve ten years in the penitentiary.

The first thing Chet taught me was how to be on the low, as in no flashy cars, jewelry, none of that. The second thing was to always, *always* have a legit job. The third—I needed a plan.

Being *fashionably late to sophomore-year orientation* for the theater department was my intention, another way to make an entrance. We were required to report to the massive performing hall at Baltimore School for the Arts. An imposing room, it was memorable for its super-high ceilings and a stage built from beautiful dark wood.

As I saunter in with my new extended rattail down to my butt crack, I immediately catch eyes with a new dude across the room who is engaged in a very energetic conversation with one of our class-mates. He's wearing a thick old-school alpaca sweater and jeans. He has beautiful brown skin with big brown eyes, heavy eyebrows, and a tiny peanut head.

The minute I turn and notice him, he's already staring at me. Me catching his eyes gives him the gumption to walk across the room and come right to me. Boldly, he smiles a big ole smile, showing off his big ole teeth, and puts out his hand to shake mine. "Hi," he says, "I'm Tupac."

I am struck by the power of that unusual name. Tupac.

His smile will become an unforgettable feature—a million watts of white teeth—and his hands feel strikingly clammy, becoming an ongoing joke between us for the duration of our friendship. The power of his presence lets me know right away that he is something special.

"I'm Jada." I smile back. "Nice to meet you, Tupac."

"Hi, Jada," he says.

From the gate, Pac was an undeniable charismatic who could captivate any room, peanut head or not. He hadn't yet told me his story or that he was already making moves as a fifteen-year-old rapper to be the next Rakim or that he had serious acting chops. But I would soon find out all of that and so much more. What I didn't expect, even with the uniqueness of his vibe, was that this young man and I would create a bond that would impact my life forever.

Chaos in the midst of chaos isn't funny, but chaos in the midst of order is.

—STEVE MARTIN

Many of us who were raised in environments of chaos as children become addicted to that chaos. These cycles of chaos will seem so normal that we won't recognize how we attract it and make consistent choices that keep us mired in disorder. For many of us, the trappings of chaos seem SO familiar, so RIGHT, that we can't even recognize the warnings when they make a blaring appearance.

———

Such cycles can mislead us into believing that the adrenaline, the roller-coaster ride of emotions, the merry-go-round of pain, is "living." The truth is we can't tell up from down when we're on this kind of high. And when we're not, we're miserable. If we're lucky, we hit rock bottom, worn out from the chaotic drama, confusion, and danger we are inviting into our lives.

———

We have a choice, but we must be patient. We have cultivated this way of life for a very, *very* long time. And for most, we can't change overnight. Sometimes, to create that change, it takes surveying the past and identifying the origins of our chaos in order to recognize it in our present circumstances and be willing to take personal responsibility for bringing the past forward.

———

Is there any aspect of your life at the moment that reflects an addiction to chaos? Does part of your life feel unmanageable and out of control? Do you seek the thrill of the roller coaster? It can be so helpful to look at what keeps you hooked on chaos—perhaps as a way to make yourself feel strong and valued for your ability to withstand? When you're willing to name that cause, it loses its power and gives you back yours.

CHAPTER 5

Advanced Degree

A**ight, Pac . . . kiss me, then."

Pac and I are standing on my tiny back porch on Price Ave., and the two of us are bantering—about how, maybe if we actually tried to be more than friends, could it work or not?—and I decide to dare him.

During our teen years, it wasn't really Pac's good looks that grabbed you, because his sculpted features and unforgettable handsomeness hadn't quite come in yet. What he did have, even in tenth grade, was pure, unadulterated charisma that was out of this world. What he saw in me at first might have been just that I was the cute feisty girl in the room. For any curious male spirit, that's the first move—to want to know her name and see what's up. Basic.

And yet all I can tell you is that our immediate connection, I felt, rose beyond the "basics," and this is what made me want to get to know him. We became inseparable from the moment we met. We were kindred spirits in so many ways, and although Pac may have had an attraction to me in the beginning, the more time we spent together, the more we could both see that there was no romantic chemistry between us . . . at all.

There were no airs between us, either. We could be raw and authentic without the constraints of having to impress each other. You got what you got. There were no butterflies, no tingles in the body, no hot desire to be in each other's embrace. Rather, there was something far more important unfolding between us—a friendship of a powerful strength, giving us the ability to hold space for each other through some of the most unbearable moments of our lives.

Being as young as we were and as tight as we were, we both found it confusing at times that we weren't drawn to each other romantically. Hence the day he got on my last nerve about the possibility of being more than friends, and I dared him to kiss me.

Without hesitation, Pac grabbed me in his arms and did just that. The kiss lasted a few seconds before we both pulled away in mutual disgust. It felt wrong. Pac pulled back with his eyes all squinted as if he had drunk spoiled milk. He wiped his lips hard and said, "What the fuck?"

I laughed my ass off. "See! I told you, dummy!"

It was literally like a sister and a brother trying to make out. All I knew though, was that it was possible to really love a guy deeply without it having anything to do with sexual attraction. I had never felt that before.

Pac made up for the lack of male protection and care I sought in my life. Unlike other guys, who wanted to flash their jewels, cars, cash as their value—because Pac didn't have any of those things to display as his worth—he offered his mind, his care and attention. Besides, I think God knew that if sexual attraction had been possible between us, we would have left each other in a special kind of ruin. Instead, God gifted us with a special kind of friendship.

Now, our bond didn't come without its challenges and costs. We were both fiery, passionate, and dangerously stubborn. This made for feral fights. We didn't take each other's shit, and unfortunately, we also knew how to hurt each other—like no other. Our tongues were the sharpest of swords between us. These fights could leave us not speaking for days, sometimes weeks, at a time. But we always made it back. Always.

But nobody could tease me like Pac. He knew how to get under my skin. He created a nickname to remind me that I wasn't as up on my game as I acted. It was brutal. He called me "Square." For life.

When I first met Pac, he owned one sweater—the same one he'd worn the day I met him—two pairs of pants, and a few shirts. That's all. Pac couldn't hide the reality of poverty in his life. Looking for an easier way of life, in part, his mom had brought him and his little sis, Sekyiwa, from New York to Baltimore. But it didn't sound like their lives had gotten much easier for them.

As Pac and I grew closer, I got a clearer picture and learned that, like my mother, his mother, Afeni, struggled with addiction. Like mine, his environment was full of instability and chaos. We really bonded as the result of riding the same roller coaster with our moms, and both suffered the pains and disappointments that came with it.

Unlike my mother, Afeni had not been able to secure work, which had only worsened their financial struggles. Pac never said so, but I could tell that getting to eat three meals a day was not a given for him. Nor were shoes that fit or getting a good night's sleep. Between my regular jobs and cash I'd started to make in the streets, I always had some money in my pockets. To help Pac, I made it my business to ensure he was straight but not on some charity shit. Pac was prideful. He had standards about what it meant to be a man and stood his ground on that, in spite of how he may have been suffering. If he was made to feel like I thought he needed assistance, he would refuse support from me. And in those instances my heart withered watching him do so.

Early in our friendship, I brought some clothes to school that I'd bought him—some shirts and a jacket. But I had to be careful. As I started to show my purchase to him, I went, "Yo, Pac. Gap was having a sale, right. So, I was getting some stuff for myself, and then I saw this fly-ass jacket and I couldn't help but see you in it. I was like, 'This would be fly as fuck on Pac.'" I held the jacket up against his chest. "Damn! I was right."

I remember the biggest smile came over his face as he grabbed the corners of the jacket. "Yoooooo! You're not such a square after all. This is dope!" He threw on the khaki jacket with pride.

I had succeeded. His sis had simply thought about him, that's all, and happened to run across some fly shit she wanted him to have. Anything different, he would have made an excuse not to take it.

If I was going somewhere to eat, I'd take him with me on some "let's kick it" shit, with a casual flow. Whether it was TGIF, to get a chicken box, cheesesteak subs, or McDonald's. We had late nights at Denny's and IHOP. Later on, when I was starting to really roll in the streets and was flush with cash, I even took Pac a few times when I went with my homegirl Fawn, Chet, and some other high-roll'n hustlers to full-on "upscale" dinners at Pargo's, our spot after "a good week." I'm talking about at least a couple of grand in my pocket. For the other players, it was a LOT more. I didn't bring Pac around often because I didn't want to pull him into the dangers of the Baltimore dope scene—the game wasn't for you if you weren't from Baltimore and didn't have your people. I wasn't thorough like that to have him on my hip. Me, I could barely cover my own ass.

On Greenmount Avenue, where Pac lived, the dudes selling dope already saw him as a threat—a young Black charismatic male they didn't know and didn't like because he had an IT factor they didn't. Young lions can always smell the blood of other young lions in their territory who might present a problem.

Pac didn't pay their foolishness any mind. He was focused and becoming known for his brazen rap battles. At fifteen and sixteen, he could freestyle and rhyme you relentlessly into submission. We were each other's biggest fans, going crazy watching each other do what we loved. I loved watching him do rap battles, and he got a kick watching my dance battles. Then there came the inevitable moment when Pac tried to convince me, "You should rap. You'd be dope, Jada!"

"I don't know, Pac."

"Come on! Stop being a square! I'll write a rhyme for you."

I couldn't refuse, because Pac was SO determined to have a female rap battle group. He put me and two other girls together and quickly arranged a rap battle for us. Pac wrote my rhyme and made me practice with him every day after school. I WAS HORRIBLE. Pac really tried, saying again and again, "Listen to me," and then he'd rhyme the rhyme for me.

Can you imagine? Pac's cadence and style were as dynamic then as when the world got to hear him. And here he was, trying to get me to rhyme like him. Pleeeasssse! He just thought my inability to do so was because I was being stubborn. Pac would be like, "What? Is your great-great-great white grandma com'n through now? Where is your rhythm? Is you listen'n to the guitars or somethin'? Get on beat, Square!"

I could never find my cadence. But I went through with the battle, and we won. I got out alive without embarrassing Pac too much, but my rap career ended there.

Pac and I were thick as thieves, and we trusted each other completely, even confiding in each other about our love interests. Pac was seemingly falling in love with someone every week, although there was ONE girl in any given period of time that he was really CRAZY about. That was the ONE HE COULDN'T GET. He would have his eye on a few, but there was always that one ungettable girl who would take hold of his mind completely, at least for a time. And that was the one who became my assignment. He'd send me on missions to put in a good word for him or deliver letters and poems to that one elusive girl in class.

On the flip side, when I had an aching crush on a senior, Pac agreed to help me out. John Cole was a visual artist at BSA who wasn't on campus often. Whenever I saw him, I had butterflies. I was so infatuated with him that instead of just introducing myself, I had asked two friends to make the introduction in the lunchroom one day.

The moment John looked at me, it was as if his eyes pierced into my soul. He was emotionally open yet mysterious. He kept to himself and his art most of the time, and I could feel in him what seemed to be a soft but tortured heart.

He was not my usual preference as far as masculine beauty goes—I liked Black dudes, street dudes, to be correct, and John Cole was neither. The exact opposite, he was pale white with white-blond hair all over. Not yellow blond but white blond. To some, he could have seemed damn near transparent. But in my eyes, he was . . . beautifully handsome. His face and body seemed sculpted like one of those classic Greek statues. He was *different,* and I was captivated.

This was new territory. I wanted Pac to get to know John for me, explaining, "He's different, and I like that, but I wanna make sure he's not on some weird out-of-pocket shit."

As soon as I introduced Pac to John, the two of them fell into a tight friendship that made it natural for John and me to become romantic. It was unexpected, unforced, and epic. We became the Three Musketeers. The only thing I tried to keep separate was my street life, not wanting to involve either of them in what was still on a limited scale at this time. I didn't want my worlds to collide.

We each had a level of dysfunction and trauma in our lives, but because Pac's life was so marred by poverty, I think he felt the stresses more. Pac stayed with his mom and his sweet baby sister, Sekyiwa, whom he ADORED, with his own spot at the back of the house in a makeshift extension.

One day I went to pick him up, and he invited me inside. He took me to his room, and I saw that he slept on a tattered mattress on the floor with a sheet thrown over it. The floor was covered by a super-thick carpet that looked like it had never been vacuumed. Me, I could post up in many projects in Baltimore. But Pac's house? Not so much. Pac's living space made the projects feel like the Four Seasons.

He grabbed what he needed, gestured to the front of the house, and then took me to meet his mother. And there Afeni was, in the dark, as Pac led the way through the very still and heavy space.

Over time I would get to know Afeni and see that many of Tupac's traits were inherited from her. Afeni was brilliant, well learned, and when she had her mind set, there was no changing it. She had a smile that could light up a room, and when she started to speak about something she was passionate about, it was impossible for her not to get your attention. Pac was the same in every way. All of this shared magic would at times be the grounds for conflict between two very intelligent, strong-willed spirits already steeped in their own individual conflicts.

"Ma, this is my friend Jada from school," Pac said to Afeni, who sat quietly smoking as the embers of her cigarette lit up the darkness.

"Well, hello, Jada. Aren't you pretty." She said this without celebration, as just a matter of fact. I don't know how to explain it, but I was immediately drawn to her rawness and her lack of desire to be impressed or to impress.

"Thank you. Very nice to meet you."

"You, too, sweetheart." Afeni then turned her attention somewhere else.

And I turned to go, following Pac out of the house.

After my first visit, I never went back to that house. John, on the other hand, stayed with Pac a couple of times, until the rats got a little too close for comfort to the mattress on the floor of Pac's room.

Before long, there came a point—between the young dealers in his hood targeting him and conflict with his mother—when Pac admitted he needed somewhere else to stay.

I knew what I had to do and had Pac come with me and wait in the living room as I went to my mother's bedroom to beg. "Ma, just let him stay here tonight. One night."

"Just one night?"

"Yes. Until we can figure something else out for him."

My mother agreed to one night and not one night more. She thought it very inappropriate for a male friend of mine to be staying with us. I didn't care about what was appropriate—Pac wasn't going to be on the street. Period! I got him some sheets and a blanket, and he slept peacefully on our couch.

The next day, Pac and I explained his situation to John, who instantly offered for Pac to come and stay with him.

My anxiety drained from me in a flash. I knew with John, Pac was straight.

And thus began a memorable period in each of our lives. John lived with his parents in Bolton Hill, a well-to-do area at the time, not far from school. John's parents loved both Pac and me, which granted us an open door to their home.

Pac stayed weeks on end in the spacious upper loft John occupied. And in time John's home became Pac's official residence. I will forever be grateful to John's parents for allowing their home to be a safe space for us.

The closer we became, the more John confided in me about his heartbreak, which had to do with the debilitating stroke his mom had suffered and how it had stolen from him the mother he once knew. Pac and I had lost our mothers to addiction. The three of us were all orphans in some manner. We had lost our mothers in different ways.

We were codependent in the best way. We would try to fill in the gaps of one another's losses as much as we could. What the three of us were going through became the glue of our everlasting friendship. I had found a new garden.

There was something so liberating about being with a young man as deeply passionate as John. He brought that passion to everything— from the music he was drawn to, to his desire to help others, to his art and how he loved. He was also passionate about sharing every aspect of life with Pac and me. He would sometimes go to Odell's with us on North Ave. and lay in the cut while I dance-battled. He'd explain later that he rarely got to see me dance because I was always surrounded by a sea of people while he stood posted as the only white dude amid a sea of hustlers. He didn't care. He was down to kick it with Pac and me no matter where we were.

Whenever I stepped off the staircase after climbing to John's loft sky, I felt free to be someone other than the Jada I knew. With its beautiful brick walls, high ceilings, and tall windows, his living space was a world full of deep feeling, art, music, and openhearted conversation. I had my first mushroom experience with John, which was a hell of a ride after I damn near poisoned myself by taking too many. He was a seasoned enthusiast; in fact, much of his artwork was inspired by his 'shroom journeys.

Pac, in these days, didn't indulge in any heavy mind-altering substances. He smoked weed now and then, and drank alcohol once in a while, whereas I could be extreme. We all shared a love of every kind of music. John revolutionized our musical knowledge by introducing us to bands like New Order, This Mortal Coil, the Cure, the Cocteau Twins, Blue Nile, and Dead Can Dance. We all became huge Kate Bush fans, especially "Running Up That Hill."

In our world together, no subject was taboo. Pac, fiery and eloquent, delivered political sermons to me and John, with particular attention to the plight of the Black community. It was in these impromptu forums that I learned about the Black Panther Party (his mother, Afeni, was an ex-Panther) and the teachers who shaped its ideology. Pac taught me so much history I had never known, and he spoke about how that history continued to influence the systemic abuse of power in efforts to destroy Black communities.

In these moments, I saw a preview of how Pac could change the molecules in the air around him in ways the world would eventually experience through his music, his movies, his interviews—and, above all, his presence.

Through Pac, I became enthralled with freedom fighters like Angela Davis, Huey P. Newton, Geronimo Pratt, Assata Shakur, and Elaine Brown. He urged me to read *Angela Davis: An Autobiography*, *Soul on Ice* by Eldridge Cleaver, *Soledad Brother* by George Jackson. Marion had given me a foundation in the history of the civil rights movement, but Pac embedded me in the history of Black Power, which gave me insight into why my aunt Karen and my mother approached social inequalities the way they did. Now it all made sense.

In my own studies, I noted that there were still gaps in the thinking of both movements that held Black women back—because we were ultimately expected to propel Black men forward. Pac and I had many intense and powerful debates about sexism within the civil rights movement and the Black Power movement and the ridiculousness of how Black men, in fighting for their freedom and autonomy, had a very difficult time believing their women deserved the same freedom and autonomy. This was always deeply disappointing to me, and Pac and I would go at it around this issue. Pac loved women, especially Black women, but he had his hang-ups. I could go as hard as he could but was more willing to give up my need to be right when he hit me with some potent truths. I can't say Pac gave up his need to be right so easily, but *man* . . . I knew how to sit him down. We both cherished our intellectual and passionate exchanges.

John was sometimes our audience and oftentimes our student. One day John and I were out shopping in a store when I realized, in my newfound radical awareness around racism, that a white female clerk had been eyeing me and covertly following me.

"Are you following me?" I finally asked.

"Excuse me?"

"I said, 'Are you fucking following me?'"

John immediately ran to my side, smoothed things out, and took me outside the store. "Hey, what's going on?" he gently asked.

"You didn't see how she was treating me? She was following me like I was going to steal something. How come she didn't do that to you?"

"Why do you think she was following you?"

"Because I'm Black, John."

John listened silently but with the deepest empathy. When I was done ranting, he said, "I get it. I'm sorry you experienced that, and I wish you didn't have to."

He was so kind, but what we both knew then was that he would never have such experiences. No matter how hard he tried to understand, I knew this would create a chasm between us. That made me question if I could truly consider white men as romantic partners. It was bad enough that most Black men didn't understand the plight of Black women, but to contend with a white man who wouldn't have the ability to get it no matter how hard he tried? Which was worse?

John could see beyond these things. He operated off of spirit, which dissolved barriers and filled chasms. Things just were. I loved how he had that ability at such a young age. I did not.

For the time being, however, I had found a measure of safety in the company of these two remarkable and gifted men. Both who loved me, in different ways, for myself.

By the summer of 1987, aspects of my life were starting to crash into each other.

The fact that I was starting to move from occasional low-level dealing to selling more often made it difficult to keep my worlds separate. John—who was very persistent—wanted to be with me in my different worlds. He wasn't intimidated or daunted, even as a striking, almost iridescent white dude in the middle of places where he had no business. His fearlessness made me uneasy. I bluntly told him more than once, "Listen, you can't go with me everywhere . . . I mean, you can't be up on me like that. I'm going to be in places you can't be." He didn't get it. He would just ignore what I said.

John thought he could be Mr. United Nations and create a demilitarized zone anywhere he went. He felt comfortable and had no reason to see himself as a possible target. That wasn't going to work with me, especially after the night he dropped me off in his baby-blue VW Bug and some dude I knew stepped to him and asked for a ride somewhere with two buddies.

John agreed. That was the night that almost got him killed. In an attempt to set John up and rob him, maybe because they thought John was carrying something for me, these dudes got in his car pretending they needed a ride to a part of town he should have never been in. There was quite a saga that followed but culminated at a red light with guns from another car pointed at John's passengers, who fled on foot. John took off in the nick of time, barely escaping with his life. *Chile*, the worst part, he wasn't fazed at all. But I was extremely fazed, so much so I made sure some friends of mine had a word with the dude who started it. John almost got his ass in some shit because of me. Never again. The intersection of our worlds created too much risk. We decided to go our separate ways, but John and I would have a lifelong friendship.

Outside of John and Pac, I had homegirls who were like sisters to me. Yet, unlike a lot of female social sets, my girlfriends and I very rarely posse'd up. We each had our own unique sisterhood—each of my girlfriends represented different flows and offered me levels of connection to something important that I needed.

Toni, my skating partner, had just moved to Baltimore from New York when I met her at the rink. She was petite like me, with a relaxed demeanor. It didn't hurt that she could SKATE her ass off, which made a perfect pairing for learning moves and showing out. None of my other girlfriends skated, while Toni and I couldn't get enough of it. We had many adventures and some misadventures too.

One day at Painters Mill, some rowdy, rough-ass chicks squared off on Toni as soon as she skated off the floor. Whatever instigated it, I didn't see—I was still skating—but within a minute or so, I caught the commotion. I peeped the scene quick, and I could tell by the stance of the girl coming at Toni that she was used to fighting boys. She had her right foot back and her left forward, hands down, clenched in fists—ready, inching toward Toni as she talked shit. Girls who couldn't really fight would be swinging their fingers in somebody's face, shouting big words with their feet in a parallel stance (that was me for sure). I knew right then we were in trouble.

On instinct, I took my skates off in the middle of the rink, ran across the floor, and jumped beside Toni with one skate in hand.

These girls were about to whip our asses, but not without a fight. Because I was so small, I didn't adhere to the rule "a fair one." I held my skate tight by the wheels, ready to smash it against the side of this girl's face if shit got stupid. Toni swung, and the girl did a quick lean back, missing the shot like a pro. The girl's reflexes were quick as hell, and just as she was about to lunge toward us, two male skate guards jumped in between us. I was so damn relieved. Scared as I was that day, the rule was and is: If we come together, your fight is my fight.

My girl Fawn and I spent a lot of time together. Tall and pretty like her name, she was a bit older than I was and had the freedom to move with me however/whenever. She was super quiet and smooth. She didn't know nobody and didn't care to. She was the girlfriend who probably knew the most about my drug activities at that time, because I trusted her. She didn't ask questions, so if I got a page and said, "I got to make this stop real quick," she simply nodded and we rolled.

Fawn's home situation was plagued with addiction, like mine. Our loneliness and dismal family lives were often cured by each other's company. We both were basically able to come and go as we pleased, and Fawn was always down for whatever.

And then there was Ramsey, who went to Baltimore School for the Arts in the visual arts department. Half-white and half-Japanese, Ramsey's looks strongly favored her Japanese heritage from her paternal side. Being mixed race made for an interesting dynamic with her white family on her maternal side, who raised her. She was orphaned, too, in a way. Through Ramsey, I was able to witness the racism that Asian American women faced—very different from the racism I faced as a Black woman. What she experienced had different nuances and complexities, yet she was as challenged by white supremacy as I was. This was especially the case since she lived right across the street from some members of the KKK.

Although we had to deal with all the external realities, Ramsey and I had so much fun together. Rams was super cute, and when she came to my neck of the woods, all the dudes loved her. She looked like your quintessential visual artist with her black turtleneck, black jeans, long black hair, and Capri cigarette in hand.

Ramsey was another one who rolled with me anywhere. I had her deep in my streets and she had me deep in her streets, populated by poor white boys from Pigtown to Highlandtown. In that mix was a weird combination of punk, metal, hip-hop, and drugs. They liked pills and acid. These dudes were in bands and were artists in their own right.

Rams introduced me to the hard-core punk scene, with bands I would see at the Loft, a hole-in-the-wall club in her hood. It was full of some of the most gutter, rugged, rough white boys the city had to offer.

My homegirl Keesha, who also went to Baltimore School for the Arts, was one friend I couldn't take anywhere because she was a homebody, more or less by choice. Her mother, Geraldine, a dead ringer for Sade and soon-to-be entrepreneur—a caregiver who would build a multimillion-dollar business placing other caregivers—worked as much as my mother did and had the same kind of hours. Keesha didn't like to be alone, so she would sneak her boyfriend in to stay the night with her almost every evening. Sometimes while I was hanging, I'd be inspired to color my hair with Jazzing semi-permanent color over the top of my platinum blonde and use the bathroom sink—much to the displeasure of Geraldine, who kept the most immaculate house. Luckily, she put up with me ruining her beautiful towels. Being at home with Keesha was a safe place for me to decompress and be still. We'd known each other since middle school, and nobody could get through to me better than Keesha, who was deeply affectionate, loving, and just downright silly.

Even when she was serious, Keesha had the brightest smile and the whitest, most perfect teeth. She was obsessed with dental hygiene. Like nobody I ever knew.

Although I loved hanging with Keesha, I loved being in the streets more. And summertime was the best time for that. Some of my fondest memories are of Fawn and me making our way to Druid Hill Park, one of the oldest public parks in America. There were gardens, waterfalls, and even a zoo where I used to go with my grandfather Grant. But the main attraction in the park every Sunday was like a big ole block party that started at high noon and went until dark. You could scope out the dopest cars in the city, driving by in a slow-moving train, and listen to the bang'n-est sound systems as joints like "Paid in Full" BLASTED with thumping bass. All us girls were looking fine as hell, and the dudes who were the biggest high rollers in the city always made an appearance.

Every feature of a car was up for scrutiny at that event, down to the detail of how well your tires shone. Dashboards, steering wheels, and panels in the car had to be shinin'. Your car had to be just as fly on the inside as it was on the outside, even down to the Tree air fresheners that hung from the rearview in black ice, vanilla, pine, strawberry. To this day, a crisp car that smells good is an aphrodisiac for me. Add to that the smell of a man wear'n Drakkar Noir—don't get me started.

How you laced your car was an art form, and it was also an indication of your come-up for that week. The flyer your car became, the more money you were making. It was also at the park where everyone followed the unwritten rule that there was to be no violence of any kind. It was the only place and the only day when hustlers from all parts of the city could convene and socialize without issues.

As soon as dark hit the park, the festivities moved to Northern Parkway and Wabash, where we watched the dopest motorcycles in the city race up and down. Sundays were fun days when the streets took a break from the madness. They were like the hustlers' holy day.

It was the cars, motorcycles, hairstyles, nails, bags, and jewelry, how much stuff you had and the quality of it, that were the signs of worth for a community of people who were constantly reminded—*you ain't shit, and you ain't never gonna be shit.* Watching those cars roll through the park was an inspiration. They were a constant reminder that a prosperous life was possible and that we deserved the better things life had to offer. Those cars kept many of us hopeful. They may have not guided us to the right path, but they gave us something to reach for instead of giving up on ourselves.

I kept all this in mind when I got my first car, not the one I wanted, because (1) I could never explain to my mom how I could afford such a car and (2) I rolled in this city, at all hours, with product and didn't want no smoke from the cops or, worse, stickup crews.

Drug money was not the only way to pay for a car, though. By this point I had already worked my first professional acting job, playing a runaway slave. The short PBS special, entitled *Freedom Station,* was about Harriet Tubman and the Underground Railroad. In addition to being admitted to the local performers' union, I earned about six grand. With that, I paid cash for my little Nissan Sentra with the patient understanding that if I played it smart now, one day I could have any car I wanted.

In my Nissan, I was the last person you'd suspect of carrying a decent amount of product and pockets full of cash. With my blue or pink or green or platinum-blonde hair, I was just the friendly, artsy girl next door who went to Baltimore School for the Arts, and, who knew, was one day maybe going to be an actor.

T*he level of sophistication present in* the East Coast drug game operating in Black neighborhoods during the 1980s to the '90s has rarely been captured in film and TV. The violence of the landscape has been portrayed on screen, but never the intelligence, the ingenuity, and the organized nature of it all. I'm not an expert, and it's a tricky subject to broach because it's actually nothing to brag about. Yet it was truly a unique era and has yet to be explored

enough to show why. What's more, there are some of us in the entertainment world today who were schooled through that street game.
We were given lessons that helped us achieve success—legitimately—
and made it possible for us to survive different types of jungles.

I came across dudes from New York, Philly, and D.C. who were
real-deal entrepreneurs and who first introduced me to stocks and
the importance of investing money. Many of them owned multiple
businesses—sub shops, barbershops, hair salons, body shops, and
shoe stores. They were kingpin/CEOs who knew how to organize
young lions, gain their loyalty, and keep them in check when necessary. I was lucky to come across a few big ballers who took a liking to
me, who saw promise in my future beyond the streets, who helped to
keep me safe, and who taught me a few things along the way. They
showed me the importance of being self-made and that nobody was
going to give you your success. They taught me how to hold my own
and persevere to get mine.

Because I was taught to always keep a legit job, my mother never
became suspicious. Ironically, though she didn't know about me, I
was aware that she had her own stint selling cocaine in order to support her heroin addiction. The fact that mother and daughter were
selling at the same time was indicative of the condition of our world.

My legit jobs, also ironically, helped me make connects with all
different kinds of hustlers. When I worked at Merry-Go-Round, they
came through to shop for themselves and the women in their lives.
The men who were really about that life were confident, had nothing
to prove, kept all things close to the chest, and carried an assured stillness that made them a walking secret. And then there were those who
were wild, reckless, violent, and unpredictable, and although folks
feared them, their days were always numbered. Arrogance, typical of
the boastful ones, covered for how insecure they were—this type was
always worried about themselves and would throw you under the bus
quick. And believe it or not, there were many who had the sweetest
heart behind the rugged exterior that shielded their wounds.

Hustlers were everywhere. The skating rink, the clubs, the record store, clothing stores, my telemarketing job, a Black family–owned candy store at the Harborplace mall. All these jobs and the people I met in those settings just helped me cultivate my instincts and better read the inner workings of others.

F rom the moment I met Chet, I wanted to learn *everything* from him. I liked the way he carried himself and his business. He was on the low, low, low, and I knew that was the exact recipe needed for success. As he rose in the game, he became my mentor and my direct connect, though I remained under BP's wing of protection.

Chet looked like a nerdy college kid with his light eyes, small frame, big head, and super-cheerful attitude. He would come around in his UPS outfit after work, giving off absolutely no impression that he was, in fact, a drug dealer. At the time, Chet was the only dealer I knew on his level who had an actual job, giving him a legit-looking appearance of being the guy next door. He did not carry a tough-guy killer persona. I don't think I ever even saw Chet with a gun. Ever. Chet would also be the first millionaire I actually knew.

My first goal of having an acting career became secondary, as I was now under the illusion that I could become a bona fide queenpin. The timing was ripe. B-more was a hub for the drug trade. A lot of product flowed in and out of our city.

Much of the product was coming in via traffickers in Florida, California, and at times, New York, although New York was tricky because of secondhand sales that cut into profit. One of the means of bringing in drugs was through independent truckers or small truck companies that could move large-scale shipments. Kilos of coke were sometimes packed inside the lining of huge concert-sized speakers put into these trucks. Once they were delivered to a warehouse, the speakers were taken apart, unpacked, and the bricks were ready to distribute. The amounts in shipments ranged from twenty to a hundred kilos. The truckers were paid based on the distance they had to drive and how much product they were transferring, five hundred to a thousand per kilo for delivery.

Laundry detergent boxes were another method to disguise product. The product had to be vacuum-sealed before you put the soap powder back into the box. Cars were also used and packed to the hilt full of drugs—door panels, motors, inside the seats, spare tires, and even the tires on the car. Once the car was unloaded, it was a clean and free titled car to be used however the receiving party wanted. Often it would be side chicks who got those cars.

Over time, more sophisticated methods developed to ship larger quantities of drugs. Legitimate companies were formed to disguise drug shipments, like, say, a pool and spa equipment wholesaler that used hot tubs to transport product. All kinds of companies sprang to life to conduct illegal business.

Other practices were developed to deal with the large amounts of money that had to be moved to pay for all this product coming in. A common system was the use of money orders to pay off smaller debts up to a hundred thousand dollars. Someone would get paid about two thousand dollars a day to run around all over the city and purchase a hundred money orders for a thousand dollars each without being flagged. Then these money orders were placed inside the pages of magazines to be shipped for payment of the product sent. Another method was tampons. Once the boxes were purchased, the tampon wrappers would be carefully removed and the actual tampon replaced with tightly rolled money, which was then placed in the wrappers to be resealed and repacked in the box. And to make it all full circle, sometimes the same speakers used to deliver product were flipped to house large amounts of cash to be shipped back to the distributor.

When I think about this now, I don't know what made me think that I had what it took to play in this province of wolves. It wasn't long before I learned that kittens don't have no business try'n to play with beasts.

That said, I believed I could defy the odds by making my mark my way. And when I found a spot in Cherry Hill where nobody was selling—for good reasons, it turned out—I was able to convince BP to help me set up shop. His reaction? "Damn, shawty, *I* never even thought about that."

The last place anyone would think I'd be was hustle'n in the zombie zone at the bottom of Cherry Hill.

This was another crash course in navigation. Cherry Hill, in Southwest Baltimore, close to downtown, was an area that was on a peninsula surrounded by water and did not operate like the rest of the city. There was only one way in and one way out—a death trap for my line of business. If you got twisted up on the dead-end side streets off the main drag, you could get trapped, get got, and get forgotten about. You rarely saw a police car, which made this territory basically lawless—although that had its advantages, of course, as I was able to roll in and out with product and money and no concern about the law. On the other hand, I had to worry about the wolves who also had no concern for the law.

All of this made for a unique and dangerous dynamic. But I saw opportunity.

The top of Cherry Hill was on the main strip, where there was a convenience store, a barbershop, a sub shop, and some other spots. This was where the majority of hustlers worked. In contrast, the bottom, where I wanted to be, was desolate. There was this small apartment complex, and I felt there was a lot of money to be made from residents who otherwise had to go to the top to be served. Whereas others may have viewed my location at the bottom of Cherry Hill as a no-go, I saw a golden egg. And as one of the first to tap into this underserved population, I'd turn out to be right.

BP had respect in Cherry Hill, and I was protected under his wing. He knew the dangers so well that he gave me a .22 for a "just in case." I set up shop inside a woman's first-floor apartment, where I served folks out of her window and sometimes through her door with the chain on.

Everything ran smoothly for a while. My pockets were fuller than ever. It felt good to be able to share a bit of my financial freedom with my girlfriends and other women (whom I might not have been tight with but who needed help to get out of a "sticky" situation).

Chet and I liked sharing with people in our community, Robin Hood–style, easing struggles where we could. Sometimes we would be in the supermarket and notice a single mother with children, or an elderly person alone, and straight-out pay for all of their groceries just because we could.

There was so much suffering in our environment, and it never really occurred to us that we were adding to it.

K ings Dominion?" was the first thing out of my mouth.
Spring was in the air in 1988, and my mother had just announced that her boyfriend, Rodney—and future husband—wanted to take us to the amusement park a couple of hours away. Adrienne loved amusement parks, everything about them, and she was so cheerful when she said, "Rodney wants to take us to Kings Dominion. Do you want to go? I think it would be fun."

I deliberated for a bit but could feel her enthusiasm as she went on about what a great time the three of us could have together. I have to admit, I wasn't that interested in hanging with an adult crew for the day, but Rodney was cool, and more importantly, it would make my mother happy. I agreed on one condition: "I'll go if I can take Pac."

It was a road trip, and Pac and I both needed to get out of the city and to have . . . some *fun*.

During this time, Pac was busy working a job John had helped him get, after school and on weekends. He was creating a vision for his future and was flourishing creatively, although, as he came into his manhood, he was frustrated he couldn't do more to help his mother and his sister. He felt like he was failing as a man, and he was hard on himself, because in his mind, he had to live up to a standard in providing for the ones he most loved.

As often as I could, I'd tell him, "Your day will come, Pac. Be patient. There is only so much you can do right now." In time, I assured him, he'd be able to do more to help his family. I said that to him because I believed this to be true in my own circumstance with my mother. My idea was *If I save myself, it will make it possible for me to save her, too.*

Pac had never been to Kings Dominion, so he was happy to join us. Besides, Pac was always down for a good time. As soon as we entered the park, Rodney dug into his pocket to load us up with cash. He obviously didn't know I had my own money. Which was best, because that would have made for a much different conversation. Rodney suggested we reconvene later, at an agreed-upon spot, and with that Pac and I bounced.

Of course, we got on rides and ate a ton of junk like cotton candy (my favorite), hot dogs, and french fries. At some point we wandered over to an installation where you could pick out a song by your favorite artist to make a music video of yourself lip-synching to it, against a green screen.

"Pac! We gotta make our own music video. We gotta do one!" I said excitedly.

He looked at the list of artists. All pop stars. Pac was hesitant. "They don't have nobody Black."

I scoured the long list. "Hold up—they have Jazzy Jeff and the Fresh Prince."

"Where?" Skeptical, Pac looked again.

I pointed. "Here. 'Parents Just Don't Understand.'"

Pac smiled. "They the only rappers on here. Damn. I don't know all the lyrics to that song. Do you?"

I shrugged, saying, "Nope. But 'Parents' is cool. We know enough to fake it."

My thing was, any chance I had to perform, I took it, and that day I also had an opportunity to have it on tape. Pac was feeling a little self-conscious, because he didn't know all the lyrics. It had already been established that I couldn't rap, so I had the easy job. All I needed to do was be his backup dancer. We went back and forth, but he finally gave in.

And the rest is history.

The Universe loves to sprinkle prophetic teasers into our lives. All the time.

Not in a million years would I have dreamed that I had just made a video lip-synching the brand-new hit song that would go on to win a Grammy as one of the first in a newly created Best Rap Song category. Not in a million years would I have dreamed that the Fresh Prince and I would become, um, very well acquainted. And I never would have imagined that this video would become a tangible memory of the last time Pac and I were simply kids together.

One morning a very short time later, without warning—other than the knowledge that there were difficult struggles within Pac's family life—I arrived at school, went to my locker, and found a letter from him in which Pac broke the news that he had left for California.

I would come to find out he had gone to Donald Hicken days before to try to find a way to stay. Pac kept this whole dilemma from me. His exit was abrupt, very abrupt, and that made me worry. Although he assured me in the letter that he was okay and that he would be in touch with me soon, my deep concern for his well-being overshadowed the fact that he was gone from Baltimore—for good.

When we finally spoke, he let me know he was okay, he was moving around from place to place, but he was safe. He got me up to speed on the why, but it was complicated. He did his best to ease my hurt feelings about his sudden departure and my desire to make shit right for him. I hated the fact that I was absolutely powerless to make his life easier.

Pac gave me addresses and numbers for whenever I needed to reach him in Marin City, out in the Bay Area of the West Coast, and kept talking about how he thought I would love Cali, and how he wanted me to visit. I promised I would and meant it.

Most of our conversations ended with a familiar refrain of his: "Aye. Don't get into no stupid shit. I don't want to have to jump back on a bus to Baltimore, Square."

He'd say it like the world was an easy place when we both knew it wasn't, just to reassure me that no matter where he was, he was still willing to hold me down.

I wouldn't give myself the room to feel his absence. I had to keep it movin'. I just kept on stepping, deeper and deeper, into the shit that I believed was going to be my way out of it all.

I
t's a warm Friday night in late spring 1988 that begins with Ramsey and me on North Ave. at a corner liquor store.

Ramsey is a senior at BSA and about to graduate. We're looking to kick it as much as possible before she goes off to college, so the plan is to get a bottle of peach schnapps and head down to the harbor and hang. Before I can buy peach schnapps, I have a check for seven hundred dollars from a hair modeling job that I need to cash real quick.

I'm in line when I notice this really tall dude in a white T-shirt and jeans standing behind me. The person in front of me leaves, so I walk up to the bulletproof plexiglass that the cashier is behind. I ask for schnapps and ask the dude to cash my check after I sign the back of it. He slides my cash toward me, underneath the glass, and I grab it. Just as I'm about to put the money in the top pocket of my jeans jacket, the tall dude behind me snatches my seven hundred fucking dollars right out of my hand and dashes out the door.

The last thing I expect is for a joka to reach over me and rob me like that. That's what I get for being short.

Out of pure instinct and rage, I whip around and charge after the dude, out of the store and down the alley. As I'm chasing him at top speed, I grab my switchblade out of my upper jacket pocket, flick it open, and do my best to catch his ass. All I can think is *How dare you just snatch my shit! Not tonight, n-gga! Not tonight!*

Ramsey's watching at the top of the alley, screaming after me, "Jada! Noooooo!" I'm out of my mind, and she can see that trying to stop me is a losing effort. The guy's tall as hell, with long legs. The farther ahead he gets, the madder I get. Clearly, I am not gonna catch him.

So I stop and try to catch my breath as I walk back toward Ramsey. Once I reach her, she's pissed. "If you had caught him, what were you gonna do?" she asks, irritated.

"I was gonna put this knife in his back and rip out that n-gga's spine!"

"Yeah, right! He could have killed you. Something is really wrong with you," Ramsey says with a slightly relieved chuckle.

We went back to the spot and got our peach schnapps and went down to the harbor, hanging out and drinking until it got really late.

The late-spring night was so nice. It was evenings like this that made me fall in love with the East Coast warm nights forever. The pleasure of being outside and hanging on nights like this was something I wanted to hold on to as long as possible. We were having such a good time, as usual whenever we were together, and I felt like whatever problems were in our way were nothing.

Then, unbelievably . . . WHO do I see? Yup, homeboy! Who took my shit. Across the street. Same jeans, same shoes, same white T-shirt. Just mobb'n like shit ain't happen earlier. But he doesn't see me.

In this moment, I have to make a choice. For several beats I look at him, contemplating whether I should go confront this dude. What I realize is without that rush of adrenaline, I don't have the same courage I had in the alley. Note taken. *I gotta stop being so damn impulsive—it's going to get me hurt.*

I tell myself, *Turn the other way and just leave it alone.* I do just that and continue my laughs with Ramsey.

Despite the earlier events, this night gave me a lasting memory of the carefreeness of my youth. In the midst of everything, with the overt violence and the undertow, there was beauty, love, and deep friendship among all these lessons I was learning at the University of the B-more Streets—*Advanced.* And considering all the other choices and circumstances that lay ahead for me, this was a very "good" Friday night in a city where you had to B-more careful 'cause you were in Murda-land now, not Mary-land. Welcome.

Find your tribe. Love them hard.

—ANONYMOUS

I am so grateful for all the supportive, meaningful friendships I have had in my life, with women and men alike. Being my mother's only child, I feel blessed to have found so many sisters and brothers in friendship who genuinely love me and look out for me. They have made sure I haven't had to walk through the dramas of life alone. These kinds of friendships are not always a given. Many times we can give more attention to the people who cause us drama than to those who want to assist in our peaceful well-being.

————

Who are the people in your life that you consider friends? Write down their names and why you consider their friendship important and nourishing. Have you told them how special they are to you and how grateful you are to have them in your life? If not, take the time to do it . . . right—this—second.

CHAPTER 6

A Gate to Many Roads

The envelope addressed to me from the Juilliard School arrived in the spring of 1989. Before I opened it, I imagined how my acceptance would begin—"We are pleased to inform you . . ." Then it would present the next step for passing through this all-important gate to adulthood.

The Juilliard School was (and is) the mecca for college-level conservatory performing arts training, and if you ascended into the ranks of the Chosen Ones there, that meant you were the real deal. At the audition, I was super confident I'd be accepted. *Then* I'd decide whether I would attend. Part of that confidence came from winning talent shows, dance battles, my training at BSA, and getting every professional gig I had ever auditioned for—since I was eight and had landed a place in the ensemble of Baltimore Ballet's production of *The Nutcracker Suite.*

In my senior year, I was cast in a professional production of August Wilson's *Joe Turner's Come and Gone* at Baltimore Center Stage—to play the part of Zonia, a young girl wanting to find her mother but not wanting to be separated from her father. What I most loved about acting was bringing a character to life by finding the part of myself that I could draw from. Besides that, I loved August Wilson as a playwright—he and Sam Shepard were among my favorites, different as they were.

The reviews of my performance were very positive, and the experience was a good one. Everybody on Mom's side of the family showed up in glorious support. By now, my aunt Karen and her family had moved in with my grandfather Gilbert to take care of him. Aunt Karen was moving into the position in the family that my grandmother once had: organizing holidays, maintaining family traditions, as well as keeping her door open to family members who needed meals or a place to stay. My family were proud of me and were keeping their fingers crossed that I'd take advantage of the opportunities being readily tossed in my direction.

My grandmother Shirley saw my path as a professional actress differently and made it a point to talk to me about my plans for the future outside of the arts. My grandfather Grant's health was now failing, and Shirley, after all those years of not wanting to leave the house, had stepped up to become his caregiver by doing the shopping, running errands, and overseeing his medical care. This was a remarkable change, in my view, and I was happy that she'd even come to see me in my play. Actually, it was Shirley who kept albums of newspaper clippings from any local press I received. But she caught me off guard when she met me in the lobby after the play and said, "Good job tonight, but you need to start planning for college—and prepare for an actual career. Acting won't pay your bills."

That was Shirley. Standing in that lobby, still high from a great performance, I held my tongue—and the bouquet of flowers that someone had just handed me.

Shirley's words echoed in my ears as I opened the envelope from Juilliard. It began, "We regret to inform you . . ." or words to that effect. I had not been accepted.

My life of auditions flashed before my eyes. I had never been rejected. Juilliard proved there is always a first time. My ego was shattered, and my feelings were hurt. I felt the self-doubt overwhelm me: *Maybe I really don't have what it takes to make it outside of Baltimore.* I took the rejection as a sign that I was meant to keep working on my other career, building my empire in the streets.

It's funny how easy it is to buy into the fallacy that it's momentous turning points and grand choices that decide our course. Sometimes it can be one small action, even one taken by someone else nudging us this way or that, that makes all the difference.

You never know who that someone might be. For me, it was Donald Hicken, who, without asking, put me on the list to audition for the University of North Carolina School of the Arts. The faculty from North Carolina, like many of the performing arts college programs, actually came to our school to hold auditions and select talent for their freshman class.

In the nicest way possible, I told him, "Thank you, but that's not the school for me."

He wouldn't take no for an answer. Donald Hicken gave me all the reasons that he was a fan of UNC School of the Arts in Winston-Salem, telling me that it was in league with the other top performing arts programs like Juilliard, Yale, Carnegie Mellon, and so on. In his opinion, I was a triple threat—I could act, dance, and sing—and conservatory training would give me a launch into a serious career.

Besides, Donald had seen enough to know that I needed to get out of Baltimore. He knew I was in trouble.

Even though I was scared I'd be rejected again (because by now, I truly believed I had no talent), I finally agreed to audition. It was hard to say no to Donald.

I decided to audition with one of my favorite monologues from *Antigone*—when she must plead for the right to bury her brother. I had done it countless times in class, and I knew it like the back of my hand. Donald had worked me to death on it in monologue class, helping me to fine-tune every moment. That drama department at BSA had brilliant teachers, and I have yet to meet their equal.

When the day came, unfortunately, Donald had to provide one last push to get me in the room to audition. I tried to make an excuse for why I shouldn't audition. "Donald, I don't want to waste anyone's time. I'm never going to school in North Carolina."

"Jada, you have more talent in the tip of your pinkie finger than most people have in their whole bodies. You don't want to see where that can take you? What are you going to do here? Huh? Keep running around with your friends, not giving yourself a real opportunity to do something with your life?" Donald was at his wits' end.

So I sauntered my reluctant seventeen-year-old ass into that room and auditioned. Donald was relieved. He'd done his job. The rest was up to me.

It cannot be overstated how much my mind was completely and resolutely made up. Winston-Salem could have been on the planet Mars for all I knew or cared, because I was not going there. I was not going to give control of my future to anybody. I was in these B-more streets, and I was gonna make my mark.

Keesha was the first person to really call me out on the choices I'd been making. She knocked me off my high horse—a bit. This had been building for a while. I could feel a growing rift between us. To smooth things out, I took her to a fancy seafood restaurant and brought along a gift as an olive branch—a piece of jewelry. Something I'd bought from a local jeweler. We both LOVED jewelry. I really believed my gift would close the distance and ease whatever tension was between us.

When I handed her the present, she sadly sighed and took a beat before opening it. To my shock, she was not impressed in the least. Instead, she had an air of disappointment and fear.

"I can't take this," she said, and handed the gift back to me.

I shifted uncomfortably in my chair, knowing exactly why.

"What are you doing, Jada?" she asked.

That was not a question I was ready to answer.

Keesha went on to tell me she couldn't understand why I was throwing my life away, that I was going to end up in jail. Or dead.

I wasn't ready to make a change, but I didn't forget what she said. Apparently, I needed a bigger warning.

That reality hit me right before graduation, when we all received devastating news about one of our beloved classmates and my friend, Isha Moses. She was such a light, so sweet and funny, and suddenly, she was gone. She died in a car accident, coming home from a weekend trip with her boyfriend. That was a cruel blow and evidence that things out of our control can take a fatal turn. It seemed so unfair and random. Her death made me take a closer look at my choices.

The fact that I graduated was a miracle. My attendance record for academic classes was so disastrous, I had to do a lot of begging. My diploma was more or less a gift that came with the understanding that I had potential—*if* I would apply myself to positive endeavors.

And as the summer moved on, I saw exactly what a positive endeavor was and what it was not.

O*ne night, on my way to* go skating at Painters Mill—dressed to a tee, my pockets loaded with cash, and a bunch of jewelry on—I went on a quick run to Cherry Hill. I NEVER went to Cherry Hill laced like that, but I didn't worry. I wasn't planning to be there longer than fifteen minutes to drop off some product.

While I was there, a dude—whom I had previous bad dealings with and promised myself to never serve again—came to the door saying he was looking to buy.

Suspicious, I say through the door, "Show me your money." Through the peephole, I see that, sure enough, he's got a wad of cash. "Aight, hold up," and I turn to make sure I've got the amount of product requested. Once I have it in hand, I open the door, leaving the chain on, to make the transaction.

Before I can grab his money, two dudes jump out, both holding 9-millimeters as they kick the door open, breaking the safety chain, and point their guns at my face.

In terror, I fall back into the recliner I'm usually posted in and pee my pants.

One of the dudes presses closer to me and points the 9 to the middle of my head. The woman who lives there, in similar terror, hides under a small round dining table as the second dude starts to scour the apartment.

"Take off your jewelry," says the dude with the gun to my head. He is so cool about it that I, terrified as hell, in pissy pants and all, can't help but talk shit.

As I'm taking off my bracelets, I jabber, "Why you fuck'n with me? Oh, so you wanna take my lil bit a shit."

This dude is not paying me a bit of mind as he looks over his shoulder at his homeboy, who's searching for any other stash I might have there. He yells, "You see anything?"

"Naw," his homeboy yells back.

He looks at me, icy as hell. "I want all the drugs and all your money."

I dump my pockets of cash and give him all the product I have on me. He takes it and some of the jewelry I've already taken off. "I want all of it. Even those . . ." He looks down at my ankles and the gold chains wrapped around them. I start to take those off, and he turns to survey the entire apartment, looking to see if there's anything else worth taking.

In that moment, I quickly rip off a white-gold necklace with a small diamond solitaire pendant attached that was given to me by my stepfather Tony and throw it under my tongue. They were not getting that piece no matter what. Not that I was so sentimental, no. That diamond necklace had become a symbol of my worth as a human. So much so, I was willing to risk my life for it.

The main dude, let's call him Cee, grabbed the rest of my jewelry, then proceeded to move out. His homeboy left first, and as Cee was backing out of the apartment with his gun still pointed at me, our eyes locked.

I could see the thoughts running through his mind: *Should I kill her, she knows who I am. I could kidnap her, rape her.* I knew he was trying those thoughts on for size. But he backed out slowly, paused for one more glance . . . then closed the door.

As soon as he left, I called Fawn, letting her know what had gone down and that I'd be late. That's what you do. You keep it moving and stick to the plan. Near-death experiences and all.

Then I called BP. His first question was "Did you have your gun on you?" Of course I had the .22 that he'd given me, but it had NEVER crossed my mind to use it. I'm not built like that. It was clear I'd been set up by the dude who came to the door with the wad of cash. How could I have been so stupid? BP immediately identified the stickup dude as Cee, who was notorious for robb'n folks in that area.

BP arranged a meeting at my request, because I wanted my shit back. BP, who came along to make sure I was straight, thought I was out of my mind, and warned me I'd be lucky to get back whatever jewelry Cee hadn't sold. The cash and the drugs were a no-go.

When we met up on a side street in the Hill a few days later, as BP predicted, Cee gave me back a few pieces of my jewelry that he hadn't sold. Our meeting was brief, but before we left I had to ask something.

"You left me there—how come?"

He looked at me for a second, with eyes that appeared as if he had never felt a warm touch in his life, and said, "You were too pretty."

You know what's crazy? That was the very first time I actually believed it.

And that was the last time Cherry Hill saw the likes of me.

Two weeks later, Cee was arrested for the murder of two drug dealers he'd shot up in the trunk of a car and was sent to prison for life. It still didn't register how lucky I had been.

Chet and I met at a car wash for me to give him whatever cash and product I had stashed at my house. Stressed big-time that I owed him a lot of dough (to recoup the loss from the robbery), I didn't want him to be in the hole because of me. I told him, "I promise I'll get you the rest when I can."

Chet looked me in the eyes and said, "You good with me, shawty, I'm glad you're still alive." He was not stressed over my setback. Besides, in the future, I would pay him back tenfold.

For the time being, I was deflated and defeated. I had been doing so well, and just like that, I was broke and in need of another hustle. So when BP told me he needed my help with a situation, I was glad that he still had trust in me. What we were trying to do is lost in the haze of memory. Something about how the basement in the house of one of BP's relatives—which he used as a stash house—had flooded. We needed to go there to move some product, along with some money, from a safe.

It was a typical summer night when BP came to get me. We pulled up to a row house on a quiet residential street in a working-class neighborhood. But as soon as BP parked the car, I felt a flash of unease. Ignoring it, I told myself, *I'm with BP. I'm good.*

The front door was open, with a screen door to allow fresh air into the house. We opened it, and as we walked through the small living room, I noticed that the house was quiet. We reached the basement door and headed down the steps.

At the bottom of the stairs, I could see about two inches of water on the floor. Other than giving off a musty smell, the water looked clear to me, not foul. So far, so good.

Then, just as BP was about to open the safe, a dude with a 9-millimeter charged down the steps. He pointed the gun at me first and demanded I go stand on top of a cot in the corner of the basement. "Back up," he ordered.

Oh shit, not again.

Everything in my nervous system went cold.

I put my hands in the air by my shoulders. Scared as I was, I didn't want to piss myself again. With whatever control I could muster, I stayed calm and did as he said. I did not break eye contact with him. I knew he meant business: His eyes had no soul, no fear, just animosity. My heart was POUNDING. I was very aware that this was a moment that could go very wrong—very fast.

I climbed up on the cot and stood there, all five feet and ninety-five pounds of me, trying not to show my fear. The dude kept the gun pointed at my chest, making it clear to BP that if he did anything stupid, I would be shot.

BP had no options. If I hadn't been there, he would have handled things very differently, I'm sure. The dude with the gun, continuing to point it at me, put his focus on BP, who was stooped down, an already compromised position, on a wet floor in order to open the safe. The dude proceeded to tell BP that he was looking for T-Row, a friend of ours who apparently owed this guy money.

A helpless spectator, I had to stand and watch as the dude took his gun off of me and pointed it at BP while the two of them went back and forth with an aggressive exchange of words about T-Row. T had disappeared weeks ago. BP was adamant he didn't know nothing about whatever money T owed.

Suddenly, in the middle of the exchange, BP seized a moment and charged at the guy. The two went at it as they began to tussle in the water. It was slippery, but the dude with the gun got his footing and enough leverage to violently pistol-whip BP across the face.

My fear was matched only by my complete shame. I was helpless.

The gunman demanded, "Open the fucking safe!" BP did as he asked, and the dude made him hand over all the product and all the money and left.

BP looked to me with a busted mouth full of blood and asked, "You okay?"

"I'm okay," I said, and tried my best to muster a steely exterior. But the truth is, I was not okay. Not at all.

We were still alive. But what played in my head was a cold truth. *There will be a day when you won't be so lucky. A day when you may not make it out alive.*

M y mother's first wake-up call was finding empty bags of product in my room, which led her to assume, incorrectly, that I had become an addict. She may have decided to search my room because girls who came to the ob-gyn clinic where she worked—Total Health Care, deep in West B-more—were constantly telling her, "You know we be see'n your daughter hanging out in Cherry Hill."

"My daughter? She does not go to Cherry Hill," my mother would reply.

"Your daughter be down 'nare all the time."

So, when she found empty plastic bags with white powder residue in them—in a hole in my wall—she came at me. "Jada, how long have you been using?"

"What?"

She showed me the bags.

"Ma, I'm not using," I replied, frustrated.

I tried to make up all kinds of excuses—let's call them lies—none of which she bought.

Eventually, I confessed that I had dabbled in selling. She didn't believe me and demanded I take a piss test.

I did and I was clean. She got off my back. For a minute.

The shit really hit the fan when she heard through the grapevine—because the streets talk—about the robbery in Cherry Hill. She couldn't believe it. "You were dealing in Cherry Hill? Have you lost your fucking mind?" Adrienne had gone red. I stayed cool because she was quick with her hands.

A few weeks prior, I'd gotten into UNC School of the Arts. I had told my mother that I didn't want to go. Before she found out about Cherry Hill, she was patient with me around my hesitation. With this new information, the patience was gone. "All this talk about you not going to school! Fuck that! You gett'n the hell up out of here, I bet you that. You understand me?"

I had my stoic "whatever" expression on my face.

Adrienne stepped over to me and snarled through her teeth, "Play wit me if you want. I'll take your ass out on that concrete." With this, I needed to pull back and get myself in respectful alignment. I had promised myself that there would never be a day when my mother and I had a physical fight. I humbled myself quick.

Adrienne was no longer in a cheery "time to go to college" mode. "Start pack'n your shit. Now."

School was to start in two weeks. But after a college loan, I still needed fifteen hundred dollars to go.

In the not too distant past, I could have paid that money no problem. I could have collected the money from all the dudes I knew with a snap of a finger. I refused. I wasn't going out like that. Besides, I was hoping the money wouldn't come through and I wouldn't have to go anyway.

But of course, Adrienne rose to the occasion and found the money.

I was being forced into exile. Insult upon injury, I wasn't allowed to take my car or have one on campus as a freshman. I procrastinated on packing until the night before I was supposed to leave.

"You listen to me. Pack your shit and be ready to go in the morning. I'm not play'n with you!"

The next morning, despite my resistance, I packed up my stuff and got in the car. There was no need for tearful goodbyes with my closest friends. In my mind, I'd be seeing them next weekend.

I didn't say a word the entire six-hour drive to North Carolina. Mom, Rodney, and I sat in silence.

But the closer we got to Winston-Salem, the more relaxed I felt.

I could feel some peace in the slower tempo. I thought about my last conversation with Chet, when I'd told him my mother was getting me the F up out of B-more. Chet was on the come-up, and I was mad I was going to miss out.

"I thought we was gonna be Bonnie and Clyde, shawty," Chet said, laughing. "I'm sad you're going." Then he went on, "I'm happy for you, too. You do need to get up outta here." I could see in his eyes he meant it.

Maybe Chet was right. Maybe it was time for me to just be a theater student on the straight and narrow. The closer we got to the school, the more willing I became to let it all play out.

For many reasons, *UNC School of* the Arts was exactly where I was supposed to go. For starters, it turned out that Mia Pitts, one of Fawn's best friends and a dance major at Baltimore School for the Arts, was a sophomore there. We hadn't been tight back at home, but in our new setting, we struck up a close and lasting friendship.

Mia was chocolate brown and fine as hell, with thick bowed legs. She talked unlike any Black female I had heard before, with a preppy, proper, upbeat manner. She didn't sound like she was B-more at all.

People often mistook her "proper" speak for softness. Those folks would have a most unpleasant surprise, because Mia had no problem throwing hands, going from zero to a hundred in seconds. She was not to be tampered with, especially when she was prancing down the halls of her dorm in only patent-leather high heels and a G-string, preparing for one of our nights out. I witnessed her mop a chick up real quick in that getup one night, after the girl came for Mia one too many times.

Mia liked to go, GO, like me, and that's exactly what we did all through my only year in college. We'd go to parties, clubbing, to homecomings, on road trips to Greekfests, to concerts—nonstop, without missing a beat at school. Mia would later work in professional dance companies, eventually landing in Hollywood in the 1990s to make a name for herself, before I asked her to work with me.

We had been in college barely a minute when she talked me into going on the first of countless weekend road trips. A six-hour drive was nothing to get us both up to Baltimore on a Friday and back to Winston-Salem on a Sunday. The beautiful part of the experience we had in North Carolina is that I could be on the go as much as I had ever been—but without the dangers I met at home. Don't get it twisted, the streets of North Carolina—and the hustlers who kept them—found me, and I had opportunity and temptation. But I got focused on becoming the theater arts student on the straight and narrow. Besides, my housing and food were basically covered, so why not be broke and make the best of being a college student? I was starting to like it.

I hadn't been in North Carolina long before I had a pep talk from Pac. "I'm proud of you. Stay focused on school. If you need something, you let me know. Don't get stupid down there. I'll send you a lil something whenever you need it."

"Nah, I'm cool," I'd always tell him, because I didn't want to ask him for a thing.

But it never failed. After every conversation we had, I would end up getting some cash in the mail from him. How the tables had turned.

At this point, Pac was mov'n and shak'n in different kinds of ways. He was doing his thing and was excited to be making some real nice connects as far as his music went. He was on his man game, and he was feeling good about it. And soon he'd be rolling with Digital Underground, which would change his life.

I kept my word, as hard as it was, to become an all-around "good" girl.

Thank goodness I met Toine, who was a year younger than I was.

He grabbed my attention and kept it. He was a trumpet player, and it was through him that I fell in love with jazz. He introduced me to John Coltrane, Sarah Vaughan, Wynton Marsalis, Branford Marsalis, Billie Holiday, and so on. He was well studied in the arts, which fed my curiosity and new desire to be "cultured." Eventually, Toine would become a highly respected jazz trumpet player. I loved that he was such a serious musician, but I hated competing with that trumpet.

This new environment inspired me in ways I never expected. Everyone around me had a passion and was focused intensely on it. There were not a lot of Black students at school, but the ABA, the Association of Black Artists, had been formed in order to ensure that the needs of Black students were recognized. Mia and I helped to organize a fashion show/fundraiser for ABA. We were able to get clothes from the happening local store and managed to pull off one grand event. And it was fabulous, Winston-Salem-style.

The theater department was reminiscent of BSA, yet the serious ambition of my classmates was new. They seemed to understand that there was more than luck and charm required to make it in the real world of show business. It was beginning to dawn on me that hustle had many applications.

Even before I went to Baltimore School for the Arts, Debbie Allen had been my main inspiration. She was the female example of having a multidimensional career. She produced, directed, choreographed, sang, and danced—there was nothing she couldn't do. In light of my revived focus, her journey provided a blueprint for what was possible.

Witnessing the power of Denzel Washington's performance in *Glory* was yet another turning point. Denzel had inspired me first in the movie *Cry Freedom*. His portrayal of activist Stephen Biko had moved me so much that I even named my beloved black-and-white cat Biko.

In *Glory*, Denzel's intensity and ability to transport you to another time and place had a very potent impact. I sat in the North Carolina movie theater as the credits rolled and a flow of tears cascaded down my face. *I want to make people feel through art, I want to wield this kind of magic,* was all I could think. And then I resolved, *I'm either going to do this or not, but it's time to make some moves.*

In my opinion, I didn't need to stay in the program at UNC any longer. A lot of what I was learning was just putting finishing touches on what I'd started years earlier at BSA.

Right before the end of my freshman year, I called my mother with my plan. "Hey, Ma," I began, "I don't think it makes sense to do three more years of college for acting. So, you got two choices—I can go to law school and become a lawyer, or I could go to L.A. and see if I can really do this acting thing."

Without hesitation, my mother answered, "Hollywood it is."

Look closely at the present you are constructing;
it should look like the future you are dreaming.

—ALICE WALKER

When we look back at our journey, we discover the choices we made that shaped the life we are living. We often forget that although many aspects of life are out of our control, our power of choice is not one of them. Behind the many choices we make (unconsciously or consciously) are wounds that can blind us to how we abandon love and kindness, sometimes taking us and others into shadowy tailspins.

———

Unfortunately, when we are immersed in environments full of shadow, it can take a long while to unteach ourselves the methods learned there.

———

But it's okay. We can make different choices with better outcomes. We can have remorse and we can atone—without forgetting that sometimes we have to live who we're not in order to know who we are.

———

You can examine the shadows within and guide them to the light through the power of choice. When we are willing to accept how we have had a hand in the condition of our lives, as we pay close attention to the outcome of our choices, new opportunities from the Universe become more apparent and available. But the first step is to own your choices and have the desire to better your life.

———

Take that step with just one aspect of your life and see what changes. And then keep going.

PART II

HOLLY WOOD

CHAPTER 7

Promise of a Perfect World

W hat's up, Square?" *Pac begins, as* always, and then bursts into that contagious giggle of his. The levity and big energy in his voice make me smile.

"Boy, what do you want?" I've just gotten home from a rehearsal at the studio. I'm tired, have Rottweilers to feed, and I'm not in a mood for his nonsense.

As usual, though, Pac couldn't care less about whether I'm tired. He's on a mission. "Look, there's this movie I want us to do together called *Menace II Society*."

What? Am I dreaming? I thought back to a few years earlier, when I'd arrived in L.A. in the early summer of 1990.

All I wanted to do was win-win-win. And I believed if I played the game right, it would deliver me the life of prosperity, peace, and happiness I had always wanted. That was the dream. Trying to make it as a queenpin hadn't offered me that dream, though the game had taught me a strong hustle—a hustle I brought to L.A.

There is no such thing as overnight success. Everybody who grabs the spotlight probably looks like an overnight success 'cause you ain't know 'em before they got on the scene. Behind each one of those stories is someone who was willing to suffer setbacks and put in the hard work, hoping for a little sprinkle of luck.

The best talisman I had was my mother's belief in me. Without it, I don't think I would have been able to pursue an acting career with such confidence. But just like everyone else, I had to deal with the classic Hollywood catch-22: If you don't have any recent or current credits, you're stuck trying to get credits, which you can't get if you don't have any credits.

How to overcome that? Your training, talent, skills, and commitment to hard work are all valuable assets, for sure. Connections, as everyone will tell you, can be helpful but can't make you. A connection can't give you a career, but it can help open a door enough to get your foot in.

And timing is crucial. There is one other asset that might seem to be a curse but can turn out to be the ace up your sleeve. For me, that was my education from the University of the B-more Streets. I had cultivated fearlessness and a no-nonsense attitude. After all I had seen and been through, I knew any trials Hollywood had to offer would pale in comparison to the trials I had already withstood. However, it was sometimes a double-edged sword, because some would say that I could come off as abrasive, distant, and aloof. I didn't seem approachable, which until now had worked as a beautiful defense mechanism and kept me safe. But here in Hollywood, it seemed as if I had a chip on my shoulder. I wasn't aware of this "edge" because that's just how we rolled back on the East Coast.

I also got lots of pushback for being "rough around the edges"—whether it was my Baltimore accent or the fact that I wasn't your clean-cut girl-next-door in my style. And, oh yeah, I was too hairy. On the East, hair was considered sexy. Hairy legs, arms, upper lip, even bushy eyebrows, were celebrated where I was from. I once had a very famous Black actor tell me at a pool party when he saw me in shorts: "Jada, promise me that you'll never shave your legs." I remember thinking, *Gladly*.

With all the Hollywood nonsense and scrutiny that came my way, my edge helped me stay true to who I was and where I came from. And that so-called chip on my shoulder was my refusal to lose myself in the very white Hollywood standard of poise, dress, and attitude that was slowly but surely being pressed upon me. Black *talent* was in vogue, whereas *Blackness off-screen* was not.

Often I heard the question: "What are you mixed with?"

"Excuse me?"

"Is your mother white?"

"No, she happens to be full-blooded West Indian," I would answer proudly.

"Oh, that's it—the Indian in you." This casting director was trying to imply that to look as I did, I couldn't be of full African American heritage. And he assumed that the Indian in my mother's heritage meant Native American.

It got to the point where I saw such comments as ignorant and ridiculous, but I could not believe how frequently I heard them. What got me was the constant look of disbelief whenever I replied that both my parents were simply . . . Black.

Ringing in my ears all the time were my aunt Karen's words about never speaking on the mixed blood anywhere in my bloodline. She'd emphasize that people would always try to use that influence in your background as an excuse for why you had any appealing quality at all, even if the one relative from another race was from three generations ago. "They'll never want to give your Blackness credit, Jada. Don't let them do that."

Whenever the questions arose, at a time when I was knocking on doors, hoping they would open for me, I thought of Aunt Karen.

Once I began to enter these audition rooms, I would come across a lot of fake wolves posing as producers, casting directors, directors, and such. The Hollywood flex was amusing, but there would be quite a few times when I let jokas know: "I ain't the one."

Compared to the real wolves of B-more, these show business jokas were more like little puppies.

Sometimes I got nervous because I always wanted to do well. But this wasn't life-or-death for me, like it was for some. I knew all too well what life and death looked like. I could keep everything in perspective and just—ride. The hustle became fun and exciting. My real edge? I knew it was all a game.

Los Angeles itself can be deceiving to the uninitiated. The palm trees, the balmy weather, and the slower daily tempo can trick you into thinking you are on holiday every day—but I learned quick that these L.A. streets weren't nothing to play with.

I was still an avid skater, so it worked out well that both the first place I lived in Culver City and my next address on Comey Avenue, off the corner of La Cienega and Venice, gave me close proximity to World on Wheels—the skating rink I hit every chance I got. Other than that, L.A. was like a foreign country to me. What confused me most were the colors and repp'n neighborhoods thing. I didn't understand what all that had to do with making money. The gangs didn't own the property they were dying and repp'n for. On the East Coast, street cliques hooked up to make money. A clique might rep an area of the city based on money made, not based on gang color.

Clearly, I was out of my league, so I kept my nose clean of all that. But L.A. trouble had a way of finding me anyway. At home, you knew when you were in a neighborhood you should not be in. L.A. was different. You could be in a neighborhood that looked like a working-class area with nice lawns and palm trees, and the next thing you know, you'd get got. In other words—robbed and carjacked.

One night, driving home from World on Wheels with one of my homegirls, a packed little hooptie pulls up beside us. I see some dudes up against the window looking as if they created a new version of pop lock'n, ready to battle some East Coast B-boys. I start laughing and tell my girlfriend, "Look, they pop lock'n."

My girlfriend looks up and her mood turns. "Oh shit!" she yells, "they throw'n signs! They 'bout to jack us. We gotta go!"

I stepped on the gas of my Civic CRX so fast and hard, we sped down Venice all the way into Culver City until I'd made sure we lost them. That would not be my last run-in with L.A.'s unpredictable nature.

For all the differences in Los Angeles and Baltimore, I found my people. We loved to frequent places like M&M Soul Food, or Silver Spoon, that couldn't be beat for Sunday breakfast. Then we'd prowl through the Slauson Swap Meet, which became my go-to where I could shop for everything, even new woofers and stereo systems for my cars. I loved going to Leimert Park to join protests or to enjoy the outside markets. Not far from there were the aisles of Eso Won Books, an iconic Black-owned bookstore that featured Black authors who focused on subject matters of interest to people of color. I found books there you would never find in chain bookstores.

Not too far from my house on Comey Avenue, over by Rodeo (Ro-dee-o on that side, as opposed to Ro-DAY-o in Beverly Hills), I was out and about when the acquittal in the Rodney King trial was announced. I'll never forget how Black people poured into the streets, rioting and looting. The community was furious, fed up, tired of a system constantly reiterating that a Black man beaten senseless by cops had no recourse under the law. We were tired of a system claiming that the Black community was not worthy of justice and fair treatment. The Rodney King beating represented injustices felt in every hood across America. Whether you were from the South, the East, the North, or the West, whether you wore colors or Timbs, we all felt the pain and humiliation of entrenched dynamics protecting those who had no regard for Black life.

My girlfriend Keesha was visiting me from Baltimore that day, and we took our frustration to the street. Within the chaos of the riots was a unified voice: "Fuck this! You WILL hear us today!" Youth + anger + passion + frustration can rightfully = impetuous acts. In expressions of anger, frustration, and the need to be heard, many got caught up in the tide that would render unintended consequences as we grabbed stuff out of local stores. At that point in my life, I definitely believed justice meant an eye for an eye. Maturity would teach me that's not always the case. That night of looting and burning down businesses destroyed resources we needed in our community, and we felt it.

We knew that what happened to one of us happened to all of us. The saving grace was that in the midst of this chaos there was a lot of love to be found in many of our homes, churches, and community centers, as reminders of our worth.

In the end, the tragedy was that not much changed to address the pain of that moment or to prevent the moment from happening again. Or worse.

The period from the late 1980s into the late '90s was truly prime time for young hopefuls like me. That was when SO many doors began to open for Black actors. Hollywood was finally gaining the confidence to invest in untapped Black potential, allowing for what I often call the Golden Years of Black Hollywood.

If you were a Black male comedian, it was practically a given that you'd have the opportunity to star in your own sitcom. This, of course, opened doors for Black actresses. But it wasn't quite the Promised Land. Black laughter might have been hot, but Black drama lagged behind in terms of what got made. There were few opportunities to become the next Black Meryl Streep.

But what I really loved about this era was the sisterhood among Black women. A success from any of us created opportunity for all of us. I'd see Nia Long, Paula Jai Parker, Elise Neal, Halle Berry, Regina King, Tamala Jones, Tichina Arnold, Malinda Williams, Monica Calhoun, Nicole Ari Parker, Lela Rochon, Queen Latifah, and so many more on the audition circuit all the time. Nia Long was one of the first actresses I met going on auditions. We became friends and, at some point, even decided to try our hand at forming a singing group. Though we didn't end up following through with that, we cheered on one another in our other endeavors. As time went on, we all became full-fledged adults with very busy lives and only managed to catch quick hellos at Hollywood events. But to this day, every time we see one another, the love and sisterhood of that time remains among us all.

When Halle became the first—and as yet ONLY—Black woman to win a Best Actress Oscar, for *Monster's Ball,* she generously acknowledged many of us and the support and belief we had for one another. I felt that her acknowledgment was a beautiful homage to that era.

We all had our own superpowers, yet we had a healthy competition. We knew at some point we would each get our due in the way that was meant. There was no beef, it was all love . . . always.

Early on, my mother came out to visit. Because she ran into other mothers in the game who were managing their children, she suggested, "Jada, maybe I should be your manager."

This was not a good idea. The process seemed easy, and some of the mother managers had offered her guidance, but my hunch told me there was more to managing than my mom could imagine. Besides, Adrienne was still struggling with addiction. With much love and gratitude, I told her that all the belief she invested in me would serve me well, but: "You gotta really know this game to do that, Ma. I don't think that's a good idea."

We went back and forth as she ran down the examples of the mothers who were managing their daughters, and all I could think was—*I get it, but . . . no.*

My instincts reminded me that the laws of supply and demand would work for me. Blackness was popp'n, with more and more Black writers and directors coming up, as were opportunities to tell the stories of our generation. Eddie Murphy had jumped from the stand-up mic to TV star to movie superstardom in comedic AND action-adventure roles, proving that Black entertainers were viable—globally. Black content was BOOMING: From *The Fresh Prince of Bel-Air, A Different World, Family Matters, In Living Color, Hangin' with Mr. Cooper, Roc, Living Single,* and *Martin* to movies from Black filmmakers like Spike Lee, John Singleton, Robert Townsend, Julie Dash (*Daughters of the Dust*), Leslie Harris (*Just Another Girl on the I.R.T.*), Ernest Dickerson, the Hughes brothers, and Gary Gray.

All of this was happening at warp speed, with a huge, beautiful cluster of Black talent. I felt welcomed into a bustling, energized extended family right out of the gate. In short, I wasn't looking for things not to work out. My future didn't hinge on all the barriers in front of me. My future hinged on the conviction that if I could get in front of the right people, those barriers could be overcome.

For my first three months in L.A., I juggled three jobs—my main gig at Music Plus, a record store near Pico and La Cienega; a second job as a temp for various businesses where I cheerfully answered phones (though I couldn't type worth a lick); and at night, another job in a personal injury doctor's office where I filled out insurance claim forms that weren't entirely aboveboard.

In my free time, I enjoyed taking the trek up to West Hollywood to the Bodhi Tree, another independent bookstore and magical space on Melrose Avenue that sold a wide range of New Age, spiritual, and self-help-type titles. In L.A. there were so many worlds I could touch, so many different types of communities and subcultures—all I had to do was find my tribe.

Pac was still in the Bay Area, and he'd check up on me frequently. Every few weekends or so, I'd drive up to see him or he'd come to see me. At this point, he was becoming known with Digital Underground and had started to be featured on records like "Same Song." Things were about to really get rolling for him, and he predicted they would for me, too.

Sure enough, within a matter of weeks, my mother's friend who had let me stay with her introduced me to her friend Daphne. She became one of my new L.A. homegirls. Daphne was dating Keenen

Ivory Wayans and eventually went on to marry him. After defying the odds as an actor and stand-up turned filmmaker with *I'm Gonna Git You Sucka,* Keenen broke all the rules again with his hit sketch comedy show, *In Living Color,* which had debuted the month before I got to Los Angeles. His show not only became a hit, but was an audacious representation of diverse talent and creativity in Hollywood. He was so ahead of the curve, launching careers for everyone from Rosie Perez to Jim Carrey to his brother Damon Wayans.

After Daphne brought me to one of Keenen's parties, I got to know him, too. He soon became a mentor in the best sense of the word. At one of those parties, I boldly told Keenen, "You need to make me a Fly Girl."

After all, I was a dance battle queen from Baltimore. Why wouldn't he want me to be part of the dance troupe on *In Living Color*?

He chuckled. "Oh really." He continued with: "Keep doing what you're doing. You got something."

Keenen had an eye for talent, and maybe he saw something in me from the start. This may be the reason he chose to step into my world and put his foot down at a critical point, and in a way that I didn't even realize was needed.

The backstory to this incident was one I thought I'd left behind. One of my former "associates" was a Philly-based heavy hitter in the drug game and part of a clique known as Junior Black Mafia. We'll call this dude JB. When I first met him, I was impressed by his calm, confident demeanor. My girlfriend Fawn and I met JB and a few of his homeboys at the Harborplace mall in Baltimore.

In that period, JB was among the many hustlers from Philly, New York, and D.C. who would come through Baltimore, especially in the spring and summer. He had his eye on Fawn. However, Fawn didn't roll in those circles without me, so whenever he wanted to hang with Fawn, I came along. This was how JB and I became cool.

At one point he invited me and Fawn to Philly. We met him at a stash house. That sticks out in my memory because when he asked,

"You two wanna go shopping?" and we said yes, he directed me to the laundry room and said to grab whatever cash we needed from the dryer.

When I opened the dryer door, I found a large black garbage bag full of cash. Being nosy, I checked the washing machine next, and, same thing, it was full of money too. Fawn and I decided to be conservative and only took fifteen g's apiece.

JB was a good friend to Fawn, but she always kept things platonic. That was just her steeze. Fawn was smart to do that. She kept things simple, without hurt feelings. Besides, dudes liked the challenge of her *aloofness*. She was not interested, and conquerors always love the chase of the unconquerable.

After I left Baltimore, the government came down hard on the street game. Unbeknownst to us, there were full-on stings happening all over, meant to take down some of the biggest operations of drug distribution on the East. Many dudes I knew were being arrested back-to-back, and JB was one of them.

When I got home in the summer after college, I paged JB. The feds called back, asking how I knew him.

I answered fast, "He didn't tell me that was his name. I know him as Harold Jackson." Made it up on the spot. I quickly explained I'd been away at college and had met this guy once at a party. Whether or not they believed me, I don't know, but as I hung up the phone, I felt my heart racing and was so sad. *Damn. They got JB, too.*

Not long after I arrived in L.A., I received a call from JB—who had gotten my number from Fawn—and he asked for a favor. In short, he was going to send me some photos. He wanted me to change the dates on them and be willing to testify in court that he was in L.A. visiting me at the time of those dates. He obviously needed an alibi.

JB was someone who had always had my back, and I had learned a lot from him. For everything he had done for me, my reaction was *Easy, no problem.*

A few days later, while I was kicking it with Daphne at Keenen's, he overheard me explaining to Daphne what I needed to do for JB.

Keenen immediately piped up. "You cannot do that." Keenen usually had the most cool, laid-back, "you can't ruffle my feathers" demeanor, but in this instance, he was ADAMANT and wanted to make it very clear that I was about to put myself in a very bad position.

"Jada," Keenen insisted, "you cannot go to court and testify about dates you changed on pictures. That's perjury. You will go to jail."

Now, my eighteen-year-old naive ass had not thought about that. All I was thinking about was that JB was my homeboy who needed my help. If you ride hard for people when they are flying high, you ride for them harder when they are down and out. Pleading my case, I said, "He asked, and I don't want—"

Keenen interrupted and spoke to me with full authority: "Lying in court is perjury. You will go to jail." His point was *What real friend would ask you to jeopardize yourself that way?*

I knew he was right. As terrible as I felt, I had to tell JB that I couldn't do what he asked. Years later, though, I was able to do him a solid and help his family.

I'm so thankful for Keenen. If he hadn't taken the time to talk some sense into my young, arrogant, thick skull, there's no telling where I would have landed.

Although JB understood, I still felt this was betraying the code I knew. Being a ride-or-die was central to my worth. Maybe I needed to relearn the code.

----

*I*n the land of Hollywood, *I* was lucky to come across practical advice early on that made a difference for me, even if I didn't put it to use right away.

At one of Keenen's bowling parties—celebrating the season wrap of *In Living Color*—I had brought a dude from Baltimore who had just been released from one of his stints in jail. In passing, Keenen introduced my friend and me to Eddie Murphy, who was there supporting Keenen.

When we asked Eddie if we could take a picture with him, he obliged. As the night went on, Eddie waved me over to where he was standing and asked, "Who is that peanuthead n-gga you're with?" I cracked up laughing. He came back fast with words to the effect of "No, really."

I responded directly, saying, "My boyfriend."

"Him?"

"Yes, him."

Eddie smiled. Then he asked what I was drinking, which was an alcoholic beverage of some kind. He told me alcohol wasn't good for me.

"What are you drinking?" I asked.

"Water. My body is my temple."

As we talked, I saw the truth of this idea in the brightness of his eyes, the vibrancy of his energy, and the smoothness and clarity of his skin. He was just shiny and full of life. I thought, *No toxic substances in the body makes one . . . vibrant.*

That was dope to me. Most of the time you heard about big stars partying with all kinds of drugs and alcohol. I was surprised by his get-down. And you know what else I was surprised by? He was kind.

Eddie and I were friends from then on. He gave me a nickname— Jada May. Of course, he could make me laugh my ass off, although he wasn't one of those comedy dudes who had to be ON all the time. He was smart, thoughtful, and a deep thinker. Eddie gave advice if I asked, but mainly, he gave me the sense that focus and intention would carry the day.

Everybody thinks once you meet famous people that they should put you on. What I was learning was that if you heed the lessons successful people have to offer and stay on your game, the successful people around you will see your effort and want to give you assists.

Nobody can do it for you, and nobody is truly inspired to help you in a real way if you are not willing to help yourself. Nor should they. To be successful takes so much more than "who you know."

In nature, this harrowing process can be seen in the journey of baby turtles. Once they hatch on the beach, if you don't allow them the struggle to the water through the sand and predators, they have no chance to make it in the ocean. And yes, most of the turtles don't make it. They get eaten by the birds that are literally waiting for them to hatch, to swoop them up and devour them. But those that make it to the water, and get to reach adulthood, do so having had to earn their strength to survive and thrive.

Hollywood is the same. When Eddie felt I had made it to the ocean and was charting my own course, and he witnessed that I could continue to make a way for myself, he offered me a grand opportunity.

But until then, I kept nagging Keenen to make me a Fly Girl. Although that was never happening, he always had a new gem to offer.

"You didn't come out here to be a dancer. You came out here to be an actress. Right? Stay focused on that." He was also quick to tell me, "But don't do extra work. Too many people get stuck there." I'd heard from others that if you worked as an extra, that could get you noticed. Keenen disagreed.

At this early stage of the game, when I was working my three jobs, I didn't even have an agent. Getting an agent was very difficult. And very necessary. But again, convincing an agent to take on a newcomer was no easy task.

Keenen explained, "It's not about the status of your agent, it's about how passionate your agent is on your behalf." He made it clear that if I signed with a big agency, it would be easy for me to get lost in the shuffle because they were too busy with their bigger clients. "Find someone who is passionate about you. That's the person who will work hard for you. No matter where they are."

All I asked of Keenen was "Can I use your name?"

He nodded with a smile. "Sure."

It was almost as if Keenen's inner voice—with that smile—was *I see where she's going with this. Let's see what she does.* I made it my mission to produce something from this nugget of courtesy he had given me.

Wasting not a minute, after scouring the Yellow Pages of the phone book and finding names of talent agents, I made the first of what I expected would be many phone calls to Nancy Rainford. Much to my shock, she answered the phone.

I vivaciously introduced myself and, without taking a breath, added, "And Keenen Ivory Wayans told me you are a great agent, and he suggested I call you."

"Oh? Really? How does he know me?" Nancy responded, apparently flattered.

"I didn't ask. He just said you were a great agent and that I should call you."

Nancy was in. I could tell from her tone. She asked me a few questions, I told her a little about myself, and then she said, "Can you come meet me today?"

That very day I went to meet her, and we were a match on sight. When I'd picked Nancy Rainford's name out of the phone book, I'd had no idea she was Black, and that was a plus for me. She owned her talent agency, and she had another client who was on the rise— Michael Rapaport, who became a dope friend at the time and who gave me rides to a slew of auditions.

Nancy Rainford was heaven-sent. Keenen was right—her passion for both me and Michael, in the early days of her agency, was worth its weight in gold. Nancy went with me to almost every audition. She had faith in me and wasn't concerned in the least about my being rough around the edges. She knew that would smooth out as I matured. Nancy was fierce, smart, and fearless. I loved that about her. I would often hang out in her very small office and watch how she conducted business over the phone. She carried the same kind of confidence I had—we knew what we were made of, we knew we had something special to offer, and you were the lucky one if you jumped on it—NOW.

In an experience that was not common for actors and actresses early in their careers, I had the opportunity to listen to how she negotiated deals for me and how she'd walk away if it was not panning out to her liking. Nancy would say no, basically, then hang up the phone confidently and look at me, predicting, "Don't worry. They'll call back in twenty minutes." She understood early that although lots of work was available for Black talent, the dealmakers loved to lowball us. Nancy, in effect, taught me how to walk away from deals that didn't represent my worth. It's a lesson I've held on to throughout my career. More than that, she showed me how the game was played behind the curtain.

Soon after I signed with Nancy, I booked my first job—a TV pilot for an ABC series called *Moe's World,* in the part of the teenage sister of a deceased boy who narrates the show and acts as a guardian angel to his family and friends. After *thirteen* callbacks (I was rough around the edges and not the look they wanted, but I wore them down), I discovered that booking a pilot as my first gig on a major network was a godsend. And rare.

Getting *Moe's World* was my foot in the door in the best way. By no means was it a guarantee that I would have a lasting "career" in Hollywood, but it paved the way toward promising opportunities. My name spread quickly in the TV world, and I had great tape that demonstrated my talent. *Moe's World* was also how I became lasting friends with Duane Martin, who had a prominent role in the pilot. This was his first acting job after arriving from New York, where he had played with the Knicks. Duane became a big brother on day one, and we have championed each other ever since.

A s the University of the B-more Streets had taught me, there is such a thing as chasing the game, up to a point, but also letting the game chase you. Both strategies can be powerful. You have to know the difference between being hungry and being desperate. You never want to be the latter.

But I couldn't help being really excited when Nancy called to say that I had a meeting with a young writer/director named John Singleton for a feature film being produced by Columbia. As soon as I heard the plot, my instincts told me that this movie, *Boyz n the Hood,* was going to be very big.

Not much stands out about how the meeting started, other than the usual greetings and small talk. Then John sat down at his desk as I took a chair across from him and the casting director, who began to read the scene with me. As we read, I couldn't gauge what John was thinking. When I lifted my eyes to his after the reading was done, however, there was clearly a problem.

Looking me dead in my eyes, John told me, "That East Coast accent, you need to lose it, because if you don't, you'll never make it in this business."

Looking dead in his eyes, I told him quietly, "We'll see." After that, we talked a little more, I thanked him for the opportunity, and I bounced.

When I left the audition, I felt instinctively that he was wrong. Yet I also understood where he was coming from. Deep down, I believed what I had to offer would overpower an accent, because the one thing you can't buy or teach is *energy.*

The postscript to the story is that John and I became fans of each other. Whenever I saw him, I'd tease him about his prediction. He'd say, "You got rid of the accent, though."

We'd both laugh, and I'd say, "You got me there."

In the meantime, I chose to stay focused on all that was working for me. I very quickly started to book guest-star roles, one after the other, on shows like *True Colors; Doogie Howser, M.D.; 21 Jump*

Street; and *Cagney & Lacey,* to name a few. If I didn't get the job, I was always on the hunt. As long as I was able to hunt, in my mind, I was winning.

Every now and then, I'd hear feedback later with some form of "Oh we loved her, but . . . how tall is she?" That's what happened when I went in to audition for a guest-star role on *The Fresh Prince of Bel-Air,* then in its second season. Coming out of the casting office on that audition, I ran into—guess who?

We'd never met before.

Our exchange was hardly memorable. "What's up?" he asked with a cheerful grin.

"What's up?" I asked in response, not giving him the time of day, and kept moving.

The next time I saw him, sometime later, was in Bullock's department store, where I'd gone shopping with my mom, who had come out to visit. Out of the corner of my eye I saw a tall, lanky, nice-looking guy trekking past me. He was wearing a backpack.

Mom asked, under her breath, "Isn't that Will Smith?"

"Oh yeah," I said with a nod. Again, he had that cheerful bounce and the vibe that he didn't have a care in the world. I mean, he had a hit television show on the air. Life was good.

My mom said, "Why can't you be with somebody nice, like him?"

"The Fresh Prince?" I exclaimed. He would teach me not to judge a book by its cover.

I n the spring of 1991, just short of my being in L.A. for a year, I auditioned for the recurring role of a twelve-year-old on the TV show *Blossom.* When I went in for the audition, I showed up in a green onesie jumpsuit with a curly bunny tail on top of my head. No question, I looked like a straight-up twelve-year-old.

When Nancy announced that I'd gotten the role, I had second

thoughts. Did I want to spend the next few years playing this role of a preteen? Nancy made it clear that the show was going to be huge and that a big break like this didn't happen often. "People spend years out in L.A. before an opportunity like this comes along."

I knew she was right, but something told me there was another opportunity coming. It was pure instinct, intuition. I could feel in the rooms how casting people and producers were responding to me, and my instinct told me to hold out. Taking a major risk, I said, "I can't do it, Nancy."

There had to be a moment of frustration for my agent, who was pushing so hard for me.

Nancy quietly checked with me one more time: "Are you sure?" And I was. She took a deep breath and released the offer, but she wasn't angry. She trusted my gut, and she had faith in what we were building.

True to my instincts, only two weeks later, a new opportunity came along. It was to audition for the guest-star role of a student who had contracted HIV on *A Different World*. The show had been on for three and a half seasons and, thanks to the stewardship of Debbie Allen, was unlike anything on television at the time. Originally, the show about student life at Hillman, a historically Black college, had been conceived as a *Cosby* spin-off. It was a sitcom but a bold departure from the standard fare, with Debbie overseeing the development of multifaceted characters, relationships, and storylines that reflected the concerns, social issues, and culture of Black college students and faculty.

My intention was to go in and faithfully portray this student who had HIV and give a great reading. After I read for the role, Debbie seemed impressed, and we started talking. I immediately had to tell her that I couldn't believe I was sitting in front of Debbie Allen in person—and that she was my only inspiration for believing I could have a multifaceted career. However the words spilled out of me, I can't recall precisely, other than my letting her know she was the artist who had given me a blueprint for what was possible. As I excitedly acknowledged her, intent on showing her every bit of appreciation and awe I could muster, I expressed what was in my heart: "You are MY BIGGEST INSPIRATION."

Debbie smiled that beautiful, maternal lioness smile of hers, saying, "Tell us a little something about yourself. Where are you from?"

Not expecting that question at all, I seized the moment for the next two minutes, mentioning that I'd gone to Baltimore School for the Arts, not unlike the school on *Fame*, where I'd studied acting, dance, and voice. I finished with much enthusiasm, "I'm going to be the next Debbie Allen."

Debbie cracked up laughing. She wanted to know more about me, so I told her my family history and how I got to L.A. Debbie was intrigued and engaged. After I recounted the broad strokes of my life, Debbie paused and looked into my eyes as she spoke, thoughtfully saying, "We are going to give this role to someone else."

I nodded.

She went on, "I want you on this show as a series regular."

"Are you serious?" I responded as calmly as I could.

"Yes, baby. I want you on this show. I am going to create a role for you based on your life."

I thought I would cry. Not because I'd just been told I was going to be on one of the hottest shows on television, starring next to the one and only Jasmine Guy, but because my idol, the woman I had admired all my childhood, *saw* me. Debbie Allen felt my presence, she saw my promise, and she believed in me. What could feel more rewarding or make me feel more worthy than that? I felt seen by this incredible woman in a way I had never felt before. More than anything else, within this experience, I felt loved. There would never be another experience in an audition room that would make me feel that way again. And there has not been a day since I met Debbie Allen that she has not loved, supported, and cared for me—no matter what. I love you, Debbie.

Needless to say, I could barely speak. This was a career-making moment like no other. The role of Lena James didn't exist before I walked into that room, and Lena James would catapult my career to the stratosphere.

The kicker was—my painful past was the very thing that allowed me and my character to be relatable, emotionally meaningful to audiences, and, to many . . . *lovable*. For the next two and a half seasons.

When keeping it real costs you.
—FAT JOE ON *RED TABLE TALK*, 2022

Whenever we look at the places where we once were and recall how we made the leap to the places where we traveled next, we're given a chance to observe all the times in our lives when certain codes (*keeping it real,* for example) cost us—or could have cost us. Looking back on the jump I made from the B-more streets to the fast lane of Hollywood, I was able to reflect with gratitude on the ways I was willing to change in order to take my life on a different trajectory.

———

The hard part is unlearning old codes and following through with the new ones. The unwillingness to change our codes is the very thing that can keep us stuck, keeping us from the insights and tools needed to enter a new territory of life.

———

As challenging as it can be to change our codes, it can be just as challenging for those who have been by our side to understand why the change must happen. The big blow for a lot of us comes from realizing that not everyone gets to go on the next part of our journey. And that can hurt, badly. In straddling two worlds, we may question our loyalties and see ourselves as frauds for not being able to uphold the very code that helped us survive.

———

Most of us genuinely want to take everyone with us. Some are ready for the new codes; many aren't. But we can honor the past and never forget where we began—without sacrificing the glory that is ours to claim. A glory we all deserve.

———

Can you identify a few codes in your life that have been hard to let go of? Can you see how holding on to old codes may be keeping you stuck? Try on a new code for size, one that allows you to continue to be real—without the cost.

CHAPTER 8

Living the Dream

Are we goin' to the club* or what?" was how I nudged my homegirl MC Lyte one Saturday night.

The two of us had met when I was a presenter at an awards ceremony for ACT-SO, a New York–based foundation that provides awards to students in the arts and sciences. When I saw that Lyte was part of the program, I felt like a dream had come true. Talk about one of the most unique and distinct voices in the game! She was my female rap idol, and she better be glad I can't rap a lick because I would have tried to steal her whole steeze.

When I'd arrived at the venue, I'd immediately gone to find her backstage, where she was sitting in the makeup chair. I was so excited that she may have felt the need for extra security.

I unabashedly introduced myself and told her how much her music meant to me and how much respect I had for her and what she did for women in rap. Lyte was the first female rapper to release a full-length rap album (1988's *Lyte as a Rock*) and by the early 1990s was on her way to becoming an icon. Plus, she was down-to-earth and gracious—everything I had imagined her to be.

From that moment, we began a friendship that grew into a beautiful sisterhood. She became one of my few close girlfriends who would witness me at my best and at my worst and love me all the same.

In those days, I could seriously drink a lot of folks under the table and still be on my feet. It was the Pinkett in me. Lyte was often at my side on those occasions when I was straight wild'n. Although she partied hard in her own right, she always maintained the wherewithal to make sure I didn't get into too much trouble.

On this Saturday night, before we even went out, I'd already downed damn near a full bottle of red wine (her beverage of choice), smoked enough weed to almost pass out, and then taken a tab of X.

Lyte looked at me in my Lena James–esque attire—basically eclectic streetwear—and responded to my slurred question by saying, "Yeah, let's go."

Before we left, I took a shot of Courvoisier to top it off. Brown liquor, in particular, usually became the gateway to my more aggressive, dark side, although that night I think it was the mixture of several mind-altering substances that got me going.

The whole L.A. club culture at this time was wack. As in BORING. Other than the gay clubs, most of the well-known clubs didn't have good music, and most of the people were on the dance floor to be seen and not really dance. But now and then, a hot DJ might come through and take over an underground club or restaurant/bar, and the word would get out. Sometimes a lively crowd would actually show up.

Once we got to the club, I headed straight for the dance floor to cut loose, doing my thing and bumping into whoever was in my way.

"Hey, watch it!" more than a few people barked at me.

"Fuck you!" was all I had to say.

"What did you say?"

"I said, 'FUCK YOU!' I'm dancing! You don't like it? MOVE!"

That brown liquor had me mean and obnoxious. And I liked it.

Lyte knew when to pull my coattails, though. She was right at my side, leaning into my ear. "Okay, little lady, it's time to go."

"I'm not ready to go!"

"I bet." She chuckled and politely grabbed me by the arm like we were about to square-dance, and we do-si-do'd out that spot. I was just warming up, but oh well. Lyte poured me into the car with another friend of ours and took me home.

All the way to my place, I continued talking shit, laughing, joking, and just being the usual raucous mess I am when I get fucked up.

Lyte got me into my house and up the stairs, where she made sure I was okay. She never felt the need to give me a lecture. Instead, she was best at holding space, and I could tell what she was thinking through her silence—how she listened, offering looks that conveyed subtle approval or subtle disapproval. That quiet way of keeping me grounded has always been far more potent an influence than a talking-to.

There were times when her looks would speak volumes: *Hey, we can have a good time, but why do you have to be so reckless?* At this point, not only did I not have the answer, but I couldn't see how my excessive, destructive behavior was a red flag.

There was a void inside me that I just couldn't fill but also refused to acknowledge. Why would I? I was supposed to be happy, and people who achieve what I had in a very short amount of time are supposed to be happy people.

I was reminded of that on a daily basis in the city that offers you, with hard work, a happily ever after.

----

*A*fter I joined the cast of *A Different World*, a lot of positive changes happened quickly.

For instance, once I knew there was going to be a steady paycheck, and a good one at that, I was able to leave the place on Comey Avenue—which *had* to happen, since my goddaughter and her mother, who lived with me at the time, were almost carjacked in my neighborhood. I moved to a townhome in the hills of Studio City, walking distance to Universal Studios and less than ten minutes from Radford Studios, where the show was filmed.

At age nineteen, though I was making good money—legally, too—nothing was ever guaranteed, and rather than spend it all on lavish decor, cars, and jewelry, I kept my life and my new place simple and modest. Old habits, like being on the low, don't die easy. The rent was reasonable for this sizable three-bedroom two-story townhome with a garage and a two-car carport, not to mention a large back patio and spacious backyard. There was a beautiful stained-glass window at the top of the front door and an earthy, rustic feel, with lots of wood throughout. My favorite feature was not one but two wood-burning fireplaces—one in the living room and one in my bedroom—which had been a childhood dream. I didn't know *nobody* with a fireplace in their bedroom, and that meant I had made it.

Whenever friends came to town to visit—Pac, Keesha, and, later, Mia and Fawn—and I ushered them in and invited them to sit on my blue velvet sofa in the living room with its cream-colored carpet, I felt like I was the queen of my queendom. It felt fulfilling to share my success with the people I loved.

Every friend who came to visit was happy for me and made sure to claim their guest bedroom. The only issue for my friends was that the place was haunted—"Somebody sat on my bed last night while I was sleeping! But no one was there!" or "I heard knocking on the bathroom door when I was in there, but when I said 'Who is it?' nobody responded" or "I can't sleep in here. Something funky's going on. I gotta go to a hotel." My invisible housemates didn't bother me, but they did their best to make overnight guests feel quite uncomfortable.

The whole vibe of my new stomping grounds was energizing. Living right off Ventura Boulevard, wherever I went, I'd run into up-and-comers from all levels of the industry.

It felt so good to experience a level of prosperity among fellow dreamers, knowing we were able to pay our bills from sharing our talents. In a world where young Black artists were at one time invisible, it felt as if we were on our way to the Promised Land. And I experienced it alongside the cast and crew of a predominantly Black production on *A Different World*.

At work, there was a family atmosphere. I could not have asked for a more supportive group of people to have at my side as I came into my own. There were Kadeem Hardison (Dwayne Wayne) and Jasmine Guy (Whitley), always in my corner, both like older siblings looking out for the young wild one. I actually first met Kadeem through Duane Martin—they were tight—so Kadeem and I became fast friends. Jas was just a down-ass chick—a girl's girl who was pretty, funny, super smart, and didn't take no shit. My kind of lady. Darryl Bell, Karen Malina White, Ajai Sanders, Dawnn Lewis, Glynn Turman, Charnele Brown, Bumper Robinson, Patrick Malone, and Lou Myers were phenomenal castmates. I was blessed to be thrown into the mix of such a superior bunch for my first television show.

Cree Summer (Freddie) was a big influence in my understanding of feminism relevant to Black women in a movement portrayed largely through a white female lens. Highly intelligent, with a razor-sharp wit, Cree put me onto books and social justice movements around L.A. She also introduced me to a vegetarian lifestyle, something I embraced enough to give up my fast-food habits.

Both Cree and author/activist bell hooks—who also became a friend and mentor in my early years—expanded my understanding of racial and gender politics in America and especially in Hollywood. Funny, sweet, and sharp, bell was a provocative thinker and writer and constantly reminded me that success was to be used to help the greater good. Building on the foundation set by my grandmother and by Pac, Cree and bell further ignited my desire to take activism seriously. That's when the dream seemed most meaningful, knowing my success opened doors to opportunity for me to uplift others, especially Black women and the Black community at large.

Another fellow activist on the show was Darryl M. Bell, who played the character Ron. Super-intelligent with a memory like an elephant, Darryl never let me forget how I convinced him to travel with me to Baltimore to speak to Black youth about the value of education and the opportunities that come from it. He was so gracious and giving of his time, helping connect his own entrepreneurial journey to the message we were sharing. Darryl and I went on to be nominated for an NAACP Image Award for our focus on youth empowerment.

When I spoke to kids who reminded me of myself at their age, I understood the blinders that come along with not being able to see life beyond your immediate experience. Education allows you to see that there are dreams you don't even know about. I became passionate about helping to create educational opportunities for those behind bars, making visits to juvenile detention centers and women's prisons in several different states. My early efforts included building libraries in underprivileged schools in Baltimore and Los Angeles. I had by no means been an academic star growing up, but books had given me a lasting lifeline.

M*y path crossed with those of* other passionate dreamseekers who were deeply inspirational to me, one of whom had risked his life to come to this country from his native Mexico so he could have a shot at the American Dream. I met him shortly after his arrival, when I needed assistance with some Rottweilers I was fostering. I'd inherited two adult Rotts and their puppies, helping out a friend in a tight squeeze. That friend sent me to this uniquely gifted dog whisperer for guidance in how to care for the dogs.

Cesar—only a couple of years older than I was—had a center in East L.A. where he would use his gifts to train and rehabilitate canines. He hardly spoke English, and his commands for the Rotts were in German. I had to navigate his broken English and learn German commands in order to work with my dogs. Later, when I found myself with four male Rottweilers, Cesar was able to make me a full-fledged leader of my first pack. Whenever my dogs and I would go see him at his facility, folks would tell me to stay away from the predominantly Hispanic area because of the violent conflicts between Blacks and Mexicans. Coming from the East, I didn't have that experience, and the L.A. street politics weren't going to dissuade me.

Cesar taught me that strong breeds like Rotts need purpose, respect, and love—as much as humans do—and don't respond to words without the energy to match. "You can't fool dogs" was his way of putting it. He taught me how to earn the respect of my pack.

Cesar Millan, long before he was a household name, often talked to me about his dreams of sharing his knowledge with the masses—opening a bigger facility where people from all over the world could bring their dogs to be trained, and eventually becoming an author and television star. His passion and confidence made us kindred spirits. There was no ceiling to his dreams. He had the drive, talent, and the IT factor to win, but there was one problem: "You're going to have to learn English if you want to reach the masses, Cesar."

He nodded in full agreement.

"How 'bout I pay for a tutor for a whole year?"

As luck would have it, my former assistant was once an English teacher in Kuwait. The two got to work right away, and Cesar proved to be as determined a student as he was a teacher.

Cesar and I were on the same trajectory. Iron sharpens iron. I admired Cesar's hustle, and in moments of self-doubt, his drive sparked mine and helped me keep dreaming and keep going—even when I didn't feel like it.

T*he mentality for me was:* If you work hard, then you get to play as hard as you want. *Play hard* was my real-deal mantra. And it wasn't just drinking and getting fucked up, it was also men. *Chile,* the dudes were abundant everywhere. I was young, uninhibited, and BOLD, and because of my success, having a lot of eyes on me, I felt entitled to reap the benefits.

I had tried my hand at committed relationships, but at this point, I had decided to forfeit getting tied down. After all, the world was my oyster. Why would I give up this state of freedom, exploration, and

FUNNNNN in the golden hour of my youth? There were all flavors and varieties. I did NOT discriminate when it came to men.

Besides, I didn't believe that one dude could have all the qualities I really was looking for. So, I resorted to my Frankenstein approach, compiling a composite picture of my ideal man. One dude would be the Intellect and talk big ideas. Another was the Artist who was in touch with his feelings. There was the Funny Guy who made me laugh. Then there was the Roughneck Bad Boy—always gotta keep one of them. There was also, always, the In the Bed Guy who, hands down, every time would be satisfaction guaranteed. The unfortunate irony is that while most of my relationships with the other guys were platonic, I preferred spending time with them—as opposed to the In the Bed Guy, who was strictly for late-night calls.

Was it unusual for me to come from a dinner date with one dude and, sitting in my lonely silence, pick up the phone and make a call? No.

"Hey, what you doin'?"

"Sleeping, it's two a.m."

"You want some company?"

"You can't keep calling me, wanting to come over here late at night. You need to call me so we can go to the movies or something."

Are you kidding me? "Fine," I'd say. "We'll go to the movies. Can I come over now? You good?"

When it became clear that I wasn't into commitment, something interesting happened—the guys who were normally cool with a no-strings-attached situation all of a sudden felt the need to tie me down. My immaturity led me to assume that most dudes would be relieved with the no-strings-attached get-down. We could simply "enjoy" each other and keep it moving. Very rarely was that the case. This was a small revelation about the notion that men don't feel and the BS that they have no need for connection. I found that the "players" were the most in need of connection and were simply terrified of surrendering to emotional intimacy. Just like me.

Sex, for me, was a distraction from having to look at my genuine need to be held, have connection, and feel loved. It fed the appetite of the little girl who hadn't had enough parental affection and attention. That dance became addictive. The feeling of entitlement that I should feel good all the time was a setup, because it could never be satisfied. Gimme, gimme, more, more, makes you greedy, and it confuses what it is you really want.

We usually talk about external addictions, drugs and alcohol, but rarely about internal addictions of the heart. These get mistaken for love, admiration, and connection. Often it's just lust, and that can further the lie that you are having your happily ever after.

Now, there have always been rumors that I'm gay—that I like women. Maybe that had something to do with clubs where I hung out, like the Catch, one of the leading LGBTQ + spots in L.A. at this time that had nights for getting up and doing lip-synchs, and where I myself, on several occasions, got up onstage and lip-synched to all kinds of songs. I killed Madonna's "Vogue" there one night.

The truth is that during those early years of exploration in Hollywood, I had a few sexual experiences with women, only to realize that when it comes to sex, I love men. Still, I cherish the beauty of women inside and out. And I have never stopped being infatuated and in awe of women of all ages, sizes, and colors. My belief is—women are the most amazing creatures on the planet, and I hold reverence for women through my friendships.

What this season of my life taught me is that every woman should have the right and the freedom to explore and embrace her sexuality unapologetically by her own definition. Sadly, many haven't. In years to come, I'd find it disheartening how many adult women I knew had never had orgasms.

This phase of "let's just have fun" with men was ultimately short-lived. I liked the excitement, but I only got a temporary high. Eventually, the addictive chase got to me. Now, I never considered myself an addict of any kind—but that's just a classic case of denial.

T*here was one person on my* neck at times about my lifestyle, and his name was Tupac Amaru Shakur.

And imagine—he was concerned about my lifestyle? Whenever Pac got in some mess (which was often), I would get a call from his mother, his brother Mopreme, or even him. Likewise, Pac would go out of his way to check on me, especially if he heard I was dealing with some fool (which was often).

"You know that n-gga ain't shit."

"Pac, you don't even know him. Have you ever spent time with him?"

"I don't have to know him. Every n-gga I know ain't shit. What? You actually think these n-ggas wanna love you? Hell no! These n-ggas just wanna fuck you!"

"Pac—get off my phone with this shit."

"Aight. I'm tell'n you. You better leave these busta-ass n-ggas alone." As he finished his lecture, he'd laugh that beautiful goofy-ass laugh of his.

Ironically, Pac was ALWAYS falling in love with somebody. And I never complained. As long as he was happy, I was happy.

But when we'd be sitting up in my living room, and he'd use the occasion to get up on his soapbox and give me a sermon about his "good girls and bad girls"/"bitches and hos" philosophy, things got heated.

"What are you trying to say, Pac? That there are women who deserve respect and those who don't? Do women hurt any less than men? We gotta understand and be cool when y'all act a fool, but we don't deserve the same? You need to chill with calling women 'bitches.'"

Pac countered with his usual "I'm not talking about you or none of your friends when I'm talk'n about bitches . . . Or am I? Is there something I don't know? I got mad respect for women who have mad respect for themselves. But if you a ho—I'mma treat you like one."

That got me to my feet. "Generalizing and disrespecting women in that way is dangerous." I was just warming up. "That's why I can't understand how Black men can't see that they are oppressing and demonizing Black women in the same way they've been oppressed and demonized by racist white people. Y'all act like we are not part of the same struggle you are. It's stupid!"

"Then be mad at the white man for my condition. Be mad at that because they stole my . . ." And so on. And so on.

We'd been having these arguments over the years about the ways Black men justified mistreating Black women. Although the virgin/ho trope was common throughout the male kingdom, it was blaring through rap music with a poisonous pervasiveness in our community and eventually the world.

In time, after many arguments, I would have the epiphany that Pac and I were actually arguing about the right to feel loved. We thought we were arguing about the semantics of how men and women disrespect each other. But underneath that was his point that Black men deserve love, and not just because they're famous and got money. My point was that Black women deserve love even if they don't live up to the idealized vision imposed on them. This was made more intense because we were both confronting these themes in a lifestyle that told us we should be loved all the time and yet weren't.

Fame might get you company, but it ain't always good company. And it's certainly not real love or real respect.

So, misogyny and objectifying women in rap were complicating what we all truly desired—to be respected and loved and to feel worthy.

That was a point I tried to make publicly when BET invited me to be part of a group on-air to talk about current events and our representation in media. On that panel was Eazy-E of N.W.A, aka Eric Wright, whom I had never met.

As soon as I saw that Eazy was going to be part of the conversation, I made up my mind that I would find a way to address misogyny in rap with him directly—given the popularity of N.W.A and their music, starting in the late 1980s with *Straight Outta Compton*. Mind you, I love me some N.W.A, BUT . . . how they referred to women in their music, I found offensive.

Once I had the opportunity to address Eazy, after the moderator asked me what I felt about his lyrics, I spoke my piece. "I met him today. I would have thought that he was a woman hater because of his music that he writes." I added that because Eric owned his own record company, he had the ability to "make a change starting from within his community to uplift us." My point was "When I listen to his music, I want to feel good about myself. I want to feel good about my people." Nobody jumped in, so I went on. "Eric, you have the power to do that, you know?"

He coolly shifted in his seat as the moderator pressed him to describe how he was going to respond. "I do say nice things—" he began.

"To *me*," I interrupted. How does that change the impact of calling women bitches and objectifying us? Other Black women felt as I did. "Me being a young sister, and wanting to feel good about myself, now, come on." I had put him on notice.

After the show was over, Eric approached me to say he did a lot for his community, adding that he was putting on a carnival for kids in need. He asked, "Would you make an appearance?"

I took a beat. Frankly, I didn't believe him. However, I decided to give him the benefit of the doubt and said, "Sure."

I have to admit, I was impressed. We kept a dialogue going about making change in the community, and about assisting the youth, and a dope friendship was born. Eazy's real passion and focus was educating young people about business and entrepreneurship. He taught me a lot about the importance of ownership of one's artistic property. That was the change he was mostly interested in—artists owning their art, no matter what it was.

In fact, when I gave him a folder of some of my poetry (which included the artwork of my ex-boyfriend John to accompany it), Eazy had an entrepreneurial idea. He was very complimentary and told me, "Publish your poetry and record it as spoken word to music. Sell the CD with the book. Own it. All of it."

This was the early 1990s, when almost no one was doing things like this. He was ahead of his time. He was a unique character. Sometimes when he stopped by and I wasn't home, he would leave a note written backward that you could read only in the mirror. When he paged me, he'd place the numbers together in a unique way that created words. His dry sense of humor was like no one else's, and he could also be very, very silly.

It didn't surprise me that he enjoyed kicking it with Keesha, who knew how to make him laugh. She teased him mercilessly about his Jheri curl and how he needed to cut his hair. Once she went further, gathering his hair up off his face and into a rubber band, insisting, "See! Don't you like that better instead of hav'n all those wannabe curls in your face?" Then Keesh laughed her bottom-belly infectious laugh while Eric stared in the mirror, shaking his head.

In my heart, I believe that Eric knew he was sick during our friendship. I do not know this to be fact, I just feel it. Whenever we saw each other, it seemed he had a cold that would never leave. I'd comment, saying, "You still got that runny nose?" Or "You need to go to the doctors and check that out, E."

He'd flat-out ignore me or quickly change the subject. Maybe I should have pressed the issue. Instead, I shook off my concern, figuring it was probably just symptoms of stress, considering all that was going on in his life post-N.W.A. He was pretty brokenhearted about how business was going down with Suge Knight, the former bodyguard turned promoter, artist manager, and cofounder of Death Row Records, who, as time would tell, would become a symbol of violent chaos to be avoided.

Eazy always seemed like he had a gray cloud over his head, as if he was heavy with sadness. In my naivete, I found it hard to witness how huge success could come with weighty, complicated problems and didn't necessarily equate to a happily ever after.

T*here's a saying, "We ain't in Kansas no mo."* Or something like that.

I knew this to be true whenever I went home to Baltimore (aka Kansas) to visit. I felt like a stranger in a place that was once so familiar. No longer. Understandably, it was very difficult for people to fathom the reality I was living. They assumed, as I once had, that with fame and fortune, all ills are cured. Shocker—I had changed, but my ills had not.

It would take me a lot of years to unravel the difference between having confidence in some areas of my life (performing, making money, and thriving in survival mode) and having a healthy sense of self-worth. Confidence can help build self-worth, but it can't substitute for self-love.

When you don't know this, you are in a constant storm of having to prove yourself. You tell yourself, *If I just get a little bit more success and learn how to do it right, I can* . . . all those things that, if we get more, if we fix our flaws, look cuter, lose weight, get a nose job, buy a new car, have a new relationship or a few of them, we will be good.

If I dared admit that I was still searching and struggling to find authentic happiness in the Hollywood glitz and glamour, it came off as ungrateful and spoiled. I couldn't tell if something was wrong or if I was actually ungrateful. It was confusing.

At home, I looked forward to not having to be *on* and to just being Jada. That didn't always happen, though part of going home was to recalibrate and get grounded, chill and be with loved ones. Many loved ones, rightfully, wanted to be Hollywood-adjacent when I was in town.

On one return to Baltimore, I went to see my grandmother Shirley and was surprised that she had planned an autograph gathering without telling me ahead of time. When I arrived, the first thing I saw was people on the porch outside and then, inside, people in the living room and the kitchen waiting to meet me. Really, what I had been looking forward to was sitting down in her kitchen and playing a game of Boggle like I did as a kid.

This was no fault of Shirley's. She was proud and excited to give everyone a chance to see me. Though I begrudgingly went along, took the pictures and signed the autographs, I wasn't happy about it.

Once everyone started to leave, Shirley asked, "What's wrong with you?"

"I wasn't expecting all these people here," I answered, hoping that would be the end of it. How do you come home to your grandmother's house and explain you don't want to be celebrated by her and her friends when that's all she wants to do? Even to me, that sounded ridiculous. But it was how I felt.

My explanation didn't go over well.

At Georgetown, where I went shopping with Chet one day, every time someone approached me and said, "You look like that girl on *A Different World*! It's you, right?" I would politely say, "No, but people tell me I look like her all the time."

Chet would ask, "How come you don't want nobody to know who you are?"

"Because today you just kick'n it with your homegirl Jada, that's why."

Chet respected that and played along.

No matter how much I tried to explain to others that success wasn't fixing my life the way I thought it would, that didn't seem possible or real to them. And I got that, because it didn't seem possible or real to me, either.

After all, I was living the dream. Right? I'd just have to do better.

I*n the fall of 1991,* I turned twenty. Birthday celebrations had always been important, and Pac was there to celebrate the occasion with me.

Pac's career was on fire. After years of roll'n with Digital Underground, he'd established himself as a rapper in his own right, and after two years in the studio, he was getting ready to release his first solo album, *2Pacalypse Now.* I was so proud of him and happy that the world would finally get to share in the gift of his brilliance.

Pac had also just starred in *Juice,* his film acting debut. There was a lot of Hollywood attention for his performance and for the movie, the directing debut for Ernest R. Dickerson. Pac was flying high, but even with his success, he was feeling the same void I was. Luckily, we could confide in each other.

We had a lot of the same worries and stresses, but his were on a larger scale, and his life was more complicated than mine. Pac had a lot of responsibility and took care of a lot of people while trying to figure out how to take care of himself. He also had to deal with the pressures of the street politics of the hip-hop game and simply being a young Black man in America who had notoriety. This placed a different kind of target on his back that he hadn't seen coming.

None of this was playing out the way we thought it was supposed to. The saving grace was that we had each other as tethers.

In the past, when I was in some money and Pac wasn't, I'd be the one looking out. And when he was in some cash and I wasn't, he looked out—like when I was in college. Now we were on parallel tracks. It was surreal, almost unimaginable, that we would be on this type of come-up at the same time.

As flawed as the dream was at times, sharing the rise was the most beautiful, unexpected part. We had each other while we were stumbling, too—attempting to learn how to manage the new influx of money and status that is always accompanied by higher expenses, more pressure to take on the financial responsibilities of our immediate and extended families and friends, and every other demand of being the "it" commodity. Nobody prepares you, especially when you are nineteen/twenty years old, and you don't know who to trust.

There were times when I felt Pac distanced me from seeing him in his new orbit. Very rarely did I spend time in his environment. This was new. If I suggested that I wanted to come see him perform, he adamantly refused. He'd show up wherever I was, no problem. But he tried to keep me from his world and all that came with it. Unexpected shit was always popping off with him that he could not always control. Looking back, I can see he wanted to keep me safe.

And because of this, I never saw Pac perform live. Of course, this was meant as a temporary arrangement. But we were always looking for opportunities to collaborate creatively. That was a must for us both.

Pac was the first to move us toward that dream by summoning me to be part of a video for his single "Brenda's Got a Baby," based on the true story of a twelve-year-old girl who gets pregnant and has to turn to the streets to survive and support her child.

Then it was my turn, when I called him about playing a role on an episode of *A Different World* that Kadeem Hardison was directing. My character, Lena, had a homeboy from Baltimore coming to visit her at Hillman, and I knew ONLY Pac could pull it off.

Pac said yes.

The in-studio live audience for *A Different World* was always boisterous, laughing and hollering, which added so much to the energy of the show, but when Pac made his entrance—his charisma off the charts—everyone out in the seats ROARED. It was one of the first times I saw for myself all the love out there for him as an artist.

He put in the work, as usual, stealing the show, and then, in the blink of an eye, he was off and running again, on to the next adventure. If my career had ended there, it would have been complete. How great that we traveled to this point together, given where we came from.

But there was more. Leave it to Pac to top it with a phone call about this movie he wanted us to do together.

He couldn't say enough about the project. He was really excited about the opportunity and went on to say that the young directors, twins, the Hughes brothers, were very talented. He was convinced they were going to make a strong film, and the sentiment was that it would be rawer than *Boyz n the Hood.*

A scenario like this rarely happens in Hollywood. In those days, for an actress to make the leap from a TV sitcom to a gritty feature film was a high hurdle. (These days there's much less of an issue with actors doing both TV and movies.) Besides, I was under contract with NBC and, as of then, not really available. Plus, I had to audition for the movie, as I reminded Pac.

"Naw," he insisted, "I already told the directors that you're my homegirl. All they gotta do is meet you. I told them you're perfect for the role."

Who knew that my first Hollywood film ever would be starring next to Pac, in a job he put me on?

Pac made the arrangements for me to meet filmmakers Allen and Albert Hughes. When we met, we all took a liking to one another. They liked my read for the role of Ronnie, a single mom. And in a snap, it seemed like the deal was done.

Not quite.

Once the offer came in, I went to see Debbie Allen to tell her about the movie, and she was so happy for me that she channeled her magic into convincing the network and the producers to allow me to do the movie while shooting the last season of *A Different World.* Debbie wasn't going to let me miss an opportunity like this. Not on her watch. "Don't you worry, bunny rabbit. We are going to work this out. My baby is going to do her movie." As promised, Debbie got it done.

Having gotten over the biggest hurdle, I was set and ready.

THEN, as I was upstairs in my bedroom one evening shortly af-

ter the deal was done, Pac called me. He had gotten into an alterca-
tion with the Hughes brothers.

I sat on the edge of my bed in disbelief. "What the hell, Pac, what
happened?"

Quietly, I listened as he proceeded to explain his side of the
story—how he had gotten into a fight with the directors and gotten
fired from the film. To this day I still don't understand what it was
about.

"Well, if you're not doing it, I can't do it." Period. The end.

No, it wasn't the end. Pac wouldn't hear it. He made it VERY
clear that he wanted me to do it regardless of his beef with the Hughes
brothers.

"That's not going to work, Pac."

"This movie is good for you, Jada. You need it. And I'm tell'n you
to do it."

Oh, now he's commanding me.

In fight mode, I shot back, "What? I was only doing this movie
because of you! How you just—"

Pac cut me off. "Do the movie, Square! I'll check you later." And
he hung up the phone in my ear.

Immobile, I continued to sit there on the edge of my bed, staring
at the telephone as if it were to blame. The dream of the two of us
together in my first movie was shattered. He was the only reason I
wanted to do *Menace II Society*.

I didn't even bother to call him back. He was lucky because I
couldn't call Debbie Allen and say, "I'm sorry, after all you did to
fight for me, I don't want to do this movie now."

All I could think as I lay back and looked up at the canopy was
What the fuck?!

When it was all said and done, I gotta give Pac props. He had what could best be called *sight*, which I did not yet possess. *Menace II Society* helped to launch my movie career in a serious, rapid-fire way and even led to the Cannes Film Festival, one of the most prestigious film festivals in the world. That doesn't happen often for Black actresses from Baltimore. Just saying. That was Pac's vision—not mine.

The voyage to the French Riviera in the South of France was a rite of passage. Nobody had prepped me, really, for walking the red carpet before the screening of our film. Nobody ever talked about having a stylist to help pick an outfit and dress for the international press. I knew nothing. What I thought was an artsy, daring ensemble turned out to be me dressed like Bozo the Clown, in pants and a long orange top with yellow and orange circles like polka dots. Not my best look.

For the most part, working on the first big project with the Hughes brothers was a liberating experience. They gave me a lot of leeway to play a scene how my gut told me I should, drawing from my own experience. The movie was a huge success, critically and commercially. Being a part of it was a blessing in every respect.

Pac never told me "I told you so." But he probably felt good about himself for helping to start what became a domino effect. He loved being by my side at premieres and such, not because he needed more of a spotlight for himself but because he got a kick out of seeing me shine. He would often tell me, "I am so proud of you. I always knew you would do it. You've always been a star. Just don't let your head get too big, Square."

I'd grab any chance to acknowledge his role in the start of my movie career, although he didn't feel he needed to be thanked. He would say more times than I could count, "You looked out for me when you didn't have to. I'm always going to love you for that with all my heart. Always."

He was a constant in my life. Whenever I called, he was coming. No matter what.

We don't even recognize how many false gods we worship.

—ANONYMOUS

Throughout my years of studying many different forms of religious practices and beliefs, I have regularly come across the idea that one should not worship false gods. For a long time, I assumed that "false idol" or "false god" referred to any god or entity outside of the tradition I was studying. Slowly, I learned that the worship of a false god is much deeper than that.

―――――――

Many of us who devote ourselves to achieving our version of happily ever after come to the stark realization that no matter how hard we strive to attain our dreams, there is a bottomless pit inside us—a void. We're forced to confront the false belief that not only will success lead to our versions of fame and fortune but that it will cure our ills and the ills of the people we love. For me, it was easy to buy into a gold-rush mindset that once I hit the jackpot, it would heal my heart, my life—my soul.

―――――――

Now, there is nothing wrong with having dreams and goals. It's another thing to make them the be-all and end-all of your existence—your false god.

―――――――

We've all heard versions of *Achieve by pulling yourself up by your own bootstraps, and the glory of life shall be yours.* The part that goes unsaid is *If you define your glory solely by winning or losing in your pursuit of goals, the part of you that craves authentic connection will be abandoned, leaving you with fleeting satisfaction and false safety.* We may find ourselves chasing and clinging to false gods or tricksters who lead us away from the truth of ourselves, the truth of love, and take us off the path to authentic fulfillment.

―――――――

Can you identify any false gods in your life? Are you willing to let go of the belief that external attainments can sustain happiness, and instead look inside to find fulfillment within your soul?

CHAPTER 9

Breakdown

W hen Duane Martin—*on set with me* for *The Inkwell,* a movie we were shooting in Wilmington, North Carolina—first mentioned that his good friend Will Smith wanted to fly in to talk to me about a role, I said, "Cool."

I had time. I was in Wilmington, for crying out loud.

"He's flying in tomorrow."

We didn't have many options for where to go. We were staying on the outskirts of Wilmington in the glamorous suites of the Holiday Inn. Next door there was Hooters, yes, home to waitresses in tight T-shirts serving pitchers of beer and carrying trays of hot wings. Our only other option was a janky, dimly lit Chinese restaurant with a Southern twang, which seemed so unnatural for some reason.

Will arrived in North Carolina from Atlanta, Georgia, where he was working on a project, and he, Duane, and I met at the Chinese restaurant. Will began by saying that he'd flown down to ask me personally if I would play his girlfriend, a series regular, on *The Fresh Prince of Bel-Air.* The sitcom had been a huge success for several seasons, so the answer was seemingly a no-brainer. The show was proven. But at this time, I wasn't interested in going back to television.

Since *Menace,* a lot of movie opportunities had become available to me. As nicely as I could, I explained to Will, "Thanks for flying all the way here, but I don't want to do TV right now. Thank you for the opportunity." And that was that.

Will was gracious and understood and left as swiftly as he had arrived.

Duane started giving me a hard time at the restaurant and then accompanied me to my suite at the Holiday Inn—not glamorous but roomy—to convince me to reconsider. His concern was that Hollywood wasn't regularly turning out lead roles for Black actresses. He also stressed the importance of a guaranteed income on a crossover megahit comedy series like *Fresh Prince*. It didn't have to interrupt my film career, he pointed out. "You can do both TV and movies, you know," he said.

I agreed. Only—"That's not what I want to do." Despite the odds, I wanted to take my shot at being a film star, even though I had nothing slated next. That was a risk. By the same token, what if I went back to doing TV and lost my hard-won foothold as a film actress?

Duane wasn't having it. He felt I was banking on longevity that was unrealistic. "How many scripts are being written for Black actresses, Jada? Don't be stupid. I can't let you turn down this kind of financial security. Get cashed up and make movies on hiatus."

Although he had a point, I stayed firm. "I don't want to."

Duane was pissed and did his best to convince me I was making the biggest mistake of my life. It was a heated exchange, but I wouldn't give in, to the point that when he left my room, I slammed the door on him.

Shortly after, he came back, knocked, and asked in a conciliatory tone, "You want to go get a drink?"

After opening the door a crack but keeping the latch on, I called back, "No, go to Hooters by yourself." Then I slammed the door again. Discussion over. And Duane left it alone.

My decision was sound, I believed then and now. Movies gave me the opportunity to do a variety of roles, go from project to project, and not be stuck in one role on TV, under contract, when you didn't always have a Debbie Allen to fight for you to do movies.

As those other opportunities came, including films like *Set It Off* and *A Low Down Dirty Shame,* and I was climbing the ladder to leading lady, I had to learn to adapt to other challenges. As a case in point, when I was up for *Jason's Lyric,* my audition process lasted until the final hours before principal photography began in Houston. Up for the title role of Lyric, a dreamer who wants to get out of the life she and the other characters are stuck in, I flew in for my final in-person audition, where Doug McHenry, director, and George Jackson, producer, would deliberate—not sure I could pull off the role because, once again, I was "rough around the edges." Doug's vision was that, like the character's name, the actress who played her would have a softer essence and quality in juxtaposition to the harsh realities of her environment. This quality was supposed to be her enchanting appeal. I was clear: I wasn't quite that.

The audition was a chemistry read with the wonderful Allen Payne, the film's lead. Allen—respectful, a gentleman, and a very giving artist—made me feel welcome right away. We had a dope rapport, no question, and the readings went very well.

At the end of the session, the director and producer began to confer, sending out for people from hair and makeup, as I stood there, unsure what was going on.

There was something not quite right about the hair on my head, I heard them say as they discussed how to remedy that. There was also talk that I was literally *hairy.* My eyebrows were bushy, and my upper lip had a bit of fuzz on it.

As I crossed my arms and stood under the microscope of "what's wrong with Jada" and her lack of "pretty softness," my soon-to-be very close friend Maxine Rennes, head of the hair department, was summoned into the room. She was tall and lovely—she reminded me of a gazelle of sorts, but less fragile—and with a sweet, cheerful voice. She looked at me and asked, thoughtfully yet confidently, "Is it okay if I touch your hair?" I nodded, and she threw her hands into the cacophony of the bushy mess. She could see that my hair had been damaged after a few films where the hairstylists didn't really know how to care for it.

What I loved about Maxine from the gate was that she had an out-there sense of style. Her hair was like a medium Afro of short blonde dreads. She was fly in her baby tee that showed a little tummy, a plaid pleated miniskirt, and high-heeled ankle boots with really long legs standing in them. So, when Maxine asked if she could cut my hair, it was how she asked, with such confidence coupled with her fly style, that made me say yes. She smiled that adorable cartoon-character grin of hers and said, "I have something so cute in mind for you." Judy Murdock, who was the head of the makeup department and Maxine's close friend, was ordered to wax my brows and upper lip.

After a complete makeover, I was presented to Doug and George. With that, and with poor Allen Payne advocating like hell for how perfect he thought I was for the role, Doug and George finally gave me the thumbs-up. Thanks to Maxine and Judy, this movie was a turning point for me, helping me to soften those edges.

Jason's Lyric was the first movie I'd done that had an explicit love scene in it—which I did NOT want to do. The producers had agreed up front to hire a body double but had a very tough time finding one that was a match to me. Later, I had the same issue on *Set It Off* and didn't see the mismatch until the screening. The body double's juicy booty, though really, really appealing, was not my less juicy booty.

I liked making movies, although the daily whiplash challenging my worth got to me. Babyyyyy, I would be constantly reminded, more than ever, how inadequate I was—while being praised at the same time. For a twenty-year-old, it was confounding. It was like being on a hamster wheel, on a merry-go-round, chasing a carrot: *Your performance is stunning.* And about the poster for *Jason's Lyric: Is that your thigh showing? We're so sorry, it's too provocative, so we are taking your thigh out.*

Also: *You're so funny . . . That dress makes you look like a Black*

girl, that's not for the red carpet . . . Your eyes do so much acting . . .
Black girls on the cover don't sell our magazines.

I was already tired of being kissed on one cheek and backhanded
on the other. It was one thing to embrace self-improvement and to
adjust to standards of being a leading lady, but where did it end? How
could you play the game without getting too caught up? To the point
where you let the game identify you completely?

I had no solutions other than swallowing my discomfort—which
I was used to doing. It was a run for the roses to avoid any gnawing
insecurities or discontent. They would only slow you down.

Maxine, *a dreamseeker in the best* sense, a native of Canada,
had been hoping to move to L.A. to work on more films
when we met on *Jason's Lyric*. After I suggested she come
on out and be my roommate, she made the move in no time.

Maxine would not take no for an answer when she said that she
was going to throw me a twenty-first-birthday celebration.

I tried to brush her off with "I don't want a party, Maxine."

"You do so much for other people, and you never let anybody do
anything for you. I just want to celebrate you!" she whined at me in
the sincerest way.

Deep down, I was afraid of disappointment. What if nobody
showed up? I resisted, but Max was determined. Eventually, I got to
"Fine!"

The biggest smile came over her face, and she hugged me so tight.
"Thank you, Jada. It's going to be the best party." And she was right.

She outdid herself, organizing a night at Creeque Alley, a
West Indian restaurant on Melrose Avenue, and oh my goodness,
I couldn't believe how many people showed up! There were ath-
letes and rappers, actors and actresses, a star-studded who's-who of
friends of mine or friends of friends. The restaurant was tiny, so the

party spilled out onto the street corner. There were all kinds of great food, a male stripper, a full bar, dope music, and a video playing on a screen as a birthday tribute—with some very special footage, including the video of "Parents Just Don't Understand" that Pac and I made in high school.

Everything Maxine did—putting so much time and care into this celebration—was out of love and appreciation. I was beyond touched. Nobody had ever done anything so special for my other milestone birthdays. My sixteenth had gone under the radar; so had my eighteenth. But not my twenty-first.

Pac came through, and when he saw the video of us lip-synching, he was not thrilled. He pulled me into a corner to ask, "Who put up that video?"

"Pac, stop tripp'n! Ain't nobody think'n about you." I laughed, realizing, oh yeah, here I was, like his sister bringing out his baby videos. Of course, Duane was there, and at one point, I brushed past Will, who was leaning against the wall, and he wished me a happy birthday. "Thank you, Will." And that was that.

It was a really good time had by all. Max was a little older than I was and knew what a rite of passage turning twenty-one was, and she wanted me to have the gift of a magnificent memory. It's one of so many fond shared moments with her that would mean even more in the future.

There was something else, however, about the high of my twenty-first birthday. My life was on such a promising trajectory, but the high couldn't be sustained. Highs, by nature, are fleeting. A fall was inevitable.

E*arthquakes are very hard to predict.* Sometimes you feel tremors ahead of time, but that's not a rule. Often, they come on suddenly. This is how I can best describe an otherwise uneventful day as I'm driving down Melrose Avenue. A girlfriend recognizes me driving by from her car and flags me over. I make a U-turn in the middle of the street to follow her car to the curb. I hop out and we greet each other.

"How have you been? I haven't seen you in a while." She says this warmly, with a gentle smile.

"I know . . ." I begin, and then realize that, suddenly, I'm not talking, and my body is hot, really hot, and I'm starting to shake. There is a war going on inside me. I burst into tears out of nowhere. What's happening? I'm both startled and confused.

My girlfriend can see I'm in trouble.

"I'm sorry, I don't know what's going on," I whine.

She reaches out and tries to grab me. "Are you okay, Jada?" she asks, but I can't even answer.

Turning to go, I climb back into my car and drive off, but in moments, I realize I'm too rattled to drive.

When I reached the next corner, I turned onto a side street, parked, and tried to pull myself together through torrential tears and an avalanche of emotions. I felt incredibly anxious, my heart was beating out of my chest, my breath was short, and I couldn't fight off a tidal wave of sadness—a despair that was going to drown me if I didn't get control of myself. It felt like fear and relentless sorrow had sucka-punched me.

When I got home to an empty house, sadness gave way to an urge I'd never experienced—that this hurt inside needed to be stopped, that it was so unbearable, the only option was to stop living. The more I tried to unthink the image of slitting my wrist, the more afraid I became that I would actually do it. For the first time ever, I didn't trust myself alone.

I called my mother. "Ma, I need you to come out here right away . . . because if you don't, I'm going to kill myself."

As soon as we hung up, Mom began to make arrangements to get off of work and come to Los Angeles. In the meantime, I desperately needed eyes on me that second, and Maxine was out of town working.

My next call was to my homegirl MC Lyte, who was also on the East Coast. "Lyte, I need you out here." I told her that I didn't feel safe with myself. She dropped everything and was on the next plane smok'n to L.A., no questions asked.

I was hopeless. I had NEVER had suicidal thoughts in my life. I had never felt this level of despair.

Once she got to me, Lyte literally brought her light into my darkness, not leaving my side for a minute of the day, not asking questions. She was such good company, keeping me grounded and distracting me from feeling unhinged. Never one to go into drama, she normalized my days, as did my dogs. Routine can be stabilizing. We'd get up, go to my favorite breakfast spot, Vivian's, and then go out with the Rotts. More than anything, Lyte was an anchor in a stormy sea, a symbol that everything was going to be okay, until my mom flew in.

When my mother arrived, my seams burst all over again. Mom was only a year into her sobriety then, and she had only two weeks to stay, during which she did the best she could to comfort me and help. After working her steps in recovery, she was in touch with how I could be affected by our history.

"You know, Jada," she would gently suggest, "you probably have a lot of stuff to talk about with a therapist, even anger toward me."

I didn't want to look at the possibility of being angry at my mother. Not at that point.

She then suggested we do therapy together. The prospect of opening up that entire Pandora's box with my mother was too much just then, and I knew that.

But I did know that I needed help. And that prompted me to reach out to Debbie Allen, a phone call that began, "I'm not doing good . . . I need some help, somebody to talk to . . ."

Debbie, as always, sprang into action on my behalf and arranged for me to be seen the next day by Dr. Sally Grieg, the sweetest therapist, who, without a doubt, saved my life. After my first session with her, she requested that I see a psychiatrist so I could be prescribed some meds.

The psychiatrist diagnosed me as clinically depressed and put me on Prozac. I resisted. I protested to Dr. Grieg, "I don't want to be on medication, like I'm crazy or something."

"Jada, this medication is simply to help get your head out of the gray clouds so we can actually deal with the issues that are coming up for you. This won't be forever. And you are not crazy." After a beat, Dr. Grieg reassured me, "A lot of people get a little assistance to help relieve overbearing depression."

She had such a warm, maternal nature, and I believed and felt her sincerity. I relinquished my resistance when we agreed to the plan that, once I'd stabilized, I would get off the Prozac—pronto.

The process took longer than expected. Once I began the medication, I was not happy that it killed my libido. That wasn't going to work for me for a long period of time. Sex was the one great thing going on in my life. However, as Dr. Grieg promised, the meds helped me get my head above the gray clouds, and therapy helped me begin a journey of emotional healing. Now, at least, I could see where the wounds came from, then slowly begin the daunting work of forgiveness and acceptance.

In my early passages of healing, I was ready to be done with Hollywood and bought a farmhouse outside of Baltimore. It required a lot of renovation, but the plan was for me to move back home. This way, I could fly to L.A. or go to New York for auditions, but I no longer wanted to be in the Hollywood mix.

I needed some peace. I needed some quiet. I needed to breathe.

Even running is part of the process. It is only human to do so, but not for long and not forever.

—CLARISSA PINKOLA ESTÉS, *WOMEN WHO RUN WITH THE WOLVES: MYTHS AND STORIES OF THE WILD WOMAN ARCHETYPE*

One of my favorite observations offered up by Clarissa Pinkola Estés, one of my longtime mentors on the page, is the understanding that running is part of our human experience and can lead us both astray and back to ourselves.

Fight-or-flight is wired into our DNA. Even while in flight, I was aware that something was welling up in me that needed to be examined. An unimaginable pain threatened to consume me, and my fear was that if I gave it more attention, it would make good on its threat. And sometimes that's exactly what happened— but not for long.

Once we stand our ground and face the source of the pain, it can't kill us. The more we ignore our hurts, the more we run, the more power we give them. This takes us out and, for some of us, to our grave.

Often our pain is simply a communication encouraging us to ask for help. With the belief that we can be helped, it's easier to recognize that our state of desperation is our wounds screaming, "HEAL ME!"

When we cease to fear our wounds and cover them in love, they begin to heal and eventually transform—into a flower, a prince, a queen, a gift. But we can't do it alone, and we are not meant to. If you can have the courage to believe it's okay to cry to the Universe for help instead of "Why me?," a door will open and healing, in some form, will come.

For those who struggle with suicidal thoughts, I pray you come to understand that you are worthy of your healing. One day at a time, one minute at a time, one second at a time. Hold on—have faith. Get help. Find someone trained to guide souls through the dark hours and to remind us that our suffering is not meant to take our lives but, instead, can lead us to the life we deserve.

Today give yourself the gift of choosing to look at a wound you may have been running from. Can you see what it might be trying to tell you? Can you accept that you are worth the help you may need?

CHAPTER 10

Trying to Find My Footing

The main appeal of the farmhouse I bought on the outskirts of Baltimore was that it was old-world tiny, with a charming hearth in the kitchen and a small pond off the deck, and it all sat on a large expanse of land. The views from the farmhouse windows were beautiful, and I was sure they would prove to be in every season. Once I made my new home habitable, I planned to fill it with a menagerie of rescued dogs and cats, maybe even a horse for my mom, fulfilling a childhood dream of hers.

Even though I intended to move into the farmhouse as my main residence, that couldn't happen right away, so I remained in L.A. while overseeing the renovations, making short, frequent visits.

Whenever I came back to the East Coast, being close to family helped me find my bearings and made me feel grounded. Funny enough, life in Baltimore felt a little simpler and a little slower than it once had. Whenever I stayed with my mom—now deeply committed to her recovery and living in Columbia, Maryland, in a new, solid relationship with Paul Jones (soon to be her third husband)—I found a level of security that I had not felt under her roof for quite some time, if ever.

The fact that Adrienne was living in the suburbs helped relieve my growing anxiety over the potential of being kidnapped and held for ransom. Part of this was PTSD from the violence I had already survived. Part of it was the reality that kidnapping was becoming a new hustle in Baltimore, and now that I was a recognizable budding star, people would assume that I was a profitable target. I moved a lot more cautiously because I didn't want to end up duct-taped in the trunk of a car. And unfortunately, I knew people that had happened to . . . and people who were doing it. My solution was to be extra-vigilant.

During this period, while on Prozac, I resolved to stop drinking or using any mind-altering substances, to avoid dating, and to concentrate on getting my shit together. This was the best way I knew to get well and find my footing again.

With the exception of Lyte, none of my friends in Baltimore or L.A. were aware of my breakdown. Nobody really suspected that there was something seriously amiss, although Duane Martin suggested I was becoming a hermit after I turned down invitations to get together. He finally called me up one evening to say, "Come out. We're right down the street."

He and his girlfriend at the time, Tisha Campbell, were at the Baked Potato, a lounge-like spot on Ventura Boulevard. As an afterthought, Duane added that Will Smith might join us when he finished work for the night. I couldn't tell Duane no, because I could literally walk to the Baked Potato from where I lived (probably why he chose it). Saying no felt disrespectful.

When I got there, under duress, I didn't plan to stay long. And then Will, charming and cheerful as usual, joined us. Shortly after his arrival, it became too loud to have much of a conversation. Someone suggested, "What about Jerry's Deli?"

We all agreed that was a good idea and bounced.

The next thing I knew, the four of us were up the road on Ventura Boulevard at Jerry's, a popular spot that stayed open late. Will was not at all the goofy guy I'd suspected him of being. He was a gifted conversationalist, highly intelligent, well read, and contagiously passionate about a wide range of interests. He went from the likes of Plato to Z-3 MC's (old-school hip-hop) to politics and to taking over the table with his dynamic storytelling. He was funny, too, and seemingly had a level of stability that was refreshing. He had an expansive vision, not just for his career, although he made no apologies about his drive to one day be the biggest movie star in the world and to take hold of all that life had to offer.

My thought at the time was *Will Smith is actually intriguing and captivating.* Who knew?

A few weeks later, my mobile phone rang during one of my visits to Baltimore, as I was walking along with my mom at a mall in Columbia. As soon as I pressed the button to take the call, I'd barely said, "Hello?" when the caller identified himself as Will Smith. Although I considered him just a friend at this point, I did perk up when I heard his voice.

My mother immediately asked, "Who is that?"

"Hold on," I said to Will, put my hand over the speaker, and turned to my mother, saying quietly, "It's Will Smith."

She gave me a disapproving look. "What does he want?"

"We're friends."

Adrienne got a look in her eye that showed up on the important occasions when she did not intend to be misunderstood. "What is Will Smith doing calling you? He's married." True, Will had married Sheree Zampino, and the two had a son, Trey, together. Before I could repeat myself, my mother insisted, "You don't need to be friends with a married man. Hang up the phone and tell him not to call you anymore."

My mother was right. I had perked up a little too much when I heard his voice, and Mom could tell this interaction was not appropriate.

I told Will somewhat sheepishly, "My mom doesn't think I should be talking to you, since you are married, and she said you shouldn't call me anymore."

Will understood, relayed that he meant no disrespect, and abided by the rules as set forth by Adrienne.

With that, we said goodbye and wished each other well. Almost a year went by before I heard from him again.

P rofessionally, *I barely skipped a beat.* The survivor in me knew better than to give any notice of my troubles, so that I was not deemed "unreliable" for work. In 1994, on any given week, I was on a merry-go-round, either doing publicity for a crop of films released that year, or in the middle of shooting other projects, or putting in hours for another batch in pre- or post-production.

One night I might be in Washington, D.C., at the premiere of *A Low Down Dirty Shame* (which was memorable because I invited Robsol and he showed up in a red leather suit, as esoteric and stylish as ever), and the next day I was flying back to L.A. for fittings on *Demon Knight,* directed by Ernest Dickerson and executive-produced by Joel Silver as part of *Tales from the Crypt.*

It was my good fortune, I felt, to have avoided getting typecast, and to go deep into character development and motivation, in drama and in comedy. During pre-production for *A Low Down Dirty Shame,* I had the opportunity to train with a fight instructor for my role of Peaches—to make it believable that I could physically kick a grown man's ass.

As usual, I went ALL IN and seriously thought, *I really like fighting, maybe I should go pro.* Many folks, including Keenen, reminded me that no one was interested in hiring an actress with no teeth. Instead, I looked for other ways to expand my repertoire and to explore other avenues—like getting into directing music videos.

After finding an agency willing to rep me as a video director, I was fortunate to connect with R&B crooner Gerald Levert, who was a sweetheart. When he wanted me to star in his video for "How Many Times," I made him an offer: "I'll be in your video if you'll let me direct it." Once we had it filmed and edited and aired, the requests started to come in.

Getting behind the camera—and coming up with the concept for the video—showed me that my creativity was not limited to being in front of the camera. Suddenly, I had a juggling act with acting and directing, so I had to be conscious about how I chose to use my time, professionally and socially. But sometimes the two came together.

Out of the blue one day, I got a call that none other than Prince wanted to speak with me about a creative endeavor—a ballet/opera he had written and recorded. He had seen some of my films and was reaching out to discuss possible collaboration.

Prince? As in my lifelong inspiration and one of my favorite artists ever, whose music had inspired me to get my first job so that I could afford to buy his records? As in the creator whose songs and looks I had impersonated in costume and lip-synch contests? This was crazy!

Within days, the meeting was set—at my house—and I was still in a state of disbelief when I opened the door. There he was, dressed all in white, wearing a warm smile, as I ushered him into my living room and pulled out my photo albums to prove that I was a serious devotee!

It didn't even occur to me that Prince would be embarrassed by my behavior, because I was so excited to show him those photos. Needless to say, he was subtly horrified (there was no likeness), which made me love him more.

What began as his interest in possibly collaborating on some project ideas soon turned into a beautiful, lasting friendship and shifted as well into his generosity to me as a mentor. While he helped me find my footing, Prince was also trying to find his, in a sense, in his battle with his label, Warner Bros. Records, for autonomy over his artistry. He was single-minded in spreading the message to other creatives about not allowing the industry to exploit your art for their profit. A constant theme in our conversations was his desire to retrieve the masters to his music, to own his art as well as his name.

I admired his determination beyond measure, how powerfully expressive he was and what he was willing to risk in order to take on the powers that be. But Prince also loved to have a good time and had the most potent sense of humor, along with a sprinkle of "hood magic"—in contrast to his dandy-esque ways.

Prince was one of the first artists I witnessed taking over a whole movie screen one night. We entered through the back exit, and as we were walking along, I must have been pressing my point about something, as per usual.

Suddenly, he gave me a look—all five feet and something of him, barely taller than me even in his heels—in the middle of my oratory, and without warning, he swooped me over his shoulder like a weightless sack.

Pleasantly shocked, I started to protest. Who knew he was so strong in those heels?

"What you gonna do now . . . huh?" he said, laughing.

All I could do was say, in a schoolgirl voice, "Oh my God—put me down!" *Chile,* I clutched my pearls, because Prince was a whole lotta man, heels and all—and a reminder to me to "Slow your roll, little girl."

When he seemed to come out of nowhere to befriend me, I was reassured by his kindness, his respect, and the value he placed on my talent. He offered me knowledge, understanding, and support that I really needed at that time in my life.

Although I wasn't up for a serious involvement, by the fall of 1994, I felt ready to end my sabbatical from dudes. Then I got a phone call that piqued my interest. In this era, Hollywood introductions were often made through publicists and managers. That's how I agreed to go out with a gentleman—we'll call him Lance. I obliged the request because . . . why not?

From our first meeting, Lance seemed very focused on locking me down. He came with gifts, trips, and compliments galore, accompanied by the declaration of his desire to have a child with me. This guy hardly knew me, and though I made it clear that I was not interested AT ALL in a serious relationship, he persisted. He wasn't hearing me, to the point where he asked me next to meet the child he already had.

I politely told him, "It's too soon, and we really don't know where this is going. We should wait on that."

Then he went all out, thinking I would bite, and offered to pay close to seven hundred thousand dollars toward the renovation of my farmhouse in Maryland. Yes, it was an expensive job, and it was tempting, but long ago I'd learned—nothing is for free. His gesture didn't feel like generosity, it felt like a way to entrap me. When I declined his gift and he got very upset, my mother pulled me up, declaring, "I don't like him, Jada. Something is off about him."

I thought her level of concern was excessive, and as naive young daughters do, I pooh-poohed my mother's reaction. But there was a gnawing feeling inside me that knew Mommie was right. He had shown signs of being easily agitated and sometimes having difficulty calming down when he didn't get his way. Being young, my attitude was *Why not give the dude a chance, in case I'm missing something?* There was a sweetness to him, and I gotta admit, all that attention—especially after my breakdown—made me feel desirable again. So I rationalized, *Maybe he is just an extremely generous person and excited about the possibility of us as a couple.*

Lance lived out of state, and I'd visited him a couple of times and enjoyed myself. For that reason, shortly after Thanksgiving, when Lance invited me to fly back with him to his home, I accepted his invitation, letting him know, "I can't stay long."

I had been at Lance's for no more than two days when a series of calls in the early morning of November 30 came through, and I needed to leave for New York.

At approximately twelve-thirty a.m. that day, Pac had been ambushed and shot outside Quad Recording Studios near Times Square. He had been struck five times and rushed into surgery at Bellevue for his most serious wound, a gunshot to the groin. The reports I got from Afeni, Pac's mom, were encouraging. Pac had survived, and we didn't have to worry about whether he would live or die.

The concern, though, was that Pac was due in court the following day—December 1—in an ongoing sexual assault case stemming from an incident in November 1993. When Pac had first attempted to explain to me the basis for the accusation, I had been visiting him in New York. We were in his hotel room, talking about his new project for Interscope Records, *Me Against the World*. I was really excited about the album and happy for him. Then, as the conversation turned to his latest legal concerns, Pac looked at me with sincere intensity and said, "I need to explain to you what happened. How I caught this case."

He didn't get very far into the story before I stopped him, holding up my hand and looking at him with the same intensity. "Listen, I don't need to hear the details. All I know is that if Tupac Amaru Shakur is ever in a room with any girl under any circumstance, she should always feel safe—no matter what."

I braced myself for an intense rebuttal, not that he disagreed with that belief but because you never knew which Pac was showing up on any given day. He could be combative, depending on his mood and whether he gave a fuck about your opinion. But on this occasion, he sat down in a chair across from me in silence. Something in Pac was shifting. His energy was filled with more humility and openness than I had seen in a minute. We sat there in the quiet for a long time, and I remember thinking that once everything was over, he was going to move very differently. His world had been going way too fast, and he had gotten off track. I saw this as a sobering moment for him.

Throughout the legal proceedings, Pac would maintain that he did not commit the alleged abuse but did take responsibility for not having stopped the others who did.

The shooting and robbery outside Quad Studios on the eve of his court appearance added one more layer of chaos. Rather than being a random robbery (of more than forty thousand dollars of cash and jewelry), it seemed that the hit had been planned. We didn't know whom to trust or what to believe.

Before I got off the phone with Afeni, she simply said, "When are you getting here?"

I gave Lance the short version. "I need to go to New York. Pac has been shot."

He was not happy. As I started to make arrangements, he said, "So you're going to leave me to go see some other n-gga?"

Here we go.

In my romantic relationships, I had often been haunted by layers of misunderstanding regarding my relationship with Pac. So I could be patient with Lance's discomfort, but the way he reacted didn't score him any points with me. "That n-gga happens to be one of my best friends," I said, calm but flustered.

Even though I knew Pac was out of surgery at Bellevue, looming questions were WHO had ambushed him and WHY, and HOW to help plan for his safety. The first line of business was to get Pac through his court day and then get him to an undisclosed spot where he could recuperate. I didn't have time for Lance's insecurities.

But Lance wouldn't stop. "Yeah, right—your friend."

I placated him, promising, "I'll be back when I can." From there, I shut him out. I had no more appeasing left in me.

The trip to New York was surreal. When I arrived at the courthouse, Pac was in a dingy hallway, accompanied by Afeni and several other people, awaiting his hearing. I will never forget my first vision of Tupac after that attack—bandaged up and in a wheelchair. I had never seen him so vulnerable. There was nothing I could do or say to make it all better. He was in pain, while dealing with an intense court case, on top of a very serious attempt on his life, along with the media circus. All I wanted to do was hug him, and I couldn't.

Everything was chaotic, and he was dead certain that somebody was really trying to kill him. The first suggestion was for Pac to come out and stay at my house, but Afeni and I reasoned that if anyone was trying to find him, my place would definitely be a top contender for where to look.

Jasmine Guy had flown in once she heard the news. As she and I were tight, she and Pac had become close friends. Afeni and I thought about Jasmine's house as a safe place in L.A. for Pac to recuperate, because very few knew of their friendship. And Jas—without a doubt—was a stone-cold ride-or-die. Jas and I had lunch that day and talked about Pac's situation, but Afeni called her personally to request that Pac stay with her. Without hesitation, Jas said yes.

It was decided I should keep my distance until we knew exactly what was going on.

In the courthouse hallway, Pac and I said our goodbyes without knowing when we would see each other again.

Everybody had their marching orders. A part of me felt absolutely useless. That hurt, but it was best for now. So I decided to go back to Lance's house. At least I'd be distracted.

But distraction was hard to achieve, as I was in constant contact with Jasmine and Pac. I'm sure that gnawed at Lance.

A couple of days went by. Nothing major happened, although I received another very important phone call. I just didn't realize its significance at the time. The call was from Spike Lee, who was interested in me for a script of his called *Girl 6*. Spike jumped on the phone and talked about the project, and he left it with: "I'll send you the script, see what you think, and then we should meet."

Even though I didn't think that particular project was right for me, I was excited to be on Spike's radar. Later, when I told Lance about the call, he wasn't interested.

The next night, Lance took me and a friend of his to dinner. Everything seemed to be relatively calm and on par. I remember looking out the window on our drive home and paying attention to landmarks that had become familiar by now. Given my new fear of being kidnapped, and my need for having an escape plan on deck, I had developed this habit whenever I was in a new environment.

We were a mere three minutes from Lance's house when, all of a sudden, a minor dispute between us erupted into an explosive reaction from him. His intensity never really felt safe, so as usual, my reaction was to try to stay levelheaded.

But the calmer I stayed, the angrier and louder he became, and the more his friend in the back tried to intervene, saying, "Hey, man, just calm down," in a respectful way.

That only threw more gas on Lance's fire. The madder he became, the more I realized—this was not going to end well. Besides, this dude was huge, all muscle, and apparently out of control. He had been drinking, and when he slammed his fist on the dashboard, I feared I could be next.

My heart thumped, and I instantly scanned the environment outside the car, pinpointing exactly where we were and how far we were from his house. My assessment came just as Lance slammed on the brakes and turned as if to hit me. At that instant, I threw the car door open and jumped out in my flat sandals and skirt and made it across the street, cutting through some backyards to get to the house before he did.

I knew he kept his back sliding door open, and I dashed into the house from his backyard, veered into the bedroom, where I quickly grabbed my black Russell sweats and my sneakers, and then raced into the kitchen, where I grabbed the biggest knife he had before running into his child's empty bedroom to hide.

As I change into my sweats, I go over my options. It's late, I know no one in the area, and there is no leaving safely. I have to make it till the morning—till I can get on the first plane out of here. Before I can finish tying my sneakers, Lance's voice bellows through the house as he comes through the sliding back door: "JADA! WHERE THE FUCK ARE YOU?"

He continues to yell for me as I realize—FUCK!—I'm stuck in a small room with only walls around me. No doors or windows. Trapped. If he finds me, as huge and amped as he is, I'm done. I have no escape, no advantage, even with a knife. I feel panic rise in me, but instead of going there, I find enough anger inside to move.

I make a choice to try to gun it for the front door. The second I step into the hall, Lance comes out of his bedroom at the far end of the hall opposite from me. We are in a standoff. Lance starts to walk swiftly toward me until I draw the huge knife and hold it out in front of me.

"Don't come any closer." My voice is low and full of fear, yet I'm determined to protect myself by any means necessary. "I swear to God!"

Lance stops in his tracks but then, in a sweet fucking Jekyll-and-Hyde way, offers a line I have heard only in movies: "You think I would hurt you?"

My heart drops. I know neither of us is going to get out of this one unscathed. He begins to creep toward me, as if to persuade me that I'm safe, which I know is not the case.

Just then, thank goodness, Lance's friend comes into the house through the front door and right away tries to deescalate the confrontation. His friend calms everything down enough for Lance to apologize for how far everything has gone.

Thinking fast, I respond by playing along, accepting his apology, and agreeing, "Of course. I understand. I know you didn't mean it. Everything's fine." And so on.

As soon as all seemed smooth, I managed to secretly call my assistant and asked her to get me on a plane to L.A. first thing the next morning.

Lance saw me packing and asked, "Where are you going?"

"Remember I told you about my call with Spike? He wants to meet with me tomorrow in L.A., but I'll come back after."

Lance knew something was up but let it go for the night, partly because I'd mentioned Spike earlier. When the car came to pick me up the next morning, Lance said, "I'm never going to see you again, am I?"

I put on my brightest, most forgiving smile and said, "Of course you will. I'll call you after my meeting."

I got on that plane, holding my breath, thankful the lie had worked. I never saw Lance again—alone, that is.

T*he most potent love language for* me has always been the language of protection. It has always been important for me to feel protected by those I love and to be able to protect them in return. You show up for each other, even when doing so comes at a cost.

This was one of many thoughts running through my head when I made the first of a series of visits to Pac while he was incarcerated. This visit was to Rikers Island, where he was locked up in January 1995—first in the infirmary wing—while awaiting his sentence. Originally, he wasn't required to turn himself in, but a judge ordered him held after he wasn't able to post bond for the $3 million bail. When we'd all stood in the dark hallway of that courthouse on December 1, 1994, the day he was convicted of sexual abuse (the other allegations were dropped), I'd never imagined he would end up in Rikers—one of the most brutal, dangerous prisons in our country.

Given my years of visiting incarcerated friends and working with young people in juvenile detention, I was no stranger to the inside of correctional facilities. And yet nothing really prepares you for a visit to Rikers.

To get there, I drove first to a parking lot where I boarded a bus, which took passengers over a bridge to the actual island. Crossing that bridge was nerve-racking. I took deep breaths, trying not to focus on the fact that I was about to enter a notorious prison on an island without any means of escape. I was at the mercy of Rikers.

As I looked down at the murky cold waters of the East River, a riptide of anxiety began to set in at the prospect of seeing Pac imprisoned. My challenge was to swallow all my many fears and put on my best face for what was to come.

When I arrived at the prison itself, I felt as if we had reverted to the Middle Ages. Everything appeared dungeon-like—dark and dank, accompanied by horrid sounds of gates slamming and bars clanging as I entered one section, then creaking open in front of me as I moved to the next. At various checkpoints, there were faceless uniformed guards who searched my belongings, asked questions, and patted me down thoroughly, and even a drug-sniffing German shepherd who gave me the once-over. This is a demeaning process that makes you feel you've surrendered yourself to do time. Not every prison gives you these feels, but at Rikers, the vibe was that one wrong move would get me thrown in a cell, too. *Except* . . . when some of the guards quietly asked for an autograph in between their moments of cold control.

Finally, I was led to a room with a small round table where I waited for my one-on-one with Pac while a prison guard kept eyes on me through a glass window. Soon the main door opened, and I watched as Pac, dressed in a brown prison uniform that looked like scrubs, completely shackled, shuffled into the room with a guard. The moment I laid eyes on his face, my heart sank. As the guard unshackled Pac, I tried to maintain composure so he wouldn't know how shocked I was by his appearance.

Pac was thinner than I'd ever seen him. Patches of hair were missing all over his head, a pattern of his alopecia that started earlier after he was beaten by police in Oakland. In his heightened level of stress and sadness, he was not himself in any way, shape, or form. For the first time in years, he was having to deal with harsh realities *without* weed or alcohol. No mind-altering assistance was there as he sobered up and awakened to a very brittle circumstance.

As soon as he approached and I was given a nod by a nearby guard, I hugged him hard, holding on to him for as long as I was allowed. He seemed so frail. Among my first words to him were: "I've been talking to your lawyer, Pac. We're going to get you out of here."

We sat down across from each other. Pac paused for a beat. "I can't ask you to help bail me out. You have worked so hard to get where you are. I couldn't ask that, and because I love you, I wouldn't ask that." Pac spoke with the deepest sincerity.

But for me, the idea of not helping him get out was unacceptable. Pac was a young artist, steeped in legal bills, on top of a great many people counting on him to support them. I knew that $3 million for bail would not be easy for him to come by. He needed help, and there was a group of us offering to step in—including some other female friends and women in his life—but Pac resisted. His refusal to have me raise money for his bail was more than pride, which I only came to see during that visit.

Considering the nature of the charges, it was unfathomable and unbearable to him that any woman should have to shoulder his problems. And in his view, as there were men in entertainment making millions off his talents, it made sense to count on them.

I pushed back, as I always did, and continued discussing how we should strategize about his bail.

"Jada," he interrupted, "listen to me. All I need you to do is make sure my mother is straight. Take care of her bills for me while I'm in here. Can you do that?"

I wanted to cry, but I couldn't. My tears would be worse than bullets at this point. "No problem. Whatever you need, Pac."

It seemed he had surrendered to something that I was not yet willing to accept—his fate. All he was asking me to do was assist him in taking care of what he needed most, not what I *thought* he needed.

I wanted to be both a good friend AND a good soldier who could follow his lead. That would ultimately be a very trying task.

Again, because of the nature of the charges, Pac wanted me to
keep my distance. What he didn't realize was that I had already been
pulled in. Calls had come in from women's groups led by prominent
Black women who requested that I disassociate myself from Tupac.
But he was my brother. I wasn't going to abandon him, though I knew
it would cost me one way or another.

Toward the end of our visit, we did our best to make small talk and
add some levity. But it wasn't possible. It was a devastating day and became even more soul-crushing when the guards took him away and it hit
me: *I'm leaving him here, and there is nothing I can do.*

I couldn't believe it. As I crossed that bridge in that stupid bus,
a tidal wave of guilt came rushing in with the thought *What kind of
friend am I that I get to go home and he doesn't?*

From the moment Pac landed in Rikers, we were in close
communication—either on the phone or in a volume of
letters—and he didn't hold back from giving me the blow-by-
blow. One of the very first letters, written at two a.m., described how
he spent his days trying to drain out the "shouts of power" of the
guards and attempting to ignore the "diabolical laughs" of "hollow
men happy to be incarcerated." He compared himself to a bird without wings, unable to fly to freedom, and to a fish "far from the sea"
unable to breathe.

I would do my best to be home at certain hours to receive his
phone calls. My schedule was hectic, but we figured out how to talk
often. We were still holding out hope that his appeal would land
him a reprieve and he wouldn't have to serve out his sentence. He
was looking at anywhere from two years to seven. The legal bills
were mounting, and a couple of times, I took care of some of them to

keep the ship moving. Thankfully, he didn't protest, but I treaded lightly.

Then I received a letter from Pac, dated February 2/3, that took me by complete surprise. It was addressed to "JK Shakur" (as in Jada Koren, with Pac's last name).

I opened the envelope and read through the letter slowly. Pac began by saying that he realized we had not been romantic in the past but that he was at a place where he believed the two of us were meant to be husband and wife. He wrote to say that when he was in struggle, others claimed to love him but "only you loved me," that when he blew up, "everybody swore they loved me," but in his view only I did. And, he continued:

> now as I have slipped from grace and the world has turned against me, a few claim to have love 4 me but once again you show me your love. After deep reflection and spiritual awakening I have come to realize the friend, lover and soulmate was there all the time. I have not seen or felt from anywhere or anyone the intensity & loyalty that you have shown me.

That was why, he concluded," I want to commit myself to you." That was why, he repeated, "I want to marry you."

The last thing I ever expected was a formal marriage proposal from Tupac. He asked me to answer as soon as possible because his entire existence depended on me saying yes.

Pac had a way with words that could paint the most idyllic picture of his heart. I knew we had deep love for each other, but not in the husband-and-wife sense. I was sooooo torn. I knew what this was. He needed solid footing. I had been that for him through so much, but what he really needed was someone to do time with him. And I had planned on doing so—as a friend. As a loving, devoted, ride-or-die friend. But as his wife?

Pac called my mother and formally asked for my hand in marriage. Pac had his old-fashioned ways, especially when it came to certain traditional values. He believed in family and loyalty, and he *loved* children. I had never dreamed of getting married—in fact, I had no intention of ever doing so. To anyone. Even so, one thing I knew about Pac was that he would eventually be married and a devoted father.

Mommie loved Pac, too, but she did not think that we should get married. She told Pac that if this was something we really wanted, we should wait to see how things panned out with his case before we made any kind of commitment. When I talked to Afeni about Pac's marriage proposal, she was very diplomatic: "I want you guys to do what makes you happy."

Everyone was a bit shocked by this turn of events, but none of them had seen Pac at Rikers. I had, and I knew what Pac was feeling. Still, I couldn't let go of the strong sense that the two of us as husband and wife would be a recipe for disaster.

In my uncertainty, I played with the possibility. That is, until I asked Pac, "Do you expect me to come there for conjugal visits?"

His answer was yes. This was when reality hit hard. Pac was expecting me to be not just a psychological wife but a physical wife. I couldn't do it. It took some difficult conversations, but eventually, Pac and I got to a place of acceptance.

Here is what I knew—Pac wanted me as a wife to get him through his jail sentence, but not for a lifetime. He didn't know that then, not while he was behind bars, but I promise you, once he got out of jail, he was glad he didn't marry me.

On February 8, Pac was sentenced in court to serve from eighteen months to four and a half years. *The New York Times* reported that he tearfully apologized to his victim while protesting that he was not guilty of the crime. A short time later, around Valentine's Day 1995, Pac was transferred upstate to the maximum-security penitentiary in Dannemora, New York.

None of us could believe it. In Tupac's words, Dannemora was "where they send you if you were to kill somebody or if you blew up the World Trade Center." Two years earlier, in fact, terrorists had attempted to blow up the World Trade Center, only to come back to finish the job in 2001. Where did they put those terrorists? Dannemora.

That's where Pac was.

O*n that same Valentine's Day of* Pac's sentencing, the other big news—at least in the entertainment world—was that divorce papers had been filed in the dissolution of the marriage of Will Smith and his wife, Sheree. Before the week was out, my phone rang while I was over at my aunt Karen's house.

A seduction began the moment I answered the phone. It was Will, cheerful, smiling audibly as he asked, "What's up? Where are you?"

"Baltimore," I told him, smiling audibly in return. I told him about the farmhouse I'd bought and was renovating.

He didn't waste much more chitchat before asking, "You seeing anybody?"

I paused. What else was there to say but "Uhm—no."

"Good," Will said. "You seeing me now."

Oh, I thought, *that's a bold approach.* And nobody had ever stepped to me like that. My reaction was a schoolgirl laugh. Bold, done right, is—sexy.

"Hit me up when you get back to L.A."

"All right," I said, defenseless.

And I bit. Hook, line, and sinker.

Naturally, we will make mistakes and fail from time to time. That's part of being fully alive. There are no guarantees. If we are waiting for guaranteed courses of action, we may spend much of our life waiting.

—MELODY BEATTIE, *THE LANGUAGE OF LETTING GO*

Sometimes, on our journey, we lose our footing. This is an unavoidable occurrence. But too often, our mistakes or confusion can paralyze us and put us in states where we no longer trust ourselves. We can become so fearful that we render ourselves stagnant. There are certain times that require us to be still, but there are also moments when it's important to keep moving.

———

We must remain in touch with our willingness to continue trying to find our way, to find our footing. Knowledge and wisdom come from embracing all the lessons life has to offer. Your steps are not always meant to be perfect, although so many will try to shame you into believing so. There are times we will step in shit—learn from it. And then there are times we will step into a gold mine—celebrate it. Either way, life is about taking risks and stepping out on faith. And no matter what, the path you need will find you.

———

Do something today to change it up: Drive an unexplored route home, extend yourself to make a new friend, learn something that inspires you to get out of your comfort zone.

———

And have fun finding your footing along the way!

CHAPTER 11

The Savior Prince

I *am drunk as hell,* and my heart is SWOONING.

What can I say? I'm in a magical season in my life. I'm in love. Yes . . . in LOVE . . . with Will Smith.

I have to be honest—me falling for Will Smith was very unexpected for me.

From afar, and even after meeting him a couple of times in the Hollywood whirl, I concluded that Will Smith would never have been on my radar—only because he was so . . . cheerful. That was a sticking point. Cheerful didn't represent itself as deep, and my young mind believed a troubled person was a deep person.

To my surprise, Will proved to be one of the most complex individuals I'd ever meet. We had more in common than I could have imagined, but it was his irresistible charm that stole my heart—and, in time, that of the world.

And here we are, after eight months of his unstoppable "charm offensive," on Thanksgiving Day in Jamaica, the small island nation that is the latest stop on our North America Young Love Gone Wild tour. Everything has been a blur, from our first jaunt that began: "Where are we going?" "You'll see. Pack a bag." "Oh, a private jet?" (This was before everybody in Hollywood had to have their own private airplane on standby for spur-of-the-moment weekends in paradise.)

With the heat of rum punch starting to surge through my veins, I'm thinking back to how Will managed to wear down my defenses early in our courtship. Gotta say, his level of intelligence mixed with his West Philly grit was compelling.

We each understood where the other came from, and there was no need to offer explanations. He also had a unique way of presenting an argument. On our very first date, we were sitting at a restaurant, having a fierce debate over dinner. Will pointed to his glass as a visual component to understanding perception.

"You see that glass? It's to the right from where you're sitting." He waited for me to agree, and I did. "But from where I'm sitting, it's on my left."

I had never thought about things that way at the tender age of twenty-three. The point he was conveying was that learning to understand someone else's perception by putting yourself in their position is a powerful skill.

Nobody around me at the time was thinking that deeply. I admit, it felt great to be courted by the most skilled man at courtship on the planet. But the greater magnet for me was my sense that Will would challenge me in substantial ways.

He was never hesitant to take on the status quos in Hollywood set up for Black Men—and Women of Color as well. He broke the rules that were entrenched by Hollywood's ignorance of the broad reach of Black talent; he broke rules so effortlessly it would set him in a league of his own.

And you know what I found to be so gangster about that? He did it with a smile. I respected that . . . a lot. I also respected that he could make me laugh like no other. He could sometimes, only sometimes, be hilariously silly. I did not find him as consistently funny as others. BUT when he did make me laugh, he knew it was genuine and made a sport out of having me literally (and I mean literally) rolling on the floor.

Will was a guy who could be comfortable in the hood or at the White House and everywhere in between. He had the ability to spread his arms wide and promise you that the world was his oyster, and he was going to give you all the pearls it had to offer.

Although I had never encountered anyone like him—that was a fact—I had no idea that he would sweep me off my feet so quickly.

Will courted everyone in my world, too: my mother, my friends, my coworkers, you name it. Will and Maxine, my roommate then, became instant friends. Everybody took to Will—who wouldn't?

It never occurred to me to question how fast we moved into our whirlwind, because that was just how my whole life had been. Everything moved at lightning speed. His life moved the same way. With that pace, at this point, we were primed for each other.

In bits and pieces, Will and I told each other our respective stories of growing up in chaos and dysfunction. In hindsight, it's clear that we were each running from ourselves and our thorny pasts, too busy adapting to the demands of wanting it all and trying to have it all, but in different ways for different reasons. At the start of our relationship, I sat him down to explain the breakdown I had gone through and that I'd been taking Prozac. That same day, I stopped taking it. In the euphoria of this storybook romance, I felt, who needs Prozac?

I don't know how he felt about my admitting what I'd come through. He just smiled and said, "Okay," and kept it moving. In hindsight, it's obvious we were showing each other red flags. He was freshly separated and running from having to face how and why his marriage had dissolved. And I was about to make him my new Prozac while running from the reality that I had been diagnosed as clinically depressed. But who cared? We were young, and the whirlwind between us was too intoxicating at the time to pay the red flags any mind.

After having avoided alcohol all this time, I started drinking again socially because Will and I loved to drink together. Will was a lightweight, which I found hilarious, considering how big he is. He'd be lucky to finish one small drink of some kind before he knocked out. Me, on the other hand, I didn't have that issue.

Being pursued with all the bells and whistles, as Will knew how to do, was the main drug, with a drink or two or three or four as the chaser. The gifts and surprises had to keep topping themselves. I'd arrive at my trailer on the set of *Nutty Professor* and see Fawn shaking her head with a smile, only to open the door and be met with dozens and dozens of roses that Will had sent, so profuse that I couldn't even get in the door.

There was jewelry and, later, cars, but from the start, mostly luxury weekends where I'd be whisked away to a private airport and then flown off to Cabo to stay at a private estate. On other occasions, I'd open my front door to find a basket of books he'd bought for me and had delivered to my doorstep as a surprise, connecting to some ideas we may have been digg'n on together, with a thoughtful note inside.

The one thing that did not work for Will was staying over at my place, mainly because it was haunted. To me, there was nothing foreboding about the spirits there. But Will, like my friends, was creeped out. He didn't mind visiting me during the day, but he stayed the night only *once*. Will would eventually ask me to move in with him, and his house became where I spent most of my time.

By that point, I was all in, and Will kept upping the ante—like this trip to Jamaica that included Duane and Tisha. And so off we flew in a private plane to Baltimore to see my people, and then we drove to Philly to see Will's people, then off to New York on the jet so Will could do *David Letterman* and Duane could see his people. From there we jumped back on the jet to go to Jamaica. Amid all that magic, because the world was now our proverbial oyster, we would wind up flying next to Aspen, where the winter wonderland awaited.

In advance of our arrival in Jamaica, Will had rented a beautiful brick house with a pool and a mainland feel—not the typical Caribbean home. The grounds were full of lush tropical greenery, one of my favorite characteristics of the island. I've always had an affinity for Jamaica's nature, especially the jungle-like rainforests, and this was, after all, the land of my grandmother's roots.

Here we are, Thanksgiving Day, finishing up a delicious Caribbean feast prepared by a local chef. For dessert, I decide to stick with rum punch, my absolute favorite.

Soon we all retire to the living room, which looks out to the pool, all lit up and sparkling. Everyone is mellow. Not me. I've had way too much to drink already, and I'm a little belligerent.

This was a complicated time for Will as well as for me. He was in the middle of his divorce from Sheree. And I didn't know a damn thing about the complexities of divorce other than what I'd observed in my dysfunctional upbringing. My biggest misunderstanding about the dissolution of marriage was the belief that divorce and a breakup were the same. I figured, once you decided to send divorce papers, that meant you were truly done. Sheree had been the one who filed for divorce, which made me believe it would be a clean break.

Divorce doesn't work like that, especially when there is a child involved. No, ma'am.

A few months after I'd really fallen for Will, he had called to announce that Sheree wanted to put the divorce aside and try to reconcile. My heart crashed.

Hot tears spilled from my eyes, but my voice on the phone held steady. It occurred to me that this wasn't about me or even us. This was really about Will and Sheree's two-year-old son, Trey. In a flash, I saw Trey's circumstance, and it made me think of all the times in my childhood when I badly wished adults had thought of me first. I wanted to do better by Trey than what I felt had been done by me.

As calmly as I could, I said, "You have to try. There is a child involved." I thought I would collapse.

In my mind, I was letting go of the best thing that had happened to me in a long time. But I knew, without a doubt, it was for the better. Two terrible weeks passed, at which point Sheree and Will both decided to continue with their divorce.

Now, months later, in my drunken agitation in the living room of the rented house in Jamaica, it grates at me that I'm hearing Will on a phone call with Sheree and family, LAUGHING and wishing everyone "Happy Thanksgiving!"

Here we go again. My insecurity spikes. From his end and how he was just gee-geeing away, to my insecure mind, it sounds like a reconciliation lovefest. So, as Will is finishing up his call with Sheree's mother, Pat (whom I will grow to ADORE), and saying his goodbyes to everyone, I yell, "If you're divorced, what the hell you need to talk to Sheree's mother for?"

Will shoots a cold look my way. Seconds later, he hangs up the phone.

"What was all that?" I growl.

The petty arrogance in my tone instantly takes Will over. His face twists in disbelief that I'm even going there. "What do you mean, why am I talking to her? It's Thanksgiving, and she's my son's grandmother."

Before I have a chance to say anything else, I watch as Will gets up from the chair in the living room and makes his way to a lounge chair outside by the pool.

It's a beautiful hot night, and the lights from the pool reflect ripples of iridescent light across his face. With too much drink in me, I decide to press my luck and follow Will outside. "What? You don't want to talk to me now?" I bark. Then I look at him sheepishly, like "C'mon . . ."

Will shoots me another chilly look with that stern "I'm not playing with you" expression I'm gonna learn all too well not to push. "You're drunk and you're talking crazy." He leans back in the lounge chair.

Something tells me I should leave it alone, but I don't. "All I was asking—"

Will shuts me down. "I'm not talking to you about this. I actually don't want to talk to you at all." He spits his words with finality, lies back in the chair, and closes his eyes.

The tone of his voice and the frosty glare he gave me have made it very clear that he's doing all he can to restrain how angry he is.

Furthermore, by now, rum punch be damned, I realize I've been out of line. This was me trying to play tough, but the truth of the matter is . . . I'm scared he's going to call everything off and leave me again.

Now, in shame and self-recrimination, I can't believe how much I showed my ass, in full disrespect of Will trying to keep things peaceful and smooth in an already difficult situation—because I was in MY feelings. Will was doing his best to manage it all, and I wasn't being helpful. My immaturity made me completely blind to the fact that Sheree, Trey, and her family were feeling great loss as well.

The bottom line is, I acted ugly, and I know it.

Not to mention, as I pace around the pool berating myself, that my childish reaction has ruined the whole seduction of the night. I was ready for a full-on sexy evening, if you get my drift.

How in the hell, I'm thinking, *can I get things back to hot and sexy?* As I look at the lights reflecting off the water in the pool and then back up to the roof of this house where we're staying, my drunk ass devises a plan.

Crazy as it is, when I go check the side of the brick house, I see that the black ironwork of the trellis is perfectly structured to serve as a ladder. Without hesitation, I put down my red cup full of rum punch, kick off my sandals, and start to climb the railing. Thank goodness it's sturdy, which gives me the confidence to place my feet in those tiny wedges in order to hoist myself to the next rung. With each step, I start to feel more and more like Catwoman in my tight-fitting hiked-up Lycra dress as I scale the side of the house.

Finally, I reach the roof, where, conveniently, there is a small black iron fencing around Duane's bedroom window. Hanging from my newfound iron ladder, I yell in a drunk, sloppy whisper: "DUANE!"

After a few moments, Duane pulls his curtain back to see me hanging from the side of the trellis. He then opens the window, pokes his head out, and bursts into laughter.

"SSSHHHH!" I can barely get my finger across my lips to signal to Duane to be quiet.

"Jada, what are you doing?" he asks with amused concern.

"SSSSSHHHH. Be quiet. I don't want him to hear me," I say in a slurry stage whisper.

"Who? Will?" Duane whispers, too, chuckling away.

"Yes. He's mad at me. I'm going to jump off the roof into the pool. Sssssh. Don't say nuff'n." A mix of serious determination and fierce concentration gives me two seconds of sober confidence—enough to pull myself onto the roof to the left of D's window.

Laughing, Duane blurts out, "Jada, NO!" He knows this is dangerous, and knows damn well he should get me off the roof, but the boy in him has to watch it play out.

Here's the thing: Once I commit, rethinking an entirely flawed plan is not my style. So now, on the rooftop, I do my best to pull myself together and get as coherent as possible. Slowly, I make my way to the edge of the roof, about twenty feet in the air. It's a lot higher than I guessed, and the edge of the pool is a little farther from the house than what I calculated from below. Through my drunk mind's eye, the path forward tells me I will have to run and then jump out toward the pool so I don't miss it entirely and break my back on the concrete.

Inhaling a deep breath, I turn toward the house and walk farther up the rooftop to get a good running start. Within a second, I whip around and start to run toward the edge of the roof. In no time, I am flying in the air, screaming, "I LOVE YOU, WILL!"

SPLASH!!!

My body slammed into the water. Thank goodness it was the deep end because I damn near slammed into the floor of the pool.

The water was freezing and dulled my drunken high. When my head popped out of the water, I was ecstatic. That quest was a hell of a thrill and was completely without injury. Quickly, I swam to the side and lifted myself out of the water. Will was sitting in the same lounge chair I had left him in as I shuffled toward him, soaked and shivering, my teeth chattering at top volume as I continued to profess my love for him. "I love you, Will, I love you, Will . . ."

By now, Duane had run down to the pool and witnessed up close my whole drowned-rat perp walk.

While I shuffled closer to Will, I could see him smiling from ear to ear. My plan worked! He got up and wrapped me in a towel that was on the back of his chair and pulled me into his lap. "You are crazy as hell, you know that?" Then he kissed me and held me in his arms so I could get warm.

This was US. And this night was a preview of the next damn near three decades of our life together. Living on edges of our own making and driving each other absolutely crazy. Sometimes joyfully and other times with great . . . dislike.

We must be about the business of saving ourselves and calling attention to all that is keeping us from being whole.

—BELL HOOKS, *SISTERS OF THE YAM*

My experience is that if someone is willing to save you, most likely, it's because they are looking to be saved, too. How many of us bought into the fairy tale that the prince in shining armor or the beautiful princess would save us from ourselves and the horrors of life? ME!

———

We all buy into fairy tales, to a certain degree, because of centuries of being fed the messaging of what romantic love promises us—permission to avoid self-responsibility by allowing someone to protect you while demonstrating how much they love you. Endlessly. Because if they really love you, they will know how to, and be willing to, rescue you from all the pain of life. What's crazy is that the beginning of most relationships feels so good that this false idea is validated as attainable.

———

New relationships can be so intoxicating that we forgo the need to take care of ourselves and often abandon the healing work or our own growth on our journey to become more whole. In turn, we continue to expect the savior to provide the intoxication, the euphoria, of saving us, so that we don't have to feel the weight of the baggage we brought into the relationship. We don't want to have to deal with our shit, and here is where the savior cycle can spin out of control for a long, long time.

———

The desire to be saved is not limited to romantic partnerships, although they are a hotbed for revealing how unrealistic expectations can set you up for disappointment. You might want to ask yourself if there is a Savior Prince or Princess in your life whom you may be unconsciously asking and expecting to save you. Are you expecting them to make you feel safe? Feel cherished? Feel worthy? Take a really good look at any relationship dynamic that is in constant flux or has a lot of confrontation in it. Where could you be lacking self-responsibility in expecting someone to care for you in ways you are not willing to care for yourself?

CHAPTER 12

Loss Unmourned

E*arly in 1995*, I received a call from Eazy-E.

"What's up, E? It's been a while. How are you?"

Eazy, in fact, wasn't well and was in the hospital at Cedars-Sinai, recuperating from pneumonia. After getting me up to speed, he quickly got to the purpose of his call. "I heard you're directing a video for Dre."

"I am," I responded. I had met with Dr. Dre about directing the music video for the release of "California Love." Dre loved my video concept, a hood version of *Mad Max Beyond Thunderdome.*

At this time, Pac was not on the record at all. This was strictly Dre's version of the song, and it was bang'n. As soon as I heard it, my imagination went wild, and I was ready to shoot the crap out of that video. We were about to go into production until—"It's not a good idea for you to be on that set. You don't need to be around Suge."

Damn it! I was so caught up in the art and excitement that I had totally forgotten about Suge Knight and his ties to Dre at the time, besides the ongoing issues with the dissolution of N.W.A. Suge had a reputation for violence, and after meeting him a few times, I could see his level of intimidation with my own eyes. The thought of Suge on the set gave me pause. "Damn, E, I didn't even think about that part."

Eazy made me promise I would step away. Instead, he had another possible video he was interested in me directing. He felt bad, I could tell, and this was a way to make up for work he thought he was taking from me. That meant a lot, and I played along and told him, "Yeah, get me the music, and I'll see what I can come up with."

Then, thanking him for having my back, I asked, "When can I come up there and visit you?"

Eazy told me that a visit to the hospital would be a hassle and he would be home soon.

I gave a diplomatic excuse to Dre's team about why I couldn't direct the video, which was put on hold temporarily, anyway. "California Love" went through unexpected changes in months to come—namely, that a different version was recorded with Tupac included on the track, which made an already bang'n song unstoppable. Here is the funny thing—Eazy was ahead of the curve, because once Pac came onto the record, he would not have wanted me to direct the video and be on set, either.

Clearly, it wasn't in the stars for me to direct "California Love." The video would eventually get made using my *Mad Max* concept, but directed by the great Hype Williams, who did it beyond justice.

When E convinced me on our call that his health was getting better, I believed him. I never thought that would be the last time I would ever hear his voice.

I was shocked when it was announced, shortly after he called me, that he had been admitted to the ICU in critical condition and was suffering from full-blown AIDS. Eric Wright, aka Eazy-E, was thirty-one years old when the news broke. Just before his death, he chose to go public to raise awareness about AIDS, especially with young people or anyone who believed that HIV affected only gay men and addicts; he was neither.

E didn't give me one inkling that his phone call, based on concern for me, would be our last conversation. I felt like an awful friend that I didn't get to say goodbye. I didn't know how to mourn for him, or how to process his death, any more than I had with many losses in the past. I did the only thing I knew how to do, and that was to set the loss aside, not mourn, and just keep it moving.

My first sight of Pac at Dannemora was a pleasant surprise. When he walked into the visitors' room of the facility, I thought, *This man is more swole than I've ever seen him.* It looked like he was spending every waking hour lifting weights, and his rebellious, fearless swag had returned. But I knew that in addition to his rigorous regimen, he'd been reading and writing up a storm. I'd been sending him books, including *Kindred* and *Wild Seed* by Octavia Butler, one of my favorite authors. Inspired, Pac loved her work and eventually wrote two scripts, one of which was called *Kindred Spirits,* and the other a fictional depiction of his legal ordeal.

In even more contrast to his mood at Rikers, Pac was smiling. I would come to find out he was damn near running the place, advocating for reforms within the prison. Most of the inmates had love and admiration for him, but that created haters as well, and sometimes beef with the correctional officers. All of this made for a dangerous concoction, because Pac had no problem getting into confrontations, including with the guards.

Pac's bravado was bigger than ever, as evidenced when, as soon as he was unlocked from his restraints, he grabbed me and kissed me, damn near swallowing my face.

I immediately pulled away and screeched, "Boyyyyy!"

Pac started laughing. "Come on, stop being a square." He went on, "I'm up here with these ugly n-ggas all day. What do you want from me?"

"Pac, please."

"Well, shit, you ain't gonna marry me. A kiss is the least you can do."

We both cracked up. We were good.

For this visit, I'd traveled to upstate New York with Lyte, whom Pac knew well, and another female rapper and friend, Nefertiti.

Nef and Lyte joined us after I'd greeted Pac, and we sat with him kicking it and listening to all the stories of what was happening with him in general. We hadn't been there long before he calmly broke the news to us: "I'm signing with Suge Knight."

Pac signing with Death Row, Suge's label? This was not good. But the three of us reacted cautiously, with the same energy of "You sure you want to do that?"

The last thing I wanted to do was press him in front of Lyte and Nef or upset the confidence he seemed to feel about the decision. Instead, I decided to come see him again on my own before returning to L.A. On the drive back to Dannemora, I took some time to sort things out in my head. One of the memories that came to me was of a call from Pac the year before and how excited he was to tell me, "I wrote a song about our mothers."

Of course, it wasn't about both our mothers—it was about Afeni. But the sentiment was our shared experience of being children with mothers who were addicts.

Instead of playing it for me on the phone, he sent me a cassette. The song was "Dear Mama." Pac had a bit of apprehension about the song and wanted to know my thoughts. In the first verse, he had me:

When I was young, me and my mama had beef
17 years old, kicked out on the streets . . .

After I listened, my immediate reaction was to cry. The song was honest but so loving and heartfelt. I'd witnessed many of the challenges he and Afeni had faced, and I loved how he could honor her and all the beauty that outshone her difficulties. The journey he narrated in his lyrics allowed me to reflect on my mother in the same way.

"Dear Mama" was a healing, hood-style, which was not an easy feat. Knowing he had trepidation about sharing this aspect of his journey as well as Afeni's, I called him back and reassured him, "I think this is the best song you've ever done." I told him I loved it and that I believed Afeni would, too. It was an anthem song for every mother who struggled and wasn't perfect, and I was grateful that it went on to receive so much critical acclaim.

On that drive, I also thought through the different glimpses I'd caught of Marion "Suge" Knight over the years. The first occasion had been when a girlfriend of mine, the belle of the ball in many circles, asked me to accompany her to Gladstones on Pacific Coast Highway in Malibu after Suge had invited her there for a dinner date. She didn't want to go alone because of his questionable reputation (which I wasn't privy to yet). From the moment we sat down at the table with him, his charm was on full blast, like a big ole teddy bear. He had me fooled in that moment. It wasn't until I saw him again at Monty's, a trendy spot, with an R&B group he was looking to manage, that I witnessed his intimidation tactics.

I tell you what—a fast glance around revealed he had nothing short of three or four straight-up killers surrounding that space where he was meeting with this group of young men, one of whom was a friend of mine. When I say "killers," I mean they weren't just muscle (there is a difference). They were strategically placed, not too close to warrant alarm, yet close enough to foreshadow what was to come if something shouldn't go Suge's way.

I watched Suge sit there calmly, a cigar stuck between his lips like he was Don Corleone, with a ring of threat around four young men who were no threat at all. That day I got to see that Suge didn't play fair. And when Eazy-E shared his experiences, I got a full understanding of Suge Knight's lethality. On the drive, it all came into view.

At Dannemora, I was on a last-resort mission to gently convince Pac that there was a way, other than signing with Suge, to get him out of jail. It was a tall order.

We talked calmly, like adults. He was in jail, and he wanted out. Period. And as Pac had been waiting for, a seeming comrade had come along to save him. But I couldn't ignore the alarm ringing in my head. Pac was about to release *Me Against the World*, which would include "Dear Mama" and debut at number 1 on the album charts, a feat never accomplished by an artist while in prison. By agreeing to sign with Death Row, Pac would gain his freedom after Suge arranged the now $1.4 million required for him to be released pending the appeal of his conviction. In return, Pac explained, "I will owe three albums. I'm going to make my first one a double album, which will count as two, and then make a third. Then I'm done."

Pac did his best to convince me he understood what he was getting into and that he had everything under control. But it all sounded too easy. "You're dancing with the devil, Pac."

Pac held his ground. "Suge's the only n-gga willing to get me out." The way he saw it, everybody else was fine to let him rot in prison.

I backed off, wary as I was. After all, I wasn't the one doing time, and I had no magic wand to make Pac's situation different. Plus, I knew Suge's promises would be too potent for anyone to intercede.

C all me Coco! Please, Jada, please, call me Coco. I'm legally changing my name" was how Maxine first announced her news. She was so sweet, with that childlike singsong Toronto accent of hers.

"Coco? No," I grumbled. "I'm not calling you Coco. Your mother named you Maxine, so that's what I'm calling you." Sometimes it was entertaining to get Max flustered, the way older siblings do with younger ones, except Max was older than I was. But in this moment, it wasn't so fun. Something was off.

Will, ever so gallant, piped in, "Okay, Coco it is." This just made Maxine/Coco love Will more than she already did.

All of this was charming, if a little eccentric, but Will and I didn't give it much thought. That was until March or so, not long after Eazy died, when I got a call from a neighbor while I was on set. My roommate was pacing around in front of the house, talking to herself, and banging on the front door, trying to get in.

The set was ten minutes from my house, so I rushed home. Maxine was naked except for a robe. "Max, did you lose your key, what happened?"

She seemed disoriented, out of it. "I got locked out. I don't know."

A few days later, I saw her wearing a short miniskirt, and if she moved in a certain way, it was clear she had no underwear on.

"Maxine . . . ?"

"Coco, please call me Coco!"

"Coco, you can't go out like that. You need to put on some boy shorts or something with that skirt. I can see your whole name and address."

"I'm fine! Don't make a big deal about everything, Jada!"

This wasn't the only time that happened. I'd cajole her into putting on shorts or changing her clothes, but she was increasingly manic. I thought maybe she was stressed out about her relationship or going through a rough patch. I couldn't figure it out. She then booked a job on location with a team connected to Judy Murdock, the makeup artist on *Jason's Lyric* who became my go-to for movies before she later worked with Will.

Something—an incident—happened on the set of the movie, and Judy was able to intervene. We wanted to get Maxine home to her mother, who could keep an eye on her. As soon as she got back to Toronto, Max received medical care in a hospital, and when the doctors thought she was well enough, she went to stay at her mother's house.

From everything we were told later, Maxine probably had a thyroid condition, which can set up a psychological imbalance if unchecked. All we could hope was that she would get better.

Throughout the summer, I talked to Maxine often. In the most heart-wrenching, pleading voice, she begged, "Please, Jada, I need to come back to L.A. Please!"

"Let's get you healthy first. As soon as you're better, you can come back."

"Jada! I'm fine! I promise you, please! I need to come back. That's where I belong. I miss L.A. so much."

I'd feel so guilty whenever we hung up, not being able to give her what she wanted. I missed her, but with her level of instability, I couldn't risk it. I felt terrible.

A few days after a brief conversation with Maxine, I got a call from Judy. Strangely, Will happened to be there with me at the time, which was rare for the middle of a day, because he was usually on set at that time for the last season of *Fresh Prince*.

Judy was upset but calm. She relayed that Maxine had jumped off her mother's balcony to her death, leaving behind only her shoes on the balcony floor.

My heart shattered. I couldn't form words. I couldn't breathe. It was too unbearable to allow myself to feel.

When I hung up, I looked at Will—who at that moment was lying on my bed next to where I'd been sitting—and said, "Maxine committed suicide." He was frozen.

I remember falling back, then rolling on top of him and us making love. It was primal, me hoping to shut out the pain. I knew better, but at least the reality of her death would be gone for these moments. I needed to feel anything other than the agony of this incomprehensible tragedy.

In the long run, the unbearable loss would catch up to me, surfacing over and over again, throwing me into sorrow I never knew how to express.

A memorial was planned, but I couldn't go. I needed to be alone and grieve by myself. In hindsight, I should have gone. There was a part of me that felt ashamed at the time, like it was my fault that Max/Coco had committed suicide. Would she have jumped if I had just let her come back to L.A.? In what was one of the saddest conversations of my life, I talked to Maxine's mother, who was inconsolable after losing her only child. Max's mom died about a year later. No doubt from a broken heart.

Again, not knowing how to grieve or how to memorialize my friend, I simply kept it moving and stuffed down the pain and guilt.

There are all kinds of loss that we don't stop long enough to mourn. Not just the loss of a loved one through death but the breakup of a friendship that soured or the absence of a parent who is unable to be present in your life or the void left in the aftermath of a divorce or separation. We are just not well equipped in our society to honor the life passages brought on by such losses.

I am haunted by a memory:

It's the first time I've seen Pac upon his release from prison—at a restaurant on La Cienega Boulevard. We're sitting together at a square table. By midafternoon, it's fairly empty.

Pac is looking fly in a suit, stylish but casual. It's a deep-navy electric blue with a slight sheen to it. I'm in a white dress of some kind. Since Pac's release, he's stepped up his style game. I love it.

Pac and I are meeting because once again he has a movie he wants us to do together. It's a crime story with a dark comedic edge, called *Gridlocked*, and I listen as he explains the script and the role he thinks I'd be good for. But there is a big old monster elephant in the room we aren't mentioning. Pac knows I'm not at all happy about his get-down since his release. His whole vibe has changed since his association with Suge. I can't make it all Suge's fault. Post jail, Pac's a little different (but who isn't after doing time?), and I believe he is allowing his bitterness, disappointment, and anger to be preyed on.

"I'm worried about you, Pac," I say, interrupting his flow.

This kicks off a hailstorm of rage as he leans across the table and into my face, aware, as I am, that we could be overheard if we don't keep our volume in check.

Pac makes it clear that I don't need to be worried about him, and that since I got all Hollywood, I've forgotten what it takes "to be a real n-gga out here."

"Where is all this going?" My genuine concern is his display of vengeance since he was shot and released from prison, and his participation in the steady brewing of the East Coast/West Coast beef. It's about to put Pac back in jail or worse.

He cuts me off. "I know what you think about me." He pauses for a beat. "I can see your thoughts in your dreams. I know what you're thinking. You can't fucking hide from me. You done gone all Hollywood, but that's cool. That's why I got my real patnahs out here."

I lean back across the table into Pac's face, trying my best to keep my voice down. "Who the fuck do you think you're talking to, Pac? Talk'n about I'm all Hollywood? You're being reckless." We are seething at each other with a calm intensity like two bulls in a staredown, fixing to charge.

"I don't even know who the fuck you are anymore," he says.

"Ditto, n-gga."

The disagreement gets more intense and goes back and forth. His gist is that I am no longer a real one, and mine is that he's mad because I'm not placating his bullshit. Pac's not having my pushback, and I'm not having his disrespect.

Next thing I knew, he was done talking, and so was I.

When I got up to walk toward the exit of the restaurant, I was so angry my legs were shaking. We didn't say goodbye to each other and went our separate ways.

As soon as I got in my car, I called my then manager, James Lassiter, who was Will's longtime friend and manager as well. In a torrent of tears, I exploded, "FUCK TUPAC! I DON'T WANT TO DO THAT STUPID MOVIE OR ANYTHING WITH HIM! I NEVER WANT TO TALK TO HIM AGAIN."

I tried to calm down, knowing, of course, I shouldn't be ranting to James. He was not built to take on my hysteria. All I could do was try to catch my breath. I couldn't believe that Pac and I had just had that exchange.

Then again, this kind of blowup between us was not new. The drill had always been that we would give each other the silent treatment. He was one of the few people on the planet with whom I could fight that harshly and still know there was no love lost between us. PISSED as I was, I knew, like always, that time would pass and we would say our apologies, hug it out, and we'd be back. But he was going to have to call me first this time, and I was not budging on that. He had been WAY OUT OF LINE.

So, let me say this: If you have a blowup with someone you really cherish, do not play the game of waiting for the other person to get wise.

A lmost a year passed. On September 8, 1996, Pac was shot in Las Vegas, and I was in Toronto shooting the movie Woo. I was on the set when I got a page from Afeni. I called her immediately.

As soon as she let me know what had happened, I told her, "I can shut the set down right now and come to you guys."

"It's okay. He's in a coma, but he's going to be all right." With no panic or alarm in her voice, Afeni continued to give me the rundown on his condition but kept assuring me that Pac was going to be fine. After surviving five bullets and everything else, he was considered invincible. That put me at ease, even though I did stop the shoot for the day.

I was scheduled to leave for New York soon—Will had planned an early birthday celebration for me with our families because he was promoting a movie out of the country and would be gone on the eighteenth. "Should I cancel the trip to New York, Fey?"

She suggested I fly out after the celebration, telling me, "He should be awake by then." She assured me that everybody was there, holding it down, including Pac's fiancée, Kidada.

Afeni didn't think for a moment that he could actually die. And neither did I. For the next five days, I checked in regularly with Afeni on Pac's condition and planned to head out to Vegas on the fourteenth whether he was awake or not.

On the night of the thirteenth, we were in our hotel room in New York as the events of the evening were winding down. Sheree called Will, and I overheard her on the phone, saying, "Pac just died."

I said to Will, "Hang up. She doesn't know what the fuck she's talking about. She's lying." I was pissed. How dare she spread a fucking terrible rumor like that? How dare she do that? Will, seeing how upset I was, told Sheree he would call her back.

Just then I got a knock on the door of my hotel room, and it was Fawn. As soon as I saw the frozen pain and sorrow on her face, I knew what Sheree had said was true.

My knees buckled. I nearly fell to the floor. My whole system crashed, and I lost my breath for a moment. I never once saw myself on this planet without him here, somewhere, on it. I felt a huge piece of love for me leave the world, a part of myself gone. In its place was rageful sadness.

Pac had been a mirror, a reflection of the best of myself, a tether. My heart felt ravaged, like a million stabbings every second.

My worst fear had come true. For too long, I drank the Kool-Aid and allowed the illusion of his invincibility to squander time. I hadn't spoken to him in damn near a year. I could not punish Pac's memory by thinking that he'd left this world in any way questioning how much I loved him. Because I know for a fact he did know. Yet I tortured myself thinking whether things might have been different if I had been strong enough to express my fears without judgment, to prevent my anger from blinding me to the fact that life is fragile. In the end, I don't think that would have made a difference. He made his choices, and he fulfilled the plan God laid out for him, but it would take me a very, very long time to accept that truth.

I'm glad I never made it to Vegas, though. I'm glad my last memory of Tupac is not an image of him in a coma. I'm glad I didn't have to share space with Suge as Pac was dying.

When I heard that Pac had been cremated, I was very upset and immediately believed Suge was the one behind that decision, which made me ask questions. I never heard Pac say that he wanted to be turned into ashes. Never.

Tupac Amaru Shakur had been murdered, and the first action was to burn his body into ashes? What if we needed his physical body for more evidence? Pac only ever talked about being buried in a casket. He spoke of it in his songs and told me of the morbid fantasies he had of his death, envisioning masses in the streets following his casket to his grave. In my mind, something wasn't right.

To make matters worse, at the private memorial Afeni chose to have in Jasmine's backyard, I answered the door, and it was Suge who delivered Pac's ashes into my very hands—in the cardboard box one is given by the crematorium. I'll never forget the slight smile in his eyes when he handed me that box, like: "There's your homie—homie."

Now, I could be putting twenty on ten because of the state I was in. Between Suge's smirk as he handed me those ashes and my assumptions about Suge's involvement in what happened to Tupac, I might have been putting a lot of color on the moment. But I tell you what, and I do myself no good to say it—I wanted him to pay. I never felt that intense need for revenge in me before, not even after being held at gunpoint.

Pac was dead, and Suge handed me his ashes in a little cardboard box like it was just another fuck'n day. No "I'm sorry for your loss." Noth'n. I felt helpless, and I hated myself for my helplessness. I hated that I had no way to get even, take revenge, confront Suge, find the joka who pulled the trigger, MAKE SOMEBODY FUCK'N PAY!

I hated the streets, I hated hip-hop and every fake-ass gangster act'n like they really on some gangster shit when, within only six months, we had two hip-hop giants dead, Pac and Biggie, and don't nobody know noth'n and ain't nobody try'n to do noth'n?

Fuck this bullshit and everybody in it.

For years to come, I would feel like I had let Pac down at the end. I had been able to show up for him for so many years, and at this most crucial time, I didn't know how to show up in a way that didn't rock the boat. It was complicated by the fact that there were people then who believed Suge had done right by Pac and his family. I knew different. Pac's life had been stolen, and as things unfolded, I would find that his trust had been betrayed as he was making moves to change the direction of his life.

There was a lot happening, and I felt I was putting a lot at risk if I kept involving myself in Pac's "matters." I knew eventually, with my continued involvement, it was gonna pull Will in. And I just could not jeopardize that.

Pac had done his best to keep me away from the danger of his world; he would not want this moment to be any different. I knew that for certain. I swallowed my pride and did the most unfathomable thing—and walked away. Thank goodness Afeni eventually put on her cape and went to war to expose how Pac had been financially exploited during his Death Row tenure. And that wasn't the half of it.

As time passed, it healed nothing. I didn't even know how to grieve Pac. So I stuffed my rage, my pain, and my shame into a forgotten place within me. And I never again felt the same love for hip-hop or the streets. From then on, it was all dead to me.

When our grief cannot be spoken, it falls into the shadow and re-arises in us as symptoms. So many of us are depressed, anxious and lonely.

—FRANCIS WELLER, *THE WILD EDGE OF SORROW*

It's not often that I see grief addressed directly, or addressed at all, when it comes to spiritual recovery and emotional sobriety. Too many of us become stuck in grief because we don't understand the need to grieve, and culturally, we are not taught HOW to grieve.

———

I feared my grief. My hope was that time and staying busy would make all the pain of loss go away. The accumulation of unresolved grief collects in the body and eventually feeds into our depressive states, into our anger, shame, and heartbreak.

———

Maturity teaches us to respect grief. The fact that life is full of losses of many kinds can be a very difficult reality to accept and embrace. But if we have the courage to make friends with the intense feelings that come with the mourning process, we give ourselves permission to be vulnerable.

———

For many of us, it's daunting to remove our armor and experience our vulnerability. But if we can't respect that place in ourselves or in others, we can't touch our grief, and we won't make safe space for others to touch theirs. It's in the respect and care for vulnerability that we can find intimacy with ourselves and others and learn to hold space with love for intense emotions like grief.

———

Are there any losses in your life that you have not given yourself permission to mourn? Do you need to know how to grieve? If so, check out the book by Francis Weller, *The Wild Edge of Sorrow*, as a start.

———

A note to those who have lost someone special—you'll never get over it, so stop looking for that moment. We just learn to accept and cope with the fact that they are no longer here, and place them upon an altar in our heart, and celebrate them there.

CHAPTER 13

The Reluctant Bride

As our families got to know each other in the beginning of our courtship—which we were keeping quiet—Will's grandmother Gigi got word from Will's sister Ellen that her grandson was dating someone new.

Gigi picked up the phone and said to Will, "Oh, so we keep'n secrets from each other now, loverboy?" Or words to that effect.

Will assured his grandmother that he wasn't trying to keep secrets, that yes, he and I were dating, and that we could all meet soon. The next thing I knew, Will had arranged to fly Gigi out to California within days, so that proper introductions could be made.

Before I arrived at Will's house at the appointed hour, he decided to have Gigi watch *Jason's Lyric*. Which, by the way, included a very naked sex scene in the woods (where I had a body double, as I adamantly didn't do nudity). Just imagine, I'm meeting my new boyfriend's beloved grandmother for the first time, and I walk in and she's sitting there on the couch, arms folded, shaking her head. She goes on to say that back in her day, it was different, her point being: "I don't know why young people feel like they gotta take their clothes off to make movies."

Mortified, I smile, hug her as a greeting, and then gesture to Will to join me in the back bedroom as I say to his grandmother, "Excuse us a minute, Gigi." I couldn't believe he pulled a prank like that, and I was pissed: "Why would you EVER do that to me? What the fuck are you thinking?"

"Babe, I promise you. This is gonna be funny later."

"It isn't funny. That's your grandmother. Do you see how she's looking at me?"

With that, I mustered all my diplomatic skills—with some acting thrown in—and went back out to Gigi, laughing like it was nothing.

To this day, Will and I are still debating whether it was funny or not. It was, however, a bonding experience for Gigi and me. From then on, I didn't have to put on any airs. I could just be myself, because I didn't have anything to hide. Literally. Eventually, for the record, I did bring up the nude scene, telling her, "Gigi, you know, that wasn't actually me on the screen," after which she just looked at me and lovingly shooed me away with her hand.

Being close to Gigi gave me all kinds of Marion vibes. Gigi was an absolute joy for me to be around, and I loved absorbing her seasoned grandmother presence. Gigi always said exactly what was on her mind—my favorite characteristic of hers.

During a subsequent visit to see us in California, while I was working on *Set It Off*, cast as a female bank robber, I was leaving for work one day when Gigi frowned and blurted out, "You look a mess. You always dress like an orphan." Before I could respond, Gigi continued, "You're a nice-looking girl, put some better clothes on."

I cracked up laughing and tried to explain, "Gigi, I'm going to work. I'm going to the set. I don't need to dress nice for that. I'm going to be putting on my character's clothes when I get there." She grudgingly accepted my explanation, but I knew she still didn't approve.

I loved how Gigi loved Will. She was not caught up in any of the rah-rah of her grandson's Hollywood success. She wanted him to stay humble, yoked to God, and to abide by Christ's teaching. When that was in place, she applauded.

We made frequent visits to see Will's family in Philly and my family in Baltimore. After growing up surrounded by the matriarchs of my own family, getting to know the matriarchs of Will's life came with ease. I had a deep affinity for Will's mother, Miss Carolyn, aka Mom-Mom. She was real, solid, and strong. I greatly admired her grace,

considering what she'd come through in her life, and how, despite a
challenging marriage to Will Sr., aka Daddio, and a subsequent divorce, she respected Will's desire to have both parents present for important events and holiday celebrations. A school board member and
activist, she was passionate about education. Mom-Mom was always
a beautiful example of what faith, strength, and patience could gift in
this human experience.

As for my mother and Will, she did a full 180 degrees on him—
from first telling me not to talk to him because he was married at the
time (a good call) and advising we not date (because he was divorced
with a child and that would be complex) to now declaring him the
most wonderful guy on the planet. All of a sudden, Will had her in
constant giggle fits. He could do no wrong. She just loved him, and
when it came to having fun, they were two peas in a pod.

The fact that our families embraced our relationship and embraced one another was a blessing in so many ways. It's not always a
guarantee that families get along, and since family was important to
us both, this was a shared core value that gave us a solid foundation
not to be taken for granted.

T he timing for us continued to be complicated. It wasn't only
that Will had not fully processed his divorce and that I
hadn't recovered from either my breakdown or the wave of
recent losses. Our careers were expanding rapidly. I was busier than
ever, and Will had started to become a full-fledged leading man in
films—*Bad Boys* had just been released, and he landed *Independence
Day* soon after we began dating.

Even though we had work to do on ourselves, Will proved to me
that I could count on him amid a lot of tragedy. He offered me a safe
space. We also had an undeniable chemistry that was beyond, and he
had a way of helping me lighten up. My Virgo mind was often very

serious and contemplative. Will, a Libra, would balance that with his ability to play and be silly all the time. His silliness is truly world-class. It would drive me crazy sometimes, but when he got me, it was refreshing, like oxygen—an escape from this heavy time in my life.

One evening we were getting ready to go out, and I'd gotten out of the shower, and Will noticed that I had missed quite a few bikini-waxing appointments. Well, let me be honest, I had stopped going. "You see, you're a guy, so you don't understand the pain of it all." I went on and on. While I made my case, Will was rummaging around in my closet. Somehow he found my black knit hat with short little black dreads all over it.

I had sat down on the bed to put lotion on my feet when I looked up at Will. There he stood in his briefs, hiked up into a Brazilian-bikini fit, with curly dreads from my hat sticking out like ungroomed pubic hair on all sides in a forest-sized bush.

"So, you okay looking like this?" Will asked as he pointed to what he saw from his point of view.

To this day, I have never been able to unsee him like that. For some reason, it's when Will makes fun of me with that level of creativity that I find his comedy unparalleled.

That was clearly his wheelhouse. And it was disarming and frustrating if I wanted to be mad at him, because he could always manage to pull out a joke. Sometimes I refused to laugh, hoping he would see that he had chosen an inappropriate moment to try to be funny. This would prove a fruitless effort.

Humor was an elixir he knew how to pour. He used his brew of intelligence to similar effect. Part of our dance of seduction was a tango based on a shared love of learning that led to intellectual banter that was hot. We could go toe to toe from sunup to sundown, talking and debating about all kinds of subjects. We would find ourselves reading the same book in order to get the great debates going. Whether it was *The Tao of Physics* or *A History of God,* we loved keeping each other on game. There is no one on this planet who can offer my mind better conversation than Will. We literally can and do talk for hours.

First and foremost, we established a friendship that was at the center of our relationship. But no relationship is perfect, and the pace of our lives left little room for your typical honeymoon period. We were also plowing into a big life, and neither one of us had the emotional maturity to handle it. Yet the challenges created a bond that sat outside of romanticism because things got too real too soon and we had to figure out how to navigate it together. And in some ways, I clung to romanticism in my desire for Will to be my Savior Prince. A classic setup for us both.

As a case in point, there was an incident that took place one afternoon a short while after I more or less moved into Will's house in Westlake (though I kept my place in Studio City) along with my dogs. The pack had expanded to include two new Rottweiler puppies gifted to Will by Jay Leno.

In addition to my daily routine with the dogs, Cesar and I met regularly, and he'd bring along his pack, which included his assistant teacher, Daddy, the most special pit bull I've ever met. We'd then work in a serious hike all together.

On this particular day, we were far out in some remote hills. Cesar came upon a section of the trail where he remembered there was a natural source of water nearby. Instead of staying on the trail, he decided to go charging down a really steep hill with all the dogs. I went charging down after them, practically flying. Partway down, I lost my footing and rolled my right ankle, causing me to fall back on my butt and sending a sharp pain through my foot and leg.

By then Cesar and the dogs were out of earshot and nowhere in sight. My ankle was way too painful for me to stand on and get down the hill. Instead, I rolled onto my stomach and used the base of nearby bushes to help pull me back to the trail.

Before long, Cesar and the dogs returned, and I leaned on his shoulder, slowly limping back to the parking lot to drive myself home.

When I walked in the house, I found Will watching television. I sat down nearby to remove my hiking boot. The boot had provided compression to the ankle and acted as a splint, keeping the swelling in check. After I removed the boot, my whole ankle instantly blew up like a balloon. It was dark purple and hurt like hell.

Given my habit to play down anything painful, I tried to white-knuckle it out of reflex, though I ran it by Will. "Can you take a look? I think I might need to go to the hospital."

He took a quick glance and nodded. "You'll be all right." Then he went back to watching TV.

Thinking he was probably right, I decided to ice my ankle and wait until the morning for the swelling to go down. Nope. The next morning my ankle looked worse, and it hurt really, really bad. When I went to Will and asked him to take me to the doctor, he had a conflict and wasn't able to do it. Instead, I called Duane. He took me. Sure enough, my ankle was broken. The doctor put me in a cast and sent me home.

The broken-ankle moment was pivotal. More than I realized at the time. Neither Will nor I was able to recognize the seriousness of the injury. My stance (and his) was *If I'm not crying in dire pain, I must be fine*. This attitude came from our upbringings. We were both hardened because of how we grew up, dealing with things far more extreme than a broken ankle. Neither one of us had been taught to slow down and take a good look when hurts came up. When they did come up, the mantra was *Ignore it and keep it moving*.

Ignoring hurts in yourself or your loved one, by the way, can come back to create far worse pain. If you don't learn that lesson early, it's much harder to learn later.

My misstep was being invested in the image of being strong and unbreakable. Will liked that. My strength was the comfort pocket. Yes, I was strong and fragile all at once—except I had no idea how to express the parts of me that needed a hug, needed to feel cared for and that I mattered.

Divorce, as I learned, is rarely amicable. It's brutal, no matter how much two people intend otherwise. Will internalized a lot of what he was going through. To his credit, he tried to the best of his ability to be a loving presence for his son, Trey, who was a toddler when his parents separated.

As a child, Trey was brilliant, energetic, and confident, with an irresistible sweetness. The first time I got to spend an afternoon with Trey, my focus was on creating an exciting, memorable outing. Where to? I thought and thought. Then it hit me—a candy store!

I mean, what kid doesn't like candy? It was not just any store. This was a candy wonderland, with every classic and new candy ever made, like Halloween on steroids. Trey's eyes were big, he was so happy, I let him pick out all the candy he wanted, and he went for a variety.

The minute we got back into the car, I said it was okay for him to eat some of his candy, and Trey went for it. By the time we got back to the house, he was bouncing off the walls, jumping all over the couch, dashing through the house in circles. He was a completely different child.

I stood in the middle of his zooming and thought, *Oh my God, what do I do? What do I do? He is literally zipping around the house like the Road Runner.* I called my mother—a nurse—to ask for advice. "Put him in the tub" was her immediate response.

So I put Trey in the bathtub, assuming my mother's suggestion would work and the warm water would calm him down. Nope, Trey was going as berserk as before. In the tub.

Finally, Sheree called to check in, and I reported what was happening and explained that he had eaten a bunch of candy. She interrupted and said, all matter-of-fact, "Oh no, you can't give him all that sugar. It makes him super hyper."

I'm like: *Oh, snap!* Lesson learned. He eventually got the sugar out of his system and crashed into sleep. I never made the mistake again, but I felt pretty embarrassed—the first time I take Trey out, I get him on a sugar freaking high that's beyond anything I've ever seen or even heard of.

Needless to say, it was also a bonding experience. Not just for me and Trey but for Will and me, too. Apparently, I still had a lot to learn about how to care for children.

I'm pregnant."

Will and I are in bed in a rented villa in Cabo San Lucas. It's late summer 1997. I am twenty-five years old, soon to turn twenty-six, and Will and I have flown down to Mexico as a reprieve from work. We are both breathing hard, in post-passion, and I am feeling something that I've never felt before, and it's TERRIFYING.

Freeze the frame right there. Let's rewind to several months earlier.

In February or March, Will and I were hitting our two-year mark, and he was out of town working. Ever since I'd started dating Will, we'd enjoyed drinking together, so I was back to drinking a lot. I wrote it off as part of our means of having fun. But one day I was given a reality check about how much was too much.

I had been hanging with my girlfriend Sidra at Will's house while he was away doing film promotion. We were drinking white wine and shared a bottle. Once she took off, I finished off a second on my own. I was going to get a third bottle when I stopped in my tracks. This thought popped into my head: *I'm here drinking by myself in the middle of the afternoon because I'm bored and lonely. Jada, you've got a problem.*

In that moment, I went cold turkey. No more drinking. For the most part, being sober felt good—clearer, more robust, more in tune with my body. I would have instances of seriously craving a drink, but they would subside.

This happened to coincide with my realization that the birth control I'd been taking—the depo shot—had a side effect of depression. When the huge mood swings started, I knew it was time to switch to a different method of birth control. Thinking I was protected after my last shot, I wasn't concerned. As I wasn't menstruating, I assumed I wasn't ovulating, either. That was correct. Most of the time.

My mother, an expert on birth control from her years as an ob-gyn nurse, warned me, "Don't fuck around, Jada."

How do you know that you have just gotten pregnant in the second when it happens? The best way to describe it is, if you've ever been into a bank vault, you know there is a lock that looks like a big round steering wheel, and when you turn it, it locks with a CLICK.

That's what it felt like in my womb.

This is what I explain to Will after he gives me a skeptical look. And I repeat, "I'm pregnant."

He sits up. He's wearing an expression that says, *You must be crazy.* He starts laughing. "Jump up and down," he suggests. "Stand on your head."

I am too devastated to respond.

He calls Duane to continue his jokes about me believing I'm pregnant before the little ones have even stopped swimming. While he and Duane are joking, I'm crying. All night long, I can't stop crying. I am *that* sure I'm pregnant. My inner monologue is so loud, I'm sure Will can hear it: *What the fuck have I just done?*

Technically, *we've* just done it. But being pregnant changes everything. It's not that I haven't imagined motherhood and lovingly bringing a child into the world. It's just that I wanted to plan first.

Two weeks later, I went and bought ten pregnancy tests. This was not to be excessive. It was scientific. Fawn came over to Will's house. I set her up with five tests and myself with five tests. Every single test Fawn took was negative. Every single test I took was positive.

Conclusion: I AM PREGNANT!

Without hesitation, I drove to the set where Will was filming *Men in Black,* marched into his trailer with my five tests, and lined them all up for him to see. He could clearly see that I was indeed pregnant and indeed *right*. Unlike the night in Cabo, he was not joking now.

Not blinking an eye, he looked at me and calmly said, "It's gonna be all right."

The next call was to my mother, who listened quietly as I told her that Will and I were going to figure it out. Then she voiced what needed to happen. From some ancient place within her, Adrienne spoke to me with deep concern. This was as the daughter of a woman who at thirteen had borne a child she had to give up. This was as a woman encouraged to marry a violent addict rather than bear the shame of conceiving a child as an unwed seventeen-year-old. My mother decreed, "Jada, you have to get married!"

Adding to my confusion and fear was the onset of morning sickness. Or all-day sickness. I was prepping for a role in a movie called *Return to Paradise* with Vince Vaughn and the late Anne Heche. I'm sure I came across as distant or chilly because I could barely stand straight longer than ten minutes without feeling like I needed to throw up. After a scene, Vince made a comment along the lines of "Aren't you a peach?"

I couldn't blame him. I couldn't tell anyone I was pregnant . . . except Anne, who was my homegirl at the time. I told her in confidence, so she got it.

Frankly, I felt too lousy to worry about what other people were thinking of me right then. My big predicament was being too scared to get married and just as scared not to get married. I was stuck.

My trepidation had nothing to do with Will—it had everything to do with my long-held belief that marriage wasn't for me. Let's face it, my mother had two failed marriages already (and wouldn't settle down until marriage number four). And although both sets of grandparents stayed married for the entirety of their adult lives, their examples didn't convince me that what had worked for them would work for me.

The one thing I was interested in was the level of devotion I witnessed with Marion and Gilbert, as well as with Shirley and Grant. Even with my desire to love and be loved in that way, I'd been in the world enough to know how husbands and wives take each other for granted—far more than loving and appreciating each other. I did not want that. And I definitely wasn't ready to make a lifelong commitment under a spiritual contract with God. This was a shoo-in to fuck up.

But I had always thought I'd have a child one day. It wasn't unthinkable that I could be a single mom or that I could have a close male friend coparent with me. Why not? I had my own career, my own money. I could be a single parent if that's what I decided to do. These beliefs were as powerful to me as any fantasies of walking down the aisle in a white dress might be to someone else. Of course, all of this was hypothetical. Until it wasn't.

And I didn't feel ready. But it was becoming clear, now that I was pregnant, that with or without a piece of paper making Will my husband, he was the father of my child, and that was a sort of "till death do us part," anyway.

Once I accepted that this tiny being inside me was having her or his way, and had chosen us as parents, I was able to listen to Will when he came to my side as I was resting on the chaise lounge I had put in his bedroom—just like Marion's. As I was lying there, trying to ease my all-day pregnancy sickness, Will leaned in and proposed by saying there was no way I was going to have a baby without him marrying me.

All I could do was cry. His proposal was beautiful and sincere, but I was scared as hell.

The next day, I went to Harry Winston in Beverly Hills and bought my ring, a nice-sized pear-shaped diamond set in a platinum band. By buying my own ring, I took some measure of control and sent the message to myself: *All right, get with the program.* A decade later, Will would completely outdo himself and buy me a ten-carat Graff diamond ring. But in this moment, I had to move quickly to make it all real and concrete for my psyche. The ring was a statement that said to my fear: *Get used to this now.*

My hard line, though, was that there would be no big, fancy, traditional wedding. All I wanted was for me and Will to meet on a mountaintop, just the two of us and someone to officiate the ceremony as we exchanged vows we had written under the power of the Universal Source that would be guiding this marriage along the way. Most important was to fortify our spiritual union.

Years later, after watching the three-day challenge on *Amazing Race,* I would concoct a more realistic idea for a marriage rite. What better preparation for couples than being thrown together in the wilds of the jungle? They would either discover they could problem-solve as a partnership and overcome really challenging adversity or realize they weren't built to run the race together. If you cross that finish line and look at each other after surviving in the shit together and still want to get married, go ahead and put on your white dress and call in your bridesmaids. 'Cause the jungle test is the ultimate marriage gauntlet.

At the time, the mountaintop wedding was all I had. Will, as always, was hyper-focused on work and wasn't really paying attention to the wedding-to-be-or-not-to-be. He usually preferred to eventize special occasions, but he wasn't voicing any opinions quite yet.

When I explained all of this to my mother, she was not having the mountaintop. Distraught, she said, "Jada, you are my only child. You have to have a wedding."

This was a bridge too far. "I don't want a wedding. I need to concentrate on what I'm about to get into."

"You are my only daughter."

Though I tried to see it from her perspective, I didn't have the bandwidth. Putting on a wedding was hugely distracting when I felt we should be focusing on who we needed to be and what was needed for a successful marriage. I was sick, I was scared, and I didn't have the energy or desire to plan a wedding to-do.

But leave it to Adrienne to plead her case to Will. After she cried her eyes out on the phone, Will took her side, assuring her we would indeed have a wedding after all. Even though he didn't need a big wedding, he did believe it was important to have a ceremony that would include family and close friends.

When I called my mother, she couldn't contain her excitement about her conversation with Will. All I could say was "You want a wedding, you do it." And she did, gladly.

Will and I chose the date, December 31—New Year's Eve—and plans were put in place for a small, intimate gathering in Baltimore, where Will was filming *Enemy of the State*. In order to avoid an on-slaught of media, details were kept under wraps. Our plan was to notify the guests of the location on the day before the wedding. My last living grandparent, Grandmother Shirley, was convinced we were doing this just to confuse her so she wouldn't come.

Now that I was going to become Mrs. Smith, Will and I had several conversations about me kicking off Pinkett as part of my last name. People had suggested that before, including my mother, who told me early in my career, "You should go by Jada Koren."

In both instances, I refused, because I wanted to honor my grandfather Grant Pinkett, the first man in my life who was devoted to me. I wanted the world to know I had been part of his legacy of love that had helped me get to where I was now. Jada Pinkett Smith had a ring to it. It was a keeper.

As the day approached, my father made it clear that he wanted to come. I made it clear that I didn't want Robsol there. This may have seemed harsh, but it was all too much.

Will heard me out.

"So, let me get this straight," I began. "He gets to decide not to pay child support ever. To hardly keep in contact with me growing up. To decide when and how he wants to be in my life. But now he wants to be at my wedding?"

Will simply said that I would regret the decision in the future if

I didn't have Robsol come. I knew he was right, but I needed to be heard. Underneath it all, I was more upset than anything that two of the people I most wanted there—Pac and Maxine—would be absent. It seemed cruel that they couldn't come and my father would get to show up. But at this point, I had to let it go and surrender to the powers who were in charge, Adrienne and Will.

That is, until the day when Will and I were in Philly for the weekend visiting Mom-Mom. Will asked me to join him in the backyard. This was winter, and the leaves of the trees were gone for the season. It was a cold day, but the brisk air felt good as I fought waves of nausea.

Will began, "You know, my team is thinking that I should get a prenup." This made sense, as he was freshly divorced and in the midst of paying alimony and child support, while also paying off a big tax debt.

I paused and looked at Will. "Well, do you think we should get a prenup?"

"I don't know," he answered simply and honestly. "What do you think?"

"I think that if you don't trust me and you need to think about our breakup before we even get married, maybe we shouldn't get married. If we're going into this marriage with the possibility that divorce could happen, then I don't think we should do this." Will didn't say anything, so I continued, "I'm not going to start the end of our marriage in the beginning."

Will agreed without hesitation and went back into the house.

And that was that.

It was within that exchange that a deep commitment was made—almost like we were making an inherent promise to each other even before we got to the altar. It was as if he was saying in that moment, "I trust you." And I was saying, "I love you enough that no matter what happens, we are going to work through it, whatever inevitable challenges come up, and for better or worse, we are in this for the long haul."

Our promise was a holy one, made without the intoxication of the fairy tale of a wedding ceremony. It was two people sitting down and being real and clear-eyed with each other, swearing an oath in front of God. In the end, I got the mountaintop moment I wanted while he and Adrienne got their wedding shebang. Everybody won.

In years to come, it would be this conversation that would carry major significance for me, because no matter what, I would find it impossible to go back on my word, given to him in that very sacred moment.

Everything we would have, we would build together. That was a given from then on until this day. Without that agreement, divorce might have been a reality, but with it, we have saved ourselves from irrevocable strife on more than a few occasions.

T*he wedding was held at the* beautiful setting of the Cloisters in Baltimore, which reminded me of a castle with its old-world enchantment. We had about eighty close friends and family. My dress was cream velvet, just like the dress Grandmother Marion wore for her winter wedding. Will wore a cream-colored suit that, like my dress, was custom-made by the designer Badgley Mischka. I did not have bridesmaids, but Fawn, my mother, and Aunt Karen also wore Badgley Mischka dresses.

Other than all the media attention and hoopla, it was a very simple, down-home wedding. Adrienne was beaming with pride at her accomplishment of being Baltimore's premier wedding planner. She was joined by the rest of my close family members, as well as my Baltimore homegirls, along with Lyte and Jasmine Guy, who had flown in. On hand were Will's entire family and his longtime friends from Philly, along with his *Fresh Prince* castmates.

As shotgun weddings go, it was lovely, but we dispensed with all the formalities. Once the ceremony began, Will and I decided to walk down the aisle hand in hand toward Aunt Karen's pastor, Rev. Dr. Marvis May from Macedonia Baptist Church, whom we had met a few days before.

A group Will was managing at the time, Tra-Knox, sang the Jodeci song "Forever My Lady"—a cappella, no less—and Will's friend Charlie Mack swore he was going to sing "She's Your Queen" from *Coming to America* when they were done. That never happened, but our wedding was thoroughly hood, which I loved.

For the most part, I had gone with the flow of the day, but as soon as we got halfway down the aisle, I was overtaken by emotion and couldn't stop crying. Straight-up bawling. I was happy and sad, hopeful and scared, triumphant and uncertain. But what I knew was that I was going to give this marriage my best, and no matter what, I was going to give my child the opportunity to have the father I'd never had.

After our vows, we all partied together and brought the New Year in on a new beginning, and that's just what it felt like—a new slate. As soon as I said "I do" and we were officially husband and wife, something instantly changed.

Will was now my everything. My heart was completely surrendered. Hearing myself referred to as Mrs. Smith was surreal, and yet it was a symbol I could finally embrace as part of my new life.

I looked at my family and friends and saw all the love surrounding us. I grabbed Trey's little precious self so he could cut our wedding cake with us. I realized that my responsibility to him was even greater now. He was no longer my boyfriend's son, he was my bonus son, and that's exactly how I saw him—as a bonus.

There was a lifting of heaviness I had been carrying for so long.

It felt like something old had died, and something new within me came in. I felt at ease. It was almost like I had been standing on a cliff with all the anticipation of what the fall was going to be like. Now that I'd taken the leap, I felt as though I'd landed unscathed. My concerns were behind me and there was a beautiful future ahead of me with the opportunity to create the family I'd never had.

Done is better than perfect.
—SHERYL SANDBERG

You want to know why there is no such thing as being ready most of the time? Because you can never really know what you signed up for before you dive into the experience. There will ALWAYS be surprises. Which is why it's a great gift when we learn to be adaptable and flexible. Life never fails to throw curveballs.

————

You know what else? Sometimes the Great Supreme has a plan that is outside of the plan we have devised for ourselves. The Great Supreme makes no mistakes and often will bring situations our way for which we need to step up our game to meet the challenge. The trial is created to work in our favor to help us to find the giants within. Trust that even if you are not ready today, it is in having the courage to go for it anyway that you will meet your own strengths.

————

Is there any circumstance in your life you don't feel ready for? Can you let go of your need for things to be perfect before you leap? What different attitude could you adopt to be more ready for the lessons ahead? Write it down or record yourself talking it out.

————

Take the dive. It's rarely what you expect—but it could be better.

PART III

RIDE-OR-DIE

CHAPTER 14

Little Gurus

My kids, *at every stage of* their growth, have loved me as the best of myself and the worst of myself without a moment's hesitation. Not flinching, not batting an eye. They are the most powerful teachers of my heart. I do not call them little gurus lightly.

Trey—so nicknamed because he is the third in the lineage of Willard Carroll Smiths—planted the seeds for my understanding of what it means to nurture a child's individuality.

From our first meetings, I felt deeply connected to Trey and became attached to him quickly. Once Will and I got married, I kept my pledge that if I was going to be the loving bonus mom to Trey that he deserved, it was time to get past any resentments and misunderstandings that existed between Sheree and me. I could not proclaim to love Trey without embracing his mother.

In the early days of my relationship with Will, there was no tutorial for how the ex and the new partner should get along. It makes no difference who wanted the divorce in the first place, because nobody likes the idea that they've been replaced. It can be all the more prickly when the new partner is playing guardian to your child at times. That can be awful. Now, for my part, being the new partner didn't give me the sense of security that Sheree might have felt I had. In my mind, Sheree would always be Will's first wife and the mother of his first son—experiences I would never share with him—and at times, that made me feel like the alternate. The runner-up.

There was one instance early on when Sheree called to talk to

Trey and I answered. Evidently, she wasn't happy about having to go through me to talk to her son and didn't hide the fact that she was annoyed.

"I don't really appreciate your tone," I said.

She couldn't have cared less.

So I hung up on her.

Being the spitfire she can be, Sheree called right back. Not mincing words, she said, "Bitch, you livin' in the house *I* picked out."

And being the spitfire I can be, I replied calmly, "Well, it's *my* house now."

At one point, I was given a report from the mother of a friend of Trey's that he had misbehaved during a playdate. Thinking I was doing the right thing because Sheree was his mother, I brought the incident up with her, saying, "We all need to sit down and discuss his behavior."

She dismissed me in a heartbeat, saying, "Get his daddy, please." In other words, *Stay out of this.*

Sheree spoke to Will and made it clear that she didn't appreciate me overstepping my bounds. Something I have always loved about Will is his level of respect for motherhood and the roles we play in our children's lives. In this instance, he deferred to Sheree entirely and doubled down on her stance, telling me I was out of line.

Afterward, I had no problem going to Sheree to apologize in person. Sheree and Will were right.

After Will and I were married, and as I drew closer to our baby's due date, I felt it was important to get past any perceived rivalry between Sheree and me. Will and I were committed to building a blended family, and for that to be successful, Sheree had to be part of that equation. Will and Sheree shared custody of Trey, and like many children of divorced parents, Trey split his time between the two households. That can be hard enough, but the toughest days are birthdays, holidays, and other special occasions. We really wanted him to be with everyone he loved for all the celebrations—including his future siblings. I didn't want him to miss out on the wholeness of family. Thinking ahead, I didn't want him to refer to his siblings as half or as anything other than *That's my little brother/sister.*

With this in mind, I decided to reach out to Sheree. By this point, we could act cordial with each other, though there was boiling water behind our smiles.

"You think we can get together and talk over lunch?" was the gist of what I asked Sheree, and she immediately agreed.

When we sat down at a spot she suggested, nothing too trendy or fancy, we started out with a bit of small talk—about how I was feeling as an expectant mom. Then I broke the ice.

"Look, I know it may take work, but I want Trey to feel, no matter what, we're all family, including you and me."

Sheree, without hesitation, fully agreed.

She had been trying in her own way, too. After the first time Trey met me, which was really difficult for her at the time (as I later learned), she asked Trey, "What did you think of Miss Jada?" and he answered, "I really liked her, Mommy." Trey had wanted to get me a present, in fact. All I knew was that a short time later, Sheree presented me with a candle and a thoughtful note.

I was touched. The solution was there all along. We both wanted the same thing for Trey—the loving, harmonious familial experience that neither one of us had known in childhood. Both of us came from a broken home and were raised by a single mother. We harbored simi-lar wounds. Our only obstacle was setting aside our egos in moments when we might act territorial, jealous, or even unkind.

Sheree had one request: "All I ask is that you love my son and treat him well."

"You'll never have to worry about that," I assured her, relieved that we were finding alignment.

We slowly became not exactly *friends* but allies, and much later, bonus sisters. In the process of making peace with Sheree, I received the gift of getting to know her mother, Pat, Trey's devoted grandmother. Pat and Trey were two peas in a pod, and because she was with him so often, that meant she and I got to spend a lot of time together. Pat embraced Trey's siblings once they were born, as her bonus grandkids. We called her Sugar Mama because she gave the kids as much candy as they wanted, even when they weren't supposed to have it.

Those early celebrations with all the parts of our extended blended family weren't stress-free. Sheree and I stuck it out, but believe me, there were plenty of times when we would have rather not spent holidays together. Before this passage, I'd never understood the idea that love requires a conscious choice. Sheree and I had to choose to love each other and learn how to do it. Without Trey as our common interest, the gift of that lesson would have eluded us both.

F rom the moment I met little Trey—whom I nicknamed "Noodle" because of his lanky limbs that reminded me of spaghetti—he had an enviable closet full of clean new sneakers. You have to understand that for those of us who grew up in the Black community with an aspiration to come up, a closet full of pristine tennis shoes, whether you are six, sixteen, or fifty, is a big deal. Well, it was a big deal to his mother and to me. Sheree kept Trey laced, and I kept that trend, too, making sure he had the flyest of the fly . . . because that's just how we do.

Trey had different ideas.

One day when he was about four or five, he had a friend over, and as I popped my head into Trey's room, I overheard his friend say, "Trey, you have really cool shoes."

Not missing a beat and not looking up from the paper racetrack he was building, Trey answered, "You can have 'em."

Trey had a habit of giving his stuff to others—toys, clothes, shoes, etc. The only thing that he wouldn't part with was whatever video game he was into at the time, and his game system, of course. I loved that about him—but giving away all of his sneakers? A short time later, I peeped into the room, and sure enough, his friend had begun to collect the shoes from Trey's closet.

Keeping everything light, I asked Trey to come into the hall for a second. Out of earshot of his friend, I said to Trey, "Are you giving away all your shoes?"

"Yeah," he said, "I don't need 'em."

"But they're your shoes, you know? We bought them for you."

"Yeah, but they're mine, right? They belong to me."

My first thought was *Well, he's right there.* What could I say other than "Yes, they're your shoes."

"I don't need 'em, and I want him to have 'em."

A bit ruffled, I asked, "Well, Trey, what are you going to wear?"

He kicked up his foot and showed me the shoes on his feet. "These." With that, my little Noodle bounced back into his room and continued his project.

Trey was not only brilliant, I had never witnessed a child with his level of concentration and attention to detail when he was engaged with an activity of interest, like creating full-scale handmade paper models of racetracks and cars. He would sit quietly for hours on a mission to finish his masterpiece made with paper, scissors, and tape, until he'd call for me to see the finished product, proud and beaming. He had such a unique mind for someone so young, and I was in awe of it. His level of attentiveness, application, and passion would inspire how I educated his siblings in the future.

But it was his generosity that taught me something very important. A closet full of tennis shoes was not what made him happy. Giving his shoes to a friend who wanted them did.

The more I looked at this, the clearer it became that I put too much emphasis on material belongings to give me value. In part, this was because they were a badge of status for those of us who grew up in an environment where the ability to acquire a large quantity of the finer things in life—whether shoes, bags, clothes, jewelry, or even food—seemed so out of reach. Wanting to have every desired cereal box in my cabinet at once and never feel any lack was my baggage, not Trey's. My lesson was to let that go and help Trey develop his own sense of values around his possessions.

To this day, whenever I see Trey's closet, he has only the bare minimum—which is consistent with a mantra of *I acquire only that which I need.* It's a lesson I'm still trying to practice.

That was the last time I ever talked to him about not giving his things away. Instead, we developed an agreement about certain items that Trey would really need—like a good suit for special occasions. In those cases, I'd say, "Trey, I'm putting this suit and these dress shoes in your closet for you to use, but they are items that belong to me. Is that okay?"

This was a method of understanding we developed that Trey and I both could rock with. But most always, whatever we gave him, I'd make a point of emphasizing "This is yours," so he felt the freedom to make his own choice to keep it or not.

Trey reminded me that kids are not extensions of their parents. They are their own beings, with their own values, strengths, and sensitivities. Trey had been the only child for a while, so as my due date approached, Will and I made a conscious effort to find ways for Trey to feel he was a part of bringing his new sibling into the world.

I *can't say that my pregnancy was* uneventful. Those nine months had both their trials and their magic. In stark contrast to how brutal my first trimester had been, as soon as I hit month four, like a sudden shift in the weather, I became the happiest I had ever been in my life. I felt calm, joyful, and peaceful in such an unprecedented way that I knew my state of being was a result of my child's energy. My child possessed an openheartedness before ever making an entrance to this world. My ultimate fear was that I would ruin that loving energy with dysfunctional parenting.

While I was pregnant, this little being did not allow me to eat meat. Just the thought of it nauseated me. In the past, I had gravitated to a vegetarian diet but would eat meat on occasion. This baby mandated a meatless diet. Eating for two, I resorted to a high-carb regimen that gifted me a little over fifty pounds and transformed me into a walking beach ball.

A few weeks before my due date, my ob-gyn, Dr. Gail Jackson, told me that the baby wasn't dropping at all and that I would be two weeks overdue. Still over a month to go! It was summer, and I was so big that walking was very difficult and I could hardly breathe. There were even false reports in the tabloids that I had a condition that had me bedridden. I couldn't blame the rumors. I would have thought the same thing about me.

The mysteries of motherhood were already so vast and so daunting that I had no idea how to get my baby to drop and deliver on time.

A few days later, I got up from watching the U.S. Open on television and walked outside for some fresh air. I found some shade, shelter from the July heat of the San Fernando Valley. The moment had come to open my heart and calmly beg my baby to make an entrance: "Mommy loves you very much, but I really need you to come out. Mommy is having a very hard time. I can't wait an extra two weeks. You are supposed to be here July ninth. Mommy is so tired, and I really want to hold you. Can you do this for me? Please?"

There were no signs that the baby was ready to leave her/his happy place. Fortunately, my mother had decided to come stay with us before my delivery and then as long as I needed her. I was grateful to be the beneficiary of her years of experience as an RN in delivery rooms. But she also kept telling me that due dates were not to be trusted, and if Dr. Jackson said the baby could be two weeks late, that could well be the case.

The days moved at the slowest pace. By this time, I could hardly move. On the night of July 7, I had just settled uncomfortably into bed, waiting for Will to get home, when I heard a loud CHIME from the security sensor as he walked through the door.

With that sound, my entire body seized with pain. This had to be a contraction, because it felt like I was being split in two.

I called for Will. He hurried in as he called for my mother, who rushed to our bedroom a short time later.

"Ma, I'm in a lot of pain. I think we should go to the hospital."

My mother was quick to observe that if this was my first contraction, it was way too early to go to the hospital. Besides, she added, "The pain can't be that bad, you probably haven't even dilated yet."

"No, this is bad," I insisted.

In Adrienne fashion, she assured me that whatever I was feeling was just pressure, and to relieve it, I should go sit in a tub full of warm water. Her motherly/nurse advice was "Girl, relax. You're probably not even a centimeter yet. You might as well stay here as long as possible so you can be comfortable."

I had heard that if you weren't at least three centimeters, they might send you home from the hospital. We had a bit of a drive to get to Cedars-Sinai, so I certainly didn't want to rush to get there only to be turned away.

Mom followed me into the bathroom, ran the water, sat up on the counter to keep me company, and held to her stance that there was no urgency and I'd feel better once the hot water helped alleviate the pressure.

No relief was to be found. The hot water just made me feel hotter, and the pain grew. As I got out of the tub, Mom suggested I do a deep squat, a great way to take pressure off the bladder. As I assumed a sumo-wrestler position, my water broke, or so I assumed while liquid gushed onto the bathroom floor.

My mother's entire demeanor changed, and she leaped off the bathroom counter, announcing, "Well, that's that. Time to go." Multitasking, she ran out of my bathroom to go get dressed while summoning the rest of our troops. "Will!" she yelled. "It's time!"

Moments later, we rushed into the garage—me, Will, Adrienne, and our nephew Kyle, who happened to be staying with us at the time. With the pain off the charts, I could barely think except to note that the only car to be seen was the cherry-red Bentley coupe with the tan suede seats.

I mustered the composure to ask, "Will? Where is the truck?" I could hear the hint of panic in my voice.

"Damn it!" Will had sent the SUV out to be serviced to get it ready for driving us to the hospital. "It's okay," he replied, "we'll just have to take the Bentley."

"But . . ." I started. Who knew what all else was about to gush from my body?

Will had an idea. "Let me get some towels." Shortly, he came back with a stack of about ten towels, placing several layers on the passenger seat and murmuring, "I'm sorry, baby, but these seats are suede."

I got my pregnant tail on the stack of those towels and stuck my head out the window so it wouldn't hit the ceiling of the car. Will drove so fast on the freeway that a drive usually taking close to an hour took only half that time.

When we arrived at Cedars, we were met in the parking garage by personal security and hospital security. I was put in a wheelchair and discreetly taken to the labor and delivery unit, where Dr. Jackson explained that she needed to examine me to see how far I had dilated.

No, no, no. The pain was overwhelming, and I had only one response: "I'm not leaving this chair till I get an epidural."

Once the epidural was administered, I became super relaxed, even happy. After a few hours, Mom was at my side watching the monitors and noticed, to her alarm, that the contractions were lasting too long and the baby's heart rate was dropping. The concern was that the longer the contraction, the harder it was for the baby to get oxygen, putting the baby at risk.

After checking me again, Dr. Jackson suggested a C-section.

"No, no, no, I'm going to relax and ease these contractions. I don't want a C-section. I'll be fine."

"Okay. Well, at least let me give you an episiotomy so you won't tear." She reminded me that the baby was big and I was small. I refused the episiotomy as well. MISTAKE!

----

*H*ours *pass. Night turns into the* morning of July 8, and at last, my child decides to make an entrance. It's a full day before my due date.

Next thing I know, my mother is holding one of my legs in the air as the nurse across from her holds the other. Dr. Jackson stands at the foot of the bed while Will looms over her shoulder wearing an expression I have never seen on his face—pure awe.

This is a first.

I have never seen Will in awe of anything. For a moment, I worry that I'm not reading his expression correctly and that something is wrong.

"We have two more pushes, Jada. Push hard," Dr. Jackson calmly requests.

I am reassured. Everything is going as it should. My mother, in her element, joins in, encouraging me, "Come on, Jada. You got this."

As I gather the strength for an extra-hard push, I spot Dr. Jay Gordon, the pediatrician I've chosen because of his natural approach to medicine. He validated how I felt—I didn't want my baby to leave my side after birth or have any medications that weren't required.

So, Dr. Gordon has come to be on deck and make sure my newborn is healthy and no one tries to fight me on how I want my baby cared for.

"We are almost there, Jada. One more push," says Dr. Jackson excitedly.

This is IT. I take in one more deep breath and exhale with a deep primal grunt as I push so hard it feels like blood vessels are popping in my head. And then I hear . . .

"It's a boy!!!!"

My baby doesn't cry immediately, which, for a moment, creates a bit of alarm. Dr. Gordon gently takes my son and gives him a good looking-over. Slowly, my baby's eyes open, and he cries a loud whine.

Dr. Gordon hands our baby boy back to Will and informs everyone in the room, "He is perfectly healthy."

This puts us all at ease.

Right away, Will brought our son to me, and I held him close. I couldn't believe how pretty he was. He was as calm in my arms as he had been in my womb. I couldn't take my eyes off his precious face, and I felt so connected to him—beyond any other connection I had felt in my life so far. Will was beaming, and I was beyond enchanted by this bundle of love lying on my chest. There is nothing like the miracle of bringing life into this world.

I couldn't believe that I was a mother.

We had not decided on a name. Will didn't like the name I had chosen, Syre. "How am I going to be the Fresh Prince but my son's name is Sire? Nope."

The next day, Will stepped into my hospital room after returning from the house. Our baby was asleep beside me in his little incubator bed. I was half asleep myself, already very much regretting my decision not to have an episiotomy. I would be sitting on a doughnut for the next three months.

Will had an announcement. "I know what I want to name him."

"What?"

"Jaden."

I paused. "Jaden?"

"Yes. After what I saw yesterday, he has to be named after his mother. I've never seen anything like that. I want to name him in honor of you."

I couldn't find words. I didn't even know how to receive this acknowledgment, and I couldn't help but think, *I'm not deserving of this. This baby is too special to be named after me.* This is what I truly believed. Even in this moment, after giving birth to our son, I couldn't embrace how Will was trying to honor me.

"Sons want to be named after their fathers, not their mothers," I finally responded.

"His name is Jaden," Will said with finality. And then he added, half-serious, half-joking, "Um, I hate to tell you this, but I don't think that thing is ever going to work again," as he pointed at my little kitten—now a boxing glove with fourteen stitches on the inside and twelve on the outside.

It had been decided. My beautiful son was to be named after me—Jaden. I made sure to keep a Jamaican tradition by giving Jaden two middle names. Trey gave his little brother his first middle name, Christopher, and I gave him his second . . . Syre.

With Jaden Christopher Syre Smith swaddled in a baby blanket and strapped into his car seat, Will drove us all home nice and slow as I looked at this magical being I already knew, and thought, *Welcome to the world, my little guru.*

Jaden has always found his own language for communicating his thoughts and feelings. Early on, I made it my business to pay close attention to Jaden's antennas and really learn to trust his intuition as he went through the different stages of his life. One of the most pivotal of those moments took place when he was only a preschooler. I had enrolled him in a summer program at a school where I was thinking of sending him in the fall.

When we arrived for the first day of the program, I parked in the school's lot. As soon as I lifted him out of his car seat and started to put on his little backpack, Jaden looked up at me and asked, "Mommy, why are you leaving me here with people who don't love me?"

I was floored. He was meeting these people for the first time that day, but he had made a point I had never considered. I explained that the program was only a couple of weeks and only half the day, just so he could try something new and make new friends.

He wasn't buying it. Jaden stood his ground and said with respectful sweetness, "I have my friends."

He was right that he had friends. Yet what really got me were memories of how I had felt when left with people who didn't love me—the ballet class where I was put in a corner in a black tutu, plus school settings where I was bullied and then shamed for trying to protect myself.

I had to reassure Jaden that I would never leave him with people he believed didn't love him.

"I'm going to be sitting in this parking lot," I said, leaning down to look into his eyes and promising to remain in the car the whole day. This way he knew that someone who adored him was nearby.

A soft, accepting look came over him. He seemed to say, *I guess that works.* He wasn't going to protest further and proceeded to enter the room where his group was gathered. There was a glass panel by the entrance door, and when I arrived about five minutes early to pick him up at noon, I spotted him posted by the door, backpack on, patiently waiting to leave.

Every day for two weeks, I dropped him off and waited in the car for half a day, and at 11:55 a.m., like clockwork, he'd be ready to go, waiting by the door. On the last day, the teacher approached me and said, "Oh, Jaden is such a pleasure. He is so pleasant, but he doesn't really socialize. You know, everybody wants to get to know Jaden, but he doesn't really interact." I listened politely. She added, "We'd love it if you guys came to the final picnic," and I agreed.

On the appointed day, Jaden and I arrived at the picnic and spotted a bench where we could sit. Jaden didn't leave my side. Kids came over and greeted him, and he was very friendly in return but showed no interest in interacting further. The teacher came over and thanked him for being part of the program, and he nodded and smiled but again stayed right where he was.

That was such a telling moment, letting me know—this child has an inner knowing that is unshakable. He held his own inner protest, as if to say: *I'm going to be here, and I'm not going to defy you, Mommy. I'm going to be respectful and pleasant, but I told you . . . I have my friends. I don't want to be where I don't want to be.*

The power and drive for self-determination was so strong in my son. Even at that age. This kind, gentle, self-possessed child standing in his own skin, feet on solid ground, not bending.

I learned early, don't mess with Jaden's inner compass, and DO NOT take his gentleness or kindness as a weakness. My job was to understand and to strive for clear communication but to never bulldoze his potent quiet power. I would only hurt myself trying.

What Jaden taught me that summer was eye-opening. He was never left in an educational institution ever again, unless by his own self-determination. He was homeschooled from then on.

My trust in him and a lesson in patience were later put to the test when Jaden asked to audition to play Will's son in *The Pursuit of Happyness.* As it was entirely Jaden's idea, I made sure to lean in to the request. Will and I were almost always aligned in our parenting decisions, and we were both wary of having Jaden go through potential rejection and all the other pitfalls of becoming a child actor.

But Jaden was quietly adamant, even with so many audition callbacks that at one point I told Will, "Enough, they either want him or they don't."

Jaden never became discouraged. Privately, I became fed up with the process that I felt put him under more intense scrutiny because he was Will Smith's son. Finally, after all the other kids were auditioned, and after Jaden's many callbacks, a consensus was formed that he was the option favored by the studio, producers, and director. And Jaden got the role. The hard-won lesson for me was to let go of my ego and fear and allow Jaden his own process.

My little Willow, oh my God, she was bold, brazen, and not to be ignored, even in the womb. She came into this world with blazing energy, a mix of lightning and thunder, with mega-sunshine and the most tender heart. It is her tender heart that, from the gate, has been one of my greatest teachers.

During my pregnancy, when we weren't sure whether we were having a girl or a boy, Sheree said she'd had a dream and wanted to share it with me. When we found a minute to talk, she described her dream in vivid terms, leading up to the fact that she had seen my new baby and "in my dream, she was a girl." And not only that, she added, but the little girl would have light hazel-greenish eyes like mine, "but lighter, and more cat-shaped."

When Sheree told me about her dream, I kept my hopes up, since Will—who knew he needed a daughter—had made it clear to me that he wanted to keep having babies until he got one. What was even more crazy was the due date of our prophesized baby girl was supposed to be the same birthday, November 11, as that of her older brother Trey. But this baby chose October 31, and I was ecstatic to see that Sheree's dream was spot-on. I almost cried! This meant I could close shop. Later on, the eyes of this baby girl did lighten more than mine and became more cat-shaped.

Willow's nickname, Bean, was given to her by her father because she was so tiny at birth, five pounds six ounces, though long. She could fit in Will's hand, like a little bean. And like me, she was primed to teach her father how to slow down, listen, and have respect for the power of the feminine, and she did so in ways that only a daughter can. Willow's feelings can be delicate and vulnerable, voluminous and intense, but always authentic. You can hear a rawness in her voice and her music, as if she is a cipher for all tender beings thrust into this harsh world.

For a mother, a daughter is a powerful and sometimes overwhelming mirror that can reflect back to her the depths of her inner world, where unhealed wounds linger. For mothers, it's rarely easy to take in the reflection and to choose whether to grow from it or reject it. The danger is that if we reject the part of ourselves we don't want to face, our daughters may feel that we are rejecting them.

Witnessing Willow feeling hurt or upset sometimes reflected back to me my own childhood hurts, which at times made me reject Willow's pain. I would tell her things like "If you're going to cry like that, go to your room. No one wants to see you upset." I was really talking to myself, finding it unbearable to manage my own intense emotions, much less hers.

Most of the time I could stay strong in crisis, though I lost it one day when I was about to drive Willow to karate class. She had come into the bedroom to say goodbye to Will, and as she jumped toward his arms, she slipped from his grasp and hit her head on the corner of our bed, slicing her forehead wide open. Blood spurted everywhere. Willow began to scream at the top of her lungs.

Suddenly, I felt the room spin and began to faint, falling to the floor as my body literally shut down. Thank goodness, Will jumped into action and handled it all.

In no time, we were in the car, Will was at the wheel driving us to the hospital, and I had revived enough to focus on Willow. It was when she looked at me and said, "Mommy, can you fix me and make it better?" that broke me. It would take me years to fully embrace whatever feelings came up from seeing her in pain. The lesson was that ignoring my own intense feelings risked denying hers or, worse, losing her. And that was unfathomable. So I set out to learn from her, as best I could, how to mother the both of us.

The Willow Wisdom approach is to feel through things, acknowledge the hurt instead of cutting off feelings by sweeping them under the rug. Willow goes through all the heartache, all the raw intensity, all the bold expression of her feelings, whereas I swallow everything and keep it moving. I get to witness her beautiful, dynamic paradox of being vulnerable yet courageous. Willow has taught me that vulnerability is a superpower.

As Willow came into language, it seemed her first order of business was to express the strength of "I love you." To this day, there is a trail of "I love you" notes that appear like bread crumbs scattered through our lives—written on paper, folded up and tucked into notebooks, scrawled on the wall (in pencil, thankfully), forever to be found as reminders. She would write me and her father and other members of the tribe what I consider love letters in her precious eight-year-old cursive hand—missives like this:

> *Mom, I love you! I am so blessed to have a mother who*
> *understands me and doesn't judge me. I love you Mommy!*

Willow, quite like her brother Jaden, has had an extreme level of independence from birth. Willow knew what she wanted when she wanted it and went for it. I could feel that fierceness in her during my pregnancy—like she was in training to do her own thing, whatever it was going to be. Interestingly, I didn't come close to gaining the weight that I did with Jaden, fortunately, and within a month, I'd lost it all and was in shape in time to begin shooting a movie.

Breastfeeding had a lot to do with how quickly I lost the weight. And I had intended to breastfeed Willow as long as she wanted. I did not imagine that her need for independence or her love for food would show up so soon and so abruptly. At one year old, Willow ate a plum. And that was it. She weaned herself there and then in one single day. I'd never known any child to wean themselves all at once, over and done, in a day. I did not know how to feel except to think, *Of course my daughter would be starting her own flow at such a young age, just like I did in my own way.*

Willow was born an animal lover, also like me. All animals. When she was a toddler, her ease with furry friends was on full display during a visit to a child-friendly petting zoo in Australia where we were able to hold koalas and feed kangaroos. At the time, Jaden was about three, and Willow was a year and some months old. When I pushed their two-seated stroller close to the kangaroos, Willow toddled right over to where the Cheerios were kept for snacks for the animals and helped herself to a little handful. She was as safe and at home hanging with the kangas as if she belonged there. Jaden stayed in the stroller.

"Do you want to get out, Jaden, and walk around and feed the kangaroos?" I asked him.

He looked up at me and pointed at the long claws on the kangaroo's feet and said, "Do you see his long nails, Mommy?" I looked down and saw that the kangaroo had some razor-sharp toenails. I chuckled at Jaden's polite way of saying *Hell no* and *Why would you let Willow run around stealing their Cheerios?* Good look'n out, Jaden. I scooped Willow up, put her back in the stroller with Jaden, and we rolled out.

By the time Willow was five years old, she wanted more exotic pets. She began by catching garden snakes in our backyard. She wanted to be connected to nature in a much different way than Jaden, who is completely satisfied with being connected to nature by walking barefoot in the grass. Willow was interested in a much more primal connection.

At six years old, she announced, "I want a pet tarantula, Mommy."

A tarantula as a pet? Now, look, I believe in allowing children certain experiences in order to self-actualize. But no, a tarantula was just not happening. "I don't know about getting a tarantula, sweetie. Mommy and tarantulas don't really get down like that."

Willow stayed on the tarantula kick until she went to a friend's pet store and got to hold one of their new arrivals—a baby red-tailed boa constrictor. She called me, overjoyed. "Mommy! I want a pet snake! I'm holding him now, and he is so cute!"

I was silent.

"Mommy, I want this snake so bad, pleeeeease?"

"Willow, those snakes eat live animals! Who is going to feed it?"

"I am, Mommy," Willow pleaded.

As I sat on the phone, I had to ask myself, *Am I going to let my own fears keep Willow from this experience? She's not scared of snakes. She's holding one as we speak.* This was her connection to her primal self and to nature. I was fascinated by her fearlessness, and as a mother, I wanted to cultivate it. My beliefs reminded me that to be a woman in this world requires boldness and fearlessness. The streets taught me, so why should I deny her lessons from this snake?

With that, I gave in. Willow happily brought home a beautiful baby red-tailed boa. We named him Beauty. That first feeding was memorable. I'll never forget how freaked out I was that we had to put live mice down into the boa's cage, and how Willow turned to me, hand on my arm, and explained it all. "Mommy," she began, "this is how life works. It's the cycle of life."

Through Willow and watching her, I fell in love with the snake. Of course, Beauty was allegedly her pet snake, but I became attached to that reptile, and as Willow gained other interests—like the two turtles she brought home that we found out were tortoises and could outlive us all—I took Beauty on as my own. I eventually got more snakes because I found them fascinating. True. Snakes respond to vibe and energy, subtle and dramatic, and your relationship with a snake is about tuning in. They taught me how to do exactly that. Yet if not for Willow, I never would have gained that appreciation or ability.

Poor Will. He never complained. I believe he found it funny as the animal kingdom rapidly expanded from felines and canines to reptiles and more, so much so that he would say, "It's Noah's Ark over here."

G*etting to watch the relationship between* Will and Willow has allowed me to witness what I would never have in this lifetime, something money can't buy—the love of a father full of daddy sweetness. I will never have a father I can call Daddy, and I will never experience the quality of love only a father can provide his daughter. It's a sweet heartbreak for me. Every time I hear Willow call her father Daddy, it makes my heart melt and cherish the blessing that she has a loving father she can depend on. The same applies to Will's love for his sons.

The fact that I provided my children the father I would never have has helped me, as an adult, to have peace around my own daddy issues. Part of adulthood is being able to have joy in watching your children experience a gift that was not meant for you. That is the selflessness of parenthood.

At every stage of their lives, I have had to remember that my little gurus are living a totally different experience from their parents. We wanted to protect them from pain and struggle, but we also wanted them to have the freedom to pursue their dreams on their own terms.

At the same time, I was always clear that any success any one of us attained was a success that belonged to all of us. I drilled that from the start. "Your success is everybody's success. No one in this family does anything alone." I preached this in multiple ways. I didn't want any sibling rivalries and needed each child to understand that they all needed one another to get through this thing called life. And if blood can find a way to get along, respect, consider, and love each other, there is no bond greater. In my observations, from my own experiences and witnessing other families, I could see that getting along with siblings is not always a given. I wanted something different for Willow, Jaden, and Trey as siblings.

Nothing I learned as a mother compared to the discovery of the power of unconditional love. My first glimpses of it came before the kids were even verbal, when we had a physical connection nightly while sleeping side by side. Call me superstitious, but having them by my side as infants and toddlers was very important to me as their protector, considering all the many mysteries that are swirling in the night. I would learn later that in Africa, familial sleeping is common and encouraged.

As infants, Jaden and Willow slept with me, and they continued to do so nightly for some years. When Jaden was about six and Willow four, I could tell Will needed a break from this sleeping arrangement, which was understandable. To give us our own space, I had even built a separate, beautiful love nest for us two grown-ups in our bedroom, complete with a domed ceiling full of twinkling stars. But over time, the kids hijacked that room as well.

One night Will finally spoke his piece. I'd just gotten under the covers, and the two kids had climbed in bed with me. Will came in the room and said to them, "Tonight why don't you two try sleeping in your own rooms?" They protested, but Will held firm. "Come on. Just try it for tonight. You guys are older now."

Jaden and Willow were very unhappy as Will took them to their rooms. My heart broke, but I thought perhaps Will was right. They were getting older.

The next morning, when I woke early and opened my bedroom door, I found both of them curled up and asleep in the hallway. This was their version of a polite protest to say they were NOT going to accept NOT being at my side at night. And I wasn't going to take that for granted. I had never felt so lovable. Needless to say, Will gave up on that.

Before long, they both made their own decision to sleep in their own beds.

Throughout my learning curve as a mom, I've made my share of mistakes, that's for sure, although one thing I do know, in spite of my flaws, is that I love my children hard—deeply and unconditionally. And I feel that they have always known how much I love them, beyond the word itself. LOVE is, above all, the most durable foundation we can have with our children.

Even when they were young, I was thrown by the fact that Jaden and Willow wanted to be with me all the time. Perhaps because my young mother had been more like a big sister, I didn't experience that same need to be with her all the time, and I was shocked whenever my kids protested about being with other people. The few exceptions were my mom, aka Gammy, who gave herself that nickname as soon as she became a grandmother, and Mirna, who I referred to as my "parenting assistant" and who became like a second mother to the kids and a member of our family.

To this day, all three Smith kids love spending time with their parents, and we feel the same way about them. There are not enough ways to express how much Trey, Jaden, and Willow have blessed me with their love. They helped me see the possibility of my worthiness through motherhood. Eventually, they broke down my walls enough that I had to consider—*There must be something really wonderful about you, Jada, if your kids love you this much.*

Out of the mouth of babes . . .
—KING JAMES BIBLE, PSALMS 8:2

There is a wonderful question to ask yourself no matter what stage of life you are in: How have children in your life been little gurus to you?

———————

Take a moment to write down your thoughts in response to that and other questions: What have they taught you? How has their wisdom impacted your life? How has a child reflected your own worth back to you? And how have you reflected their worth back to them?

———————

Don't ever overlook the God-given intelligence of a young soul.

CHAPTER 15

Swallowing the Key

Perspective is everything.

Will had made that observation on one of our first dates—when he pointed to the glass on his left that was simultaneously on my right—and it stuck with me. At the time I thought he was handing me a clue about how he navigated the world. Soon enough, I began to see the principle as something I could apply to our relationship. As in: *We may disagree strongly or react differently to various situations, but by acknowledging our differences in perspective, we can avoid rejecting the other person's point of view in order to feel heard.*

But how can we understand a significant other's perspective if: (a) we don't have the experience, maturity, or desire to identify differences; and (b) we lack the ability to recognize there is no right or wrong (except in situations where abuse is evident)? Often, with the inevitable misunderstandings and even heartbreaks that come along with most serious relationships, we forget that our opinions, priorities, and needs aren't better than our partner's, they are just different.

Unrealistic expectations are not our fault. It's the fairy tale of romanticized love that has instilled the many false beliefs that enforce *If we love each other, we must think alike.* Right? *If you really love me, you must know all my needs at all times without me having to tell you.* Right? *And if you don't live up to these expectations, I have the right to disrespect you, treat you like an enemy, and look for what I need elsewhere because you are choosing not to give me what I need.* Right?

No, no, not true.

Still, we frequently feel betrayed and unloved when our significant other is oppositional in perspective to how we think things should be. In our discomfort, we ignore that not allowing for differences is unkind to the person we say we love so deeply. It's also unkind to ourselves.

We rarely pause to measure or even identify the damage done to us by romanticized ideals—from movies, songs, TV shows, books, ads, and other people's glossy narratives of their dreamy lives. With those happily-ever-after fairy tales in our heads, we dive into committed relationships as if we know how to have healthy, deeply loving bonds. Because those stories make love look so easy, showing partners always in agreement, we think that's what real love must always be: *If you agree with me, you love me. If you love me, you agree with me.*

Though I don't consider myself a romantic, I expected Will to save me and heal my past hurts—as if the traumas, chaos, and depression experienced before we met would magically disappear within the ether of our ecstatic love.

If I hadn't been caught up in the fantasy of how my Prince Charming would make all my pain disappear as he rode me off into the sunset, I'm sure that, as a new wife and mother, I would have given more space to my own history. I would have acknowledged that I had only recently tried to extract myself from the Hollywood life in the hope of making a smaller, more intimate one in Baltimore. Or maybe I would have been more thoughtful about my choice to stop therapy once I went off Prozac—not long after a series of devastating losses that I hadn't processed.

In many ways, Will and I were like so many young couples who grow up with instability and dysfunction but do not acquire the tools to confront them. We were starting our journey after being thrust together into expanding families, booming careers, and big shifts in fortune and responsibility. Besides that, Will and I were trying to figure it all out under the increasingly hot lights that come with being celebrities and having to live up to a fantasy version of married life. True, not everyone deals with the glare of the public eye. Yet most newlyweds have everyday challenges, some expected and some not, and need to show the world that they've won the sweepstakes of marital bliss. Admitting to growing pains is severely frowned upon.

While fairy-tale thinking gets in the way of accepting differences in perspective, the other trap for me was perfectionism. Denying the humanness of the people we love is a trap. My thinking was *I'm sorry, sir/ma'am, but in our relationship, you can no longer be human. I've been hurt enough. From here on out, you better get every damn thing right. And don't worry about me, because I'm on point when it comes to loving you, even if I'm full of pain.*

Oh yeah, I was textbook.

Love is hard enough to define on our own terms, and harder still in relationships where we're bound to have different points of view on what love is, how to love others, and how to love ourselves. And the thing is, in the game of love, we are all depending on each other while navigating those different perspectives at the same time.

One of the big challenges I faced in the beginning of our marriage was that, rather than expressing disappointment or bruised feelings, I held fast to the motto *Never let them see you sweat.* My fallback position, rather than showing vulnerability, was to hide, cover my feelings, or fight. Whether overtly or covertly.

Being a graduate of the University of the B-more Streets, I was quick to pop off in the early days of relating to Will when there were disagreements between us. Will could talk circles around me at the time, so when I felt he wasn't listening and was being disrespectful, that would piss me off. Once, in a heated argument, I let go an F-you, fighting in the style I knew best.

Will wasn't having it. He said, in effect, "I can't be in a relationship with you. This isn't going to work."

He broke up with me on the spot. His explanation was that, considering the abuse he had grown up watching between his parents and how things had escalated rapidly from verbal to physical, he was not willing to participate in this kind of intense interaction with me.

"So you're going to break up with me over some words?" I asked.

Will answered, "Yes."

Over the next week, I tried to consider his perspective. My experience was different from his, but in certain relationships in which I felt threatened, slinging words was one way to protect myself.

Still, I could see that there was a more respectful way of handling communication.

We were only broken up for one week. However, Will had set an important boundary. And he did so in a way that I couldn't ignore. It was one thing to add profanity to the expression of ideas or viewpoints but another thing when it was used in a personal attack. My eyes were opened to how words could become weaponized and just as violent as blows. Similarly, disrespect can lead to emotional violence, another reason to be mindful of how words are spoken.

Will made it clear what he was willing to tolerate. "If we are going to be together, we can't do that to each other."

I agreed. After that incident, I didn't curse at him again. Not for decades at least.

Our agreement not to use profanity or disrespectful language or tones led to improved communication. But the unintended consequence of our more "respectful" talks was that they were often devoid of the honest expression of emotions, sometimes overly intellectual or analytical. Imagine having to sit down and speak about the moments when some women flirted with him in front of me and having to be cool, even-toned, analytical, and dispassionate about it. This pattern kept us safe from talking about real feelings but also from experiencing them.

Some couples manage to argue authentically. In our case, our arguments verged on being too sanitized and controlled, to the point where I'd lose genuine expression and suppress deep feelings.

There would come a day when I'd wake up and feel fully disconnected from emotional honesty—my inner compass. And that would wreak havoc. But we'll get to that.

B *y the time we were married with children,* it was obvious to me that Will and I had very different perspectives about the trappings of fame. Ripples of our differences showed up early in our relationship, but I tended to ignore them because the ride was all-consuming.

"Magic Mountain?" My homegirl Keesha was excited. "You sure it won't be too crazy?"

"It's a weekday," I assured her, and went over the plan I'd put together for her and her family—who were out visiting me—to join Will and Trey and me on an outing to a nearby area amusement park.

Will was on his way to becoming the undisputed champion of the box office and had already spent more than six years on TV screens in the homes of millions of people around the world. Being welcoming to fans was part of his work ethic, but, increasingly, it was hard to go places just with our crew to have a good time. For that reason, we tried to go out when things were less crowded so we could wander freely and enjoy ourselves.

Everything was rolling pretty smoothly, as I recall, until a group of fans spotted Will and began running toward us, practically in hysterics as they tried to get close to him. It was like a loud, excited stampede.

With a primitive survival instinct and probably some PTSD kicking in, I started screaming, "BACK THE FUCK UP! BACK UP!" In full fight-or-flight mode, I couldn't stop myself, even with Trey standing in between Will and me. Terrified and feeling trapped, I was ready to swing wildly and dared anyone to come closer. The crowd paused and looked at me as if I were insane. Will included.

When I looked up at him, he seemed bewildered by the intensity of my reaction and could only ask me to calm down. Physically, we had two different perspectives because of our different vantage points. At six-two, Will could see over the crowd enough to know that there was no real threat. I'm five feet tall on a good day, tiny compared to everyone charging at me, and in my wash of adrenaline, all I could see was the oncoming rush of bodies. All I could hear were screams as hands went reaching across my face. Will managed to calm the horde, and we all went about our day unscathed. But I was shaken.

To him, I had overreacted, even though I'd been in an unconscious full-court-press trauma response. To me, he was underreacting and unwilling to see how getting mobbed would make me feel that we were all being threatened.

This was classic. You could take this example of conflicting perspectives and apply it to everything else in our entire marriage and get the same result. Sometimes you can find common ground to balance out your differences. But if you don't attempt to reconcile the warring viewpoints at play, resentment, anger, and regret will only grow.

Our perspectives were reversed when it came to paparazzi. For Will, photographers brought out a trauma response similar to the one I had with crowds. For him, taking unwanted photos was a violation, and he perceived that as a threat. It raised his alarm system for fight-or-flight. With paparazzi—though they can be annoying—I didn't feel the same lack of control I did with swarming crowds.

I learned early in my career to create my own comfort zone by acknowledging the people with the cameras and saying, "I'll give you the pictures you want, but you gotta back up. Give me twenty feet." As long as they didn't come up right in my face, I was good. "No problem, Jada" was the response I'd usually get. So, the paps and I shared mutual respect.

But all of this—crowds, fans, paps—came with the territory. And I would have to learn to deal. I also learned that being in Hollywood didn't mean we'd left where we came from behind. I mean, I was living the supposed dream and one of my closest friends was murdered, even though he was music royalty. And it was here where, in adapting, Will and I shared a perspective that our responsibility was to provide for and to bring as many people as we possibly could along with us on our ride. Some might call this survivor's guilt.

This meant that he and I were usually the first calls whenever anyone in our circle needed help. Those startling calls, during the hours when you know it ain't good news, would roll in. Folks needing bail money, help after an accident, or funds to pay for a funeral when a person's son got murdered. Or someone had an illness and was in need of a special doctor. Someone was in trouble and had to pay for a lawyer. We had the resources, wanted to help, and felt obligated to do so if we could.

Every time a call came in, I was humble and grateful that we had come as far as we had. But I did realize that even with our combined success, we didn't have the magic to banish all woes and make life problem-free for our family, friends, and extended community—though others might have hoped that was the case. We spent a lot of time trying to be heroes for a lot of people while not focusing enough on ourselves and one another. It was as though saving others came to define our worth.

We were like so many people in every walk of life who, though well intentioned, find our value in overextending ourselves on behalf of others, to the point of being incapable of self-care. Will and I were equally clueless in this respect.

Some of our differences in perspective weren't problematic. Will wanted to be one of the biggest names in Hollywood and was always surprised that I didn't. For my part, I admired his drive, his tenacity, and his courage to push the boundaries of what some deemed acceptable for an artist of color. He set out to show the world that an actor of color was as viable with global audiences as our white counterparts, and to open doors for others in underrepresented communities. I was proud of him for that.

With both of us balancing career and family, there was even less time left over for us to check in with each other and address differences in a deep way. Every attempt to resolve our competing perspectives ended up with us kicking the can down the road, and Will's decree, "We'll get to that later." That became the theme song of our relationship.

Everything blew up fast. Time was the commodity we did not have.

       Will was on his fast train to stardom, and I was putting in my own fuel, doing my best to live up to the unattainable standards of being a perfect wife and mother. I had no one to blame. Not only had I signed up for this ride, I had taken my seat on it within my hand-made gilded cage. Then I swallowed the damn key.

       By the time Jaden was a toddler, our household was rapidly out-growing our home in Westlake. The guest rooms were always filled with visiting relatives and friends of Will's who'd been by his side for years. There was Charlie Mack, for one, who, mind you, lived with us before Jaden was born and liked to blast Chico DeBarge at five a.m. damn near every morning . . . until we had a conversation about it. The great thing is that Charlie is like my big bro, and we could be on some real talk, always. After just a few words, he smiled and even looked surprised that he had been so unaware. From then on, I never again heard Chico as the sun came up.

       Will deferred to me when it came to most of the decisions related to running our bustling household. During this time frame, we were most likely the only Black couple in our neighborhood, which made for some interesting encounters with the mostly white service provid-ers, who, though polite, appeared unaccustomed to being hired by young Black homeowners, famous or not. Most of the time, I handled whatever issues came up, but if there was something I really wanted Will's input on, of course I would ask. That's what I did on the day I called him at work after an incident with an exterminator.

       I could tell by the tone of Will's voice when he answered his phone that it wasn't a good time. Being as succinct as possible, I prefaced my recap by saying, "I've always felt like I had a good rapport with this man. We were cool." However, I went on, since our pest problem had been resolved, I'd informed the exterminator that we wouldn't need his services any longer, adding, "We'll call if anything changes."

       With me inside the kitchen and the man outside my kitchen door, he'd forcefully insisted that we did need to continue his services. I held my ground, thanked him again, and asked him to bill us as he had done in the past.

"NO!" the man said, indignant, as he stepped through the door into the kitchen. "You are going to pay me now!"

"Who do you think you're talking to?" I said.

"You no longer want my services, then you pay me now!" With his chest puffed up, he inched toward me, raising all my safety alarms, not only for me but for Jaden, who was in the house.

A switch flipped inside me to protect mine at all cost. In fight mode, I grabbed the glass blender jar off my kitchen counter and raised it, warning him, "You better get the fuck out of my house!"

The man immediately backed out of my kitchen door and was gone. What shook me most wasn't him, it was me—where I was willing to go. That place within me hadn't been activated in a minute, but it was definitely still primed to explode. The other piece was that I was hurt that someone with whom I had been cool could be so disrespectful and violate the safety in my own home.

Will heard me out, saying little until I let him know, "I'm okay, but can you believe he did that?"

His brief response confirmed he was in the middle of something. He basically said that I had handled it, and we would talk about it when he got home.

Then I did what I usually did. I bossed up, got steely, and hid my need for reassurance. With a quick "Cool," I said goodbye, and we hung up.

We didn't talk about it later. We should have. It never should have been okay for me to gloss over someone making me feel violated in my own home, so much so that I'd felt it necessary to back him down. It never should have been okay for me to let Will gloss over it, either.

Had I clearly expressed my feelings? In hindsight, I'm almost positive that I had not. That is a confession. Even to this day, it is difficult for me to express how I really feel at any given moment. Any vulnerability makes me feel uncomfortably vulnerable.

My inner monologue was going off: *Will should know I need him and bring his ass home.* Period! The biggest mistake I constantly made was thinking Will thought exactly how I did, and that I shouldn't have to tell him how I was feeling. He should already know. Does any of this sound familiar?

So many conversations and so many aspects of our lives got away from us. We had to learn on the fly to handle the issues of growing a family, running a household, organizing the details of being constantly on the go. Ours was a classic version of learning to fly an airplane while we were still building it, as more and more passengers wanted to come on board.

And of course, we wanted to share our lives with people we loved. If we were heading to Aspen for Christmas, it wasn't just us and the three kids. It was us plus forty—family, friends, team members.

The first time Will and I went to visit Aspen, I fell in love with the winter wonderland in the Colorado resort town. It reminded me of an old-fashioned holiday card. Once we had a family and wanted to show the kids a white Christmas, Aspen became our holiday destination of choice, and in the season that always gave me joy, I loved going all out. But we had no idea how this was done. We were on a constant learning curve, not to mention that every year we would have to top ourselves. Besides Christmas planning and all that it entailed, one year Will had a brainstorm: "We should throw a New Year's Eve party for our anniversary."

Oh my God. I love a good party, but this soon became an annual celebration that I had to figure out, and a year-round planning job as the guest list expanded to include every celeb in Aspen during that time.

There were endless logistics. Will—the showman and emcee—was like the executive producer, dreaming up experiences for all to enjoy, whereas I was the assistant producer, information point person, and for a while, everybody's girl Friday. Who was flying from where and getting picked up when, how many were at the house and who all was staying in hotel rooms? Who needed ski lift tickets and local transportation? And where were the toothbrushes? Even though I had Mia and Fawn to help, I was the on-the-ground communication hub at this point.

As a new wife and mom, I was often overwhelmed by trying to adapt to an ever larger whirlwind. Until I was able to put systems in place and hire more team members to help me, I kept putting one foot in front of the other, hoping to accommodate everyone's needs in our expanding world.

Everyone around us saw only the glitter and excitement of our lives. Very rarely were people in touch with what was involved when forty-plus family and friends went on a Christmas vacation. Or how exhausting it was to corral everyone on New Year's Eve 1999—my second wedding anniversary, when the world was supposed to end and I really just wanted to be quiet with my husband and family— and fly off to D.C. to stay overnight at the Clinton White House. The news broke in September:

> Actor Will Smith will host Washington's ultimate party of '99,
> the multimillion-dollar New Year's Eve celebration on the Mall,
> for which a who's who of rock music will sing backup.

This was a celebration on a scale never attempted by a president, at a pivotal moment on the planet when millions were terrified about the cliff we were going over into a new millennium. Our family's inclusion in history was thrilling beyond words, but when Will told me we were invited to stay overnight at the White House—after a long tiring night with young children—I had to say, "This is too much."

"Jada, it's the Lincoln Bedroom. We get to sleep in the same room as the Emancipation Proclamation."

"Will, I get it. But after that long night, I'm not trying to stay in Lincoln's dusty-ass bedroom."

Will thought I was being ridiculous. He couldn't believe it. "Sorry, babe, this is history. These kids will remember this all their lives." I didn't bother to tell him that fifteen-month-old Jaden would have zero memory of it.

Long story short, I was overruled. And we went in style. Gianni Versace designed outfits for us both, and Will rocked the stage. The world did not end, and I survived, although I was able to say "I told you so" to Will about all five of us trying to sleep in that small-ass bed in that dusty-ass bedroom, Emancipation Proclamation and all.

I*t's inevitable for anyone willing to* take a ride on someone else's bullet train that at some point, you start to feel lost while traveling to that person's destinations. It happens to so many of us, not just in the entertainment world but in many facets of life.

To prevent this, I fought hard to have my own professional identity, separate from Will. But to my shock, after I happily became Mrs. Will Smith, it was as if it was the only name I ever had, even after years of establishing myself as Jada Pinkett. It was like everything I had done before my marriage, all I had built, no longer mattered. My identity had never been hijacked in a relationship before. It was no fault of Will's, of course, but of the age-old tropes that portray women who marry successful men as doing so for their entire validation. She dare not try to have an identity beyond who she is in service of his identity.

Before long, I noticed people who wanted a piece of me because they wanted to get to Will. That wasn't what I expected when I went in to meet with Harvey Weinstein about a short film I had produced with the wonderful Ann Carli that we wanted to adapt into a full-length feature called *When Willows Touch*. It was written and directed by the then-up-and-coming, truly gifted Shonda Rhimes; I had starred opposite the extraordinarily talented actor Jeffrey

Wright. The meeting with Harvey was to talk about acquiring the script to make the movie. He was all business, which I appreciated. But he made it clear that he would be interested in moving ahead only if Will's name was attached to the project as an executive producer.

When Harvey said this, I was quiet and had to think hard. I couldn't do it. I understood, from a Hollywood perspective, Will Smith was the big brand name. But so was Denzel Washington, who was very interested in starring in the project. Although Will and I had projects we developed together in those days, the projects came about organically. We never collaborated as a play to get things made. I could see the trap. I knew if I yielded to that request on this project, it would be expected the next time, and the next time after that, by everyone else. With regret, I withdrew the film. I refused to trade on Will's success.

Our most profound difference in perspectives was a clash in our visions of what happiness looked like. Will was living his dream, and that meant I must be living mine, too—through him. He couldn't understand why I was often unhappy. His attitude was *Why would you want for anything? Look at the life and opportunities I provide for you, all we get to have and do and be.*

My attitude was *Yes, you have a point, but I have hitched a ride on someone else's train, someone I love, except I don't know how to jump off from time to time to ride my own train. It feels like I can't grasp my own journey. At times I feel resentful and angry. Mostly, I DON'T KNOW WHAT TO DO ABOUT IT.*

We can be overloved, underloved, overworked, underworked . . .
each costs much.
　　　　—CLARISSA PINKOLA ESTÉS

Whether it's love or work, over or under, all of it can feel like a cage, and any of us might swallow the key. And do you know what that key unlocks? Our power to create a fulfilling life we are proud of. So many of us are willing to swallow the key to our own treasure troves in order to have the love and acceptance we desire from others.

_____

Too often we feel the need to be MORE in order to be loved and not abandoned. Women are chronically burdened by having "to prove that we have value and therefore should be allowed to live," as Clarissa Pinkola Estés puts it.

_____

Sometimes the key we swallow is the truth-telling part of us that questions whether a relationship is feeding or starving us. If we swallow the key, we can't ask the questions. It's hard to look at our traps, even when they make themselves obvious. One example is when we are being objectified and used for enjoyment instead of being sought as a partner in a quest to be seen and loved. Or when we are expected to simply be compliant and fun, and never complain, because we fear these words—"You know there's a side chick dying to take your place."

_____

Here's the deal: When we abandon ourselves by swallowing the key to our happiness for the alleged happiness of someone else, there is no happiness to be found by either party. You still feel pain, and the other feels your resentment. But if we are courageous, life can offer another kind of pain that's far more sacred: pain that will deliver you your pride, your power, your happiness, instead of self-betrayal. It's up to you whether you're brave enough to face that pain. Only you know what's holding you back from spitting out the key and using it to open the gates to your inner kingdom.

_____

Do you want your key back? Write down how you may have lost it and consider why you want to regain it. And if you have been through an arduous passage of retrieving your key already, why not write down your "key" lessons? Take a moment to pat yourself on the back and be prepared to share that story with someone who's in need of how to do the same.

CHAPTER 16

Wild Banshee

The story I'm about to tell you has many entry points, but if I didn't trace the main thread back to my years in Baltimore, I would miss the chance to honor my grandmother. Marion wanted me to be able to explore worlds different from my own so that later on, no matter who I met, we could share some common ground. My openness and love for all kinds of music starts there—from the classical composers I heard in her house to the R&B, disco, classic rock, and even country my mother loved, from the reggae and Caribbean rhythms played at my aunt Sondra's to the club music and old-school hip-hop I heard on the dance floor and at the skating rink, from the 1980s alternative bands that Pac, John, and I obsessed over all the way to my exposure to hard rock and heavy metal in the home of Uncle Leslie and Aunt Marsha.

My uncle listened to *everything.* Led Zeppelin, Iron Maiden, Queen, Black Sabbath, Metallica, the list goes on. I'll never forget holding the Ozzy Osbourne solo album *Bark at the Moon* and seeing him actually howling at the moon, like a werewolf with fangs. I was captivated. Ozzy was hauntingly compelling. Listening to his music, in its hard-edged, melodic glory, I was transported. Coupled with his badass lead guitarist, thematic storylines, and melodic hooks, he stole my imagination.

R&B may have sat in my soul more than other musical forms, but metal/hard rock had a different kind of power and sway over me. It spoke to something deeply primal within. So much so that I had always wanted to do it myself, to express that energy within me and let

281

it rock out, for real. The actress and singer Tichina Arnold once said in my birthday video that she believed there was a white man trapped inside me somewhere. Metal brings out a fierceness in me, and that genre of music allowed a safe space for its release. By the time I was fifteen and Guns N' Roses appeared on the scene, I was hooked. My dream of dreams then was to be the first female Axl Rose. There were some iconic females who rocked hard and whom I admired— Suzi Quatro, Doro Pesch, Joan Jett, Heart, and Stevie Nicks—but at the time there weren't many Black women, to the best of my knowledge, on the rock scene. It wasn't until I was introduced to the London-based band Skunk Anansie, fronted by Skin, a remarkable bad-as-hell lead singer, that I found a Black woman who could rock like that. Of course, Big Mama Thornton, Memphis Minnie, and Sister Rosetta Tharpe had been pioneers in the rock game, but their contributions as Black women are often underplayed.

Sometimes it takes only one exception to the rule to prove that you, too, can go against the grain. Other times, you have to become your own exception to the rule. I'd always had a secret desire to form my own rock band, but with juggling my roles as wife and mother, and a career of my own, that dream fell to the side and soon felt out of reach.

For the most part, my acting career continued to be fulfilling, with new opportunities to tackle a range of characters and film genres. But Hollywood had a certain formula, a requirement to abide by rules of conformity, that wasn't natural to me.

There's only so much rebellion tolerated in the Hollywood game. For instance, on *Tales from the Crypt: Demon Knight,* which I took as a chance to work with the delightful director Ernest Dickerson, and in the horror genre which I loved, I showed up for a costume fitting after cutting my hair very short and dyeing it sandy platinum blonde. Executive producer Joel Silver, who was very influential and powerful at the time, called me to his office. When I auditioned for the role, my hair was dark, he reminded me, blasting me for thinking I could just change my look because the idea had struck my fancy.

I didn't interrupt Joel. There was a part of me that knew he was right. I could understand it wasn't professional to switch up your look after being hired for a role sporting another, approved aesthetic. But there was the more impulsive nature within me that was not willing to have its energy challenged. I nodded respectfully, trying to be contrite, though I couldn't stop myself from saying, "But it's hot. You gotta admit it."

Joel glowered and sent me on my way. Interesting. Despite his loud disapproval about my hair color and style change, he didn't request any changes—a clue that he thought it was dope as well. I was not used to asking for permission for *nothin'*, especially when it came to what I wanted to do with my person.

Hollywood never seemed to know how to tame me, and I didn't want to be tamed. Part of that meant being myself, no matter whom I was sitting in front of. That tended to be a double-edged sword. It was Warren Beatty who later offered me a gentler perspective after I gave my feedback on his script for *Bulworth*.

This was one of those scripts that Warren wanted to keep quiet, so I had to go to his office to read it, as he was thinking of me to costar. After doing so, I gave him my honest opinion: "This is not realistic." I felt it was culturally inauthentic. "I can't do this."

Warren was impressed, though my tone and approach may have been off-putting as I continued to critique his script. Warren listened with his charming smile and veteran patience. He could see, however, that my edgy tone, accompanied by raw honesty, wouldn't always go over well in a town full of grand egos.

After I decided the movie wasn't for me, Warren invited me to lunch. In so many words, he pointed out that maybe it would be to my benefit to soften my approach a bit. He expressed that I was talented, funny, and charming, but at times, I could come off as abrasive. He was asking me to allow more of the delight under my hard exterior to peer through.

This was the first time anyone had taken the time to put this to me in such a nonjudgmental way, and I appreciated it. He didn't make me wrong for being who I am, he was just asking me to be willing to show more sides of myself. He made it clear that I didn't have to betray myself by softening my edges, either. That was fair. Taking his input into account, I also realized I needed to find a space outside Hollywood for the wild banshee within, the one who didn't give a fuck about being soft or delightful.

It was time to move, to venture into a different world. Magically, the world I needed found me.

When I fall for a passion of any kind, I fall hard. And I go *all in*. That's how I felt when Will brought home the deck for *The Matrix*. At that point, he was the filmmakers' first choice to play Neo. Though it looked more like a comic book when I first flipped through it, the images immediately captured my imagination and had me creatively salivating. I was a hard-core anime fan, and I believed that if they could pull off cinematically what was imaged on paper, this movie would be one of the greatest of all time.

"Oh my God," I said to Will, overwhelmingly excited, seeing the possibility of turning Japanese anime style into gravity-defying live action.

He glanced down at the deck that I was holding.

"How are they going to pull this off?"

"They have some new technology they are working with." He gave me the rundown of the filmmakers' plan.

"What? Hell no! That's gonna be crazy!" Not only would their approach to action be insane, but the plot was revolutionary: a story in which humanity has to overcome all their differences to fight a war against the machines. *The Matrix* was a promising endeavor all around.

Will wasn't seeing it. We clearly had different perspectives, but he was further torn, as he was considering the role of Muhammad Ali. Soon enough, he chose the latter, the right choice for him at the time.

The Wachowskis—so ahead of their time—threw the widest and most diverse casting net, which, for me, was one of the most promising and impressive components of the project. Before Hollywood attempted to jump on the diversity bandwagon, the Wachowskis understood the importance of diverse representation that spanned way beyond ethnicity. As directors, they were expressing how they saw the world, beyond heterosexual white folk surviving in an apocalyptic future.

Once Keanu Reeves took on the role of Neo, as if it had been written for him all along, the next quest was to cast Trinity, the female lead. When I got the call to audition and became a serious contender, I just about lost my mind.

Though they had begun by wanting a Black male lead, when that didn't work, they were open to casting a female lead of color opposite Keanu, including Salma Hayek, who was also in the mix for Trinity. Salma and I both went through a series of physical movement auditions to make sure we could pull off the martial arts that Trinity would command. Luckily, I had done extensive fight training for previous films.

After Laurence Fishburne signed on as Morpheus, the cast diversified further, which made me want in on the project even more.

I felt like the role of Trinity had my name on it, and I was so happy when the directors liked my audition and asked me to come in for a chemistry read with Keanu. This was sure to be a walk in the park. I mean, I was a huge fan of Keanu's. Guess what? We had absolutely no chemistry in the reading. Absolutely none. Zero.

I could not have been more shocked.

Usually, when I don't get a role I really want, I find myself thinking that I would have been the better choice. But to this day, I can't think of anyone who would have been a better Trinity than Carrie-Anne Moss. She was the dopest. This is one of the few roles I lost to another actress where I'm here to tell you—I couldn't have embodied that part the way Carrie-Anne did.

So, it seemed that being part of the *Matrix* phenomenon wasn't in the cards. That is, until the Wachowskis decided to launch a *Matrix* franchise and chose to write two sequels.

Cut to: I'm as busy as ever, in my last trimester with Willow, when I get a call that the Wachowskis want to meet about a role in the sequels. The answer is yes before I even get the details. I sit in front of them in their office, with Willow as a big ball in my tummy.

"We have a character named Niobe that we wrote with you in mind," one of them says. Ever since my Trinity audition, the other says, I've been in their thoughts for a future character.

Now, I cannot explain how honored, excited, and flattered I was. I sat there as cool as possible while they went on, asking when the baby was due, because shooting and training would start in November. Willow was actually due in November, but I blurted out, "Oh, I'm delivering in October."

I was not missing this opportunity and later would have to admit that my statement was a bit of a stretch. This meant that whenever Willow was born, I would have to lose the baby weight and get into top shape really fast. It was going to be tight, but I assured them that I'd be ready. Fortunately, Willow kept me honest by bringing herself into the world on Halloween, two weeks early.

While still pregnant, I cranked up my usual gym workout. I had a start date at the end of November for three months of shooting. I had to be ready, and I had a month.

After Willow arrived, I doubled down in the gym, embarking on one of the most intense training regimens of my life with the one and only Darrell Foster—the same superstar fitness and fight trainer who helped Will get ready to play Muhammad Ali. I began my motion capture work in pretty darn good shape, baby Willow and toddler Jaden with me, my homegirl Fawn, and Gammy, who would be on the set while I shot all day. My mom would bring Willow from my trailer to the set every hour on the hour so I could breastfeed. Whatever baby weight I'd gained fell away fast, and nursing Willow helped.

But before long, I gained fifteen pounds of muscle after working up to pressing ten plates on either side of the leg machine and managing to bench-press 175 pounds as one press. I had never been so ripped in my life. Over my two-year journey with *The Matrix,* Darrell had me so conditioned, we even thought about me competing as a bikini bodybuilder. I was doing gymnastics class, fight-training with the cast, and weight-training with Darrell. Working out became my life.

I got so strong and rammy that I would even try Will sometimes, playfully bucking up on him and saying things like "I can kick your ass now."

Now, Will was in his best shape ever after *Ali,* strong as hell, and had no problem proving me wrong every time. Let me just say, when you want to test your strength with someone who is heavyweight-ready, remember to tap out when they tell you to.

My little muscles had me tripp'n.

After The Matrix *was done and* the cast was on the press tour, I had a series of conversations with Keanu about what we were looking forward to doing next.

Knowing he had a band called Dogstar, I mentioned that music was calling me. With vicarious interest, I asked, "How do you feel when you're onstage with your band?"

He thought a moment before he answered, but when he did, I could see a whole other side of Keanu. He talked about how fulfilling it was, and I could see how freeing the experience could be.

Yes! That's what I needed. I needed something freeing for myself.

I confessed, "You know, I've actually thought about putting a band together, but . . ."

"Do it. Why not?" Keanu said.

The logistics of putting a band together couldn't be that hard, I figured. I had so much I wanted to say, so much I wanted to express. Before I ever began, Keanu gave me the best advice. "Ignore what people have to say," he urged. People would talk shit, I realized, but as he said, "That's not your problem." His lasting wisdom: "Just have fun."

I had seen that example in Cree Summer and her band, back in our *A Different World* days. Watching her rock out onstage gave me a vicarious thrill, with her crystal power rays bursting across the crotch of her pants. In razor-sharp songs like "Curious White Boy," she hit hard on issues of race and gender, speaking to the soul of "the well-written-upon woman" and especially Black women. Cree was the baddest. Between her and Keanu, I was inspired.

As soon as the family got back to the States and we settled into our new home in Hidden Hills, I told Will about my decision.

He was all for it. From there, a whole new world outside of my handmade gilded cage opened up—where I could kick, scream, spit, and growl.

T*he announcement I never in my* life expected to hear a few years into my metal music journey was: "Next week, at the Viper Room, Sharon Osbourne is coming through to hear you play."

What?

"Yeah, Sharon wants to check you out for a possible slot on the Ozzfest tour."

My band members and I were all clear that Sharon—the wife of

Ozzy Osbourne and the power center of Ozzfest, the biggest rock and metal summer festival in the world—was the one who would make the decision based on the performance she was there to see that evening.

Of course, we'd been around only three years, and I didn't want to get my hopes up that there was a chance to be part of the festival. We would just have to go out there, give it our all, and hope our eclectic metal sound would make the cut.

This was such an amazing opportunity, and we had fought hard for it.

When we got started, it didn't take long for me to come up with Wicked Wisdom as the band's name. "Wicked" was a salute to my West Indian roots—meaning dope, excellent, or even unusual—and "Wisdom" was the state one attained when the deepest truths had been absorbed and practiced. Songs poured from the pit of my heart and bowels as if they'd been waiting there for years, screaming to be heard. Titles, lyrics, and melodies came to me effortlessly and filled up notebooks, scraps of paper, even napkins.

Wicked Wisdom was composed of a very talented group of Black male musicians, starting with lead guitarist Pocket Honore. Pocket—the name he earned because he was always in the pocket of the rhythm, intensity, and feeling—was originally from Baton Rouge, Louisiana, and he had a musical sensibility that added a unique rhythmic hump to our metal sound. Pocket put a whole lot of soul on that driving metal guitar. For one of Wicked Wisdom's first incarnations, other band members I was fortunate to have join were Cameron Graves (rhythm and keyboards), an exceptional musician who can also play classical and jazz music; Rio Lawrence (bass, may his soul rest in peace); and Philip Fisher (drums). They all contributed to our sound, which was eventually dubbed "nu-metal." Over the years, others would add their talents, including Taylor Graves (keyboards), Aaron Haggerty (drums), and Thomas Pridgen (drums), who would join a later incarnation of the band called Wicked Evolution.

In the beginning, we were more in the lane of R&B-flavored

rock, but the more we played together, the harder we pushed toward an edgier full-metal sound.

In one of my first conversations with my manager, Miguel Melendez, about my new venture, he seemed baffled. A big bro, partner, and trusted adviser on many fronts of my acting/producing careers, Miguel asked in a respectful but skeptical tone, "Metal?"

He had to admit, out the gate, that he wasn't familiar with how to move in the metal music scene. Rather than discourage me, Miguel brought in Dennis Sanders, a promoter and manager who had worked with Papa Roach, knew the terrain, understood my vision, and started booking us in every venue he could.

Dennis would book us here, there, and everywhere, the plan being for us to cut our teeth. As long as there was an address of some sort, or a spot on the map alleging to be an arena/club/bar, or a cornfield with a falling-down shack in the middle of it, Wicked Wisdom went.

There was a method to the madness—you can't really know what's working or not working until you get out there and play. With this came a lot of trial and error and raising of eyebrows. Still, it was that vibe, in early 2004, that helped Dennis book us a two-month gig as the opening act for the European leg of Britney Spears's Onyx Hotel Tour.

Music critics were puzzled. Reviewers got the old-school rock-and-soul part but didn't understand why we were opening for the reigning Princess of Pop. They weren't entirely wrong. Then again, we learned quickly how to put on a show and build energy in front of huge crowds. We learned even more being on a major tour that had so many moving pieces.

One of the things I loved most about traveling on a tour bus overseas was being able to share the adventure with Jaden and Willow, who were six and four at the time. At different stops, depending on his schedule, Will would join us, too, but often it was just me and the kids. Between shows in different cities, I'd have a lot of downtime during the day after our rehearsals. That meant the kids and I could hang out, they could have music lessons with the different band members, or we'd do a little sightseeing.

Traveling the United States after our return from Europe, I saw my country as never before and exposed the kids to as many walks of life as possible. We saw America. We traveled the highways and the byways. Some of the most fun we had was when we had to sleep overnight in our bus at a truck stop during a major snowstorm. We ended up having breakfast there and hanging out with truckers. We had the best time.

We were given the gift of going places that weren't exactly tourist destinations—like Paris, Texas—that we never would have had a reason to visit if not for music. Many of our stops were in what are known as the flyover states, where, yes, many of the metal fans are white men and women who had never seen a band like Wicked Wisdom perform for them. One of my favorite, most euphoric moments was in such a setting.

The first sighting of this place as we drove up made me think there had been a mistake. It was basically in the middle of a cornfield. It looked like a big shack. A makeshift shack at that. In the middle of absolutely nowhere.

We walked in, and it was packed to the rafters with white kids who had no clue what to make of us. We could also see by their numbers that they were ready to rock out and throw down, even if they were a bit skeptical. We were used to that.

The lighting also looked like it had been rigged awkwardly. Somebody had scattered some big work lights around—the kind you see at night for road repairs—that did little to illuminate the large space.

Some indoor venues had a gate that separated the stage from the audience below. These gates were thought to be useful as a barrier between performers and unruly members of the crowd, so no one got the bright idea to climb up onto the stage. This shack/club had those gates out in front of the stage, and the kids were already pressed up against it, waiting to see what we could do.

After we finished setting up and doing a quick sound check, the shack's manager came up and pointed out the very low ceiling, with tons of wires hanging down. He warned me, "Don't try to reach for the ceiling. You could electrocute yourself."

At most shows, I would climb out on top of those barriers to better connect with the crowd. This ceiling was so low I could have used it to help stabilize me. You use what you have. Right?

Once the show started, I got more and more hyped, and the audience got more and more hyped, and I forgot myself. The crowd paid tribute to what they were hearing by assembling into full-blown mosh pits, thrashing into one another with abandon. Doing what I was used to doing, I jumped up on the gate to be closer to the crowd. Overtaken by the wild banshee within, I completely forgot about the open wires in the ceiling, reached up to grab a bar for stability, and damn near electrocuted myself.

For a split second, I felt a very light surge and instantly regained the memory that I was not to reach for the ceiling. I quickly removed my hand and relied on security to hold me up by the waist on that gate.

What was crazy about the night was that as different as our places of origins were, those kids in that club/shack embraced us and went nonstop bananas. Every preconceived notion they must have had— *Who is this Black metal band with a Black female lead singer?*— vanished. Every preconceived notion I had—*Who are these white kids in this shack out in the middle of this cornfield?*—vanished. Color lines, economic differences, cultural differences? All vanished. We shared one reality: the need to have a good fucking time. We were all raging so hard together, we had communion. We shared a true escape from all the worries, discomforts, judgments, and pain that life had to offer. We reveled in connection through music, in a genre most believed had no place for Black folks, especially Black women. ESPECIALLY a famous Black woman. Our differences were moot on the common ground of rock'n the F out and leaving everything we had on the floor.

After we played, many of the kids thanked us for coming to their neck of the woods. In so many words, what I heard them saying was *Thank you for coming here and SEEING us. For giving a fuck that we are here. We know you didn't have to, because so many don't.*

In my metal journey, I learned about the countless white Americans from lower economic to working-class communities who feel unheard and discarded by a country they think has abandoned them. Some blame people who look like me, or blame the government for being corrupt.

In five years on the road, I also came to understand racism on a deeper level by being in the belly of the beast. We fear what and whom we don't know. When we get past the fear, we have to give up some of our biases—which I did after seeing the deprivation of the white hood and witnessing white poverty firsthand. I discovered similarities between poor Black folk and poor white folk in this country, because poverty strips all people, no matter their color, of their dignity and self-worth.

My eyes were opened to the reality of a world where, if you're white, you are thought to have no business being poor, to have no place or value. Hence the idea of "white trash"—the discarded people—yet a people who have been raised to believe this country is more their birthright than anyone else's. Now, being a Black woman, I'm not here to express the experience of poor white Americans. I can only express my limited perception and understanding of what I witnessed while on the road.

Seeing the commonality of struggle, from poor to working and middle classes, helped rinse away some of my prejudices and misunderstandings. This unlikely cultural immersion gave me a new experience of how art can bridge the chasms that divide us.

O ur *"audition" for Ozzfest took place* on the night of April 15, 2005, a Friday—when we played the legendary Viper Room on the Sunset Strip in Hollywood.

Compared to most of the dives where we'd been playing, the Viper Room—leather booths, jewel-tone lighting, moody and sexy—was pretty glamorous. But that's not what made this night special and exciting. This was the night that Sharon Osbourne, as promised, came to hear us play.

As always, we took a moment backstage to connect as a group, say a prayer—showing some gratitude before we hit the stage. Then I added my usual "Let's go fuck shit up."

Passion is contagious. That's one thing with us that was never in question. As a vocalist, I'd grown a lot, learning how to sing and growl at high volume without losing my voice. Our nu-metal sound worked with my voice and my expression, for sure, although where I felt most in my comfort zone was in my showwomanship. I loved absorbing the energy of the audience and delivering a memorable performance. Plus, my band was BADASS.

I had a great time that night, which I hoped meant we had a great show. Once I got offstage, Dennis grabbed me from backstage and brought me to Sharon's booth. We went through the formalities of introducing ourselves and got through some small talk and then—

"Jada," she began, and held me in a second of suspense before she went on, keeping it short and sweet: "I'm putting you on Ozzfest. Get ready."

So excited, all I could do was hug her with a big thank-you all over it.

Sharon smiled and nodded, showing that she was happy for me as well. I thought I understood what "Get ready" meant, while Sharon, in the moment, knew exactly what I would be up against. Her subtext was that if I wanted the shot, she was going to give it to me, but it wouldn't be an easy ride. As I reflect back, I see that she had as much to risk as I did, really. I wasn't the only one to face a barrage of criticism for my Ozzfest run that summer. Sharon was scathingly criticized for giving me the shot.

The truth is that Sharon didn't have to put herself through that scrutiny . . . but she did, and I'd be forever grateful. Her decision made way for one of the most exciting, terrifying, enlightening experiences in this period of my life.

By no accident, from this experience both Jaden and Willow would find themselves at home in the world we traveled and continue on their own paths in music. Jaden found his own love for rock 'n' roll and tour buses and Willow took it even further and would learn to pick up a guitar, rock stages, and unleash her own wild banshee.

I*ronically, the first official announcement that* Wicked Wisdom was going to Ozzfest happened right before I was going out for a live interview for BET. I was so excited, I couldn't help but let the audience know the great news.

Word spread quickly through the metal community, and the backlash was fast and furious. Eventually, I would become a Jedi of letting the most ridiculous and malicious rumors roll off my back. Listen, gossip magazines and online outlets can be disgusting and demoralizing. But nothing compares to actual threats like "We are going to stomp her, rape her, cut her head off, and put her naked body in a ditch," especially when you are a performer in live settings.

Though I tried to take all the venom in stride, I didn't always succeed. Thousands of entries on Ozzfest Web forums went from predicting I wouldn't last the whole tour to saying Wicked Wisdom would ruin Ozzfest forever. One post said, "Wicked Wisdom will be pelted by every loose object on the Ozzfest grounds." Another was "This is going to cause a f-ing riot . . . bring your steel-toed boots."

The death threats were so specific, and there were so many of them, that the head of my security detail was firm: "We are suggesting you don't go. It's too dangerous."

Ain't gonna lie—I was shook. But at the suggestion that I turn down this opportunity because of people's ignorance, I held fast. "I'm going" was all I said.

Will respected how important this was to me. Although he was concerned about what I was going to face, he knew it ultimately had to be my call and supported my decision. If this were today, in a time of rampant racial violence, I would have reconsidered. And I surely would not have taken my kids out on the road with me.

The deciding factor was recognizing everything that had been overcome by my ancestors in far more harrowing circumstances than being a Black metal band on Ozzfest. This was not the Middle Passage, or escaping on the Underground Railroad, or walking through the doors of a white school flanked by federal marshals, as six-year-old Ruby Bridges had done in 1960, or even facing the barrage of hate hurled at Black entertainers and musicians who traveled across a segregated America at the risk of their lives, while merely trying to earn a living and share their gifts. No, playing this summer festival was not that.

Because of the strides of our forebears, we knew an audience was somewhere out there for us. So I sharpened my vigilance and took to the road.

The first time we faced the reality of the threats was in Camden, New Jersey. Before our slot, I was informed that a sizable group of neo-Nazis was in the crowd. The guys and I conferred with one another, put on our armor, and said, in effect, *Let's do what we do.*

To counter the neo-Nazis were JC and an army of his homeboys working the festival. JC, a six-three, 225-pound, baldheaded, tatted, Viking-looking white dude, knew ahead of time that we would face some difficulty out on tour. If you decided to judge a book by its cover, he looked more hard-core than any of those neo-Nazis. And as soon as we were told what was happening in the crowd, JC assured me, "That shit ain't going to fly like that." I had no reason to doubt him.

"BOOOOO!!!" The air filled with the roar of angry skeptics before we even hit a note. We started to play, and the "Heil Hitler" salutes appeared. Before we finished the first song, I saw JC running from behind me to make a Herculean stage dive into the crowd of Nazis, brazenly banging his body into them.

His vibe was very much *What's up? You wanna fuck with somebody, fuck with me.*

And you know what they did? They cowered. Those men had so much heat to throw my way but wanted no smoke from JC. I got to see that day that most of those dudes acting so hard and full of hate were actually cowards. JC constantly reminded me, "Any man that treats a woman that way is a sorry-ass motherfucker."

From that moment in Camden, no matter how chilly or hostile the vibe, I made it my business to walk through the crowd before and after the show, to remind myself that there was nothing to be afraid of, and if there was anyone in the crowd who wanted to hurt me, *Well, here I was.* For the most part, folks didn't even notice. At the end of the day, people paid their money to have a good time. If we could deliver that, and maybe change some hearts and minds, we were good.

One of the most refreshing aspects of being immersed in the world of metal and getting to step from behind the velvet rope was that nobody gave two F's about the machine called Hollywood. They had real life to think about, and that helped me keep focus on the same.

I *think I'm coming down with something,"* I confessed to Will at the hotel where he was meeting up with me and the kids.

We were in the Bay Area after an Ozzfest performance. I

hadn't been feeling well for a while—just excessively tired and very drained. Sitting down with Will, I knew that whatever it was, I couldn't ignore it any longer.

Will suggested we find a doctor to check me out. When the physician came to examine me, it would turn out there was cause for serious alarm. After a thorough physical exam, he determined that every single lymph node in my body was inflamed. The doctor was emphatic: "I need to get you to the hospital right away."

My look of resistance prompted him to explain that he had to rule out cancer of the lymph nodes. In no way did I expect this frightening possibility.

Will accompanied me to the hospital. Once the doctor drained fluid from my nodes (not a pleasant experience, trust me) and ran some tests, he came back with his findings: So far, no evidence of cancer. I was relieved but still worried. His concern was *For your body to be reacting as it is, you must be under an enormous amount of stress.* The doctor strongly suggested that I leave the tour. He believed that by putting my body through this ongoing pressurized intensity, I would end up very sick.

It was hard to see how stress was the cause of how bad I was feeling, but I knew I had to consider taking a break. Sitting next to Will on the couch in our hotel room, I took a deep breath and said, "I don't think I'm gonna be able to finish."

Will looked at me. He spoke very deliberately. "I don't care if I have to have an ambulance follow you to every show or if you have to go onstage with an IV in your arm . . . but you're gonna finish this. You have to finish what you started." He explained, "Because if you quit now, you will regret it."

I started to protest but didn't have the energy.

Will said it again. "If you don't finish, you will regret it. And I can't let you do that. That's what all these people want, is for you to quit. They're waiting for you to do exactly that, and I won't let you."

A part of me agreed with him, but I was also angry at how he had laid it on the line so strongly. No matter how pissed I was, I couldn't overlook the fact that Will was more right than wrong.

I sat there on that couch in the hotel room and thought of another moment when I'd been afraid to finish something I'd started. There was a lesson I needed to remember.

It had happened not long after I'd worked on the movie *Collateral,* which was a wonderful opportunity to become really good friends with Tom Cruise. Unlike many people I've come across in different settings, Tom had the rare ability to see through my great act of having it all together all the time. Without saying it, he picked up on moments when I was feeling far less than worthy. Sometimes I would hold back on the red carpet or when doing press. Tom always had a powerful reminder for me in those instances. "Hey," he would begin, and look me right in the eye, "never forget how smart and talented you are. Now go out there and make somebody smile because you shook their hand on the red carpet today."

That was so helpful. All I had to do was get past my fear.

Early in our friendship, Tom and I found out we shared a love of motorcycles, and I was super excited when we made a plan to ride on his dirt-bike track. There was no holding back or being small when the opportunity came. In fact, I was really feeling myself—from the moment I sat on the dirt bike he'd selected for me and revved its engine to rip on the track as we took off. Enjoying the ride, I had no qualms about trying to jump off a small ramp, only to feel the thrill of catching air. The problem was that after going up, the bike and I descended rapidly to the ground, and I couldn't manage to land the bike.

As soon as I hit the ground, I was thrown from the bike and landed on my back, hitting my head hard. Thank God I had on a helmet.

"Jada, are you okay?" Tom asked, rushing to my side and kneeling down.

I took off my helmet, and though I was shaken up, I said, "I'm fine."

Relieved but concerned, Tom let me know I'd done some good riding but that I should stop for the day.

Bringing myself to my elbows, I looked up at him and asked a really important question of him and of myself: "How many times have you reminded me to not let fear stand in my way? If I don't get back on this bike right now and do another lap, I may never get on a bike again."

Tom paused for a moment, said nothing, and then smiled the biggest smile. He stood up and put out his hand, which I grabbed to pick myself up off the ground.

"Okay, one more round."

I was scared as hell to get back on that bike, but the lesson was— it's not about NOT being scared when you need to move past fear. It's about finding the courage to freaking do it anyway, even if you don't think you can. Doing it again is the only way to prevent the fear from conquering you. Finding the courage is easier when someone has confidence in you—like Tom with me getting back on the bike and Will with me finishing the tour.

This memory amplified the idea that it wasn't about trying to prove something to other people, but about proving to myself that I could finish what I started.

Not only did we complete the run of Ozzfest, but we finished with a bang in a massive thunderstorm in Palm Beach, Florida. I remember getting a lot of daps from bands on the tour who hadn't believed we would stick it out. All I could think about was Will and how right he had been. The exhilaration I felt for soldiering through was incredible. I had set out to achieve a goal, to let my primal self be free, and I had done so.

I tell you what, having the opportunity to watch masterful bands like Black Sabbath and Mastodon play live every day gave me some of the best times of my life, as well as sharing the stage with the dope female lead performer from Arch Enemy at the time, Angela Gossow, who killed it at every performance. I learned so much and made so many friends—like the crew from Bury Your Dead, Brent Hinds from Mastodon, and many more.

I found so much commonality with people of different backgrounds whom I met in that time. Not every single gig reached high notes, but there was almost always a connection that we could acknowledge—*Man, we have lived this moment, this piece of life, together, and it was fun.* Even though I used to call myself a wild banshee onstage, it wasn't about being wild and out of control for its own sake. No, I got to shake off the domestication that had wrapped around me over the years.

I needed the wild banshee who used to prowl the streets of Baltimore at midnight. The one who loved walking on the edges of danger. So many of us forsake our primal callings because we have to make a living, be the dutiful daughter or son or PTA member, and adhere to guidelines that make us worthy in the eyes of others. There are many outlets besides metal music that we can all seek in order to escape whatever boxes we've put ourselves in.

Our inner banshee wants us to give her some space to breathe—to rattle her cage, to get dirty, and to escape all the societal demands to be acceptable, appropriate, and, frankly, perfect. Perfectionism and its more dangerous cousin, romanticism, if unchecked, can cut off your oxygen supply.

I am grateful for it all. The victory was, whether you liked our music or not, you could not question the heart of Wicked Wisdom.

Just as *Ozzfest was ending, we* got an astonishing offer—to be one of the opening acts for Guns N' Roses on their 2005 European tour. It was beyond imaginable.

We barely had a breather before we needed to go out on the road again. During my brief downtime, I hightailed it up to San Francisco, where Will and Jaden were about to start principal photography on *The Pursuit of Happyness*.

As soon as I arrived, I faced a crossroads. Although I desperately wanted to go out with Guns N' Roses, there was no part of me willing to leave Jaden's side while he made this very intense movie. It was his first major role, and Will would not have the bandwidth to play his father on-screen and be Daddy off-screen. Not for a movie that told such a story. Will needed me there as well, to make sure Jaden had what he needed emotionally for this experience.

Seeking my own counsel, as is my preference, I walked out into the San Francisco night air and thought of Jaden and all the time he'd sacrificed, traveling all over the world with me so that I could live my dreams, whether it was going to Australia for a year and a half for *The Matrix* or being away from all his friends to travel on a tour bus with me so I could perform with my band. Now it was my turn to sacrifice for him. I decided to let go of the offer to be an opener for Guns N' Roses.

We still made our second album, and we still went on to perform at some fantastic venues, including going out on tour with one of my favorite bands, Sevendust, and playing the Download Fest the following summer in the UK. Then we put a pause on the band. I never regretted any of those decisions.

Pursuing a dream of getting to rock hard for nearly five years had given me myself in a way that nothing else could. At the time when I stopped, I had gone as far as I needed to go, even if I could have continued. My children were growing up and starting to build their own lives and pursue their own paths. I didn't want to miss out on watching them soar. They'd been with me on my flight, and I wanted to be with them for theirs.

A woman who is starved for her real soul-life may look "cleaned up and combed" on the outside, but on the inside she is filled with dozens of pleading hands and empty mouths.
—CLARISSA PINKOLA ESTÉS, *WOMEN WHO RUN WITH THE WOLVES*

One of the biggest traps for women is the pressure to cut off the most ugly, primal, wild, and unapologetic parts of ourselves so we can feel accepted and worthy. Traditionally, men were given outlets, more so than women, to express their more primitive selves. In recent years, though, men increasingly suffer in silence because they aren't allowed their primal screams, either—as if the nature of masculine energy itself is criminal. We're just starting to talk more about the need for men to be willing to heal so the world can feel the beauty of balanced masculine energy.

―――――

As women, some of us fear revealing our less domesticated sides. We're mired in the bargain that if we act clean and proper, we'll be rewarded with love everlasting, delivered in a big red box with a bow. Otherwise, we might be expendable. We're afraid that if we don't live up to certain standards, we will be exiled by family, friends, culture. We make sure we're never caught with our nails dirty, teeth snarling.

―――――

When we lose touch with that feminine feral force inside us, we end up losing a vital energy that cultivates fervor, fearlessness, boldness, zeal, sincerity, and the drive to love hard, fight hard, dance and play hard. This cutting off of the primal, whatever our expression of it may be, can leave us hollow, angry, and starved. Watch out: A starved woman can be one of the most dangerous creatures on the planet.

―――――

What aspect of yourself do you believe you need to cut off to be accepted, respected, loved, and cared for? Is there an outlet that offers that untended part of yourself a safe place to roam free? Do you like to paint, dance, go camping, climb trees, kickbox, travel, go on wild adventures? Can you push yourself out of your comfort zone? Are you willing to roll in the mud a bit? I dare you.

CHAPTER 17

No Soccer Mom Here

Everything grows.

If I had learned anything from the gardening lessons with my grandmother, that one truth stood above the rest. *Every* step is important in the care and nurturing of what we hope to see grow and thrive—preparing the soil, adding nutrients, planting seeds, providing the proper amounts of water and sunlight, and, of course, understanding how growth depends on weathering the changing seasons.

Not only do roses and strawberries and trees grow, but so do the pesky bugs and weeds if you don't stay on top of them. The simple but lasting lesson was, when in doubt, focus on protecting the flowers. In life, that meant the people and the relationships I treasured most. In doing my utmost to see loved ones grow and thrive, I still had to ward off negative influences. Obviously, when you see the first signs of trouble in your garden, you can save yourself much heartache by nipping the threat in the proverbial bud.

These gardening principles may help to explain why I raised my kids as I did; how I tried to cultivate an open, realistic line of communication in my marriage; and how I tried to honor my own growth as the seeker I am. Some of my choices were unconventional, quite like my own upbringing, maybe even controversial. In the early days, the judgment I faced for how I appeared to be breaking away from the collective was not surprising. Eventually, I would have to learn how to not be defensive and to understand that I couldn't let others' scrutiny and judgment direct my life. Besides, it was *my* life. No one had to fear that my going against the grain was contagious, as if it could make them swallow their values, or change their lifestyle. Yet many reacted as if I could.

I rarely felt the need to please or placate the chatterers or to refute every ridiculous rumor that popped up. Later on, when controversies got out of hand and folks believed Will and I were swingers (or that we were both gay and playing as each other's beards, or that we were sleeping with whomever we chose, whenever we chose to), all I could do was sit back and shake my head. It got so ridiculous.

One traditional aspect of our marriage is that we put family first, and for a few reasons, we were both adamantly against divorce. Children of divorce ourselves, we understood the challenges to the family unit that almost inevitably arise when marriages are severed. We both believed in the vows of "for better, for worse." You can sprinkle some abandonment issues in there for both of us as well.

We also had some issues that were traditional. In archetypal male fashion, Will was on his Hero's Journey, trying to be the superhero off conquering and charging for the flag at the top of the hill with fierce determination. In archetypal female fashion, I prioritized my roles as mother and wife, keeper of hearth and home. This didn't stop me from trying to be a superheroine in a multifaceted career, like so many of us trying to do all and be all.

My biggest issue was also fairly common—fear of abandonment. This fear fed through our too busy lives, a constant, and there was always so much going on, with the running themes of me being overwhelmed and him being emotionally unavailable, that I found myself in a chronic state of discontent.

After a therapy session one afternoon, Will and I had a conversation about this apparent disconnect in our priorities. It was a telling moment, just him and me sitting across from each other at a table in our library, a room full of books that we love and collect.

With some frustration, I tried a new way to get him to understand my point of view. He listened as I asked, "If we didn't have this house, our careers, and all the things, and it was just the two of us on a deserted island together, what would we have? What would we have between us, just you and I?"

Will paused and thought about the question but didn't answer right away.

I continued, "We need to work on our connection. We need to strengthen the love and connection between us."

Will immediately responded, "We'll get to that later."

Classic.

This was a reasonable response for someone who grew up without stable financial security and who formed the idea that material gain was the key to safety in this world. For high achievers, that then becomes the utmost priority and a display of love. His way to show his love was by making sure I wanted for nothing. Although I was grateful for his ability to provide all of that, with my history, my utmost priority and key to safety in the world was from feeling he loved me above ALL else and having ALL of his attention. Maturity and time would prove us both wrong.

We said little more that was memorable that afternoon. Then we both got up from the table, still with our difference in beliefs as to what would make for a strong union, and went about our day.

As I mentally replayed the conversation later, his assurance that we would get to *us* in the future seemed to suggest that someday his days of empire building would be behind us, and then we could slow down and connect more. None of this was helpful to me, considering that (a) our love and connection could be put on the back burner while he pursued and lived out his dream, and (b) as he pursued his dream, he would be working with and in the company of some of the most sought-after women in the world.

I was not so naive as to believe that all of a sudden, Will would be temptation-resistant in what was going to be an onslaught of opportunity. Good luck to anyone in their late twenties/early thirties who has that down pat. Some significant others might expect an incredible amount of willpower (no pun intended) in service of the ideals of matrimony. If that works for you, many blessings, but in my case, I wanted to be aligned with that which I deemed inevitable. This was less about Will but, rather, about my own experience with the nature of temptation.

I knew for myself what it felt like to walk into a room and be the one with all that attention. I also knew how seductive that energy could be. It's overwhelmingly intoxicating. And, to be blunt, certain work environments are conducive to a certain level of intimacy and time shared.

We had already run across a few situations that made me want to come up with a proactive solution to protect the sanctity of our trust. As a child, trust had been nonexistent in my home, and it was something I desperately wanted in my marriage. As long as we had each other's trust, we could work through anything. The solution then was to create an agreement to help build that trust by which we would never be in a position to lie to each other. In other words, a relationship of transparency, which is different from an "open" relationship. The agreement was never *You can go sleep with whomever you want, whenever you want.* Instead, it was *Hey, when those temptations are in play, let's trust each other to come together in partnership with the truth, talk, and work as partners through them.* In this way, we eliminated any possibility of betrayal.

And yes, this sounds like a recipe for abusing trust. It's not a strategy for the faint of heart. But as I learned early in my life, painful as it is confronting the truth, it is so much more painful being left in the dark.

Later on, talk of our open marriage was somewhat misleading because it wasn't the free-for-all it sounded like. But the term became an easy explanation for much more complicated issues going on between us in that era.

I don't believe our solution is for everybody. And in hindsight, considering I was so young and didn't understand all that would come with this decision, I definitely would make some adjustments if I could go back. This was a decision that I felt I needed to make at the time in order to trust what we were building together and to protect myself from being abandoned. Of course, in the process, I abandoned myself.

Another controversy that lingered was the way in which I chose to educate my kids.

Homeschooling is not for everyone. I get it. It's a ton of work for the parent willing to become educated about all different approaches to learning, as well as in the different subjects covered in mainstream academic settings. It's not that I'm against public or private schools. In fact, when Will and I established a charitable family foundation, one of our priorities was funding programs for education—especially arts education—in marginalized communities in this country and around the world.

The main reason I wanted to homeschool my kids was that I wanted them to be able to travel with Will and me while we worked. It was important that they be with us. With this, one of my goals was to give my kids the strongest possible fundamentals for lifelong learning, much as I'd been given by Marion. I also understood there was so much learning that could happen from being exposed to new places, and from being in contact with children from communities very different from their own. It was also important that they had teachers and peers of color in a setting of inclusion, which is why, as time went on, we expanded our approach and built a full-fledged school to include other students who came from a range of backgrounds.

Some of the controversy about my approach to education probably had to do with the use of the Study Technology learning method that I'd discovered when I was introduced to Scientology. Study Tech, although it came from Scientology, is legally defined as secular.

Because of my experiences on Sundays at the Ethical Society, and my Christian, Islamic, Judaic, Buddhist, and Sufi studies throughout my adult life, I didn't hold the same stigma around the Church of Scientology that most do. I have also never been a fan of organized religion, though I appreciate spiritual study and observance of all kinds. I was very clear when I stepped into the Church of Scientology that becoming a member would not be possible, nor was it my goal. My goal was to embrace the Basic Study Manual to educate myself about a method of learning.

The main focus of this method is on helping a student achieve 100 percent proficiency with a subject, as opposed to memorizing and regurgitating but not gaining any command over said knowledge or skills. Study Tech has a component for helping a child gain a sense of self-determinism with respect to whatever is being taught. The system offers many different processes for how to engage children in their education and to create habits that make them become lifelong learners.

Although Jaden thrived as an independent student throughout his schooling, Willow at one time in her middle school years wanted to attend a traditional school. My one condition was that she commit to the entire year. When Christmas vacation came around, Willow decided she did not want to continue her new school.

"Willow, I told you that once you started, you would have to finish the year."

Willow huffed and puffed a bit but returned to school and finished the year. I was actually impressed by the skill sets she attained, including new methods of organization for her studies as well as time management. She was very proud that she had completed the year and was happy with all that she had learned. Overall, she believed attending traditional school was a worthy experience.

As a mother, I found it gratifying to see my kids love to learn and develop the openness to question and, in time, to craft their own approach to self-education. In the process, I learned a lot, especially how to facilitate my kids' individual educational needs. And I don't regret a moment of it.

Eventually, I stopped paying attention to the criticism and judgment of others about how to raise my kids. There are no cookie-cutter ways to raise children, and the only concern any of us should have is making sure we're paying attention to what our individual child needs. No parent should be judged when trying to facilitate ways for their child to thrive. Because guess what? We're all guessing anyway, while doing our best.

I *really want to come back into* your life and have a chance to be your father" was not what I expected to hear from Robsol when he visited in July 1999. More than twenty years had passed, but I had never forgotten that day in Baltimore when he announced that he couldn't be my father. Now, apparently, he was having a change of heart.

At this point, Rob seemed to be in a good place. He had been clean for years, although his addiction was such that he could stay sober for a good while and then fall off. Nonetheless, he was healthy and handsome as ever.

The two of us found ourselves in the living room, sitting on the couch together and mindlessly watching television, when he made this sudden declaration of wanting to be in my life as a father.

Surprised and insulted, I blurted right out, "I'm married, building a family of my own. I don't need a father now." My inner monologue went much further: *Oh, now I'm worthy enough for you to be my father because of what I've made of my life?*

Sadly, I didn't have the maturity yet to grasp that it's never too late to make amends and that people are often unskilled at doing so. It was Robsol's timing that made me question his sincerity.

He went silent and returned to watching television. So did I. And that was that.

About six years later, my brother Caleeb (the son of Robsol and Carolyn who lived in California, and whom I call Caleb) called to tell me that our father's addiction was at its worst, and if I didn't bring Rob out to L.A. from Baltimore, he would, without a doubt, die.

Two warring positions took hold in my mind. At seven years old, I had accepted the edict that Rob was not to be my father and believed we had relinquished all responsibility to each other. But I couldn't leave Rob to die.

Knowing there was no one else to step in, I made the decision to bring him to L.A. and enter him into Narconon, a program affiliated with Scientology. Narconon was designed to help people with debilitating addictions, and I could only hope that they could help my father.

Robsol was in disastrous shape. Drugs had ravaged his body. He was so sick that he could not walk and was confined to a wheelchair. Weak, thin, and plagued by illness, he was clearly on the brink of death.

Even though we had little contact while he was in the residential program, I learned that within less than a month, Robsol was drug-free, out playing basketball, no less. His health, body and mind, was recovering speedily.

It was nothing short of a miracle. By the time I saw Robsol next, he was fit, fresh, with a new haircut and a spark in his eye. He was bright, strong, and mentally sober in a way I had never witnessed before. He wanted to continue his recovery in L.A., and in a moment of good timing, we had space for him in a guesthouse on a property we had just moved from and where my brother Caleeb, my sister-in-law Trish, my niece Jade, and my nephew Jahlil were temporarily staying until they moved into their new home.

This gave Rob an opportunity to spend time with his grandchildren. They got to experience the magic and beauty of Rob's mind, imagination, and talent—still as super smart and eclectic in his thinking as ever and still an artist in his own right.

Robsol Pinkett, unburdened by his addictions, was who he had always been—a man before his time who was always contemplating existential concepts in search of higher truths. We made up for lost time, somewhat. The power of DNA became more evident to me, because even though we had inconsistent contact in my childhood, I was very much like him in my eclectic approach to life and my desire to search for deeper meaning. Nothing was off-limits for Rob in the same way nothing was off-limits to me. We were alike in the sense that he would try pretty much anything if he felt it might encompass a higher truth. Rob was very clear that Narconon had saved his life when we all believed there was no hope, which was why he kept going further into his studies in Scientology.

One day Rob came to the house and asked to talk. He brought me into the library, and we sat down at the table together.

"I am so grateful for everything you have done for me and for allowing me to continue my studies at the church, but I won't be going back."

Out of curiosity, I asked, "Why?"

"I love Jesus, and some of their spiritual beliefs conflict with mine." His concise answer was fair. He got up to leave, then thought for a beat before turning back to me and saying, "Stay where you are. You don't need to go beyond there."

I nodded, saying in so many words that I had no plans to do so.

I had been clear all along about what I wanted to study and the lane I was going to stay in. Maybe there would have been more pressure for me to become a member of Scientology had I not drawn the line, several times. In any case, after Rob stopped his studies, mine came to an end soon after.

Like so many addicts who struggle to stay clean in the harshness of the world, Rob would fall into his addiction again. It was heartbreaking for everyone. After he fell off the wagon, he went back into a rehab facility that I paid for, but he kept using, which ultimately made me extremely angry. I came to the decision that he should go back to Baltimore and bear the consequences of his own choices.

He reached me on my cell while I was on a set somewhere, to tell me how unhappy he was with my decision to get him back to Baltimore—without my assistance once he left Los Angeles. I was all the more frustrated, because he felt entitled to my continuing to pay for his lifestyle as his sole financial support—even though he was still using. We had a terrible disagreement, but I held firm.

There comes a moment when you have to let go and let God. The pain of confronting a parent's addiction yet again was too much. I felt that continuing to pay for care and lifestyle would only enable Rob's addiction. It is never easy for the child of an addict to understand how to create healthy boundaries—when to step up and when to step away. This confusion made me even angrier. The never-ending roller coaster was enough.

In early 2010, before arrangements could be made for Rob to go to Baltimore, while he was still in rehab in L.A., I got a call when I was out of town.

The minute I heard my brother's voice on my phone, I knew. "Rob's dead, isn't he?"

"Yeah . . ." Caleeb went on to say that Rob had died from an overdose.

Because I was out of town, my brother took on the responsibility of handling everything, identifying Rob's body and making all necessary arrangements. We all then flew to Baltimore to attend the funeral. At the burial, reality struck me hard. His addiction had killed him. In my teens, Adrienne was the one we all thought wasn't going to make it. Rob would always bounce back.

Stories can surprise you, the way they play out. The funeral was a blur, but I have one clear memory—of looking over at my grandmother Shirley. I never thought I would have to watch her bury her son. On this tragic day, she stood strong. With all her loss and pain, she never lost her faith.

After Robsol's death, I began to make peace with the memory of who he had been in my life. With that came the recognition that my father never felt like this place was his home. He never felt that he belonged anywhere and was lonely in a crowded room. Increasingly, I could relate to him in that way, and found an entry point to feeling more empathy and compassion toward him. As time has passed, I have learned that Rob deserves honor for giving me life and that his struggles and shortcomings were not to be taken personally. He was not born simply to be my father but to play out the role designed for him by the Great Supreme. He did the best he knew how and deserved love, even in his struggle. He lived out the plan of his Father God.

Robsol had said it best: "Nobody gets out of life alive."

My father taught me a morbid but valuable lesson—that if I am in a disagreement with someone, I ask whether the conflict or upset would exist if that person was on their deathbed. If I can answer that it wouldn't matter in that instance, I know I should let it go.

Once my father died, I began very small steps toward the acceptance that people are not born to live out the purpose I might see fit for my needs. Nor I for them.

At this time, *Jaden and Willow* were both going through major transitions.

After the success of *Pursuit of Happyness,* it was clear that Jaden had risen to the challenge of a demanding role with an honest performance. As he gained public attention, I watched him, at eight years old, carry himself with real charm and maturity. My ongoing lesson as a mother would be to continue to trust him and his instincts, but doing so was not without challenges.

A pivotal moment took place when Jaden was training in L.A. for the filming of *Karate Kid.* Everything about this movie, including the five-month shoot in China, was tough. Yet Jaden approached his role and his training as an ardent, devoted student. During a session at our home with his coach, I stood off to the side, staying quiet as Master Wu asked Jaden to go into a split. Complying, Jaden hit the floor in a full split, leaving only a few inches between his body and the floor. Then I watched as Master Wu put his foot on Jaden's back and pressed him down to deepen the split until he fully hit the floor.

Tears fell from Jaden's eyes—from sheer pain. Although I had mad respect for Master Wu and understood that he believed he was doing what was best for Jaden, as a mother, I thought it excessive.

"That's enough," I said.

Ignoring me, the trainer lifted his foot from Jaden's back and said, "Do it again."

Directly to Jaden, I said, "I think that's enough. You don't have to do it again, Jaden."

Jaden got up off the floor and took a minute.

"Are you okay? I think you've done enough for today."

Jaden wiped the tears from his eyes and said, "I'm okay, Mommy," and then he turned from me to look at his trainer and said, "I'm ready. Let's do it again." Jaden left my side and went right into his split, hitting the floor fully on his own.

The exchange communicated so much. With all of us, Will had always pressed the point that pushing yourself to your limits—creatively, athletically, professionally—was where you discovered your weak points and you could then strengthen them. Jaden had begun his career so young, but in heeding his father's teaching, he wasn't going to miss this opportunity to strengthen his inner warrior.

This day was a rite of passage for my son, as he was letting me know: *Mom, I got this.*

It was a rite of passage for me, too—Jaden gave me the signal that in this stage of his life, he was ready for a bit more push, a bit more touching the edges, things so difficult for a mother to watch. This helps explain why, in some cultures in Africa, fathers will steal their sons in the middle of the night to take them into the jungle for the ritual journeys into manhood, without warning the mother. Sometimes it's painful for a mother to witness the process of a son becoming a man.

As Jaden got older, though, I found that as a Black mother, having a Black son in this world brought out all kinds of PTSD. I'd lost so many of my homies to murder, the judicial system, and other predatory factors that come with being a person of color. I was quite clear, through Pac's journey, that fame for a young Black man could also make you a target to the streets and the police. All you can do is educate your kids and make sure they develop their own sense of vigilance for when and wherever danger lurks.

In observing how my son moved in the world, I had to trust his instincts for staying safe. Still, I caution him every time he heads out, "Be vigilant." To this day.

Jaden would time and time again expand my definition of what it means to be a young, strong Black male. He showed me and continues to show me the many different shades of Black male strength.

While in Beijing, Willow—who was seven at the time—came to a decision about her future. In China, she had been studying music and Mandarin at the same time, both of which she loved, but she wanted to go further. What did that mean? Well, as she announced, "I want to record music." It was clear she was a natural musician.

We took her desires seriously, and she proved to have the chops. So much so that by the time she was nine, she had recorded "Whip My Hair" in the studio at home. Will's lifelong friend Omarr Rambert had found the song, and when Jay-Z heard Willow's recording, he knew immediately it was a hit and signed her to Roc Nation. From then until this day, Jay has been one of the most incredible supporters of Willow's musical development, along with Roc Nation cofounders Jay Brown and Ty Ty.

It was crazy. "Whip My Hair" was a hit song straight out of the gate. Willow was on her way into the stratosphere, and in a rare moment of timing, Jay was able to acquire movie rights to the musical *Annie*, to be produced with Overbrook (the production company headed by Will and James Lassiter), with Willow set to play the title role.

Everything was moving forward until we took off on a brief vacation to the Dominican Republic. There were golf carts that we used to explore the resort where we were staying, and Willow asked if she could talk to me as we set out one day, with her driving.

We drove along for a while, until she stopped and burst into tears, telling me, "I can't do this, Mommy. I can't do this."

Emotion poured out, almost from every pore. I sat with her and simply listened. It occurred to me that she was not just saying no to the *Annie* movie but to a promising pop music career. This was seemingly the dream of dreams for many young artists, and she was ready to let it go.

My first thought was *So much has been set up, and so many have invested in this.*

Fear and panic set in. For a minute, I thought that maybe I should say she would be turning down a great opportunity to have the most fantastic career and future, but I had to stop myself with some tough love—*Look at her. Drop it. It's done, it's over. She doesn't want this. It's too much. You're going to have to help her and support the dismantling of all of this. And help her father understand.*

I recognized myself in her. We have dreams, and we are not aware of all that comes with those dreams. Willow loved the creative aspect of achieving her dreams but not the pressure and chaotic schedules that came with it. She is strong but fragile, and that kind of pressure would not work for her mental health. I understood completely.

I said to her, "It's okay. I get it." She didn't want to disappoint people. She was grateful, but she knew instinctively, the way her life was going, that continuing would be to her ruin.

I was looking at her in awe and thinking that, as an adult, I didn't have the gumption to say no to people close to me who thought they knew what was best for me. Here was Willow telling the giants in her life—her dad, her mom, Jay-Z, the world—*No, thank you.*

Damn.

That conversation in the golf cart was a defining moment. She was putting herself on a journey to self-discovery as a young woman and as an artist. At freak'n eleven. She was doing the hard work that I hadn't even learned to do yet. My heart ached for her, but she was ready to design a life of her own making, by her own hands. I was hella scared and hella proud of her at the same time. My promise was to support her in every way possible.

Not only was I scared for Willow, but I couldn't bear the idea of failing her—while also trying to figure out how to do what she was doing, to build a life for myself made by my own hands instead of the hands of others.

Here's the refrain: *Everything grows. Little* baby resentments and angers, deep sorrow unmourned, the buzzing of despair ignored.

Once I got off the road with Wicked Wisdom and didn't have my music as a distraction or outlet, my interior world began to crumble and take me down with it. I had been a high-functioning depressive for so long, but all that so-called functioning was ending. All that had haunted me in my early twenties—everything that had led to my first breakdown, and which I believed love, marriage, children, and success would save me from—came crashing down on me with a vengeance. You can only ignore the haunting for so long. Unanswered questions demand to be answered. This time, the breakdown promised to take a greater, different toll.

With the certainty that I was not allowed to fall apart, because I believed it was up to me to keep everything moving in all the parts of our great big life, I shut down. In 2008 I was in Beijing, and Mia—who was there helping coordinate our living quarters during the *Karate Kid* shoot—picked up on this when she came to check in with me in my hotel room.

We were standing by the window, one of those floor-to-ceiling picture windows that gave us a full view of the city below.

Whatever gave me away, I don't know, but Mia turned to me as I continued to stare out the window, and she asked point-blank, "Are you all right?"

"Oh, yeah." I shrugged and blew off whatever she had sensed about me as stress from a challenging production situation.

Mia and I had history, with a journey that began at Baltimore School for the Arts and North Carolina, and now I was grateful she was at my side as our estate manager, aka "all things important in our lives" manager. Mia had become indispensable to me. She could also read me like a book.

"You know you can talk to me. I've known you a long time, and something is not right," Mia pushed, giving me a look of deep concern.

"I'm good, Mia. Thank you, though" was all I said.

Though Mia was my friend, she had a lot on her plate, too. I didn't want to burden her. But honestly, I was more afraid of opening the Pandora's box of my emotions. I thought I might lose what little ability to function that I had left.

I was perched high atop Beijing but felt like I was at the bottom of an abyss. If I tried, I could see how I got here, but I couldn't possibly see how to get out. Hopelessness became my unwanted companion.

By the following year, those feelings intensified. I embraced a series of healing rites, any alternative modes of exorcising the doom and gloom that I could find. To no avail.

My thoughts were jumbled, at times fixating on the fact that I was turning forty, that my best days were behind me, and that I was past my prime, not worthy of being alive. Other times I'd try to connect to what was happening in my day, but all I could think about was past losses.

The gilded cage I had built felt like a prison, and I had walked in here on my own. I couldn't come up with a solution. And I couldn't remedy my shame about being unhappy. The soundtrack was a broken record: *What's wrong with me? Am I inherently broken? Why can't I just be happy?*

More and more, I realized that Will wasn't the cause of my despair. Still, I wished he could fix me, fix it. Of course he couldn't, but that didn't keep me from being angry that he wasn't able to. Hadn't I held up my end of the deal? The boxes I had checked came to mind. I had sacrificed to be a friend, a lover, a wife, and a mother. We had a family, a successful blended family. We had amazing kids. He had his dream of being one of the most famous actors in the world. Was I demanding too much to think that now it was my turn for him to make some sacrifices for my happiness, like I had done for his?

Here's the catch—I couldn't see that I had made those choices voluntarily. Nobody forced me.

Up until this point, I had used resentment to give me righteous anger to get through the day. It kept me going, so I fed it. Anger was more palatable than despair, less debilitating. Many women opt to get mad rather than sad, although we're often scorned for it—especially those of us labeled "angry Black women." Few who do the scorning bother to see that beneath the anger are the burdens of disappointment, debilitating hurts, and deep wells of anguish. All we know to do is use our anger to keep everything moving.

For a time, I kept up a brick encasement of my rage. Nobody could touch it, not even me. As long as I could make the rage Will's fault, it was useful. That meant there could be a reason for my pain, and I wouldn't let him forget it—whether it meant giving him the silent treatment, withholding gratitude, or just loathing him. Looking back, what in the world is someone supposed to do with that?

Eventually, the brick encasement of anger and blame no longer held. My capacity for discomfort kept me going. But why keep going? I'd been suicidal at an earlier time in my life and had sought help. Not this time. Thoughts of ending my life became hard to control. Just getting out of bed every morning and managing to function, somehow, took everything out of me. The darkest, most foreboding stretches were from when I got up until about four in the afternoon. If I could make it until four, I knew that I had survived another day.

At the end of my thirty-ninth year, I woke up one morning with dread and realized that a vision for my future was nonexistent. I literally saw nothing. Right then it hit me that I had never even imagined a life past forty, as if there was no way possible I'd ever make it that far. The fact that there was no vision for my life ahead—no sight, no dream, no desires, nothing besides a black void—terrified me.

My origin story, like that of many of us young Black folks from the streets, is that we live hot, fast, and reckless, putting one foot in front of the other until the inevitable day we meet our demise earlier than expected. It tormented me that I hadn't met a demise, yet so many I loved had. Compounding that torment was this: I was alive, and not only was I alive but living the so-called dream, with a beautiful family, and I could not, for the life of me, find a way to enjoy it. That, in itself, brewed another cup of hot shame.

I didn't imagine making it past forty, but I was doing everything I could to make it another day.

That saying "*check on your strong* friends" is a very, very real suggestion.

As my fortieth birthday approached, in the midst of free-falling, I hoped that Will could see I was in no position to handle any big to-do. I was very fragile and told everyone that I didn't want a party for my birthday.

I believe there is a certain degree of intense self-focus that multiplies within the cone of pain and prevents it from showing. In our disconnection from others and even ourselves, all we can focus on are the all-consuming feelings of discomfort. In another state, I might not have been upset that nobody seemed to be listening to me when I said I did not want a party. But this chapter of my life could be called me hitting rock bottom.

A concerned friend who knew of the huge extravaganza being planned for my birthday called to take my temperature, knowing that I might not be up for it.

"I feel terrible telling you this," my friend began, swearing me to secrecy as I was told that Will, in the love language he knew how to use, was planning a most unforgettable experience for my birthday. One that anyone would undoubtedly be thrilled to receive.

There was only one reality—I didn't have it in me to fake it through such an event, during which I would be required to be *on*. That would make me feel worse, reminding me of how debilitated and lonely I was, even in a huge room full of people.

All I could do was to express to Will once again that I was not in a condition for a party. The issue, though, was that he had been planning for months. It was impossible to cancel the entire event. Instead, we decided to go forward with a very, very small gathering of only those closest to me in attendance.

The party was to take place in Santa Fe, New Mexico, in the Land of Enchantment, over the course of three days. We traveled there to enjoy a much more intimate version of what Will had envisioned. For a few moments, I got to just BE, as I was, with people who I believed really loved me.

At dinner the first night, we sat, all of us, at a long table. It was so nice. And still.

There was so much love in the room, I was given a much-needed embrace in the simplicity of it all. And even though the undercurrent of hopelessness still lurked, for the moment, it was nice to feel what I desperately needed, to simply feel loved and held. I felt it, but in my fog, I couldn't express my appreciation to Will and to everyone who had made it happen.

One of my longtime and dearest friends, Ramsey Naito—my homegirl from Baltimore School for the Arts—was in attendance. We had both gone from running the streets in Baltimore and getting drunk off peach schnapps to landing in Hollywood. She had become a leading studio executive, eventually heading up the animation divisions at Paramount and Nickelodeon.

The second afternoon, Ramsey came to my room to check on me. She started with small talk, but I could tell she had something on her mind. Finally, she asked, "What's going on? I feel like something's wrong."

Holding back tears, all I could say was "I don't know, Ramsey."

"You don't seem like yourself. I have never seen you so fragile."

I paused, desperately trying to put my words together in a way that didn't make me seem too pathetic or out of control. "I'm so unhappy, and I can't figure out why or what to do."

She responded, "I'm really worried about you."

Ramsey sat with me in the room, giving me a safe harbor. It was just us there, talking. She would later reveal that she was worried because I seemed so isolated, so alone, in a room full of people. I tried to reassure her that I'd be okay. She wasn't going to let me off the hook. "Maybe you should talk to somebody," she suggested.

I nodded, letting her know in so many words that I had tried therapy, but . . . here I was.

Just having her check in on me like that was a gift. At a point when I felt no one had listened to the fact that I did not want a party, I had been expected to rise to the occasion, and I couldn't, and Ramsey could see that. She was willing to listen and not make me feel ungrateful or crazy.

Ramsey wasn't the only one. Miguel caught up with me midwalk toward the end of that second evening, asking if there was anything he could do. "You seem heavy." He was in his big-brother mode, just touching base.

I wanted to say, "I'm going through something, but I'll be okay." But I couldn't, because I didn't know if that was true.

Over the next month, I came to the conclusion that I would never be okay.

After scouting different sites for driving off the road at just the right angle to kill myself without having it look intentional, I finally chose the spot. That was when I pulled over and looked down. Now all I had to do was decide when to carry through with the plan.

A week or so later, by Divine guidance, Jaden—a hint of enthusiasm in his eyes—came to grab me from the kitchen to join a conversation that led to a lifesaving experience.

OJAI, CALIFORNIA
January 2012

Terrified as I am to head down the driveway to the Medicine Woman's house, my heart damn near beating out of my chest, my initiation into the ayahuasca ceremony on night one is nowhere near as intense as expected.

The Medicine Woman has an immediate calming effect as she leads me to my seat on low meditation pillows in the middle of her space—a quaint, comfortable room with powerful thangkas of Tara, a statue of Quan Yin, a picture of Jesus, and, on her wall, a bronze sculpture of an Egyptian symbol.

The Medicine Woman appears experienced. I can tell she's not on no play-play, no fairy beam, moon dust, freak'n crystal wands with affirmations and shit. Her calm intensity makes it clear she is serious about this work.

At eight p.m. on the nose, the ceremony begins. The Medicine

Woman brings out a brass tray with a plastic cup and pours the brew until the cup is about a third full. Then she holds out the tray for me to take the cup.

And so I drink . . . oh my God, it is the nastiest taste I've ever had in my life. Even to consume the plant is a passage in itself. It's so terrible, you can rethink your entire effort.

My guide takes her seat on a pillow on the floor, her legs crossed like mine. For the next hour and fifteen minutes, we sit in silence, no sound other than the music she has curated especially for this journey. After all that time, I am surprised that I feel . . . nothing. But I'm not about to say anything.

Finally, the Medicine Woman speaks. "You need more?"

"I think so." Clearly, I am so defensively layered, I need much more to break through.

My next gulp is bigger than the first. It's as awful as before. Maybe worse. Another forty-five minutes of silence follow. Not much seems to be happening. The Medicine Woman brings me a third serving, and I swallow it fast. A few moments later, I AM IN! I am gone! I'm in another world—an altered reality. Very little time passes before I am replaced by a panther.

My favorite animal has always been the black panther, and I am nothing short of thrilled. My assumption is that she came to me in this ceremony because she is my spirit animal, but I was to learn that the panther, like the rainbow serpent, frequently appears as a guide in the ayahuasca journey.

I can see her and through her as she leads me into the darkness of the jungle, showing me the way.

Here we go.

For the rest of the night, this most majestic black panther and I moved deeper and deeper into the woods. I was not afraid. The journey began to feel like a beautiful midnight prowl into new territory. We walked through the jungle all night within alluring, mysterious darkness. By three a.m., I began to emerge from this first leg of the journey. I had lived. I was grateful and drove safely back to my friend's guesthouse.

The second night began much the same as the first night, except this time I needed only two doses. Once again, I became the black panther in the jungle. Lulled into believing I was skilled at this ceremony and enjoying my prowl into the unknown, I felt almost fearless by the third night.

Big mistake.

The Medicine Woman asked, "Are you ready to drink?"

With a kind of bring-it-on attitude, I took hold of the plastic cup, gulping the unpleasant brew. Then I took another dose, drinking even faster. Two doses at once.

The medicine took hold quickly, much more so than previous nights. Between the medicine and the music, I soon became a little overwhelmed by all the thoughts and sensations whirling in my mind. Oh no. I could feel a different level of intensity taking hold of me. I was losing control.

Now I'm scared. I can't get a hold of myself, my feelings, my thoughts, and all kinds of pictures that are flashing in my mind's eye. My mental state is a big, murky tornado, and I've lost all my bearings.

STOP! I'm screaming inside my head. *I DON'T LIKE THIS! STOP IT! NOW!*

I've plunged off a cliff into a dark pit, and voices crawl in like hissing snakes.

"You're worthless! Fucking kill yourself!" "What are you waiting for? Fucking do it now!"

The voices get LOUDER and LOUDER. I want to put my arms up to shield myself, but what good will that do? The voices sound like they're coming from outside and inside of me, all in a barrage like gunfire.

"You're a miserable, stupid person, you don't deserve to live. You don't do shit right anyway." "Nobody will miss you." "SO KILL YOURSELF!"

Why? I'm pleading, crying, gasping. "I'm sorry, I'm sorry."

Out of the corner of my eye, I see the Medicine Woman as she watches me, not saying anything.

On my knees and with my forehead to the ground, I'm desperately pleading with the voices, confessing my sin: "I'm so sorry that I tried to look for myself in the eyes of other people." What else? Anything that I can think to be sorry for, I say, trying to find an answer so these voices will stop. As if trying to run from the gunfire, I make it to my feet and go into the small bathroom to face myself in the mirror, all while being chased by taunting voices: "Jada, just do it. Just fucking kill yourself. Just fucking kill yourself. Your kids will be better off without you here. All they need is Will. All everyone needs is Will."

I will later understand that Mother Aya is showing me my own suicidal thoughts. She is showing me all the unloved parts of myself needing light and love within me to purify these lies. In those minutes, I have no idea that these voices are MY thoughts. I am convinced that evil has entered me, that I am possessed by the devil.

The voice I hear next is different. It's deep, low, and matter-of-fact: "Just kill yourself."

Fleeing the bathroom back to the company of the Medicine Woman doesn't help. There is nothing she can do besides hold space. I'm forced to witness this dense black shadow within myself.

The night turns into early morning, and I'm in that dungeon, wrestling with the devil. He won't leave, no matter how much I try to bargain. The more I fight, the more I wrestle, the more everything coming at me intensifies. My panther has vanished, and I have ventured into the exiled lands—the exiled part of myself. It's now just me with me, living in a horror movie within my mind.

You break the rules, and you become the hero. I do it, and I become the enemy.

—WANDA TO DR. STRANGE IN MARVEL'S *DR. STRANGE IN THE MULTIVERSE OF MADNESS*

Just as it's important to comply with the rules at times, sometimes it is important to know when to break them. When we're so trained to check boxes, we become a prisoner inside them. It's a scary moment when we have to risk the fallout—whether it comes from other people's judgment or from giving up our need to be the always available, reliable, and compliant one.

———

Uncheck some boxes. It can be terrifying to let go of that which is familiar and to lean into that which is not. If someone doesn't love or approve of you because you have decided to venture outside the box or because playing by the rules no longer works, they are not for this part of your journey. And that's okay.

———

There are lessons to be learned inside the box and outside it. Take the opportunity to diversify your experiences. You may fall on your face, but if you so choose, you will not leave the experience without the gift of knowing your own courage. You may not find your treasure, but you will be taking one big leap in the direction of it. Even having the courage to uncheck the old box will empower you in ways you can't know until you do it.

———

Go on. Choose to simply LIVE by your own rules! What boxes are you ready to uncheck, and why? When you clarify this answer, you'll be ready. Then . . . DO IT!

PART IV

TO THE EXILED LANDS

CHAPTER 18

Feeling the Rain

Night turns to morning. This is supposed to be the end of the three-day ceremony. But as I'm gathering myself to return to my friend's house to pack up and go home, I'm still very much in the clutches of an overpowering shadow.

The irony, looking back, is that even though I never drove my car off a cliff, on this third night, the cliff appeared. And there I am, down at the bottom of a ravine, having gone from fighting off the voices, to trying to control my thoughts, to begging and pleading for reprieve. Nothing's working. All I want is to get out of the dark pit, but it's seven o'clock in the morning, and I have not slept.

Finally, I look over at the Medicine Woman and tell her, "I can't go home like this. I feel like I'm possessed. Something's wrong." She nods with empathy. I go on, "I cannot go back to my children like this. I need another night."

"No problem," she says, and lets me know that I can stay with her until it's time for the fourth night of ceremony.

In the meantime, she prepares food for me to absorb the plant medicine and restore my energy for the night to come. Trying not to wolf it down all at once, I'm so grateful for an extra night. As scared as I am to confront another evening like the last one, I'm *more* scared to leave and put whatever is on me on my children.

"You can sleep if you want," she says, but I can't close my eyes.

For the rest of the day, I am awake, too afraid to sleep. In my best attempt to sound like everything is fine, I call the kids—thirteen-year-old Jaden and eleven-year-old Willow—"Hey, um, I have to finish another night of ceremony, so I won't be back tonight like I thought I would."

"Okay," Jaden says, "we'll see you when you get home tomorrow." And Willow echoes him, "Okay, Mommy, I love you."

"I love you guys, too."

When night falls, for the fourth time, the Medicine Woman brings me the tray. I take the plastic cup and swallow it down fast.

Tonight, unlike the other nights, I need to drink only once. Forty-five minutes pass before I feel the familiar hot wave come over my body. As fear begins to overwhelm me, I try to talk it down, saying, "It's okay," out loud to myself.

Sitting off to the side, the Medicine Woman gives me the first set of instructions I've heard. "Don't talk," she says gently, "just be still."

My heart beats faster as my fear runs up on me even more. I start to resist, trying to find stillness in a comfortable seated position. The less I say or do, the less threatening my fears seem. There's no way to control this experience. I have to trust and let the medicine conduct the ride.

The instructions to be still allow me to take a first small step toward cutting off the blood supply to my ego. No longer fighting, I relax into the storm, surrendering to stillness and sitting in the terror of my fear. All the horrible pictures, all the voices, all of the shadows, start to wane.

Though I don't know it yet, I will learn that after a psychological storm, a cleansing follows. And that's what this is—a cleansing, a purification of thoughts, beliefs, and energies that are not born of light and no longer serve me.

Suddenly, it hits me—my whole ordeal has been one of my own making. I've been taunting myself with false beliefs about my life and who I am. I exhale, surrendering more deeply, allowing the pictures to simply be, to watch them move past me and know they are only a movie.

Fear was soon dissolved by iridescent images. Abruptly, a bright light accompanied by iridescent blades in half-moon shapes, like the blades of a ceiling fan, dominated my vision. They made a tick-tick-tick staccato sound and moved at an extremely rapid pace before my eyes.

Within moments, I felt a warmth in my heart that surged throughout my entire body. The brightest of lights cascaded over me, washing over everything, with a holographic shimmer to it. And it was an inner sighting that made me gasp. What followed felt like I was being wrapped in the most blissful love—a love I had never felt before. *This must be heaven,* I thought. *This must be what it feels like in the bosom of God.*

The bath of this stream was where I wanted to live. Always.

I had always believed there was a God, but I had never felt the presence of the Divine. In this transformational moment, I did. I could finally feel who and what I truly am, a beloved child of the Divine, always and forever, worthy and deserving of being loved. Tears poured from my eyes in deep gratitude that I had made it through the shadow of the valley of death, and my reward was the embrace of God's love and the gift of being alive.

"You did well," the Medicine Woman said to me with a soft smile.

I couldn't stop thanking her. On a high like no other, I couldn't wait to get home, to see my children. I needed to hug them and tell them how much I loved them, how they had been my beacons of hope for so long.

On my drive home from Ojai, I called Jaden and Willow and told them everything. As we talked, I felt how contagious authentic joy can be. Not the joy we pretend to have, not the joy we try to conjure from our worldly experiences, but the joy that is birthed from the love of self that comes from a connection to the Divine. Willow and Jaden were so happy for me, and I could feel their lightness through my lightness.

When I got home, I blasted Bob Marley and I ordered dozens and dozens of long-stemmed white roses. When they arrived, I made arrangements with all the roses in different-sized vases and placed them all over the house.

All I could think was *This is the mother my children deserve to have.* And I prayed for the strength to hold on to this light.

T*he biggest change to come from* that first aya journey was that never again would I contemplate suicide. There was much more work to do in exploring parts of myself that had gone long ignored. One insight I missed was that the further I got into my forties, the deeper I waded into a classic midlife crisis and the burning question: *Outside of my marriage, my kids, and my career, who am I?*

Even with my new deep willingness to live, I couldn't escape feeling dull, withered, dry, and brittle. I remembered myself in my late teens and early twenties, hoping one day to live the dream, being at the threshold of possibility, feeling free and ALIVE. What happened to *her*? How could I reclaim that vibrancy, that fearlessness and freedom?

My kids were there to remind me what fearless freedom might look like.

One evening in late 2013, Willow and I returned home and were met by music blasting from the other side of the house. The sun had just gone down, and the house was dark except for one light that I saw spilling out of the multipurpose room. Willow followed as I went to investigate.

Will and I both loved the concept of the multipurpose room when we built the house at Her Lake. We could entertain in it, host fundraisers, gather all our extended family members for special occasions, or simply use it as a space for creativity. We dubbed it the Ballroom, which sounds fancier than it is—just a spacious room that comes to life, whatever's happening in it. On this particular evening, Jaden, charcoal in hand, stood alone in front of a large canvas.

At fifteen, Jaden had been working for years in the entertainment industry as an actor and recording artist. From a very young age, Jaden, Willow, and Trey had heard me talk about the importance of using their art, their personas, and their talent, not only as entertainment but to become a movement unto themselves in order to create change in the world.

Jaden, at age ten, started to focus on everything related to water pollution and the devastating effects of massive dumping of plastics in the ocean. At age fourteen, he came to me and Will to present his vision for JUST Water, a start-up that began by packaging natural spring water in recyclable boxes instead of plastic bottles. We helped him get it going, but Jaden was at the helm, working with a team that has kept it growing ever since. Before long, his 501(c)(3) nonprofit helped to develop and install mobile filtration stations to tackle water contamination in ignored communities like Flint, Michigan.

None of this had surprised me. Jaden was an early bloomer, wise beyond his years, and a restless seeker—pushing against the status quo. I once said to Will, "We'll be lucky to keep him here with us till sixteen."

So, when I walked into the room and saw him drawing on that canvas with charcoal—with words and phrases of his frustration—I knew something was up. He didn't turn to me, not so much because he was angry but because he was burdened by a heavy weight.

"What's going on?"

"I need something different, Mom. It's nothing personal. I love you, but I think it's time for me to leave."

I said nothing.

Jaden turned to me and paused to look me in the eyes as he continued to explain how he was feeling. He finally confessed, "I need to feel the rain."

I knew exactly what that meant. He had to be feeling trapped, in a certain way, and the change he sought was necessary for him to get some space. He needed to spread his wings in the way he felt was best for him.

We lived in rarefied air, in a remote setting, far from the rough and tumble of it all, and he was a fifteen-year-old boy wanting to chart his own course. We had always encouraged his independence, but how independent can you be, living in the bubble? He had to break out of the confines of the life that was not of his own making. He needed to know himself outside the world his father and I created.

For a moment, we were all quiet. Will was out of town working, and my first impulse was to say, "Hold up, let's talk to your dad about this." But Will left most decisions with respect to the kids up to me, and I thought this needed an immediate response. Either way, I knew this was going to be really hard for all of us. Maybe, I thought, I could suggest putting a pause on Jaden's exodus. Maybe we could postpone his departure to wherever he needed to go—to sleep under the stars, ride the rails, or heed the voice of his inner calling.

No, we could not, and I knew my response to this pivotal moment was important—because I believed he was going to leave either way. I could either be in partnership with him or against him. The latter could possibly break the power of his determination to face life's adversity on his own terms. Or worse, I could risk losing him for a very long time. I did not want to lose Jaden in that way. As scary as every image was that flashed through my mind, I knew that if I didn't let him go, on his terms, it would hurt him more than help.

You can't preach independence to your kids and then change your mind when they listen to you. In our youth, Will and I both had found much magic within ourselves from living on the edge. Jaden wanted an opportunity to find his magic on those edges as well.

That being said, I was ready to fall apart, especially when I discovered that Jaden was already packed and set to go. He would be moving in with Moises and Mateo, who were coming to pick him up. Moi and Mateo were also young men in the entertainment business and navigating the same terrain. Jaden wasn't exactly heading off alone into the wilderness.

Willow and I waited for Jaden in the foyer while he went to

his room to get his things. When he came downstairs, he seemed resolved—and perhaps relieved.

"How can I help?" I stammered. "You need a ride?"

Jaden thought for a moment, then agreed that I could drop him at the Lookout, on the side of the road not far from our house.

"Okay. I can do that."

We loaded up the car, and the three of us rode in silence up to the Lookout. There was nothing to say. This was happening. As soon as we came around the corner, I spotted Moi's car and pulled up behind it. All I could see were his red brake lights glaring in the night. Everything else was shrouded in darkness.

Jaden hopped out of our car and grabbed his stuff from the back. "I love you, Mom. I'll talk to you later," he said. Then he walked to Moi's car and jumped in the back.

Within minutes, he was gone.

A flood of tears fell from my eyes. I did my best to keep from wailing, to maintain some control in the midst of the worst heartbreak I had ever felt. I didn't want to alarm Willow, but there was no holding back. My heart crumbled as I sat there drowning in my own tears in front of my baby girl.

Willow said quietly, "It's gonna be okay, Mommy."

All I could do was nod. I knew, deep down, that Jaden was going to be fine and I would assist in whatever he needed on his new journey. That's what mothers do. The pain was simply because I wasn't ready to let him go. But I knew, with certainty, I had to.

After he left, the hardest parts for me were the change in the rhythm of the days and not feeling his presence in the house. We still talked all the time. He learned a lot about the everyday stuff of life, as we all do when we leave the nest.

About a year and a half after moving out, Jaden had a revelation, although he didn't move back into the family home. He had come to talk to Will and me to let us know what it was like to feel the rain. The responsibility that comes with the freedom of being a full-fledged adult was more intense than he'd thought—everything from paying bills to putting food in the fridge, from making sure he kept up with schooling, all the way to tending emotional well-being. He admitted that he understood why we had been so protective. At sixteen and a half, he recognized the gift of family, the power of unity and togetherness, that we had created—not to control him and his siblings but because we love them.

"I just want to thank you and Dad for everything," he said with deep sincerity. "I love you guys. Thank you for all that you've done for me." He'd left to feel the rain and discovered the true meaning of gratitude. It's a gift that has remained with him since.

I n these years, Trey was grappling with his place in the world as he made his way into young adulthood. During high school, he had made the decision to live with us, as Sheree, remarried, was relocating and Trey wanted to finish school without having to move. As a star football player, he had received several appealing college offers to play football, even to consider playing professionally. After wrestling seriously with whether that was what he wanted, he ultimately turned the offers down, and, instead, did a great deal of soul-searching. In the process, Trey began to explore the musical talents he'd had all along. Although he enjoyed producing and DJing, none of it seemed to be fulfilling at that juncture. In Trey's search for meaning, in years to come, his interests in unraveling the mysteries of the Universe led him to look into the healing properties of plant medicine. In this way, he was able to feel the rain. The timing was such that he and I could connect even more with our shared interests and abilities to hold space for one another. We can talk for hours about deep, complex questions of our existence, and often do. He reminds me frequently of the beauty and blessings within the rain.

Willow *had been pushing boundaries for* years now, on multiple fronts. At age eleven, not long after her decision not to move forward with *Annie,* Willow decided she wanted to shave her head—just like Gammy, who, at the time, wore her hair very close to the scalp.

Usually, your daughter comes to you and asks if she can cut bangs. Willow went straight to wanting to be damn near bald. My response was "Okay, let's just do it in steps."

We first shaved her sides and kept her hair long in the front. That lasted only a little while before she came back with "I'm ready to shave it off."

She was so clear on it, I wasn't going to fight her. This was about *her* hair. As a mother raising a daughter, I wanted to establish her ownership over her body—early. And we were talking about hair here. It would grow back. We arranged for an appointment with her hairstylist, and I watched Willow's transformation as her beautiful thick hair fell to the floor. The whole time, my daughter beamed with an elated smile, and I couldn't have been more proud. She would say later that it was an act of rebellion, as well as part of her exploration of beauty and identity as a young Black female.

I was in awe. How does an eleven-year-old shrug off the opinions and judgments of the world? Similarly, as her musical evolution unfolded, Willow continued to follow the beat of her own drum. To me, she was a prodigy. I'd hear her playing guitar in her room night and day or listen to her doing vocal warm-ups or pop into the recording studio to see her developing her own sound—and I could tell that she was off and running on her own Heroine's Journey.

Mom, *you will not believe what's* happening. Did you know there are girls my age who are being sold for sex in this country?"

My immediate response—since I'd always assumed this was a third-world issue—was "No, that doesn't happen here. It's only overseas."

Willow had recently watched a short film called *Kony 2012,* a documentary about human trafficking, released on YouTube. The film focused on Joseph Kony, a warlord from Central Africa who trafficked and abducted children for use as child soldiers. Willow had then launched into her own research, only to discover that human trafficking was the second most prevalent and profitable global crime, after drug trafficking, and that millions of children and adults were increasingly being stolen or sold for use in forced labor, for sexual exploitation, as soldiers on battlefields, to the black market for human organs, and more. The numbers on children and adults being trafficked in the U.S. proved how wrong I was about it only happening elsewhere.

Willow insisted, "I want to give my voice to this. People have to know this is happening."

It was a no-brainer that the two of us would work together to raise awareness on this issue. Learning from activists, leaders, and lawmakers already on the ground, seeking solutions was a priority. One of my first calls was to Angelina Jolie, then in the trenches on behalf of refugees around the world. I had long admired Angelina's commitment as an activist. She generously put me in touch with a lawyer named Adam Waldman, who soon introduced me to survivors, whom I met when I visited safe houses in cities around the country.

The stories we heard were shocking and heart-wrenching, and I was certain that if more people in positions of influence heard them, they would be moved to act. Within months, Willow and I visited the Capitol to meet with lawmakers, and Adam arranged for me to testify in front of the Senate Foreign Relations Committee about the need for stronger legislation to more effectively prosecute the crime of trafficking. What really made the difference were the stories of the survivors I brought with us—including JAMM, Minh Dang, and Withelma "T" Ortiz—so that they could, in their own words, share their horrific experiences of being trafficked in the United States.

This cause became deeply personal. Over the years, I came across stories from my travels so tragic and unbelievable that at times I was left to question how a good and just God could allow this to exist. One of the most disturbing realities was the rising number of boys being trafficked. Because of the stigma for boys who are exploited sexually, they're less likely to speak out and look for help; the lack of resources, including fewer beds or programs that accept males, leaves many of them to be exploited further. And the exploitation of transgender youth is even more confounding.

Another haunting reality was learning that many of the survivors I met had been trafficked by people they knew and thought they could trust—family members, friends, lovers, employers, law enforcement, you name it. My false assumption had been that most were kidnapped and exploited by strangers. In sharing these stories with the media, my emphasis, and I couldn't say it often enough, was: "There's no human being on this planet who should ever have to endure such treatment, and especially not a child."

After traveling to Mexico and speaking to leaders there, as well as to American policy representatives, I wanted to do more to help raise awareness in Latin communities, where trafficked women, men, and children were disappearing in droves, most never to be seen again. This was something brought to my attention years prior, when Salma Hayek called me about a march she was organizing in Juárez, to rouse action on behalf of disappeared women and children in Mexico. Salma also wanted to shine a light on the mass graves where bodies, mostly women, were being discarded in the middle of nowhere.

When Salma called, I was not available to join her, but I do remember questioning how I would play a relevant role, even telling myself—*A Black woman marching for Mexican women feels like what's happening there is not my issue.*

Once I became more versed in the realities of human trafficking, I could see how wrong that thinking was. The truth is that "one woman is every woman." All the separations we try to create—from color to economic or social strata—are false. If we were going to have impact, our responsibility was to do so within all communities, all over the world. To make amends for my former ignorance, I decided to learn Spanish to have greater reach. One of my first ventures was writing and recording a song in Spanish—"Nada Se Compara" ("Nothing Compares")—about human trafficking and asking Salma to direct the video. She jumped on board without blinking an eye. I then put my skills to use by doing outreach on Spanish media in multiple markets. Willow and I traveled to Miami and did press, and I went on to Spain.

No matter what language or demographic or, frankly, the specific issues being raised, I strongly believe that, as women, we all need to recognize our connectivity to one another, the necessity to uplift one another, and to protect our children and the world. Together, we have the unstoppable power to do so.

Willow had been the catalyst for raising awareness at a time when few were paying attention, proving you're never too young to effect great change.

Like mother, like daughter. And that was not limited to our activism. It also applied to how she liked to push edges and walk on fire, not so different from me.

But when it comes to jumping off cliffs for the hell of it, *that* she gets from her father.

There are signs along the edge of the ocean in Kauai, near the top of the path that leads down to the Queen's Bath—a natural shallow swimming hole—with dire warnings such as "Waves will sweep you out to sea" and "Many have died here."

When fourteen-year-old Willow and I went for a hike along the cliffs one day on vacation, I must have missed those signs. Given my outsized fear of heights, I didn't need to be warned. My days of trying to drive off the side of the road were behind me, but I was still sensitive to the ghastly pull of ledges and cliffs.

As we start out on the narrow trail along a ridge, I'm already having twinges of fear. Not Willow, who looks down and then out at the choppy seas before reaching the Queen's Bath. "You know," she says, "I wonder what it would feel like to jump off of here?"

My brain does a double take. I glance over the ridge on my right side, shake my head, look away, and then—oh SHIT! Next thing I know, Willow, moving with feline agility and speed, goes flying off the edge, vanishing out of my sight. I run to the cliff just in time to see that she has barely cleared the rocks to make it into the churning ocean below.

OH MY GOD! WHAT THE FUCK?!

All I can do is scream her name. I frantically look around for anyone below who may be close enough to help as I watch her struggling to swim to shore and lift herself up onto the rocks.

There is no one in sight. Once again, I think of the Buddhist story of the armless mother who watches her child fall into the river and get swept away by its current. Willow, straining hard to pull herself out of the water and onto the rocks, is truly in God's hands. All I can do is watch and pray, horrified, terrified, and armless. Finally, Willow pulls herself up with all her might, preventing the rough waters from washing her out to sea. Then she gingerly finds a path through the rocks to eventually make it back to me.

I was too relieved and too grateful to be upset, especially after witnessing what an exhilarating experience it had been for her. Instead of delivering a lecture—*What were you thinking?!*—I hold back. Besides, I had seen her obvious alarm while hoisting herself out of the water, and I had to trust that Willow had learned a big lesson. I was pretty sure she'd never try that again.

As Willow ran toward me, I was silent.

"Mom, did you see that? That was great!" Willow burst forth with unbounded enthusiasm.

"I did," I said, staying cool as we kept walking away from the edge and back toward the trailhead. Calmly, keeping my feelings grounded, careful not to pull Willow out of her experience, I continued, "You jumped out of nowhere. You gotta take more time to check out your surroundings, Willow, and see what you're getting into."

Willow paused a minute and thought about it, then continued with, "I did get scared for a second while I was struggling to get out of the water."

"Pay attention to that. That's all I'm saying. That was dangerous. That water could have swept you out to sea, and there would have been nothing anyone could do."

"Yeah . . . you're right." Willow made her own decision, glancing back at the jumping-off spot, and shook her head and smiled. She was still tasting the experience with exhilaration and delight.

After we were far enough from the cliffs above the Queen's Bath, and my shock and fear had subsided, I made a point to say, "That was pretty badass, though," and Willow's beautiful face lit up.

Everybody has different edges they like to walk, and different ways to feel the rain.

More and more, my way of walking edges and feeling the rain was through plant medicine ceremonies. After my first aya experience, a year went by before I dared go back into a ceremony. That third night had been like being trapped in a haunted house with no way out. But still grappling with a midlife crisis and searching for paths to remedy it, I gathered the courage to return to my inner world. Before long, I was in ceremony every two weeks. That's some hard-core searching.

And with these visits to the exiled lands inside of me, I believed my work in aya had certified me as wise and enlightened. Yeah, I was that one, the pseudo-guru, the spiritual neophyte who has yet to scratch the surface of true wisdom but believes she has more answers to life than anyone. Well, there is such a thing as getting tripped up by the pitfalls of the pseudo-guru. That was me, setting myself up to fall off the edge of high-and-mightydom. I didn't know shit.

One of my pitfalls was my steadfast belief that *if only* Will could catch up to my level of enlightenment, things would change. We actually had a few aya sessions together, and afterward I did see him differently.

When Will and I went into ceremony together the first time, we had no great expectations. But that night, we got to witness each other's innocence, the power of our union, and how much we love to laugh together.

Afterward, he and I went to the kitchen to get something to eat, and we were laughing so loudly at one point that Willow and Trey came out of their rooms late to investigate.

"Hey, are you guys okay?" Willow yelled down the stairs.

"Oops, sorry, we didn't mean to wake you," I said, followed by more laughter. Here we were, like the teenagers in the house, getting checked by our kids.

Trey chimed in, chuckling, too, "Okay, you guys have a good night."

I got to see the little boy in Will, who just wanted to play and didn't need applause. That authentic part of him showed me how healing and magical his humor really is. I had never been able to fully appreciate and honor his innocent joy, and how he can use humor to dispel the clouds even in the most challenging moments.

As much as I wished the night could have fixed everything, that time spent together also revealed the daunting work that needed to be done. We were each the leading player in our own fractured fairy tale presented as two separate realities. We both believed our version of the story was right, and that made the other wrong.

After almost twenty years, give or take, it seemed that nothing was going to change between us. By his own admission, feelings were not a priority for Will. How he felt, how anybody felt, was not a priority. That was a difficult reality for me to continue to navigate and accept. How many years had I been clinging to "we'll get to that later," the time when I could express my need for deeper emotional connection?

In hindsight, I see clearly that my fortieth birthday was our breaking point. Will's love language of material and experiential extravagance was how he knew to connect; it was difficult for him to hear that I didn't need all of that—I just needed *him*. I needed his heart, his willingness to emotionally connect with me, to receive me and see me. Without that, he couldn't possibly know what I was going through. And without that, I couldn't find the ground on which to build the appreciation he wanted to feel consistently.

It was nobody's fault. As much as I wanted him to love me, that would never happen if I didn't love myself. And the same applied to him. Will and I had pictures in our mind of what a happily married couple was. And our pictures didn't match.

Inevitably, we came to the proverbial stage of irreconcilable differences. That realization became starkly apparent by 2016.

We had been here before. There had been several on-again and off-again attempts at salvaging the marriage. We were tired from not finding a middle ground. We'd been on a seesaw for too long. Highs and lows. Hot and cold. But even with that, and even though we flunked out of marriage therapy, there was this *thing* between us. We had an underlying unbreakable bond, this fundamental friendship, even if we couldn't nurture it properly.

With all our ups and downs, divorce was a real option in my mind at times. However, despite rumors to the contrary, I could never find the heart to meet with one single lawyer. I could never break the promise I'd made all those years ago in Will's mother's backyard— that we would never be in a position to need a prenuptial agreement because we would never need a divorce. Throughout, I had chosen the discomfort of staying in my ailing marriage over destroying our family and the community we had created. I was smart enough to admit I was too immature to launch a legal battle without creating a bloodbath. Lawyers would have taken advantage of my emotional state, made sure they got a big check, and left me in deep regret. Will and I had our problems, but what we had at the core deserved better than legal warfare.

I'd always pledged to myself that if we were really going to end our marriage, we would do so with an amicable partnership to keep together the family we both valued. We'd have to work as members of the same team. There had to be a way to lovingly uncouple without being put under the microscope of the world. In other words, we would choose to divorce without divorcing. That is, to split up, to separate on our own terms, without legal interference.

So, at the end of 2016, Will and I looked each other in the eyes and decided to separate in every way except legally. For us, what mattered most was mutual agreement and informing the children of our separation. We would remain family-strong, not lose our friendship, and maintain our policy of complete transparency—i.e., no secrets about what we were doing and whom we were doing it with.

We didn't believe we owed the public any specifics, which was, without a doubt, a slippery slope. The pitfall for me in this plan—and I stepped right into it—was believing I was evolved enough to manage this alternative approach to ending our marriage. The pseudo-guru—who uses rationale and borrowed wisdom to tell you what you want to hear—insisted that because of my nearly four years of plant medicine work and spiritual growth, this decision was elevated and correct.

Oh, what fools we mortals be. The reckoning was to come.

I *was first introduced to the concept* of the Red Shoes in *Women Who Run with the Wolves.* Clarissa Pinkola Estés describes a woman's starved psyche and soul in these ways: "A woman who has been captured knows no better, and will take something, anything, that *seems similar* to the original treasure, good or not." And: "In this state, she will take any food regardless of its condition or its effect, for she is trying to make up for past losses." And finally: "We can better understand the woman who dives into excesses—the most common being drugs, alcohol, and bad love—and who is driven by soul-hunger by noting the behavior of the starved and ravening animal."

Clarissa illustrates this condition by exploring the experience of the adopted girl in the Hans Christian Andersen story "The Red Shoes." The girl has lost connection to her primal longings and soon obsesses about having her own red shoes in which to dance and move through the world. Once she puts on the shoes that she makes for herself out of scraps, she is taken over by them. As Clarissa writes: "Here her acute starvation of soul and meaning forces her to once more grasp for the Red Shoes, strap them on and begin her last dance, a dance into the void of unconsciousness."

Though I knew this story, I could not know that I was about to be trapped in my own Red Shoes. Like the girl in the story who is gratified by her Red Shoes, unaware of their destructive power until the rapture turns to pain, I got preoccupied with making up for lost time and reclaiming the days of my youth. The warning of the story is that once her dance begins, the orphan girl can't remove the Red Shoes no matter how hard she tries. The only way to stop the dance is for her feet to be cut off.

That's the backstory to what I call an entanglement.

Let me clarify. In referring to entanglements as such, I don't think of them as affairs. I associate affairs with cheating. (But if you choose to refer to an entanglement as an affair, that works, too.) In terms of Will and me, there were no secrets, so there was no affair. (Hold on, we will get to that *Red Table* conversation later.)

So, after Will and I separated, I put on my Red Shoes and fell into an entanglement. You know the expression: "Oh, what a tangled web we weave." That's where I was.

The word must have been in my subconscious when I first used it. I'd learn later that Buddhist and Bhakti traditions use "entanglement" to describe human interaction in the physical world that is not steeped in spiritual understanding. We can become entangled with our entitlements: addictions that are self-gratifying; combative beefs and rivalries; spending money we don't have; indulging in excess; sharing in unkind gossip intended to hurt or gain an upper hand over others; vengeful acts; or simply looking for fulfillment in all the wrong places. If your human purpose is to live your time on the planet learning how to love, any time you step away from acting from a pure place of love, you run the risk of becoming entangled with self-negating energy.

If the Red Shoes give us only fleeting pleasure that turns to chronic pain, why is it so hard to remove the shoes? Because many of us enjoy pain. We like the chaotic roller-coaster ride that gives us an illusion of exhilaration, messy dramas that are all-consuming. Yes, many of us are addicted to pain. To our romantic suffering. Some of us use pain as a blanket to blame, as a justification to avoid recognizing the part we play in creating our dysfunctional lives.

For the record, my partner in the entanglement (*entanglee*, if you will) was not, as it would be said a lot, my son's best friend. When we met, he was not shy about expressing how he was suffering from depression, unresolved grief, and, later, issues with his health. I wanted to help, and since we both had suffered enormous amounts of loss, we met there. This is how a friendship unfolded that, much later, and very unexpectedly, turned romantic.

When it ran its course, I decided to step away with the intention of remaining friends, while continuing to be supportive. But in de-entangling, there can be bruised feelings. He may have assumed that I was going back to my marriage, when that was not the case. In any event, he made the choice to sever communications with me, which I chose to respect.

This period was when I had to confront the entitlement of the Red-Shoe-wearing pseudo-guru in me. The pitfall happens when she thinks she has arrived at a place in her healing where she can distinguish between healthy sustenance and the poisoned honey of false beliefs. Until she recognizes that the poisoned honey will never quench her craving, she will be eternally unfulfilled. To save herself, she will have to do something as radical as cutting off her own feet—to be rid of the Red Shoes she so desired. Only then will she be able to grow new feet without the shoes.

And here's where these pitfalls are meant to be great teachers. They show us our unhealed parts so we can lean into the unglamorous, arduous work of self-inventory in order to transform and grow. When you can have gratitude for the experience, the deep healing process has taken hold. With that said, I am deeply grateful—for it all.

Why? Because my biggest lesson overall was that the problem was me. No one else. Not my entanglee. Especially not Will. And although it takes two to tango, I can only analyze and take responsibility for my part. In so doing, I felt enough discomfort to fall from my perch as a spiritual know-it-all. I had to submit to the fact that once again, I had tried to escape my deeper work and had gotten off track. And I knew nothing. I was back at square one.

In 2018, with the end of the entanglement, I hobbled on scorched earth on my little ankle nubs—after cutting off my feet with those Red Shoes—and fell into another kind of despair. At forty-six, I had not realized my dream of happily ever after and it was nowhere in sight. Unlike in my twenties, when it had been easy to pick myself up and go back out to conquer the world, at this stage I couldn't even see my place in the world at all. I had to mourn the reality that what had been would not be again. I could succumb to the classic fate of the bitter aging bitch OR muster the courage to continue the journey on my own.

Willow's lyrics said it best:

And I'm taking this adventure on my own
Walkin' through a darkened forest, goin' home
Curious/furious, I feel alone . . .

What I didn't expect was how far I would have to travel to learn to embrace the rain.

Just because someone stumbles and loses their way doesn't mean they are lost forever.
—CHARLES XAVIER, *X-MEN*

That's some real talk.

CHAPTER 19

A Place at the Table

"W hat are you doing with the *Red Table*?" were the first words out of Ellen Rakieten's mouth when the two of us were introduced.

A behind-the-scenes powerhouse, Ellen—cocreator and producer of *The Oprah Winfrey Show* for twenty-three years—had been referred to me by Ken Hertz, the entertainment lawyer and branding maestro, who had known Will since his *Fresh Prince of Bel-Air* days and still works with our family. Ken's instincts were usually gold, so I listened when he said that Ellen was someone I should meet.

What was I doing with the *Red Table*? Ellen was talking about a Mother's Day special that my mother, daughter, and I had posted online some years earlier.

"Nothing."

"Well, you should be."

I laughed.

Ellen was serious. Striking, with her long golden waves of hair, she had a combination of confidence, inquisitiveness, and assertiveness that made me lean in.

Red Table Talk's origin story began one day when Willow, then a preteen, said out of nowhere, "I want to know who you are, outside of just being my mother."

What a beautiful question for a young daughter to ask her mother. She wanted to know who I was before I became a wife and mother, as in: *Who were you before you came into all of this?*

Her question floored me. It struck me how many daughters don't really know who their mother is, and how important it is that they do.

"Wow" was my first response. My second was "In order to know my story, you gotta know Gammy's story, too."

This was going to be a deep conversation, I realized. Why wouldn't we, as mothers, find the time to share our journeys with our daughters? Was it because we judged our stories and couldn't get beyond whatever shame lingered? Was it because we couldn't see the value and necessity of our experiences? All of us have chapters in our lives we wish we could erase. Yet those are the chapters in which we slayed our most menacing dragons; those are the moments that, if they didn't kill us, made us stronger. The key is to set aside our shame and find a safe space where we can talk freely and openly. In the process, through everyday storytelling, our daughters will have a chance to honor and accept our journeys as worthy—and embrace whatever strength they find to take on their own journeys.

When I told my mother that I wanted to have this conversation, she was fully on board. For Willow, getting to hear the history of her mother and grandmother would give her the gift of knowing her matriarchal legacy—and, in turn, teach her more about herself. It occurred to me that it would be good to preserve this conversation by filming it. By sharing it widely, I hoped to encourage other mothers to get past the fear of telling their stories to their daughters, and maybe inspire them to have their own intergenerational conversations on their own terms.

At this point in my life, I'd come to see that the Heroine's Journey, for most of us, will not look demure, passive, or safe. True, we often deny parts of ourselves and our stories by having had to live up to the standards of being a "good woman." Instead, I hoped that if we could share our unvarnished stories with one another—Willow, Gammy, and me—we could shine a light on how multidimensional our journeys can be. We could check our self-judgment at the door—and the judgment of others while we were at it.

And this is how the concept of the three of us at a round table was created. The idea was inspired by the universal kitchen table, where women gather to cook, talk, share stories, and commune. This was the classic dinner table, where families come together and tell the stories of their day.

With a round table, there is no hierarchy. Nobody sits at the head. Everyone's place is equal. The choice of red was feminine—red for roses and the red-hot flame of a woman's passion. The red-table concept also conjured the feeling of sitting around the campfire at night, the magic of people captivating one another with story. The tradition is in our DNA, dating back to prehistoric times when our ancestors gathered around the fire to dance and sing with ritual and ceremony.

The red table, representing fire, safety, and warmth, is also the color of the blood that represents life, connection, and transformation. Through communication, through confession, and through expression, the red table is where we can purify our hearts and our souls and clear up the confusing dynamics within us and between other people. And so, conceived as a place for truth and unfiltered dialogue, the first-ever *Red Table Talk* was birthed, a Mother's Day gift to women of all ages.

Over the years, Gammy and I had never talked at length about her story before becoming my mother, her own traumas of being a teenage mom, or the details of her addiction and recovery. I knew parts of it, of course, the parts I was there for, but she had never pieced everything together in so clear and honest a way as she did that day. Up until this conversation, Gammy would bristle if there was any reference to her as a recovering addict, rather than recognition of her miraculous journey to sobriety.

Seeing my mother overcome her shame and narrate her history—in front of cameras and to her grandchild—was a cathartic moment for me and, I believe, for her. When you bring your story from the shadows and into the light, you step out of your own handmade prison and give the experience—that you once thought shameful—wings. And that's what Willow and I got to witness, as did viewers who reached out to express how moving Adrienne's story had been for them. Many shared their own struggles with addiction in their family dynamics.

Willow was amazing. On her own, twelve years old, she came to the Red Table prepared with in-depth questions she had written down in advance. Willow was enthralled with our stories and listened with enthusiastic curiosity and great empathy.

The husband-and-wife production team who helped turn my vision into reality was Mike and Moni Vargas. Their creativity and dedication made the results more than I could have asked for.

The effort was meant to be a one-off, although after it streamed, we received offers to create a show around the concept. But Willow was still so young, and I just didn't think it was time. Besides, I felt we had accomplished our initial goal.

And that was that. Or so I thought.

Five years later, when Ellen Rakieten told me I should be doing something with the *Red Table*, the timing was different. Willow was turning eighteen, and I was seeking my next step. Ellen was also persuasive: "You know, I believe that this concept—three women from the same family, three generations, sitting at a table and talking about important subjects . . . it's a really powerful idea for a show."

There was just something magical in the way she presented this to me. I opened my mind to what might happen.

From there, we all went to work, and *Red Table Talk* was reimagined as a nontraditional talk show with topics explored from our different, unfiltered perspectives. True to its origin story, the show was shot in a warmly lit room in our home, and we kept it real and welcoming, with the intimacy of a family gathering.

Within a month, and after receiving offers from numerous outlets, we decided to go with Facebook. I felt that Mina Lefevre, head of Facebook Watch, got the show right away and was open to giving us, Ellen, Miguel Melendez, and me, free creative range. Miguel and

I had produced Queen Latifah's talk show and knew how important and rare this kind of freedom was. What's more, it was the most lucrative deal offered that also let us retain ownership of the brand. Once I'd talked to Sheryl Sandberg, COO of Facebook at the time and an immediate champion of the show, I knew we would be in good hands. They ordered thirteen episodes, and we went to work. This started off as a passion project, and for the first season, I assumed it would remain that way.

In all my imaginings for my future, becoming the host of a talk show had never been on my radar—nor for Gammy and Willow. They were thrilled, and we loved doing it, although when we made the deal with Facebook, we had no idea that it would turn into our day jobs. We never suspected how successful it was going to be.

During the run-up to shooting the first season of *Red Table Talk,* I had been grappling with something of a health condition that I had been ignoring for a while.

It showed up one day when my hairdresser at the time noticed a big indentation on the side of my head near my temple where I had a significant amount of hair loss. She pointed it out, and I looked in the mirror, felt it with my hand, and said, "You know, it's like I've lost some bone density," and we could see that, subtly, the side of my head was sort of caving in. I was concerned about the bald patch and the indentation and started watching both more closely

My hunch was that maybe I was wrapping my hair too tight at night. That was an easy fix. Besides, in these days I had so much hair that I didn't have cause to worry. No big deal. Even when I started to see other little plugs of hair falling out, I still didn't stress about it too much.

Though I fully intended to follow up with a doctor, to look into hormonal changes—as pretty much everybody assumed it was "just hormones"—I kept faith that whatever was happening would correct itself. And I was right. After a month or so, the condition went away, much to my relief.

Years passed. In late 2017 there came a jolt I couldn't ignore: I'm in the shower on this particular morning while spending time by myself in Utah, enjoying the winter season that I love so very much. As soon as I start to wash and rinse my hair, I'm shocked to see that I have a wad of hair in my hands, with more falling on the tile of the shower and flowing down the drain.

In a body-shaking panic, I freeze. Though I'm scared to continue to rinse my hair, I proceed as delicately as possible, which does little to stem the amount of hair sloughing off of my head.

I've been in panic mode in my life but nothing like this. My heart is quaking with *Oh my God, oh my God, WHAT IS WRONG WITH ME?*

That's when I flash on Pac first getting alopecia from the trauma of being beat up by the police in Northern California. Of course, Pac looked good bald. The thought that I could be suffering from the same issues is not acceptable, so I stick to the theory of hormones.

As I get out of the shower, I pat my hair with a towel and wrap it loosely. I'm not touching a strand.

I found a doctor in Utah who believed I was suffering from alopecia areata but that it was probably temporary and brought on by stress. He told me there were steroid shots I could get to stem the loss, and injected me with my first round.

For close to two weeks, I didn't even look at my head. That's how scared I was to confront reality. Finally, I unwrapped my hair and gently, gently started to brush it. No reprieve. Hair came out in chunks. I could see the round circles where the roots of the hair had come out entirely.

Refusing to go into a depression over what I believed was caused by aging and years of overworking my hair, I decided, *What the hell, I'll cut it.*

Problem solved. I still had a lot of hair, and my short cut was styled to cover the patches where the hair loss had happened. For that I felt lucky and grateful. Soon enough, it very much felt that my hair was coming back, healthy and strong. Was it the shots? I didn't know, but I was thrilled that my hair was growing back.

Time would prove that the issue was far more complicated. In the meantime, I kept my hair in a hot little style and put my focus on the exciting adventure of *RTT*.

O ne of my goals in framing the tone of the show's conversation had been inspired by the candor and wisdom shared with me after I'd reached out to three special women during a tough time. Each of them—Pauletta Washington, Salma Hayek, and Ruby Dee—had provided me with a safe space for real talk.

Ruby Dee was one of the first women to see past my usual façade. We always ran into each other at industry events, but I had never had the chance to speak to her at length. At one such event, I went over to speak to Ruby, and she took my hand, looking at me with veteran discernment. Leaning in, she softly told me, "You make it look easy, but I know that it's not."

Damn, I thought, *I'm found out.*

I will never forget how Ruby looked at me with so much understanding—that lovely, generous woman-to-woman nod of knowing. This gesture planted a seed in my heart that let me know her door of earned wisdom was open to me any time.

Before long, I walked through that door. In her late eighties, a fierce powerhouse, Ruby Dee had a multifaceted career—iconic actress, poet, playwright, producer, and lifelong activist. For her nearly fifty-six years of marriage to Ossie Davis (who passed away at age eighty-seven in 2005), the two were so intricately linked—as husband and wife and as creative partners—that you rarely heard either of them mentioned without the other. What I took from Ruby was an assurance that marriage was hard and not a linear journey. Marriage has multiple ups and downs, and stops and starts, and changes through the seasons.

Sitting from where I was at the time, I had to ask, "Do you have any regrets? If you could go back and do it differently, would you?"

Ruby said something profound: "One of my biggest regrets is that I wish I had laughed with him more." Once Ossie was on his deathbed, none of the contentious, painful times they'd been through mattered anymore. All that mattered was how profoundly, passionately, and fully they had loved each other through everything. Her cautionary advice was simple: "Just keep that in mind—laugh now, because you're gonna laugh later." In other words, all the troubles that are making you cry now, with wisdom and time, will make you laugh in days to come.

Pauletta Washington—whose arts education began at North Carolina School for the Arts and then Juilliard—had a career as an actress and musician before she married Denzel. One of the takeaways from our conversations was how having a spiritual center was important in every union. Salma Hayek reinforced the importance of staying true to oneself and also not overlooking the things in a marriage that are going right.

The most wonderful part of having these free-flowing conversations with women I respect was the realization that my challenges didn't make me as special as I thought I was.

My conversations with these three also made me wonder—*Why don't women open up and share our experiences and wisdom with one another more often and in a deep way?* That's what I wanted for *Red Table Talk.*

The gift of RTT *was that* for the first two seasons, it wasn't a job as much as a continuation of the meaningful, healing, entertaining exchanges I'd begun to have with my mother, my daughter, and my close female friends *before* there was a table and a camera.

What a joy, getting to go to the table with my mother and daughter. Naturally inquisitive, I found that getting to be part of unfiltered conversations put me in my happy place. Gammy offers strong opinions along with well-earned wisdom, while Willow has superpowers of empathy and vulnerability, combined with fierce intelligence, that draw in all age groups. The three of us bring our different strengths and points of view to the table.

Our guests, from the start, came from a wide range of backgrounds and ages, and were both women and men—experts, authors, friends, folks with unforgettable stories, celebrities who needed a safe space to let down their guard. Many of our guests would say that being at the table led to a catharsis. More than a few quipped afterward, "This is better than therapy."

RTT became a forum for us to meet our audience members where they were in their lives, and they could meet us and our guests where we were. The connection was powerful. Our engagement—through comments and viral sharing of episodes—told us that our subject matter resonated in so many demographics around the world. After two seasons, viewership had risen to an accumulated 265 million.

Red Table communities began to sprout all over Facebook. *RTT,* as a brand, blossomed into a lucrative asset for our new producing company, Westbrook (cofounded by Will and me, along with Kosaku Yada and Miguel Melendez), with our last three-year deal closing at close to $100 million.

One of the hardest lessons for me, as I moved into my late forties, was overcoming my fear of being vulnerable in public. When you are playing a role in a story that's not your own, it's easier to open up in order to bring that character to life. But when it's your story and you aren't playing a role, it's not so simple.

Gammy, Willow, and I could bring insights to the table that often reflected each generation. My mother was a classic baby boomer who had clear ideas about what was wrong and what was right. Willow, a Gen Zer, was all about challenging and questioning that which was supposedly right or wrong. As a Gen Xer, I sat in the middle and enjoyed the interplay.

The topics we tackled never followed a formula. Most of the time, and I give so much credit to Ellen and our team for this, we approached sensitive subject matter that was considered taboo but was very much in the public mind. We hosted parents who had lost their beloved sons or daughters to suicide, police violence, sexual assault, or domestic abuse. We delved into topics like the rise of white supremacy and hate in America; how families can do more to support their LGBTQIA+ family members; what polyamory is all about and why it's more common than you know; women and porn; the mental health epidemic happening around the world; and narcissism and its varieties. Just to name a few.

We welcomed all topics and all people. In the early days of *RTT,* the programming flowed from our personal interests—mainly what Gammy, Willow, and I were thinking about or were going through. At the end of 2019, a lot was going on with me—though I wasn't yet sure how to talk about it.

H*ere I was in a state* that I'd never imagined for myself. Married but not, and alone. At this point, my intense focus was on my inner life, after I'd taken a vow of celibacy as a more conscious approach to my spiritual work.

In addition to plant medicine, I was in therapy and working at detaching from the life I'd known before—which became increasingly difficult when the COVID-19 pandemic hit. Up until this time, Will had been working and away for the most part. But when the shutdown happened, we were under the same roof and together for an extended length of time, which hadn't happened in a while. We both thought it was important to create a sense of security by hunkering down at the house, which became a pod for our extended family and friends during this uncertain time.

In early 2020, while most of the industry had closed down, *RTT* was able to be mostly self-contained as a production, because we shot the show at our house and were able to bring in experts and guests via video technology. Our first show during this season, "Managing Our Anxiety & Fear During COVID-19," included Jay Shetty, a former monk turned successful life coach, author, and podcaster, and Dr. Ramani Durvasula, clinical psychologist, author, professor, and podcaster of *Navigating Narcissism*. We didn't want to ignore the elephant in the living room that was the isolation of being in quarantine during a worldwide pandemic, so we met it head-on, with topics that included what COVID actually is, how it spread, and how to prevent getting sick. We also addressed ways to cope with addiction while in isolation; how to handle relationships; and differences in views about the pandemic itself.

We tried to infuse some humor into what we filmed during that time. We called one episode "A *Girls Trip* Coronavirus Quarantine Reunion"—which is just what it was, a reunion with my castmates Tiffany Haddish, Queen Latifah, and Regina Hall from *Girls Trip* (a movie we'd made four years earlier), held on Zoom. It was hilarious and inappropriate, as only the four of us can be when we're together.

We started laughing about—what else?—hair. Latifah was complaining about having to press her own hair. Tiff was showing off her quarantine weave, while Regina proudly shared her simple do. I tried to change the subject, shrugging and pointing to the ball cap I'd put on, saying it was better than the scarf I'd been wearing. Regina reminded us of how envious she was of my hair and my edges.

"Not anymore," I came back, faster and louder than I'd intended. Nobody seemed to have heard me, thank goodness.

Right before lockdown, my hair had started to fall out again. I resumed the steroid shots. The prognosis, considering that alopecia is an autoimmune condition and every case is different, was hard to determine. My hair loss could go on for a short time, a long time, or the rest of my life. It could get better or become more severe. My doctor told me, "We will have to just wait and see."

Later on, I discovered there were issues with my gut that were contributing to hair loss and possibly to the indentations that appeared every once in a while. Once I cleaned aspects of my diet that were supposed to be healthy but were actually hurting me, my health, emotionally and physically, rebounded. As for my hair, I was still waiting and seeing.

The only other memorable episode of *Red Table Talk* during the COVID-19 quarantine season aired in July. It was titled "Jada Takes Herself to the Table." It is responsible for introducing a new meaning to the word "entanglement" into popular culture.

You're welcome.

I n the spring of 2020, there had been a surge of interest in the entertainment press as to what had happened two years earlier, due to statements made by my former entanglee. My immediate reaction was *Why now? Are you kidding me?*

I never thought he was built like that. On top of the fact that this was water under the bridge, I had tried my best to respect his privacy, without even considering my own at times. But as the saying goes, *All is fair . . .*

In my experience, talking back to a media frenzy is a no-win venture, because you only make a story bigger and more susceptible to fictional add-ons. However, in this instance, I was ready to explain my actions, not with blame or self-defense but by taking responsibility. With all the work I'd been doing on myself, that's what felt most important.

I was not willing to allow someone else's narrative to put a shroud of shame on me. I felt that coming to the table to tell my story was imperative. Besides, I couldn't ask others to tell their truths at the Red Table and not do the same.

This was not supposed to be psychodrama. My narrative would encapsulate: (1) how the entanglement happened when Will and I were separated; (2) how it had been over for nearly two years; (3) how there were no secrets whatsoever between Will and me, so there was no cheating.

When I told Will what I was planning to do, he—by his own choice, without any prompt or request from me—decided to join me at the table. Frankly, I was surprised. Pleasantly so. Considering we weren't together, and given where we were sitting in our relationship at the time, that was unexpected. But he suggested that he did not want me to go to the table alone. That seemed to me to be a powerful offering, in line with our intention to be more of a united front. In our life partnership/spiritual partnership/"we don't know what the hell this is yet" partnership, we weren't quite fully united, but we were working on it.

The "not quite there yet" part became glaringly apparent when we sat for that conversation and the cameras started rolling. Beforehand, Ellen had done what she usually did, and that was to pre-interview guests. Will and I were in agreement that we would come to the table to talk about what our journey had been. We were going to honor our life partnership, yet speak openly and honestly about how that partnership had changed and how we were still figuring it out. We wanted to say that divorce wasn't an option and that family would remain our top priority.

The timing for our shoot wasn't optimal. It was late, Will had just returned from a trip, and we were going to leave for a family event the next day. On top of that, our set had been taken down for the season, so we had to reset cameras and lighting, which took much longer than planned.

Once the conversation finally started, now very late at night, we began with ease, but midway through the table talk, I could feel the conversation beginning to turn.

Although at this point Will had been free as a bird for the last four years, living his life on his own terms, he seemed to convey that he had been done wrong. At my reference to having had an "entanglement," he sternly reframed it, with a laugh, as a "relationship." This came across as if this had all been a secret to him, when that wasn't true, and that he had somehow "found out" about my "relationship," as if I had not told him about it.

Here's where I should have stopped the conversation. But instead, my habit of self-betrayal overwhelmed me, and I swallowed my own voice. After a few more failed attempts at regaining the narrative, I resigned and abandoned the purpose of why I had come to the table in the first place—to tell my truth and to show how we were in partnership in working through being separated but not divorced.

Of course, I did what I was trying never to do again—that is, fall right into my martyrdom bag. It was clear that Will and I were no longer in alignment, that the train had gone off the track. Because I didn't want to oppose Will publicly, in my codependent way, I took the blame and played the pleasing and appeasing role I knew so well. This trauma reaction was an old friend I thought I'd kicked to the curb, but clearly, it could still be activated when I was in fear of being abandoned or not feeling protected.

I wonder if Will was feeling the same way. It was hard to tell, with him sitting there with his tired, watery, weepy eyes. To be fair, Will's eyes water ALL the time. And it was very late.

Chile, unhealed trauma will do you dirty. Every time. Despite how its remedies and responses wear the guise of being appropriate, caring, loving, familiar, and safe.

You would have thought after all the intense work I'd been doing on myself, through therapy and spiritual focus, that a car crash of this nature would be avoidable. But another aspect of my lack of self-worth revealed itself that day.

No matter what, I was not going to throw anybody under the Red Table but myself. Even if it meant wearing the scarlet letter. And then there was my street code that came into play. This was my mess, so it was my bid to serve. To do anything other than taking the blame felt equivalent to going to Miami, getting ten keys of cocaine, and driving back across the Maryland state line, then getting caught, only to snitch on my homie in Miami to soften my consequences.

That was not an option. So I decided to do—my time.

Will jokingly referred to himself as the man who stood by his woman on the steps of the courthouse after she was tarnished by her "transgressions." I understood that the situation was humiliating for him, and that was never my intention.

Will managed to inject humor into the conversation, enough so that by the end, we could fist-bump to our slogan of "We ride together, we die together, bad marriage for life." It said so much when, at the very end, Will got in a final stinger. Laughing but truly serious, he proclaimed that we were okay, but with the caveat "I'mma get you back first . . ."

Laughing but serious myself, I interrupted with a rebuttal of "You gonna get me back? I think you've gotten me back . . . we're good on that." In that moment, at least, my voice returned as I took a more honest stand on my own behalf, knowing all that had transpired between us.

When the time came to post the conversation, I could have decided against it. Many implored me not to put it out.

Miguel simply said, "You're giving the message that it's all you, and that's not true. You're going to take a big hit for this."

"It's my mess, so it's my hit to take."

Ellen wasn't as adamant as Miguel, but she suggested that I sit on the video for a bit and maybe return to the table alone, as I'd originally intended.

I honestly just wanted it over. If that meant taking the hit so we could move on, cool. So I told Ellen, "No, I think we should put out what we have."

Once everything settled, I had to sit with my feelings of genuine hurt and betrayal. Even if part of that betrayal was on me, it felt unfair. The loneliness that soon set in was excruciating.

Would I have chosen otherwise if I had it all to do again? Yes and no. Yes, if I could have revisited it, I would not have gone to the table so ill-prepared. But no, I learned everything I needed to know about myself and more from going to that table ill-prepared. Being as hardheaded as I can be, I know that without the experience, there were things I would not have seen about myself or others that the Red Table revealed.

Besides, I met a fierce warrior within myself during this time. She had been in hiding, but now she was willing to go into the arena and battle shame. And for that, it was all worth it.

A part of me was willing to be torched by public opinion as a path to discovering my authentic value in the embers of what remained. If I could survive telling the truth while also taking the brunt of a lie, I could finally let go of all the pictures that I thought defined my worth. I knew—as painful as the journey would be—this was my opportunity to let go of self-judgment, without which other people's judgment has no power. With this, I would truly be free.

I was torching the handmade gilded cage in front of the world. Once and for all.

When I look back at all of this, I have to laugh. One thing is for sure, neither Will nor I, in all our splendid dysfunction, was at all equipped for that conversation at that time. We were a classic comedic mess. In the aftermath, everything felt like it was the end of the world. But as Ruby Dee said, "Laugh now, because you are going to laugh later."

Thank God that's true.

Oh, and I had to laugh after a prophetic dream I had in this time period. In it, I was attending a function, and no one would speak to me. I would walk up to people I knew, and they'd act like I was a stranger.

In the dream, I called Will and said, "Why did you do that to me? Why would you ever do that to me?"

While I continued to rant, Will waited patiently and finally replied, "The bigger question is why would you do that to yourself? It's your show, you didn't have to put it out."

WHAT DID HE SAY?????

All of a sudden, my arms bulged into huge muscles, and my entire body burst into the form of a grotesque werewolf, and I snatched Will by the top of his head through the phone receiver and delivered us both into a setting of a dark forest under a full moon. As a gray, grotesque werewolf, I stood over him at ten feet tall, panting and salivating, staring him down. He started to speak, and within seconds, my claws ripped him to shreds.

And then I devoured him. I howled to the moon with blood dripping from my jaws, and then I looked to the ground to find the one thing that was left of him—a bloody, severed index finger.

I took my grotesque werewolf foot and kicked his index finger over a canyon through the moonlit sky.

I abruptly woke up. At first, startled, I had to ask, "What the hell was that?"

Then I had to chuckle: *Why did I have to kick his finger over the canyon like that?*

A lot of boundaries that we are missing are the boundaries that we need with ourselves, around how we operate in our relationships with other people, and how we operate in relationships with ourselves.

—NEDRA GLOVER TAWWAB, *SET BOUNDARIES, FIND PEACE*

To a wounded spirit, healthy boundaries can feel like a violation of intimacy and loyalty. Healthy boundaries can feel more like an inconvenience than a necessity and can trigger fears that we will not be loved if we draw healthy lines. Creating boundaries within family and intimate dynamics can be the toughest.

————

These unhealthy principles have played a part in how so many of us have allowed ourselves to be removed from tables (even ones we've created) because we are so unconscious and unskilled at how to set healthy boundaries for ourselves. When we have not mustered enough self-worth, we can forsake the rights and freedoms that are at our fingertips. Healthy boundaries are not only an expression of how we love ourselves, they also teach people how to love us in a healthy fashion. Believe it or not, when we are able to draw loving boundaries, that is a show of love to the person we are interacting with as well.

————

Can you think of a time when you gave up your own place at your table? Were you able to reclaim your place? If so, how? If you weren't, why not give it a try now?

CHAPTER 20

Surrender

Why an index finger?

The more I thought about my crazy dream, the more I was reminded of lessons I learned in my spiritual journey. I had forgotten that, in many spiritual disciplines, the index finger represents the ego. In my quest to find full surrender in peace, the major obstacle was *my* ferocious ego—not anyone else's.

Sure, I had set aside the know-it-all of the pseudo-guru, but now I was convinced I was on my way to sainthood. At this time in my life, I'd stripped myself of every vice in my repertoire; I had no relationship to escape to; and I was practicing abstinence from alcohol and sex in a disciplined fashion unlike never before in my life. This left me staring at the werewolf of my ego in all its manipulations, cravings, and deceit. Yet I'd only scratched the surface of what I needed to become.

Clearly, I was not qualified to take this ride alone. In the words of the Buddha, when the student is ready, the teacher arrives. And I sought teachers everywhere.

We met in person or on their pages, and I sat myself down at their feet, heart wide open. I reread many of the religious texts I'd studied in the past, along with the worn pages of my soul guide Clarissa Pinkola Estés, everything by Pema Chödrön, and a new find, *Reclaim Your Heart* by Yasmin Mogahed. I dug into illuminating passages about what it meant to walk with Jesus, to be devout as described in the Quran, stories of the many sides of God from the Torah, wisdom from Sufi mystics. I was acting on the foundation Marion had given me, now in practice.

My focus then turned to learning more about the holy women in different religions—including Fatima, the daughter of the prophet Muhammad (may the blessings and peace of Allah be upon him), and her dedication to her family and her God even in persecution. I read of the majestic Indian saint Anandamayi Ma, who was born of purest heart and spirit, so much so that people could experience the Divine by simply sitting at her feet. Then I learned of the rebel Tahirih, who had been the first female martyr of the Bahá'í Faith, and the Sisters of the Beguine Order and the Sisters of the Holy Family, Black Catholic nuns in New Orleans. The devotion to Allah of female Sufi saint Rabi'a helped me understand the need to create a bridge between God's love and my heart. Discovering the soul food offered by remarkable and unsung women gave me the spiritual sustenance I'd been longing for.

One of the most applicable spiritual axioms I learned early in my studies came from Ram Dass, American-born yogi and author of *Be Here Now,* who introduced me to a tough concept. He said, "We have to learn how to have an open heart in hell." That means finding forgiveness and compassion for those who hurt us and others, seeing the presence of the Divine even in suffering and chaos, and, in short, learning how to love as God does.

When ego raises its index finger, that kind of love is a difficult state to achieve. But what happens when you get to meet someone who has achieved that state?

Right before the pandemic, I was given the blessed opportunity to find out.

"*W**here are you?*" *asked my brother-in-law* Harry Smith, Will's younger brother, on one of my last days in Singapore, where I'd been shooting a project with Gammy and Willow. The two of them were heading back to the States, but I was thinking of extending my stay and maybe traveling on my own.

Harry and I were close, especially during this era, as we were both adjusting to new lives. It was a challenging stretch for us. We checked up on each other regularly.

"Singapore, 'bout to wrap up. But I'm thinking of going to Vietnam before I return to L.A."

"Really? You know your boy Thich Nhat is there now."

Thich Nhat Hanh, a most revered Buddhist monk whose YouTube videos had been medicinal for both Harry and me, was someone I'd never thought I'd meet. I had been a student of his ever since the late 1990s, after reading his book *Living Buddha, Living Christ*.

"I think he is still in Europe."

"No . . . he's there, Jada. You should find him and go see him."

"Harry, are you positive that he's in Vietnam?"

"I'm positive."

Well, that changed everything. Thich Nhat Hanh in Vietnam? There was no question. I had to try to see him. I heeded the call: *Go for it*.

Taking a trip of this nature by myself was something I hadn't done in a great while. Being alone in a foreign place—detaching from old ideas of life—can be a gnarly experience, considering it would be just me and my ego. And yet I was excited.

My plan was to visit two cities in central Vietnam and then head south, because it was rainy season in the north. I would head to Hue because Thich Nhat Hanh's monastery was there. I didn't have confirmation, but even walking the grounds of a place that once was his home would be meaningful.

My security, Ben—a former Navy SEAL of Samoan heritage who is laid-back and without bravado but is exactly whom you want at your side when things go awry—was the perfect person to go with on this adventure. Ben and I first landed in Hội An, a beach town with many five-star resorts. The air was full of heat and moisture, but it wasn't oppressive. Even in the hustle of getting off the jet and being greeted by customs, there was a stillness that put me at ease. In that tropical climate and calm, my body let down its inner guard, and I started to relax.

On our drive to the hotel, I saw a huge Quan Yin statue that I made a note to visit. Quan Yin was a figure I knew well, as she is deeply revered in Vietnam. As is Buddha, which creates a beautiful balance between the male and female energies of the Divine. In this area, there was another attraction I was able to visit—a Buddhist temple hidden in a deep mountain cave where wounded soldiers were taken to recover during the Vietnam War. Hiking is always a pleasure for me, but after the steep ascent up the mountain, stepping into that temple within the cave and feeling the power of worship there was transformational. Inside the cave—often a symbol of the heart or the womb or a cocoon, as in a place of rebirth—I deepened my embrace of this season of rebirth that I was in. Being alone was necessary and not a punishment.

Vietnam itself feels like a temple island. The atmosphere is soft and inviting, with a swirl of devotion in the air that you can't ignore. Within a few days, the heaviness that I'd been carrying for so long seemed to lift. I had never experienced an environment that opened my heart and lessened my defenses to that extent, which made it all the more difficult to imagine that such a violent, devastating war had taken place amid all this beauty and peace.

When we arrived at Hue, where we were going to stay—at the aptly named Pilgrimage Village Hotel—I learned that we were a mere five minutes from Thich Nhat Hanh's monastery. My excitement was palpable, even though I didn't know for sure whether he was there.

Later, on the evening of our arrival, Ben knocked at my door. "You won't believe this," he said, in his classic, dry, monotone but with something tantalizing underneath his words.

"What?" I said, like a kid on Christmas.

"When I asked the woman at the desk about getting a tour of the grounds, we got into a conversation, and I told her that you admired Thich Nhat and you have been following his teachings for a while.

She then told me that he was on the grounds at the monastery."

My heart skipped a beat. "I gotta see him, Ben."

He smiled with amused patience. "I'm working on it. She goes to the monastery every night. She is going to see what she can do."

I had to give Ben props. He was as determined as I was to make this happen.

I closed the door and dropped onto my knees in my room and prayed for the opportunity to be in Thich Nhat Hanh's presence.

The next day, the wheels of possibility began to churn. Ben and the woman from the hotel brought me to the tearoom, where I was introduced to Nina, a beautiful bald woman who was beginning her process of becoming a Buddhist nun and would meet that evening with a nun from the monastery who was assisting her. Nina (and the group she was with) invited me to stay and meet the nun in the hope that it could help open the door for me to visit with Thich Nhat Hanh.

To do so, I needed to pass through many gates. Unlike other settings where doors would open easily to a celebrity or a spotlighted person, I knew here I would face more scrutiny than most as to whether I was sincere in my quest to have an audience with such a holy man. His health was a consideration as well.

That evening, the nun from the monastery arrived in her brown gown and commenced her conversation with Nina and her group. Shortly after, I was introduced. Mind you, no one really spoke English, so the young lady from the hotel did her best to translate as I explained my affinity for the teachings of Thich Nhat Hanh. After the meeting, the young lady from the hotel smiled and let me know that the nun would like me to come to the monastery. "Tomorrow."

Deep breath. "Tomorrow?"

"Yes, it is arranged." She added that Nina, her group, and I would roll together.

When the appointed hour arrived, I was led to a section of the monastery where I was met by a young nun who announced that I was to meet Thich Nhat's right hand, Sister Chan Khong. Also beautiful, bald, and adorned in brown garb, Sister Chan entered the room, and I recognized her from Thich Nhat's videos, as well as her lectures. She exuded kindness and strength. We talked about why I was there, and she shared with me how a desire to understand the meaning of love had informed her journey. It was as if she was reading my inner biography.

Sister Chan then gave me a copy of her book *Learning True Love*, which she signed and I held on to as a magical keepsake. After we vibed together a bit longer, I felt as though I had passed through the final gate. She stood up, announcing that she would take me to meet Thich Nhat Hanh.

I was to learn that women were not usually allowed to enter the men's side of the monastery, where Thich Nhat was, but that an exception would be made for me, since I would be entering with Sister Chan and Nina and a small group of other devout nuns.

My heart was so full as Sister Chan gave me the signal to walk at her side. We followed the paved walkway through a grove of mature trees that lent serenity to this monastery dating back to the 1800s. Before long, we arrived at the area where he was, just off the courtyard. When I first caught sight of Thich Nhat Hanh, I beheld him seated peacefully, his eyes closed—not unlike many statues of Buddha I had seen.

He was seated in a wheelchair, so it was evident that his health was in decline, and I understood he was not speaking much. But with a nod from the sister, I was able to step toward him and to bow at his feet, showing my gratitude and feeling his Divine energy. Nothing can compare to being in the presence of a spiritual master. I felt an automatic clearing, a spiritual purification. It was beautiful.

In surrendering to this moment, I recalled Thich Nhat Hanh's words that there is no greater communication than silence. That silence is the language of the heart, where the peace and purity of love that surpasses all logical, sensory understanding reside. And that was what I was able to experience firsthand from the holy master himself.

When it came time to raise my head and lift myself to my feet, that was the lesson that filled my heart and will last a lifetime.

I n the aftermath of the Red Table conversation with Will, I was fortunate to have the support of Jay Shetty and his wife, Radhi Devlukia-Shetty, who appeared magically at my side at a time when others were running for the hills. Jay and Radhi's embrace was nourishing. Jay had been a Bhakti monk for three years before pursuing a secular life, and Radhi was a devout Bhakti in her own right. Both entrepreneurs from England, of Indian descent, they'd moved to the U.S. determined to share a practical approach to applying spiritual principles to daily life.

Jay emphasized the idea of surrender to me, telling a very powerful story of a woman named Draupadi, whose husband lost his possessions and her over a game of dice. When she is brought to the court to be turned over to the men who now own her kingdom and her, one of the men begins to pull at her sari to disrobe her in view of all the subjects.

Jay went on: "In full surrender, she lets go of her sari and throws her arms in the air toward Krishna"—who in the Bhakti tradition is considered Lord Supreme—"as the man continues to pull at her sari to disrobe and humiliate her in front of everyone." He explained that in her full surrender, she takes shelter in Krishna, who adds more and more cloth to her sari so that she cannot be disrobed. After hours and hours of pulling at her sari without disrobing her, the man gets so tired that he stops. Because of her faith, Krishna protects her.

I was silent. The parallels were obvious.

"There is only one place to take shelter, Jada—God," Jay said.

I knew Jay was right. I had already been on the path, but it was time for me to throw my hands in the air while others pulled at my sari. I took shelter at God's feet.

Soon after, I started regular study of the Gita (the Bhagavad Gita, one of the most sacred Hindu texts, which I had not read) with Jay and Radhi. Jay introduced me to the teachings of Bhakti Tirtha Swami, a Black swami from the hood in Cleveland. How could I have gone this many years and never heard of him? When Jay surprised me with the gift of Bhakti Tirtha Swami's book *Spiritual Warrior: Transforming Lust into Love,* it seriously CHANGED MY LIFE! I became obsessed with Bhakti Tirtha's teachings, watching everything there was from him on YouTube and reading all his works. Here was a Black man from Cleveland narrating his journey of spiritual transformation, along with many challenges met along the way that I could relate to.

Inspired by Bhakti Tirtha Swami's book *Surrender,* I turbocharged my abstinence. Beyond abstaining from sex and alcohol, I went deeper—letting go of excesses in the material world (shopping only for necessities), adding regular fasting to my practice, avoiding violent TV and music. The goals were clarity and emotional sobriety. Other than colorful language now and then, I became an urban nun of sorts.

And then one day, Jay asked me the golden question: "Would you like to meet my teacher, Radhanath Swami?"

I had to take a few deep breaths. I couldn't believe Jay was offering me this opportunity. Radhanath Swami—whose lectures I'd also followed—is one of the most revered Bhakti swamis on the planet.

My first reaction was *I am not worthy!* But that was old thinking, which I was trying to dissolve.

My lessons with Radhanath Swami began immediately over Zoom. This was during the global shutdown, and though he lives primarily in India, he was in his hometown of Chicago for the time being. The minute he appeared on the screen in his beautiful saffron robe, my nerves vanished in the glow of his sweet smile. His energy, even via technology, had an immediate warming effect. American-born, the son of Jewish and Eastern European immigrants, Swami had begun his spiritual journey in childhood and in his search for enlightenment decided to dedicate his life to Krishna. A scholar who had immersed himself in the study of many religions, he could deliver wisdom from any of them in one session. Off the top of his dome might come a quote from the Quran, a passage from the Old Testament or the New, the story of a Hindu saint or a Sufi master. I was in awe. Swami was in his early seventies and had a mind so sharp and a heart so elastic, I learned simply from being in his holy presence and as a witness of his mastery of Divine knowledge from all these many faiths.

Swami was the teacher I needed. He helped me understand that the path to deepen one's surrender crosses the path to understanding what it means to forgive. After many Zooms, I had to admit, "Swami, I'm having such a difficult time with forgiveness."

"You know, Jada," he began, speaking with certainty, "forgiveness is humbling ourselves before God in the face of all that we have done, and being willing to change and let go."

Hmmmm. A part of me wanted to reject this truth or qualify it by saying, "I'm not talking about forgiving myself, I'm talking about forgiving others." But I sat quietly because I knew Swami had more for me.

"God's love is supremely forgiving. Let go of the impediments of the past. In our humility, we understand that we can only take shelter of God's forgiveness." He gently went on to point out that once you do the work of forgiving yourself, it will show you that you have little to forgive in anyone else.

Presented this way, it was clear that our human condition—in our offenses and our struggles—evens the playing field.

What we can't forget, Swami said, is this: "We have to believe in our potential to grow and in the potential of others to grow. The heart is like a seed, and like the seed, the heart must break to grow. No matter how long the human heart has been a garbage dump, we can transform it any time and turn it into a garden. It's the natural journey of going from darkness to light. This is what interconnects life in all its forms."

My heart swelled. I saw in that moment that I was no different from everyone I needed to forgive. We're all just trying to do the best we can. He made it clear that instead of focusing on someone's transgressions, we should pay attention to their potential to change, while setting loving boundaries for ourselves and becoming a well-wisher. That's all we're being asked to do.

When I mentioned to Swami that spiritual rehab wasn't easy in Tinseltown, he pointed out that what he called the "Holy Woods" could be as potent a teacher as a cave in Tibet. Sacred wisdom comes from everyday life, while washing dishes or typing up a résumé or dealing with media frenzy, and can even arise when you're having fun. To my surprise, golf was that fun outlet for me, where so many sacred lessons could come through—several of which were amplified when I had the opportunity to be given a golf lesson from the one and only Tiger Woods for his TV show.

The experience of standing next to Tiger's ease, generosity, and level of mastery instantly dissolved my ego and allowed me to surrender to the game itself—which, to me, is equivalent to the game of life. Who knew that golf could teach one to let go of all notions of winning and losing, and instead to simply be present, and to play one shot at a time?

During the spring of 2021, I revived the spirit of that little girl I once was, standing up on the high-diving platform, scared to jump into the cold water of the rock quarry below but refusing to give up. That was the metaphor for knowing it was time for me to move out of Gammy's guest room—where I'd lived for close to a year—and into my own house.

My mother's house was not far from the family home where Will and I had raised our kids and lived for twenty years, and because that family home also served as the set for *RTT,* I had been able to move out without having to feel that I was banishing myself. On the contrary, after packing only my necessities and adapting to a small bedroom and a little closet, I found a beautiful oasis the minute I took up residence at my mom's. The peace of a simple life without excess, and without being surrounded by so much energy all the time, was a much-needed reprieve. I loved it so much. My grandmother Marion had offered my mother, my aunts, and my uncle the same safe haven in her family home, and each one of them at different times had moved back in to heal and renew. Safety hadn't been there for me in my childhood under Adrienne's roof, but in a time of deep need as an adult, it was the only place I desired to be.

The guest bedroom at Gammy's faces the east, which meant that I could wake up every morning and watch the sunrise and feel its energy during my morning meditation/prayer practice. It was a time for me to surrender and have the patience to see what the Universe had in store.

Unexpectedly, in the cave of that guest bedroom, in healing myself, in finding a new intimacy with myself, I gained a new perspective on my marriage—as a holy path toward self-discovery. In this sense, the marriage vows are made not only to each other and to God but to the self. I was finally becoming the woman I've always wanted to be.

The time had come to set up my life as a garden of my own potential. That meant letting my mother have her own garden, and having the courage to build a new home of my own.

Along with me would be my puppy, Bandit, a pocket Frenchie given to me by Cesar Millan for my forty-ninth birthday. I love this dog, just as Cesar said I would. Bandit has no idea he is little. He has the heart of a lion, and you have to earn his trust. He can chill hard and play hard and wants nothing more than to be at my hip at all times.

My main criterion for a house was its location, so I could be close to the kids and my mother, which narrowed the search. After almost a year, I got a call from Miguel, whose wife, Lauren, had found a house they thought I should look at.

"Check out the email I forwarded you," Miguel urged me. "Lauren and I think you might like it."

Over the years of my marriage, I had been able to make some very profitable real-estate investments, and I didn't want this purchase to be any different. Plus, Lauren had great taste. I was intrigued. With Miguel on the phone, I opened the email to a listing I'd seen before. "Yeah . . . I've seen this before, but it doesn't look like it has the flow I want."

"I think you should at least go and see it. It may surprise you."

I stopped myself from dismissing his suggestion. Miguel and Lauren were trying to help me at a time when I was consciously working on being willing to accept help. Besides, it was in the same hood where I'd been living, near my people, and, on paper, had everything I needed.

With some reluctance, I made the appointment and went to see the house. By now, I was used to a beautifully photographed on-line presentation of a house being much less inviting in person. So I prepped myself for another disappointment. What I found when I arrived took me by surprise. The house was very open, set in nature, with lots of big windows and a view of the hills in the distance, and it *was* actually much nicer once I saw it with my own eyes. It was beautiful but simple—the aesthetic that let me focus on what was important. It was a home that I could fill with love, connection, patience, rest. It also had rooms for Trey, Jaden, and Willow in case a day ever came that they needed to do what I had been doing—return to a maternal haven for some reprieve. The kids came to see the house and loved it, too. In fact, they were more excited than I was.

Before committing to the purchase, I sat with myself to have a serious powwow. None of my fear, grief, sorrow, or uncertainty was invited to join the discussion, which went something like this: *Jada, you are about to buy a house. You will officially be leaving your old life behind. Are you ready for this?*

I took a deep breath and replied: *I'm ready.*

I bought my own place, thinking of it as a fiftieth-birthday gift to myself, and went to work to furnish it in a way that felt serene, like a warm embrace.

I n July 2021, *two months away* from my fiftieth birthday, I was in the Bahamas with the whole family and many friends to celebrate Jaden's birthday. One morning, alone in my bed there, I woke up with hair all over my pillow for the last time. That was the day I waved the white flag and surrendered to a decision I had avoided for a long time.

Not many months earlier, Willow had shaved her head for the second time in her life. She was onstage when she cut it off, and it was an act of both protest and self-love. At almost twenty-one years old, she was really coming into her own as a creative force and a serious rock musician. My girl. She was gorgeous with or without hair.

Willow had never urged me to consider shaving my head, but having witnessed all the ups and downs I'd experienced, she thought it was time.

I made a decision to see my hair loss as an aspect of my spiritual journey. The decider was going to be God. In a place of true gratitude, I talked to the Great Supreme and said, *Great Mother/Father, if you want my hair, you can have my hair. I give my hair to you in gratitude. I'm going to offer it to you with a smile. You've given me so much, and if my hair is what you're asking from me in return, then have it.*

The more I thought about the blessings of my existence, the more grateful I felt for my problems. They had afforded me the ability to become closer to the Divine and to learn how to surrender. And so

I shaved my head and, surprisingly, felt all the more lovable, all the more worthy.

My bald head was now a symbol of a covenant between God and me.

There were millions of people around the world, women and men, suffering, bullied, and even considering suicide as the result of much, much worse cases of alopecia than mine. My alopecia was mild in comparison. If sharing my story could empower them and bring their struggles to light, then I wanted to do that. In fact, I was welcomed into a new community with love and acceptance that I could give in return.

In celebration of my new life and a milestone birthday, I decided to plan my own party. For all the years I'd been married to Will, I hadn't planned my milestone birthday parties, so this was uncharted territory. And this year, for the first time in almost three decades of my life, it was very possible that Will would not be joining the celebration.

In my younger years, the thought of turning fifty had seemed so ominous, but I'll never forget waking up on the morning of my actual fiftieth birthday, in my own bed, alone, in my new house—with Bandit on the floor beside me—and feeling so full of yummy joy simply because I was me. The morning of my fiftieth, I could love all the warm honey inside of me. I didn't need a new car or an expensive piece of jewelry.

I was the jewel. This journey, all that struggle, had been worth it.

I took a deep breath, opened my heart wide toward myself, and allowed my most grateful tears to fall. I asked for guidance to carry this feeling with me, in every new season to come, in the shadows and in the light. I went into the bathroom, looked in the mirror, pointed at my reflection, and said out loud, "Damn! You *fifty*, bitch!" and burst out laughing.

My party was at the family home. And all the family was there, including Will. He and I had a fist-bump, and it felt like he was saying to me, *Wow, look at you, congrats.* He had been in full support of my independence and was happy to see where I was in my life. For the festivities, I'd been able to build an old-school skating rink—a reminder of the part of my younger life that had brought me so much joy. Because this was still in the time of COVID-19, the gathering was small and held outside, but the music was flowing, and the laughter was loud.

Ellen and my *RTT* family put together an unforgettable fiftieth-birthday special for me, with shout-outs from friends and familiar faces from my years in Hollywood. They even managed to have my homegirl Toni Braxton come and sing "Happy Birthday" to me. Then Willow outdid herself and surprised me by putting together a reunion of Wicked Wisdom and performing one of my favorites of our songs, "Bleed All Over Me."

My life was coming full circle in real time before my eyes—so perfectly that it was almost surreal. Right at the end, leaving no stones of love unturned, Trey and Jaden topped off the show with the most loving birthday cheer ever.

I had turned fifty and I had finally found my way home.

Jada—I have one question. Are you willing?
—ISHMIEL LOUNSBURY, INNER WISDOM GUIDE

One must be willing to surrender. I have a practice of asking myself several times a day whether I'm willing to let go of whatever is gripping my heart and mind, and whatever is blocking my kindness and compassion. When I ask the question, it puts me in touch with whatever unwillingness in my body, mind, or spirit is preventing my surrender. It's usually the resistance of my ego. There are plenty of moments when I have to simply surrender to the fact that I'm unwilling to let go of my ego. That's when I choose to practice patience, love, and respect for myself. Loving on our unwillingness with kindness and patience is as much a beautiful practice as our willingness.

———

Are you willing to be willing to be willing?

———

If you are, would you be willing to write down a situation that has brought you difficulty? Are you willing to find peace with yourself about it today? Are you willing to identify any unwillingness to make peace with yourself about it? I love the practice of taking fifteen minutes in a quiet place, with your hand over your heart, to breathe into your willingness in order to accept and embrace your surrender. If you're not willing, use this practice to breathe patience, kindness, and acceptance into your unwillingness. This is self-love that eventually delivers you magic. Trust me.

CHAPTER 21

The Holy Joke, the Holy Slap, and Holy Lessons

March 27, 2022

THE DOLBY THEATRE
HOLLYWOOD, CALIFORNIA

I'm sitting frozen in the front row, just to the left of center stage, during the live broadcast of the 94th Academy Awards. I am confused.

In what can only be described as one of the more surreal events of my life, I'm trying to stay composed, while trying to grasp what just happened, and urge my brain to catch up. As I watch Will march down the steps from the Dolby Theatre stage to return to his seat next to mine, the air in the room feels completely still and is hauntingly quiet.

Everyone in the house appears equally confused about what just happened. I'm still not quite sure if what I witnessed onstage between Will and Chris Rock was a skit or real.

When Will drops into his seat and we catch eyes is when I first suspect that what just transpired was not a "bit." I quickly grab Will's hand to reassure him—*I'm here*. And then I look deeper into his eyes, hoping to gauge where he is. He's sitting in his seat, but it feels to me that he's in another place and time.

My mind is trying its best to mentally rewind the tape and review the past few moments.

From where I was sitting, the whole confrontation looked fake. My angle prevented me from seeing that Will's swing actually made contact. That was confirmed to me only later. (Hold on, I'll get to that.) Until then, my mind didn't register it. For several reasons.

Will had been going back and forth from his seat to backstage all night, so that's why my first thought was: *Is this a skit he and Chris planned earlier, when they ran into each other backstage? Did he just not tell me?* Plus, when Will swung, open-palmed, it looked like Chris pulled a stunt move and ducked the shot. And when Chris was still standing afterward, I believed my observation to be true . . . *Aha, this IS a skit.*

I'd witnessed professional fighters laid down by the force of Will's hands in the boxing ring. More than once. This had to be staged. Otherwise, how could Chris be on his feet like nothing happened?

It's not until Will yells from his seat back up at Chris to "keep my wife's name out your fuckin' mouth," and then repeats it, that I perceive the gravity of the situation, and that, no, it had not been a skit. Even so, I am unclear on the reason why Will is so upset.

We had been living separate lives and were there as family, not as husband and wife. But when I hear Will yell "wife" in the chaos of the moment, an internal shift of *Oh shit . . . I am his wife!* happens instantly.

This is when sixteen-year-old Jada appeared—I'm back in a club back in Baltimore, a fight has broken out, and shit could start popp'n. I'm aware that I'm at the Oscars in a beautiful but very *heavy* forest-green dress with a high neck, a zipper bodice, and a train a thousand miles long, and I've had to stay seated all evening. But no matter how much growth I've recently experienced, my old mechanisms are driving, and my mind is racing with *Oh shit, if I have to fight or run, I'm done! I can't even get up!*

But no matter what, Will and I are in this together.

And you know, the craziest thing about that whole evening was, there was a point when I wasn't even planning to come with Will at all.

There's a lot of backstory with that.

Over our many years together, Will and I had worked side by side in our philanthropy, in business, and on many creative projects. When we decided that our marriage was going to move into more of a life partnership—with family and holidays always a constant—Will and I saw no reason to part ways in our creative and business collaborations. We were ardent fans and believers in each other's talents, very yin and yang when we came together in that way, and it worked. The same differences that made us collide were the same differences that created exceptional magic.

It was in this context, not long after Sundance in early 2018, when I had been part of the film festival's U.S. Dramatic Competition jury, that I made a passionate recommendation to Will, who was set to star in *King Richard* as Richard Williams, father of Venus and Serena. No director had been found. I had a great feeling about Reinaldo Marcus Green, whose film *Monsters and Men* I had seen screened at Sundance.

Octavia Spencer—also on the panel—and I had both fought tooth and nail to make sure this powerful, haunting film received its due and that Reinaldo left Sundance with an award in hand. So much so that we created a special dramatic category, Outstanding First Feature award. That's how impressed we were by his work and how determined we were that this talented Black director be recognized for it.

In a conversation about the ongoing search for a director for *King Richard*, I told Will, "You should meet Rei. He is an extremely talented director, and I believe he could have an eye for this."

Will took my advice and watched Rei's movie. To my delight, Will believed, as I did, that Rei would be perfect for *King Richard*. Will then asked if I would come on board with him as an executive producer. He also wanted my help making sure that the production authentically reflected the voices of the powerful Black females in the cast, specifically the mother of Venus and Serena, Oracene Price, whom I loved and whose elegant strength I believed needed to be a potent part of the story.

The offer for me to come on board was gracious on Will's part, and I accepted.

The day I saw Aunjanue Ellis read the part of Oracene in our living room, she embodied the role so naturally, so powerfully, I knew that this character was in the best possible hands. Aunjanue—who had an outstanding body of work—was bad to the bone with every nuance. I was damn near jealous of her natural presence and the exceptional quality of her talent.

Unfortunately, before production began, Will and I had a falling-out, a symptom of our trying to navigate our separate lives and different needs. I thought it would be best to be taken off the movie.

Will pushed back, saying that he wanted me to be part of a film he believed held important themes we both cared about: Black/female representation in a sport that denied so many women of color; the importance of family; the challenges of parenting; and the universal power of perseverance.

"But I don't want my name on something that I didn't participate in fully."

"You found Rei, you helped me with the script, and I know this movie is going to be special. I want you to be a part of the history this movie is going to make."

I left it alone, and life went on.

As awards season approached, I was happy to see the many nominations the film had received and, of course, was proud of and excited for Will when it became clear he was the favorite in the Best Actor category at the Oscars. Getting the film nominated was the big prize, but if he won, after two previous nominations (*Ali* in '02 and *Pursuit of Happyness* in '07), that would be icing on the cake.

This coincided with a shift I was seeing in Will. He had just finished filming *Emancipation,* which was very challenging for him psychologically. Playing that character rattled him in a way that led him to a therapeutic setting—allowing him to begin to unpack all that embodying the role of Whipped Peter had brought up for him. In the process, Will suggested the possibility of us taking steps to go back into therapy with new counselors. I resisted at first, but that changed when I met Don Rosenthal and Ishmiel Lounsbury. These two men and their approach would be life-changing.

When Will asked me to accompany him to the various award shows in early 2022, culminating with the Oscars in March, I was pleasantly surprised.

For every special moment in our lives together, we had been there for each other. I welcomed the gift of this opportunity and the continuation of our bond in that way. After all, we were now at six years of not living together as a married couple but still legally married. However, our movement back into therapy and his invitation for me to be at his side for awards season told me that we weren't ready to give everything up just yet. We still had an inexplicable connection, an attachment that didn't want to let go. That couldn't let go.

My answer was "Of course."

So there we were, sitting at the Oscars, living out Will's belief that *King Richard*—with six nominations, including Best Picture and Best Actor for Will—was going to make history. And, as the world is our witness, we did make history—only not quite how we thought.

This is only part of the backstory. There is more. There is much more.

I *had my own premonition right before* the incident on the Oscar stage. It flashed through my mind as Chris Rock's face came across the screen as one of the presenters that night. In fact, my stomach clenched. He had been known to take swipes at me—and from the Oscar stage, no less. That had been in 2016, six years earlier, during what became known as #OscarsSoWhite.

That was the year when the Academy Awards nominations came out and almost all the talent was white. When I spoke out about the lack of nominations for industry members of color, the online chatter declared that I had an ax to grind because Will was not nominated for *Concussion,* which couldn't have been further from the truth. What I didn't take into consideration was that Will and everyone with *Concussion* had been campaigning for nominations, so I could see how my outpokenness could have been misconstrued. But there was no ax because I knew that he would have another shot at a nomination. My concern was, What about the actors of color who might never have another opportunity?

What I also didn't take into consideration was how Chris, as a Black male host that year, would be affected or the pressure he would be under. Nor did I imagine that he would take offense to a question I posed in a video I made—as whether we should continue to support the Oscars that weren't consistently celebrating talent of color.

Let me add here that, contrary to Chris's claim in 2023 that I called him and asked him not to host the awards, that didn't happen. Ever. In fact, in the video I made about #OscarsSoWhite, I tried to acknowledge Chris's tough predicament by saying, and I quote:

> *Hey, Chris . . . I will not be at the Academy Awards, and I won't be watching, but I can't think of a better man to do the job at hand this year than you, my friend, good luck.*

Maybe he took the sentiment as a backhanded vote of support, but that surely was not my intention. The reason I mentioned Chris was my way of saying: *You are actually the best person to host the Oscars in a moment when what's needed is some witty social-political commentary. That could make for some powerful learning moments for everyone.*

Maybe I mistakenly assumed that a hard-hitting comic like Chris Rock wouldn't take offense to such a comment. By this era, Chris and I had developed a friendly rapport. I had been given the chance to see another side to him when we worked together on the animated feature *Madagascar* and were out promoting it. I found him to be quirky, with an unexpected sweetness, and very intelligent, with a biting wit that's impressive if you are on the right side of it. At one point, during rumors that Will and I had divorced, Chris even called to ask me out on a date. Once he found out I wasn't divorced, we laughed, and he apologized profusely, and life went on.

So, I never thought he'd see my comment as taking a swipe at him.

In hindsight, maybe I should have called Chris personally, checked on him, and wished him luck in a situation that was clearly difficult.

That was the lesson learned after others mentioned that I was a target of Chris's opening monologue for the 2016 Oscars. Why me, when there were so many others who had been even more vocal? The subtext that night was *Why refuse to attend the Oscars when I wasn't invited anyway?*

In the aftermath of those swipes, Chris reached out via text with a heartfelt apology. I reached out to my team, including Will, who were all pretty upset with the comments he'd made about me, to let everyone know that I would be responding and burying the hatchet. I then sent my apology to Chris in return. From there, I believed us to be cool. And six years went by without any contact, until, once again, we were at the Oscars—the first show in person after the pandemic— and when he came out on the stage, I immediately felt a trainwreck coming.

Trying to be optimistic, I told myself, *A lot of time has passed, it's the Academy Awards, there are no new misunderstandings, and I'm sure he'll play nice.* But another thought was *He's not going to be able to help himself.*

The plot twist here that many people don't know is there had been decades of disrespect between Will and Chris—starting in the late 1980s, before either of them even knew I existed. Like many old beefs, it began with a big ole misunderstanding that I don't have enough therapists or lawyers to begin to explain. And it just kept festering. As a result, over the years, like a lot of celebrities who are seen as fair game by comedians, Will and I both were dragged across many stages by Chris's jokes. To an extent, you have to know that it comes with the territory. That being said, lines do get crossed.

What you do is learn to laugh on cue and pretend it doesn't bother you even when it does. Laughing in response to scathing delivery, even when it's mean, becomes a coping mechanism.

T*he rolling of my eyes. Might* I explain?

When Chris came out to present an award, made some jokes, got lots of laughs, and, like comics do, decided to milk his time onstage, he saw me and my bald head and ad-libbed: "Jada, I love ya, *G.I. Jane Two,* can't wait to see it."

Just like I'd thought, he wasn't able to help himself, and I rolled my eyes.

It was not because of the jab at *my* alopecia but, honestly, about the people I had met whose condition was far worse than mine. That was indeed a very light joke, as many expressed, but it was not about me. I was frustrated that the majority of folks can't seem to understand how devastating alopecia can be. My heart broke for the many who live in shame, the children who have committed suicide after being teased and taunted by their classmates. And now the Oscars, in all its political correctness, was telling the world it was okay to make jokes at the expense of a woman suffering from alopecia?

It was disheartening. And I didn't take personal offense. I took offense because the condition of alopecia was being mocked. I was going to be fine. This was just another day in the salt mines of the world we inhabited.

My eye roll was me reacting authentically and simply being . . . human. I didn't feel like fakin' it anymore. Besides—*Really, Chris? We gotta go through this again?*

Did it later shock me that a multitude of opinion-mongers would point to my eye-rolling as proof that it was my fault—*You know she gave Will the side eye and made him go up on that stage to slap Chris?* No, I was not shocked. Some of it did surprise me, like the insinuation that I could have stopped Will in his tracks as soon as he got up from his seat, or I could have told him to sit down and relax and leave Chris alone.

The vitriol in the coming days did come faster and more furiously than I'd predicted.

Blaming the woman is nothing new. And I was clear on that. It was easy to spin the story of how the perfect Hollywood megastar had fallen to his demise because of his imperfect wife. The patriarchy depends on pinning the downfall of humanity on poor Eve. The Adam/Eve dynamic wasn't necessarily on display at the Academy Awards, but let's look at the context—women are increasingly being marginalized, in one way or another. What's sad is how many women have become the gatekeepers of this marginalization, within the patriarchal construct, and are fierce participants in the shaming and blaming of women.

I have to point out, when a man, any man, commits a displeasing act, how bizarre it is that a woman can be fully to blame. How is it that a woman can be so irrelevant *and* culpable at the same time? It's absolutely mind-boggling and quite a fascinating riddle.

When it came to Oscars 2022, I had to think about the narrative out there of me as the adulteress wife who had now driven her husband to madness with the command of one look. I had to take responsibility for my part in aiding that false narrative's existence. I also had to chuckle at the idea that the world would think I wielded that amount of control over Will Smith. *If I had that amount of con-*

trol over Will, chile, my life would have been entirely different these damn near three decades. Real talk!

Where the night's confusion intensified was when Will returned to his seat and Chris remained onstage as the clips of the nominated documentaries were being shown on the screen. Everyone in the room seemed frozen from shock. As the clips played, Chris—who was now at the edge of the stage—saw me, in the front row next to Will, and said, "Jada, I honestly meant no harm."

Will barked back at Chris once again, conveying his frustration with Chris talking to me.

Rattled myself, I couldn't absorb Chris's apology and threw my hand up in the air, saying, "I can't right now, Chris, all this is about some old shit."

Then the action resumed onstage, and Chris went back to announce the winner, Questlove for *Summer of Soul*. After his acceptance, a commercial break was taken. Denzel Washington and Bradley Cooper were both nearby and went to Will and huddled up, trying to ground him.

For the next couple of minutes, I continued to sit there by myself, trying to find my own steady ground, and was grateful for the men gathering around Will, because I was at a loss. Let the men handle this. I remained still and present, ready when I was needed.

At the next commercial break, Will's publicist Meredith and my publicist Karynne came to our seats to figure out what to do next. Meredith had just been backstage and informed us that Chris had left the building and was not going to press charges.

"Press charges—for what?" I asked.

Meredith confirmed what I had missed: that Will had in fact made contact with Chris, who had not, as I'd thought, ducked.

I looked at Will in shock. "You actually hit Chris?"

Will nodded and said, "Yes," a bit surprised that I had missed the moment of contact.

I took a moment to collect my bearings.

In the fog of it all, though we could have left, we didn't know whether we were coming or going. Given our history of coping with disruption of this magnitude, we did what we knew to do, which was to move through and try to get back to normal as fast as possible.

From my point of view, that's how we all responded to the events of that night in that room. It was a collective response: *Let's get back to normal.* Nobody came and said, "Leave," or "Omigod, what have you done?" The fog from The Slap disoriented everyone.

At every commercial break, different groups of people came over to check in. One of the first people to say something to me was Lupita Nyong'o, who was sitting right behind me. She leaned in to ask, "Are you all right, Jada? I'm so sorry."

Reeling and numb all at once, I tried my best to assure her that I was okay. And then Nicole Kidman and her husband, Keith Urban—who are always so sweet and generous in these settings—hurried over, too. I reassured and thanked them for their warm concern.

During another break, when I was sitting there by myself, I looked up and saw the one and only Ramsey Naito rushing to my side. She knelt beside me and said, "Jada, I'm here, are you okay?" Once I saw Ramsey, my facade cracked enough for me to let her know I had no clue if I was or wasn't. Then Tiffany Haddish came over, and Queen Latifah made her way to us as well. This made me feel . . . tethered. At least enough to shake off a bit of my disbelief.

Ramsey later told me that she had never seen me so alone and isolated, except for ten years earlier, at my fortieth birthday. The difference was that this time, I could stabilize myself in the storm and find the inner fortitude to keep my head up. My concern was Will.

I can't tell his story of why he did what he did, but I can tell you it had everything to do with Will's own personal battles, which unfolded on a world stage.

And what I knew, for the first time in six years since our breakup, was that I would stand with him in this storm as his wife, no matter what. I had not felt that way in a long time. I would not abandon him, nor would I fight his fight for him like I had tried to do so many times in the past. This fight was his.

There were other emotional subplots that collided for me at the 94th Oscars that I couldn't untangle in the moment. What happened on that stage was a deeply difficult, complicated, painful moment, and my heart broke for every single person affected, including the viewers. No question. It was agonizing and shocking to watch a hero have a human moment as his trauma splattered all over that room for the world to see. It crushed the romantic idea that if we achieve enough, we're exempt from our shadow. And then seeing conflict of that nature displayed between two Black men on a "white" stage was disturbing, as was watching a Black man insult a Black woman on a "white" stage. Once again.

What's more, women of color are damn near never defended. For that reason, even amid the chorus of voices ready to blame Jada for The Slap, I recognized that there were women from every walk of life who were secretly screaming, "Fucking right! 'Bout time!"

A slight whisper of that sentiment spoke to me, too, and made me feel—*Thank you, Will, for defending me.* But I also knew he was defending more than me and much that had nothing to do with me.

There was a lot of blaming, and Will for sure got his share—for stealing the magic of a night that should have been remembered for great wins for filmmakers, actors, and other truly talented artists being given their due. I did take comfort in the fact that there was no blood on the stage, and there were no guns drawn, and these two privileged men would walk away intact, with no police interference. This is not at all to minimize the humiliation of the clash that evening, but since I know that fame and stages don't keep you safe, it brought me ease that these two were able to walk away, not unbruised, but safe and alive.

Will, it seems, was suffering from the trap of his own handmade gilded cage. Turns out he is human. As we all are, including Chris.

And here's what ten years in the valley of the shadow had taught

me: Everyone's hurting. As the old saying goes, hurt people hurt people. Often, when we are finding our way, we end up bumping into
each other's hurts on the path. Welcome to the human experience.
What I was learning was not to take any of it personally.

Toward the end of the live broadcast of the Oscars show, I had
a revelation that it wasn't my place to try to steer any ship.
My job was to be in loving presence for myself and Will.
There was no fixing or avoiding the storm that was to come. The way
out was the way through, and this night was the opening of a new
door into yet another unknown.

One of the Holy Lessons of this night was how to practice loving unconditionally. All that thorny history of our complicated life
together became a nonissue. Will was going to need my support. I
knew that people who once proclaimed love for Will would turn their
back. I knew how that felt, and I knew he didn't. My heart broke for
him, but I couldn't prepare him for the onslaught. The only thing I
could guarantee was that I wasn't going to leave his side. We came together, so we were leaving together. We were in this together. Period.

Ride-or-die, Bonnie and Clyde, call on all the romanticized versions of all the outlaw shit you can think of. This is where my mind
was sitting. Through all the bullshit between Will and me, when it's
all said and done, this is what I do! I'm a ride-or-die.

This night proved for me that conflict can indeed amplify love
and compassion. Loving someone in ideal circumstances is easy. But
what do you do, say, if someone decides to make a comedy special full
of lies and unwarranted insults? You love them as God does, and you
say to yourself when people hurt that it could be they believe they will
feel better if they lash out. Can I honestly say I've never been there?
The answer is no. And that's where compassion and well-wishing
come in.

As difficult and challenging as the events connected to Oscars 2022 were for EVERYONE involved, I call it the "Holy Slap" and the "Holy Joke" because of all the Holy Lessons there to be learned for all of us.

In the media frenzy that followed, I realized I was not any different from every hater and critic when it came to Will Smith. I had been willing to accept and embrace only that which I considered pleasing behavior from Will. I did not know how to love him in his shadow states. The Holy Slap helped me learn how to walk hand in hand with Will, with all the bats and gremlins, the part of him that had been banished deep into his darkest exiled lands, and to be a torch of love for him until he could find his own.

Shadow-walking with a loved one takes a lot of practice, but it is the birthplace of unconditional love.

The Holy Joke was my own shadow walk. Chris had hurt my feelings in the past, and it was like poking an old hurt when it came back around. And although I wanted to hold on to my resentments, I'd learned that would hurt me more than him. I'd seen another side of Chris beyond his hurtful jokes, and I could not unring that bell. He deserves my concern and my consideration despite how he may decide to drag me on stages. That's his issue, not mine. From spirit to spirit, he is my brother, and if it weren't for his Holy Joke, I would not have been able to embrace this teaching so deeply.

The Holy Slap taught me the importance of learning to love Will in his shadow, how to continue to love myself through so much misunderstanding and vitriol, and how to love you, dearest reader, no matter what your thoughts may be concerning me, Will, our family, our marriage, or the Holy Slap. You have a right to think it all, and I will love you anyway, because you are lovable and worthy, too, by the decree of the Divine.

Blessed Be. So It is. Thy will be done.

One does not become enlightened by imagining figures of light but by making the darkness conscious.
The brighter the light, the darker the shadow.
Shadow work is the path of the heart warrior.
—THE ONE AND ONLY CARL JUNG

Wooweeeee! Say it again, Carl, so the folks in the back can hear!

———

What is a personal shadow? Carl Jung explains, "Shadow is the unconscious part of our character and personality that does not align with the ideal version of what we are aiming for." When a disturbing event occurs, our personal shadows rear up and unite to create a collective shadow; a raging ball of fear forms to demand order and compliance to our shared rejection. Aka the judge and jury of cancel culture.

———

The Shadow is absolutely defenseless before light and love, which have the power to banish fear. Taking inventory of our shadow selves, whether personal or if we have joined a collective, is tough work in an unsafe and threatening world. It's easier to join the fray and hit back.

———

If you are willing, take a gentle look at a fear you have, then sit in a quiet place and imagine breathing warmth and light into that fear. Does the fear begin to ease? Is your fear willing to teach your heart something new? Remember that your courage, like your kindness, is powerful medicine to bring light into the world of shadow.

CHAPTER 22

Putting the Crown on the Queen of My Heart

E ver since I was a little girl, I have been drawn to the mystery of magic. From the magic of the earth in my grandmother's garden to the magic of her love that has carried me through my life, and that I have been able to share with my loved ones.

This is probably one of the reasons I have such an affinity for ayahuasca and its mysterious, magical, medicinal properties. It guides you to the love of self and to the magic of Divine love. Ayahuasca opens portals to lost worlds where the language of love and magic dwells. There's an explanation for that, because a thousand years ago, when indigenous people of South America gathered as tribes to drink the aya brew, their tribal ceremonies for healing included the desire to access the magic of the unseen world where their ancestors roamed.

It bears repeating that ayahuasca is not the only pathway to magic, though it's a medicine that *can* help you find your inner magic of transformation. It's a medicine that has worked for me, but it's not necessarily a medicine for everyone. You know what the most powerful medicine for accessing my magic was? Willingness. I had to be willing to change, I had to be willing to suffer, I had to be willing to let go, I had to be willing to confront the shadows of my fear. And I had to be willing to love. No easy task.

Whatever your mode of transportation, your willingness will guide you to your magic—and even allow you to share your magic with those you love. About a year after the Holy Slap, I had an experience that did just that.

For a long time, several members of our family wanted to have a ceremony together, so I decided to organize an aya journey with facilitators who have been conducting circles for almost thirty years. They brought with them a group of musicians who would be playing ceremonial music throughout the eight-hour journey for both nights, as well as assisting us during the process. Will was there, as were other close members of my tribe.

A little over eleven years had passed from that very first night in Ojai in the Medicine Woman's driveway, with me bearing little more than my fruit offering. I had traveled a very long way.

Most of us were not new to ceremony, but it was our first time sharing the experience in a circle together. What I loved about this plan was that it didn't matter where we were in our individual journeys—on these nights, we would each see to our own self-discoveries, our own healing, all while holding space for one another by simply being together. In all of our beautiful vulnerabilities, in all of our love for ourselves and each other.

For many of the years I'd been doing aya, I had not seen my panther often. But this time she visited me once more, and she walked her feline prowl less in front of me and more beside me, taking me more deeply into my inner world—as a preview perhaps of a new journey to come. Some would say that the Black Panther is malformed because she is actually a cougar or jaguar with an excessive amount of pigmentation to hide her spots. But a panther's so-called imperfection is her very power and beauty. The panther is a magician, transmuting her imperfection into unparalleled confidence that allows her to prowl through the shadows of the night undetected.

The panther is a guide of protection, with deep sight, courage, and strength, and is the symbol of death and rebirth. Part of her magic is that she helps one retrieve light from the grips of shadow. I was happy to see her again.

After our last night of ceremony, we all resurfaced shiny and bright, with full, open, and nourished hearts. There was a moment before we ended when I had a chance to look around at everyone— family members and friends—and I thought of everything we had endured together and apart. This moment of love was what all the trials and misunderstandings and willingness to keep learning had brought us to.

I looked over at Chet, who seemed to have shed lifetimes over the past two nights. After he'd come home from prison five years earlier, I had brought him out to L.A., and here we were, together, from the dangerous streets of Baltimore and the days of sling'n dope to doing a whole new level of "work" together. What a miracle. He had not wasted time in creating a program called Jefe Lifestyle to help empower people in their search to feel worthy and to be bosses of their own lives. And then there was Mia, who had walked arm in arm with me through many battles since high school and was now sitting with a level of peace I had never seen in her. This had been her first aya ceremony, and she soon told me tearfully that it had been life-changing.

The magician in me glanced around, and I recognized the tangible but invisible golden threads of love connecting each of us to one another. Memories of others who had been so much a part of my life but were no longer present in physical form let me know that they had been holding my hand at every turn. As I started to cry from the overwhelming feeling of loving and being deeply, deeply loved, I looked over at Will and felt . . . differently. Our multilayered, complicated history didn't change the undefeated truth—that I could no longer deny our spiritual bond.

He saw that I was about to say something, and he waited.

"You are a King of my heart," I said.

Will's eyes lit up, as if he were allowing his heart to blossom unexpectedly. Then he told me that I was a Queen of his heart. After a pause, he laughed, still staring into my eyes, and added, "You'll have to cut off your spirit's wrist to break free of our Divine handcuffs."

We both understood that these declarations were not of a romantic nature. This was not a fairy-tale ending but a fierce acknowledgment of a connection that had been forged in some extreme fire. And within that cauldron fire, we had burned away so much that no longer served us, and we were able to bask in the truth of what remained—unconditional love.

He was a King, and I was a Queen. I could feel my powerful contribution to the making of this magical kingdom that I had wandered long and hard to find—only to learn from the journey that the kingdom was here all along. It brought me joy to bask within the glow that night, with the people I love so very much. I had everything I had been searching for in this very moment.

There had been so much focus on the external, but now we were more balanced and attuned to the golden kingdom within us, between us, within our family. And it was now ours to cultivate, in whatever form that was going to take.

Sorry, Mr. Hero's Journey, if the grail is enough for you. The heroine needs more. The heroine is in search of her kingdom of love. The Queen's power is the golden thread of love that she weaves throughout the kingdom, that gives her the understanding of the world unseen. She can hold many worlds, many hearts, many spirits at once, while surrounding and offering her King love, offering her sight and knowledge. She stands beside him with her velvet sword, as I have learned from Queen Afua, while he brandishes his sword of steel, and together, they make their universe. She is the unseen power that matches the potency of his tangible power. It takes them both to make life whole. (A note: When I speak of this analogy, don't think of King and Queen as gendered; think energy that is yours to choose.)

A Queen must wander to find the knowledge of how to forge a crown upon her heart. How to weep with her hands in the air in full surrender, pleading to the Divine to keep her afloat in her sea of tears and guide her way. How to find her torch within the darkest caves of her fears and how to compose lullabies that sing dragons to sleep. How to stitch, with her own hands, her holy shrouds to protect her boundaries lovingly. How to conjure the courage to dig for the jewels hidden behind tender pain. How to remove the debris from the wounds of her heart and allow her tears and self-soothing to magically transform it all to gold. It is with this gold that she makes her crown. Her journey is for a lifetime, and along the way, she continues to collect precious gems of self-knowledge and Divine knowledge to place upon her crown. These gems awaken eyes within her heart. With these eyes, she has no doubt that she is lovable and worthy, as is every soul she encounters.

A Queen is her own savior. Her magic is quiet, potent, and mysterious.

My hope is that you will recognize that every piece of your journey is to lead you to your own crown. I hope you will discover your own magic, your own power, your self-love. My hope is that you'll find the golden threads to weave the inner kingdom that supports the making of your chosen life. And may you share the golden threads that you'll discover, to help usher other heroines and heroes to and through their journeys.

Love and guidance are always there for us, to see us through the shadows of our hearts and valleys of our souls with the remembrance of our beauty and light—to help the pieces of us that are lost to find their way home.

When there is a woman, there is magic. If there is a moon falling from her mouth, she is a woman who knows magic, who can share or not share her powers. A woman with a moon falling from her mouth, roses between her legs and tiaras of Spanish moss, this woman is a consort of spirits.

—NTOZAKE SHANGE, *SASSAFRASS, CYPRESS & INDIGO*

Every woman is a Queen.

————

Every man is a King.

————

Honor every Queen and King in your midst on your journey to forging your crown.

————

And may God and your soul become friends along the way.

ACKNOWLEDGMENTS

There are so, so many to thank when it comes to how this book became possible. For this page I am going to thank those who had a direct hand in the making of the book. My personal life thank-yous will be at www.ourworthyjourney.com.

Thank you first to the Great Supreme for ALL things.

Thank you, Miguel Melendez, for spearheading *Worthy* and being the best big brother ever!

Thank you to Cait Hoyt, my literary agent, for your constant belief and support. Kate Childs and the rest of the team at CAA, thank you as well.

Carrie Thornton, my editor extraordinaire, thank you for your immediate interest in my story, your desire to have my voice heard, your passion, and the amazing book title. You are gangsta!

My gratitude to Liate Stehlik, for welcoming me to such a great publishing home.

Thank you to Ploy Siripant and Jesse DeCosta for bringing my vision for the cover to life. To Renata De Oliveira for the interior design, and to Ben Steinberg, associate publisher, thank you.

More thanks to Drew Henry for all you do, and to the marketing and publicity goddesses Allison Carney and Heidi Richter. Thank you to the entire Dey Street family.

To a handful of you who keep me on task, I couldn't do it without you—Carlos Molina, Zach Moe, Angela Golightly, Sadao Turner, Lukas Kaiser, and the entire Westbrook Media Team. Many thanks to Karryne Tencer for years of friendship and heading up publicity for me for nearly three decades. I am grateful to Nicole Perez-Krueger for your PR guidance on *Worthy*. Thank you to the team that makes sure my life is on point—my Her Lake family and the Smith Family Circle crew. Thank you to Chet Pajardo and Mia Pitts for checking on me every day and making sure I've eaten.

To Duane Martin, thank you for your constant belief in me.

To four people who always make space for my tears—Marque Henri, Trish Pinkett, Lauren London, and Toni Braxton—thank you for always showing up for me.

A special thank-you to Jay Shetty. Without your persistent nudges, *Worthy* would not have seen the light of day.

Mim Eichler Rivas, my coauthor, you held my hand and my heart through a grueling process. You have taught me so much through your laughter, experience, patience, and playfulness. You are an incredible lady, and I guess we are best friends now.

To every reader who picked up this book, thank you, from the bottom of my heart, for allowing me to share my story with you.

DEYST.

HarperCollins books may be purchased for educational, business, or
sales promotional use. For information, please email the Special Markets
Department at SPsales@harpercollins.com.

FIRST EDITION

DESIGNED BY RENATA DE OLIVEIRA

Library of Congress Cataloging-in-Publication Data has been applied for.

ISBN 978-0-06-332068-0

23 24 25 26 27 LBC 5 4 3 2 1